150 Years of Ministry

This illustration of Christ is reprinted from *Chisago Lake Evangelical Lutheran Church, 1854–1954,* a history written by Emeroy Johnson for the congregation's 100th anniversary.

150 Years of Ministry

Chisago Lake Evangelical Lutheran Church

1854–2004

Part One translated by William Johnson
Part Two by Emeroy Johnson
Part Three by Eunice Johnson Anderson

Edited by Carolyn Flittie Lystig

KIRK HOUSE PUBLISHERS • MINNEAPOLIS

Publication of this book made possible in part by a bequest from Elizabeth Aadland.

Manufactured in the United States of America

10 9 8 7 6 5 4 3 2 1

Library of Congress Cataloging-in-Publication Data

150 years of ministry : Chisago Lake Evangelical Lutheran Church, 1854-2004 / William Johnson, part one translator ; Emeroy Johnson, part two ; Eunice Johnson Anderson, part three ; Carolyn Flittie Lystig, editor.
    p. cm.
    ISBN 1-886513-96-1
      1. Chisago Lake Evangelical Lutheran Church (Center City, Minn.)--History. 2. Center City (Minn.)--Church history. I. Johnson, William, d. 1991. II. Lystig, Carolyn Flittie. III. Johnson, Emeroy. Chisago Lake Evangelical Lutheran Church, 1854-1954. IV. Anderson, Eunice Johnson. Next 50 years, 1954-2004. V. Minnesskrift, 1854-1904, Svenska Ev. Luth. Församlingen, Chisago Lake. English.

BX8076.C44A15 2003
284.1'77661--dc22   2003058916

This book was designed and set in type by Carolyn Flittie Lystig, Linnea Publication Services, Lindstrom, Minnesota, printed by Bang Printing, Brainerd, Minnesota, and published by Kirk House Publishers, Minneapolis, Minnesota.

Photographs courtesy of: Ed Cahill Photography; Olan Mills Church Directories; Joel Thorson, Reference Archivist, Evangelical Lutheran Church in America, Chicago, Illinois; Sally Barott, Archive Room, Chisago Lake Lutheran Church; Ellen Glenna, Chisago County Press; James Almquist; Eunice Johnson Anderson; Charles D. Anderson; Gordon L. Anderson; Duane Arnold; Sally Barott; Darlene Blair; Elaine Benson; John Fahning; James Froberg; Esther Grimm; Nancy Grossman; Lorraine Hasselquist; Rebecca Knutson Herrmann; Virginia Johnson; Paul Knutson; Barbara Lundstad-Vogt; Carolyn Flittie Lystig; Nancy Gausman Nickelson; Gladys Peterson; Tamra Peterson; Carol Sandgren; Lisa Sandgren; Mildred Tengbom; John Voelker; Bernette Wikelius; Debra Barott Wiler; and many unnamed photographers.

Chisago Lake Church

Beckoning heavenward it stands
And holds the cross on high,
A temple raised by willing hands
God's name to glorify.

How oft its bell with accents clear
Has called to prayer and praise,
To tuneful singing and to hear
God's precious word of grace!

Chisago Lake! God watch o'er thee
And keep thee ever true!
His Holy Spirit dwell in thee
His blessed work to do!

Chisago Lake! Till in the sky
Is seen the returning Lord,
Exalt the cross of Christ on high
And beckon heavenward!

WILLIAM JOHNSON

"Currents of Change" by Mary Pettis commemorates the European emigration and settlement along the alluring Saint Croix River Valley. Used by permission. www.marypettis.com

Contents

Part Three: The Next 50 Years, 1954–2004   251

Full-Page Illustrations, Photographs, and Poems

Editor's Preface

CHISAGO LAKE EVANGELICAL LUTHERAN CHURCH OF CENTER CITY has a rich heritage. As a worshiping community with laymen conducting worship services, baptisms, and funerals, it is the earliest group of Lutherans in Minnesota, dating back to 1851. The congregation, organized May 12, 1854, by the Reverend Erland Carlsson, is the second oldest Lutheran congregation in Minnesota. This heritage is recognized annually on the Sunday closest to May 12. Other Swedish Lutheran congregations organized in 1854 by the Reverend Carlsson were First Lutheran in Saint Paul on May 6, 1854, and Elim Lutheran in Scandia on May 19, 1854.

The above photograph of a couple at the church doors was taken in the early 1900s. Hulda Elizabeth Anderson and Rolland Gausman came from Europe, she from Sweden and he from Germany. Hulda and her twin sister came to Minnesota because of the large Swedish community immigrating here.

Books by the Swedish author Vilhelm Moberg continue to bring

Swedes to America and Americans to Sweden in search of ancestors and history. Moberg's epic tetralogy, *The Emigrants*, *Unto a Good Land*, *The Settlers*, and *The Last Letter Home*, made the Chisago Lakes area famous in Sweden. He did his research in this area the summer of 1948, riding his bicycle. A statue of him on his bicycle is in Chisago City. His fictional characters, Karl Oskar and Kristina Nilsson, can be seen in Lindstrom, where a replica stands of the original statue in Karlshamm, Sweden. Willard ("Smitty") Smith, a Lindstrom business-man, commissioned sculptor Roger David to design a copy of the stat-ue of Karl Oskar and Kristina in 1969.

A photograph of this statue begins chapter 14 of this book, illus-trating what is true for many of us—*looking back, missing the familiar; looking forward, anticipating the new*. Joris-Pelle (Per Anderson, a found-ing member of this congregation), is the real-life person on whom Vilhelm Moberg based his fictional character Karl Oskar.

In the summer of 2000 Anders Åhslund from Hassela, Sweden, and Sally Barott, congregational member from Shafer, conducted a tour from Sweden and a return tour to Sweden (*Tur och Retur 2000*). The Swedes came here in June; about 30 Americans, many of whom were descendants of Erik Norelius, Daniel Lindstrom, and Per Anderson, traveled to Sweden in July. On July 8, 2000, the group visit-ed Per Anderson's home place, the former Pelle farm, and joined in the 150th anniversary celebration commemorating the emigration to North America of Joris-Pelle (Per Anderson), Norelius, Lindström, and about 100 others who left Hassela in 1850 and came to the Chisago Lakes area. There is an internet site about this 150th anniver-sary celebration in Sweden.*

This book shares much of the congregation's history in three parts. Part One, "A Jubilee Celebration," is an edited version of the translation by William Johnson of the happenings, speeches, talks, and sermons from the congregation's 50th anniversary celebrated May 12 to

---

* http://w1.691.telia.com/~u69102447/mottiland/2000/joris/index_eng.html

15, 1904. This was first published in Swedish as *Minnesskrift,
1854–1904, Svenska Ev. Luth. Församlingen, Chisago Lake*. The forward to
Minnesskrift is signed by the publicity committee: Pastor F. M. Eckman,
P. R. Melin, and F. A. Porter.

Part Two, "The First 100 Years," is an edited version of the book
written by Emeroy Johnson and first published by the congregation as
Chisago Lake Evangelical Lutheran Church, 1854–1954. Gordon L.
Anderson, son of Eunice and Louis Anderson, scanned the text and the
photos of Emeroy's book, which greatly aided the process of editing
and designing this book on the computer. He also offered encouragement and advice along the way and read the final manuscript.

Part Three, "The Next 50 Years," was written by Eunice Johnson
Anderson, a niece of William and Emeroy Johnson, who were brothers. Her decision to organize her writings according to the years the
pastors served provided the shape for the edited versions of Parts One
and Two. Eunice also wrote prefaces to each of the three parts.

Two main sources for photographs besides those scanned by
Gordon L. Anderson from Emeroy Johnson's book were the church's
archive room, where Sally Barott, then chair of the historical committee gave extensive help, and the ELCA's archives in Chicago. Joel
Thoreson, reference archivist, gave extraordinary help time and again.

May this knowledge of our past inspire gratitude in us—gratitude for those who have gone before and for those who lead us now.
To God be the glory.

CAROLYN FLITTIE LYSTIG

Carolyn graduated from Saint Olaf College, Northfield, Minn., with a bachelor of
arts degree in Christian education. She was a production editor at Augsburg Fortress,
Publishers for more than 10 years. She has had many years of experience as a writer,
editor, and designer. Her husband, Lawrence, served Chisago Lake Lutheran Church
from 1998 to 2001. She was actively involved in the congregation during that time.
While still a member of the congregation she offered to help Eunice Anderson, who
said she needed an editor, and they have continued to work together.

This photograph, "Kyrkan i Chisago Lake," is reprinted from *Minnesskrift,* published on the occasion of the congregation's 50th anniversary in 1904.

Part One

A Jubilee Celebration

1904

∾

WILLIAM JOHNSON, TRANSLATOR

William Johnson (b. March 28, 1906; d. July 26, 1991), is a son of Chisago Lake Church. He translated *Minnesskrift, 1854–1904, Svenska Ev. Luth. Församlingen, Chisago Lake,* a book published in Swedish with the happenings, speeches, talks, and sermons from the congregation's 50th anniversary celebration, May 12 to 15, 1904. Part One, "A Jubilee Celebration," is an edited version of this translation.

Preface to Part One

On Thursday, May 12, 1904, Chisago Lake Swedish Evangelical Lutheran Church celebrated its 50th anniversary. This event was marked with several days of meetings. Several former pastors and synod dignitaries attended the festivities. Pastor Eckman, who was the resident pastor at the time, wrote a history of the congregation. A book entitled *Minnesskrift* was published shortly after the celebration. It contained the history, sermons, speeches, and addresses presented at the festivities, as well as other parts of the program. This, of course, was in the Swedish language.

In June 1987 I attended a church secretary's conference at Gustavus Adolphus College in Saint Peter, Minnesota. At this conference we were told that it would be advisable to have any historic documents of the church that were written in a foreign language translated into English. Soon thereafter, William Johnson of Hinckley, Minnesota, was asked if he would be willing to do this translation. He readily agreed.

William Johnson was born in the Chisago Lake area. He was baptized and confirmed at Chisago Lake Lutheran Church and continued his membership there until the late 1960s when he moved to Hinckley. He knew the Swedish language and had translated other Swedish writings, including a history of the Hinckley fire.

Mr. Johnson enjoyed writing poetry and had several poems published in *The Lutheran* magazine. Professor Leland B. Sateren composed music for Mr. Johnson's poem entitled "Calvary," and this hymn was first published in the *Service Book and Hymnal* (the red hymnal) in 1959. It is also in *Lutheran Book of Worship* (*LBW* 100) under the title "Deep Were His Wounds." It is also found in the Presbyterian hymnal.

Mr. Johnson died in 1991 at the age of 85.

Part One of this book is an edited and revised version of the English translation of *Minnesskrift*.

EUNICE JOHNSON ANDERSON

Pastor F. M. Eckman

Chisago Lake Lutheran Church, 1896–1913
Welcome · Thursday, May 12, 1904

FIFTY YEARS AGO TODAY a group of emigrants from Sweden, this community's first pioneers of Lutheran confession, gathered in the so-called "Berg's haymow" located only a few stone casts east of the knoll where the church now stands. The group consisted of not many more than 50 persons. Outwardly everything was so simple, even cheap. But it was a festive day. A service of worship was being celebrated, the first one in this area under the leadership of a Swedish Lutheran clergyman. Dr. Erland Carlsson, at that time a strong young man but now gone to his eternal home, whose picture you see here in front, was the long awaited clergyman. That day also became memorable as the day of the organization of this congregation. The group has grown. Today I see in this beautiful temple the flock grown to nearly two thousand. I greet you, beloved Chisago Lake congregation. I bid you welcome to come before the face of the Lord to celebrate with praise and thanksgiving this anniversary. On behalf of the congregation, I welcome the honored president of the Augustana Synod, Dr. E. Norelius; the honored chairman of the Minnesota Conference, Dr. J. Fremling; former pastors of this congregation, specially invited guests, fathers and brothers from near and far. A hearty welcome to join us in celebrating this anniversary to the glory of the Lord. Welcome, friends from distant places. Many of you have formerly been members of this beautiful neighborhood. May childhood memories awaken here along these lovely shores and in fellowship with relatives and friends kindle blessed recollections. And you, our good friends and faithful neighbors in nearby congregations, you are most heartily welcome to join us in rejoicing during these festive days.

May we not only outwardly bear the stamp of festivity, but celebrate in our hearts as we consider what great things the Lord has done for us.

1904

> Blessed is the people that know the joyful sound: they shall walk, O LORD, in the light of they countenance (Psalm 89:15 KJV).

Dr. J. Fremling, D.D.

President of the Minnesota Conference of
the Augustana Synod

Ascension Day Sermon · Thursday, May 12, 1904

God is gone up with a shout, the Lord with the sound of a trumpet. Sing praises to God, sing praises: sing praises unto our King, sing praises. For God is the King of all the earth: sing ye praises with understanding (Psalm 47:5-7 KJV).

THE 47TH PSALM presumably refers to the Ark of the Covenant being moved to the sanctuary in Jerusalem, as this ark was according to God's promise a seal of the presence of God. Thus when the ark had been brought up on the Mount of Zion with jubilee and the sound of trumpets, the singer could say, "God is gone up with a shout," and he exhorts Israel to praise God. "Sing praises to God, sing praises."

It sometimes happened that the Ark of the Covenant was brought along into battle and, after victory, was returned to Jerusalem; the victory was then ascribed to God who by means of the ark had been along in the battle. Then again it was said, "God has gone up with a shout." As victor over the enemies of his people, he has gone up and resumed his place on Mount Zion, the city of the living God. We can also regard these words, "God has gone up," as being prophetic, as in Psalm 68:18:

> Thou hast ascended on high, thou hast led captivity captive; thou hast received gifts for men; yea, for the rebellious also, that the Lord God might dwell among them.

In these words the Apostle Paul sees a prophecy of the exaltation of Christ as he quotes them in Ephesians 4:8.

As the Ark of the Covenant was a type of Christ, so the bringing of the Ark of the Covenant into battle may be regarded as a type of his humiliation and strife against our spiritual enemies, sin, death, and the devil, and his glorious victory over these enemies. So the return of the ark to the sanctuary signifies the ascension of the Lord Christ into heaven. In regard to this we can truly say, "God has gone up."

1904   Today we celebrate the ascension of our Lord Christ into heaven. And it is a day of jubilee— and for this Christian congregation a day of jubilee in a double way, the 50th anniversary of the congregation and also the day Christendom celebrates the ascension of our Lord Christ into heaven. Certainly no sound of jubilee was heard on earth at the ascension of Jesus, nor was there trumpet-sound. But there was not silence in heaven when the Son of God entered the most holy place and was seated on the throne of majesty.

On this our anniversary day, we are reminded of the jubilee of the heavenly host and we are exhorted by the holy singer:

> Sing praises to God, sing praises: sing praises unto our King, sing praises. For God is the King of all the earth; sing ye praises with understanding (Psalm 47:6-7 KJV).

> Afterward he appeared unto the eleven as they sat at meat, and upbraided them with their unbelief and hardness of heart, because they believed not them which had seen him after he was

risen. And he said unto them, Go ye into all the world, and preach the gospel to every creature. He that believeth and is baptized shall be saved; but he that believeth not shall be damned. And these signs shall follow them that believe: In my name shall they cast out devils; they shall speak with new tongues; they shall take up serpents; and if they drink any deadly thing, it shall not hurt them; they shall lay hands on the sick, and they shall recover (Mark 16:14-18 KJV).

So then after the Lord had spoken unto them, he was received up into heaven, and sat on the right hand of God. And they went forth, and preached everywhere, the Lord working with them, and confirming the word with signs following. Amen (Mark 16:19-20 KJV).

The joyous ascension of our Lord Christ and his sitting on the right hand of God.

1. The ascension of Jesus Christ into heaven is described especially by the Evangelist Luke in the first chapter of Acts. After his resurrection, Jesus revealed himself on several occasions for a period of 10 days, partly in Jerusalem and partly in Galilee and by many proofs showed himself alive and let himself be seen by them and spoke about that which belongs to kingdom of God. Finally on the 40th day after his resurrection, he brought his disciples up on the Mount of Olives, in the neighborhood of Bethany, and after he had renewed his promise of the Holy Spirit and had blessed his disciples, he was taken up in their sight and a cloud removed him from their eyes. Thus simply was the ascension of our Savior accomplished, but how wonderfully!

1904

We want to notice two expressions: "received up" and "raised." The evangelists say that he was received up and the Apostle Peter that he was "raised by the right hand of God" and Paul says that "God hath raised him."

The ascension of Christ was thus the work of God, the heavenly Father, as was the resurrection, and was a sort of result of, or compensation for, the deep humiliation of the Son of God, his humility and obedience unto death, for this God has now exalted him above all things. But it is also stated that he has himself ascended: yes, in Hebrews 4:14, "that he has passed through the heavens." As he had power to again take up his life, he also had power to ascend into heaven—as he had himself said, "I ascend unto my Father, and your Father; and to my God, and your God."

2. What is meant by Jesus' ascension into heaven? The very expression "ascension into heaven" tells us where Jesus went. As the disciples of Jesus "looked steadfastly toward heaven" as he went up, behold, two men stood by them in white apparel, which also said:

> Why stand ye gazing up into heaven? This same Jesus, which is taken up from you into heaven, shall so come in like manner as ye have seen him go into heaven (Acts 1:11 KJV).

He ascended into heaven—God's dwelling place, where his glory shines most beautifully, where God has his throne surrounded by countless hosts of angels, cherubim, and seraphim.

1904

It cannot be computed where heaven is located, but the ascension of Jesus shows the way up. The ascension of Jesus indicates that he has raised himself above all that is temporal and mortal. He has passed through the heavens, above all the created worlds into the eternal, glorious, and imperishable sanctuary.

The ascension of Jesus indicates that he, who was sent from God, returned to God. Yes, his ascension implies the complete glorification of Jesus, for which he prayed in the high priestly prayer (John 17):

> And now, O Father, glorify thou me with thine own self with the glory which I had with thee before the world was.

This glorifying began with the resurrection but was completed with the ascension. His human nature became elevated to divine honor and glory. As God and man he assumed his throne on the right side of the Father. It says in Hebrews: "He sat down on the right hand of the Majesty on high."

3. We shall now consider the ascension of our Lord Christ as being joyful. For whom the ascension of Jesus is joyful, yes, for the Lord's faithful ones, the congregation of the believers, it was the first fruits of the congregation of Jesus who witnessed his ascension, and in spite of the fact that in regard to his visible person they would always be separated, they were not distressed, but entirely calm, and doubtless also happy in daily fellowship and zealously faithful in prayer. The congregation of believers joyfully celebrates the remembrance of Jesus Christ's work of salvation, his birth and his death, his resurrection and ascension.

Why do we celebrate the ascension of Jesus with joy? Well, because we now have a brother at the right side of God. Jesus partook of our nature and was truly our brother and is not ashamed to call us his brethren. He sent this greeting to his disciples, "Go tell my brethren."

This brother of ours, who for our sake had to suffer death on the cross, and was insulted and blasphemed, has been raised to divine honor—his human nature has become partaker of divine attributes. He has not ceased to be man—he is and remains our everlasting brother. Oh, what an honor! What a cause for rejoicing! "Our brother is the only Son of God" and the Son is "one with the Father."

1904

"He sitteth on the right hand of God." This calls attention to his divine power—the unity of his being with that of the Father and the Holy Spirit.

Just as the resurrection constitutes the strongest proof that Jesus is the Son of God, so the ascension constitutes the strongest proof that Christ has resumed the glory that he has had from eternity.

The ascension of Christ is joyful, because we now have a perfect atonement in heaven and a compassionate defender with the Father.

Certainly our Lord Christ, through his death upon the cross, has accomplished an atonement for the whole world, an atonement which is eternally valid. This atonement became sealed by the resurrection of Jesus.

By his ascension he has, as our high priest, entered into the greater and more perfect tabernacle, into heaven itself, to present himself into the presence of God for our good.

The significance of Christ presenting himself into the presence of God for our good is explained by the Apostle John:

> If any man sin, we have an advocate with the Father, Jesus Christ the righteous: and he is the propitiation for our sins; and not for ours only, but also for the sins of the whole world (1 John 1:1-2 KJV).

What a comfort and joy for the poor children of God, who in spite of all prayer and watchfulness, all strife against temptation to sin, never succeed in becoming free from sin, but are daily plagued with this evil and daily suffer from this evil and daily feel that judgment of the law for this evil—what a comfort and joy to have in Jesus, their brother, who has ascended into heaven—to have in him a defender, a sympathetic high priest, who always prays for them, always stands in the presence of God for their good, stand there as their atonement and as their righteousness… Therefore they can joyfully sing:

1904

> My Righteousness is seated
> At the right hand of the Father, on heaven's throne,
> And the enemy, however angry and bitter,
> Can't harm them in the least.

> Hallelujah! I now can sing:
> Laud, honor, praise be Thine, O Jesus Christ,
> Until in heaven with transfigured tongue,
> I praise Thee with all saints at last.

The ascension of Christ is, for the faithful ones of the Lord, joyful because through his ascension he has taken his throne at the right side of God. Nothing higher can be imagined than the right hand of God or the right side of God. He thus has, as God and man, divine honor, power, and glory. His throne represents his royal power and rule. But this lordship of his is revealed in various ways, depending upon the various natures of his created beings.

In Psalm 8:6 it says, "Thou madest him to have dominion over the works of thy hands; thou hast put all things under his feet." Paul says in Ephesians 1:20-23:

> Which he wrought in Christ, when he raised him from the dead, and set him at his own right hand in the heavenly places, far above all principality, and power, and dominion, and every name that is named, not only in this world, but also in that which is to come: and hath put all things under his feet, and gave him to be the head over all things to the church, which is his body, the fullness of him that filleth all in all.

We notice from these and other passages of scripture that Christ, together with the Father and the Holy Spirit, rules over all creation. And this is a subject of joy for the congregation of the faithful, which has Christ as its Lord and king, that he sits at the right hand of God and has all power in heaven and on earth. The congregation of the faithful is that holy community, which consists of all such as believe in Christ as their Savior, their righteousness, and their life. It is the congregation of Jesus Christ, which he has himself founded, chosen, and called. By his own blood he has purchased and acquired the congregation for himself. By his humiliation and exaltation he has acquired for the congregation spiritual and heavenly gifts, especially that great and glorious gift, the Holy Spirit.

1904

Even at the beginning of his prophetic office, he began to draw the hearts of men to himself in order to form his congregation. The holy apostles were the beginning of his congregation. That divine doctrine which he proclaimed to them he gave to the congregation. Thus he gave to the congregation the means of grace which he delivered to his disciples.

He has given to the congregation the Word, the Word of God— the Holy Gospel, as he says in his high priestly prayer;

> Now they have known that all things whatsoever thou has given

me are of thee. For I have given unto them the words which thou
gavest me; and they have received them, and have known surely
that I came out from thee, and they have believed that thou didst
send me (John 17:7-8 KJV).

In regard to the proclamation of this divine Word, he made provision
before his ascension, when he commanded his apostles:

> Go ye therefore, and teach all nations, baptizing them in the
> name of the Father, and of the Son, and of the Holy Ghost;
> teaching them to observe all things whatsoever I have command-
> ed you: and, lo, I am with you always, even unto the end of the
> world (Matthew:28:19-20 KJV).

So this is a royal decree, come forth from the almighty king. It is
his plan to conquer the whole world, to make disciples of all nations,
and in order to accomplish this great conquest he first sends out a little troop of 11 apostles, who would soon increase to 12 and 13 and later
to a large flock of evangelists. But how does he arm them for this great
warfare? With what kind of weapons? Nothing but the Word and
Baptism and the Holy Supper. That is the whole armament. But within these simple means there lies a divine power— the Spirit—the
Spirit of the Father and the Son. One person in the Godhead is the
wonderful power who is at work through the Word and the
Sacraments. "Go ye into all the world."

1904

Monarchs have been found who have striven after great power
and have aspired to become world conquerors. But they have never
attained the glory for which they have yearned. But Christ has taken
his seat at the right side of God in order to spread his kingdom over all
the countries of the world and his plan for the preaching of the gospel
to the whole creation will be accomplished and is even now well on the
way to fulfillment. The gospel is the joyful message that Jesus Christ,
the Son of God, has come into the world to save sinners. The gospel is
the word of atonement that God has through Christ wrought atonement with himself. The gospel is the teaching of the humiliation and

exaltation of Christ, about his saving work and his saving love.

With the preaching of the gospel, Christ has united the Holy Sacrament of Baptism, which consists of water and the Holy Spirit and which through the Word and the institution of Christ are so united that the one who is baptized with water in the name of the Father, the Son, and the Holy Spirit, is baptized not only with water but with the Holy Spirit. And therefore, baptism, like the preaching of the gospel, is a powerful means of atonement, which brings about the forgiveness of sin, saves from death and the devil, and gives eternal salvation to all who believe what is implied by God's word and promises. He that believeth and is baptized shall be saved.

So the Holy Supper is also a gracious means of salvation because Christ by means of bread and wine unites his body and blood for us to eat and drink. These means of grace, however humble, frail, and meaningless they may seem, are quite powerful and active. There is in them a power from on high, a power from the glorified king, who sits upon the majestic throne in heaven. For that reason these means are active upon the hearts of men.

1904

We hear from our Holy Gospel what promises Christ has made to his believing congregation (Mark 16:17-18). These promises were fulfilled literally in the early times of Christendom, as we read in Acts. But these signs and wonder-working powers necessary at the time of the foundation of the Christian church, are no longer needed; we have the Word and the Sacraments. Where these means of grace are rightly used, they are accompanied by inner spiritual signs.

Preaching in the name of Jesus drives out evil spirits in the pagan world and among reprobate Christians who hear the word and pay attention and permit it to bring about a change of heart. Then there are spiritual movements; there is remorse over sin and fear of the wrath of God and the judgment of the law. From the depth of the heart there are questions about salvation, the need of grace, and longing for a Savior.

And when Jesus Christ is proclaimed as the Savior and atonement of the world, as the only mediator between God and man, as the throne of grace to whom sinners may flee for refuge and find grace and help at the right time, then there is enlightenment for the soul in the darkness of unbelief. Then the star of hope and faith arises and the sun of righteousness, Christ, is seen with blessedness under his wings. Then one hears such a soul, together with all the saved, born again, and made righteous souls, speaking in new tongues and telling about the mighty works of God, praising God for the forgiveness of sin and for the great grace of the kingdom of God. And as the preaching of the gospel is effective in bringing about a better life, faith, and sanctification, so the sacraments are effective both in kindling and strengthening spiritual life.

They are certainly not irresistible, but man can in unbelief resist the power of the sacraments. Therefore, it says: "He who believes and is baptized shall be saved.... And these signs shall follow them that believe." The preaching of the gospel is a preaching of faith, which indeed produces faith but also requires faith; it is likewise in regard to the sacraments.

1904

How these things can be united, bring about faith, and require faith, is a part of the mystery of the gospel, which is revealed to the simple and the heavy-laden who are in need of grace. The means of grace which Christ has given to his congregation are to be administered according to the order he has himself instituted. Even as he has given to the congregation the Word and the Sacraments, he has also instituted the office of the preacher who is to administer these precious means of grace. These are in a special way the servants of Christ and messengers in his place and stewards of the mysteries of God. The Lord and king enthroned on the right side of God in this way carries on by humble means and instruments the cause of his kingdom, strengthens, supports, and establishes his congregation and extends his kingdom toward the goal he has set.

The ascension of our Lord Christ is joyful because our Savior, exalted to the right side of God, is with us always, unto the end of the world. Just because he has in his human nature been glorified and become partaker of divine nature, he can be with us on earth at the same time as he is in heaven. But this matter of being with us involves more than his omnipresence; it involves his inner union with the congregation of the faithful.

> God hath put all things under his feet, and given him to be the head over all things to the church, which is his body, the fullness of him that filleth all in all (Ephesians 1:22 KJV).

By this expression, head and body, the apostle means the mystical relationship that exists between Christ and his body, that inner fellowship that characterizes the head and the body. From him as the head the congregation has proceeded and come into being. From him proceeds those spiritual life powers that are active in faith, which warms it and engenders love and all good works, which encourages it to prayer, intercession, and thanksgiving, which enables it to confess Christ, live for Christ, and labor and suffer for his name's sake. Yes, Christ is the life of the congregation.

1904

But the congregation is also said to be his fullness, who filleth all in all. Christ, together with the congregation, constitutes a complete body. The congregation thus becomes the fullness of Christ. But it is so-called not merely because it forms a complete body with Christ as the head, but because it is filled by himself in whom the fullness of the deity dwells in bodily form. From Christ, the living water, the congregation receives the water of life, the manifold gifts of the Holy Spirit, such as faith, hope, love, patience, and endurance, and all spiritual powers. And as he fills his entire congregation, the whole Christian church on earth, he also fills each local congregation and each believing Christian with himself and the treasures of his grace.

So we see that this congregation's living fellowship with the Lord Christ is a result of his ascension. It was through his exaltation he could pour his Spirit into the hearts of his faithful ones and it was by the Spirit he could enter into the most intimate fellowship of life and love with his own, as he says:

> And the glory which thou gavest me I have given them; that they may be one, even as we are one: I in them, and thou in me, that they may be made perfect in one; and that the world may know that thou hast sent me and hast loved them, as thou hast loved me (John 17:22-23 KJV).

We are still further assured of our glorified Savior's identification with the church by means of the Holy Sacrament of the Altar whereby under bread and wine he gives us his body to eat and his blood to drink. Being glorified, he can convey himself to us and in his love he desires to be one with us as he is one with the Father.

That great promise, "I am with you always," thus implies his intimate fellowship with us. This fellowship with Christ, the Son of God, implies life and blessedness even now in this temporal life. "Whosoever eateth my flesh, and drinketh my blood, hath eternal life."

1904

But this life is still concealed, a life by faith and a blessedness in hope. It is a life that grows and develops with much strife against evil in the world and in our nature, yes, with a constant dying and killing of sin in our nature, with a constant sighing after deliverance from evil.

And this sighing is not in vain.

> For we are saved by hope; but hope that is seen is not hope: for what a man seeth, why doth he yet hope for? But if we hope for that we see not, then do we with patience wait for it? (Romans 8:24-25 KJV).

And what is it for which we wait? What is it for which we hope? We hope to see again our Lord Christ. We hope and wait for his return; he, who ascended into heaven, shall so come. "From thence he shall come to judge the quick and the dead." And when he comes, he shall be glorified in his saints, and be admired in all them that believe. He shall awaken them from death and the grave.

He shall change our vile body, that it may be fashioned like unto his glorious body, according to the working whereby he is able even to subdue all things unto himself (Philippians 3:21 KJV).

And as the resurrection of Christ is a guarantee for the resurrection of our bodies, so his ascension is a guarantee for our ascension.

Joyful was the ascension of our Lord Christ. God has gone up with a shout. How joyful shall be the ascension of his congregation! What a rejoicing in the camp of the saved! What trumpet sound and what songs of praise from the accompanying hosts of angels, saying:

The kingdoms of this world are become the kingdom of our Lord and of his Christ, and he shall reign for ever and ever. Amen.

1904

Pastor F. M. Eckman

Chisago Lake Lutheran Church, 1896–1913
History Speech · Thursday, May 12, 1904

IT IS BEFORE THEIR ALTARS that every group of people set the direction of their own history. The history of a congregation thus becomes an important part of the history of the community. To a high degree that is true in regard to the Chisago Lake Church and the community which has from of old borne the same name. The church and the community have grown up together, and as far as the people are concerned, have been almost identical. It is true that the Chisago Lake settlement was three years old before the congregation formally came into existence; yet, as we shall see, the pioneers here were from the beginning interested in religion, and the idea of a congregation entered into the program of their lives from the beginning. Yes, it was a matter of first importance more than is true with the majority of pioneers in our times.

The first Swede to feast his eyes upon the clear waves and smiling shores of Chisago Lake was doubtless Erik Ulrik Norberg. In the winter of 1850–51 he wrote a letter and sent a map of the lake to an acquaintance, Per Anderson, who at that time was in Moline, Illinois. The result was that Per Anderson and his family, Per Berg and his family, and P. Wicklund with his family moved to this area in the spring of 1851. They and the Anders Swenson family, who on a trip from Saint Louis joined the group, became the first settlers at Chisago Lake. The group arrived in Taylors Falls April 23, 1851, and immediately continued on to Chisago Lake and founded "the first Swedish colony in Minnesota."

Norberg had already taken possession of the land on which Center City is now located, which area for a long time was usually called "Norberg's island." Here he had built a temporary dwelling house with bark for walls and roof. Norberg left later in the summer and returned to Bishop Hill where he died a couple of years later. His land was then taken over by A. Swenson. The first house to be built belonged to P. Berg and is said to have been erected by four men in one day. It was ten feet square and eight feet high.

1904

During the summer of 1851 several Swedes arrived, one of them being the present janitor of Chisago Lake Church, Claes Dahlhjelm. In September of that year Per Anderson wrote to E. Norelius, "We are now nine Swedes who have started farms here." There was, however, no considerable influx until '53 and '54, at which time quite many, most of them from Småland, moved in, and so in 1855 the settlement was reported to include 500 souls. Småland, and especially Kronoberg County, furnished the lion's share of immigrants to Chisago Lake, which might therefore properly be called America's Småland. Genuine Småland dialect is still spoken here by the third and fourth generation. The times were at first quite trying. On this subject we quote the following observations by Pastor Cederstam:

> Almost all were poor when they arrived, none owned any beast of burden and few had a cow. Berg owned an ox and had made for himself a cart with two wheels and with this rig he drove. Farm

implements were simple in those days, an axe and a hoe; with the axe in the hands of the Swedish man and the hoe in the woman's, the wild forest was soon changed into fruitful fields. And it was a charming view to see around the lake, with its many bays and points, that on the shore there was a little cottage here and there, surrounded by fields of corn and potatoes and other crops, and beside the doors and windows beautiful flower beds. They were all so contented, happy, and thankful that it was a joy to behold. Each one felt he had the prettiest location by the lake and would not want to trade with anybody.

At this time there was no flour mill in the neighborhood. But as the ground was cultivated and there was a beginning of harvest, the people acquired large coffee mills and on these grain was ground for bread and gruel. The clear ice on the lake often served as a threshing floor with the threshing being done with a flail in the genuine old Swedish way. With an abundance of fish in the lake and game in the woods one did not have to buy much for food. However, one had to "set the mouth according to the lunch basket," that is understandable. One could hardly buy for five cents on credit in Taylors Falls. Until one could afford to buy a stove with an oven, bread was baked in a large iron kettle, and it is claimed that it was remarkably good bread. When the Swedish clothing began to wear out—which was probably not very soon—one made spinning wheels and looms and made one's own clothing. One did not need so many garments in those days. If the man had a pair of homemade trousers and a ditto shirt, preferable red, he was dressed up. Homemade wooden shoes were used very generally, which was the reason Americans called the Swedes "the wooden shoe people." It is better to have wood on the feet than to have it in the upper story.

As far as religious needs were concerned, the Swedes here had to take care of that themselves as best they could. In this respect Per Anderson seems to have been particularly concerned. We find from his letter to E. Norelius that they assembled for services outdoors at first.

1904

The first time indoors was the First Sunday in Advent 1851, when the people gathered in Per Anderson's house, which was then just recently finished.

Christmas services were also celebrated there and also services on New Year's Day 1852. In several letters, Anderson expressed his wish and hope that a congregation be established here.

> The soul's life is burdensome here... We have a lovely summer and a most appealing nature. If a church and a congregation were here and as flourishing in a spiritual sense, I would consider the area to be twice as valuable (May 1852).

In September of the same year, Chisago Lake was for the first time visited by a Swedish pastor, an Episcopalian, Pastor G. Unonius of Chicago. He preached and conducted the Lord's Supper but does not seem to have won the real confidence of the people—at any rate not of Per Anderson. Unonius wrote the following year and offered to become the pastor here, but nothing resulted from that offer, probably because of Anderson's influence. The second Swedish pastor to visit the area was a Methodist, Pastor Agrelius, formerly a pastor in the Swedish State Church. There are people still living who remember that he was here in the winter of 1853. In the summer of 1854 he appeared as a rival against E. Norelius, who at that time was here preaching and conducting a school. Norelius describes him as "a stately, honorable, gray-haired man." He spent most of his time in the Marine settlement, where he later made his home near Big Lake and died there not very many years ago.

Among those who accompanied Pastor Erland Carlsson when he left Sweden in 1853 were several who were bound for Chisago Lake. Their acquaintance with him became, in the providence of God, the occasion for him to come here the following spring and become the first Lutheran pastor to visit this area. He intended to make that journey in the fall of 1853, but fearing that the river might freeze and hinder his return, it was postponed until the spring. On May 12, 1854, 50 years ago today, he was here and a meeting was held with "the

Swedes of Evangelical Lutheran Confession." In the introduction to the minutes of this important meeting, it says:

> The Swedes who had come to live in this place had for a long time felt the need of an orderly churchliness and as they were being visited by a Lutheran pastor, Pastor Erland Carlsson of Chicago, a public meeting was announced to take place this day for the purpose of the regulation of churchly needs.

Thus the time had come when "the Lord of the harvest" was to answer prayer. The first resolution was "that we unite into a congregation by the name of the Swedish Evangelical Lutheran Church on Chisago Lake." Next was a resolution about the confession, the reception of members, etc., after which were followed the same rules as prevailed in the congregation in Illinois and which later were incorporated into our present congregational constitution. In regard to a congregational teacher, the minutes read as follows:

> Since the congregation has no teacher and it is of utmost importance to get one, it was decided to unite with the Lutheran Church in St. Paul in its call to Pastor C. M. Svensson of the Dioceses of Växjö to come and take charge of these congregations. This congregation will, nevertheless, now as formerly, gather each Sunday for our common edification and also join in faithful prayers to God that he may graciously soon send us a faithful shepherd and soul carer.

1904

(Note: The church in Saint Paul was organized at the return of Pastor Carlsson to Chicago. It seems that preparations had been made earlier.)

In a letter of July 10, 1854, Pastor Carlsson wrote to Dr. Fjellstedt about his visit here:

> From St. Paul I journeyed to the Swedish settlement at Chisago Lake, fifty miles from this city and ten miles from Taylors Falls on the St. Croix River. I stayed here for almost eight days. A Swedish Evangelical Lutheran congregation was organized and of the two hundred Swedes, who live here, all but two families became members.

There is no record in existence of those who became members of the congregation at its organization, but from existing records and oral information we have found that the number of communicants was 57. Among them the following ten are still members of the congregation: Mattis Bengtson, Mrs. Lena Stina Molin, Carl Linn and his wife Lena Kajsa, Claes Dahlhjelm, Lorentz Johnson, Mrs. Johanna Wiberg, Johannes Linn, P. M. Johnson, G. J. Wiberg.

The first deacons of the congregation were Hakan L. Svedberg, Petter Anderson, and Carl Peterson. The first trustees were A. M. Dahlhjelm, Per Berg, and Anders Swenson. A. M. Ahlstrom was the congregation's first song leader. P. Berg promised the newly organized congregation that it might have its meetings in his house, but even at the first business meeting it was decided to build an "Ev. Luth. Meeting House," which was to be built in such a way that it could also be used as a school house.

The site for the building had already been decided to be on A. Swenson's land. The size of the building was set at 18 "alnar" long, 14 "alnar" wide and 5 high. [An aln is equivalent to 45 inches.] During the summer, until this building was completed, the congregation met in Berg's haymow, located near the present organist's dwelling place. The congregation was thus born in a stable.

During the first summer, from May 25 to September 10, the congregation was served by E. Norelius, at that time a student. He kept school and preached and received $25 as wages for that period. He also preached in Taylors Falls on Sunday afternoons. His stay in this area became very meaningful, especially in that Minnesota appealed to him and aroused his interest to the degree that he became the principal exponent and defender of church work among the Swedish people in Minnesota. It is almost a miracle that after half a century he is today, still a powerful man, with us to take part in this festivity.

Pastor P. A. Cederstam became the first resident pastor of the congregation. Because of a letter from this area it was decided at that meeting of the Chicago and Mississippi Conference in April 1855 that he was to be stationed here. Cederstam was not yet ordained but had a so-called "license." He was ordained in September of the following year. On Pentecost Sunday 1855, he preached here for the first time in the completed school house.

During his time of service here, two important questions in regard to the outward development of the church were decided: the building of a church and its site. The school house that had been built was altogether too small. On July 4, 1855, it was decided to erect a church 70 feet long, 48 broad and 18 high, and "after much talking and strife" the site was set to be near the place where G. Hultquist and J. Carlson now live. The decision about the building site was, however, not satisfactory and there had to be new attempts to bring about unity. It seems there was so hot a strife about this matter that the congregation experienced a threat of division. Pastor Cederstam wrote about this many years after the struggle had come to a happy ending, and from this writing we quote at some length because it gives us a clear picture of the situation at the time.

1904

> When the congregation was organized by Pastor Carlsson, a site for a church building was selected near the place where the Methodist church now stands. Later in the summer another place had been selected and the woods had been cleared away; this was on Peter Swenson's land east of the lake, not very far from the present residence of A. Molin. Several bodies had been buried here. Such was the situation when I came to Chisago Lake. However, the people were by no means in agreement about this new building site. At this time a poor American man was subsisting in the settlement and he and P. Anderson laid out a plan for a city on the land Mr. P. Shaleen now owns and here was to be a big city. It was given the name of Center City because it would be the central point in the settlement. Now it was clear that here was the place where the church should be; lots were available on the lovliest location a bit east of the place where the present parsonage is built. It was decided to build the church

here, but those who lived south and west of the lake protested, although they were in the minority. Upon this, those who lived south of the lake started to pick out a building site for a church on P. Glader's land, and also west of the lake near the so-called "fish channel" there was talk about building a church; and those who lived near the so-called "Little Lake" felt that they could build a church there, too. We tried in vain to get them together; it all seemed hopeless; but they all said, "If we can get two acres of Mobeck's land free we will unite and build the church there."

I was very sad and did not know what to do. One day I got the idea of going to Mr. Mobeck and offering him $50 for two acres of land. Fortunately I had received money for a subscription to *Hemlandet* [*The Homeland*] and so when I put it all together, my money and *Hemlandet's*, it amounted to exactly that amount. I put the money in my pocket and went over to Mr. Moberg, who was now living on his land. At this point I want to reveal the Mr. M. had become offended and stubborn as a result of many unfriendly remarks and sharp barbs he had heard because of having bought this land, which it was believed he knew the settlers wanted for a church, cemetery, and pastor's land. He was willing to donate enough land for a church site but the people wanted enough for a cemetery, too. After a moment of talking about the deplorable dissension, I said I had come to buy land and laid my coins on the table.

"Look," I said, "here's fifty dollars in gold and silver that you can have, Mr. Mobeck, for two acres of land for a church building site. You could go to Stillwater tomorrow and at the United States Land Office buy forty acres near by, and you would have more use for that."

Mr. M. did not believe that the congregation would accept the offer; they did not want to buy land. I answered, "I'm the one who is buying land and it will be my loss if this doesn't work out." After a moment of conversation and after Mrs. M. had mediated for me, M. replied, "Well, if I may deal with the pastor and designate the south boundary of the acres, I'll let it go." Thereupon he extended his hand and Mrs. M. laid both of hers over ours while she wept for joy. After we had read the Word of God and prayed

1904

together, I left, very happy and satisfied.

I now hurried over to Uncle Svedberg to tell what I had done. He laughed at me and said, "You're brave, Pastor," but nevertheless thought it was almost hateful to pay so much for that land. I answered, "If we can win unity, it isn't too much." "That's true, Pastor," he said, and was pleased.

The news spread rapidly in the whole settlement. Some thought it was crazy, others did not know what to think. The following Sunday after the close of the service, I said that I had heard with sadness that there were plans to build several churches in the settlement and pointed out as well as I could how foolish that would be; and since I had heard that all were agreeable to building on Mobeck's land, they could now get two acres there, if they wished. They answered, "Well, that's fine, but what will the land cost?" I answered, "The land has been bought and paid for and will be turned over to the congregation if it will agree to this plan."

They were satisfied; no one voted against it. Then I added, "I have bought the land and paid for it; but you all know that I'm poor and I did this for the sake of unity; for that reason I ask that if any of you would be willing to contribute 25 or 50 cents, it would be welcome." All were satisfied with this and we parted happy that this strife was at an end. Within a couple of weeks, $60 had been contributed for the purchase of the land.

1904

Thus we see that the beautiful location of our church, so admired by many people, did not come about without quite serious trouble.

After the question of a building site had been decided, there was a decision about building a church. A large building committee was set up. P. Glader was named as master builder, and in November 1856 the work was ready for inspection. However, it took several years before the church was fully completed with furnishings and painting. The cost was figured as $1,795.25, of which $935.40 was cash, $463.85 donated building material, and $396 donated labor. Although this church was at the time considered to be very large, it was necessary after some years to build an addition. This took place in 1869 at a cost of $932.05. A church bell was purchased as far back as 1860. It was bought from Staples in Stillwater. A pipe organ was bought in 1871 for $1,200 and was to be installed in time for the meeting of the synod, which convened here that year.

Pastor Cederstam never received a permanent call from the congregation. On September 9 he was called for one year. In December of 1857 he announced that he would leave the following spring, which he also did. Pastor Cederstam was a faithful worker and he laid a good foundation during his three years of service here. In his concern about both major and minor matters, especially during the time of the building of the church, he may very well have been the messenger boy and the hired man of the church, a position for which the present age probably praises him more than his contemporaries did. To what extent the congregation was concerned about his support I do not know, but the minutes say nothing about remuneration until 1857, when it was stipulated that for half a year he was to receive a dollar from each communicant.

1904

Upon Cederstam's resignation from the congregation, it was again attempted to get a teacher from Sweden, but without success. After waiting in vain a whole year for an answer from a Pastor Magni in Växjö, it was decided to call some one of the teachers in this country. Three candidates were presented: Hasselquist, Norelius, and P. Carlson, who were to be called in turn until one gave an affirmative answer. Carlson received the first call, Hasselquist the second; as E. Norelius had just moved to Chicago, it was not considered worthwhile to extend a call to him. Thus a new group of three was set up, consisting of A. Andreen, J. P. C. Boreen, and C. A. Hedengran. From 91 ballots cast, Hedengran received 80 for being the first one to be called. Hedengran accepted the call and took office in October 1859. In regard to salary, the minutes state:

> For the first year free dwelling house and free use of 29 acres of land, $200 cash and, from each settler, two bushels of grain, consisting of wheat, rye, corn, and oats, one-fourth of each kind,

which would at present amount to about 200 bushels, but as the congregation will probably grow larger, the amount of grain will also increase.

This was in effect until 1866, when the pastor's salary was set at $550 once and for all, and the communicant membership fee was set at $2.50 for farmers, $2 for each male person, and $1 for each woman.

The congregation increased a great deal in membership under the leadership of Pastor Hedengran and had, when he resigned in 1873, about 800 communicant members. There were many children and young folks. In the year of 1872, the confirmands numbered 60. The work was becoming too strenuous for Hedengran's frail body and for this reason he gave the congregation the choice of securing an assistant pastor or calling a new teacher. The congregation chose the latter proposition. The congregation should not be faulted for this, as it was probably best, although at the time it seemed somewhat harsh toward a sick and faithful teacher. The congregation softened the circumstances by granting its old teacher an annual pension of $300 and the right to live on the congregation's property—this last item also applicable to his wife until her death.

1904

The trying years of the Civil War took place during the time when Hedengran was here. When the government called men to bear arms, they came from these woods too, from their pioneer farms, from wife and children. Some of these men never returned, but found their grave under the southern sun. The greater number, however, returned and, hardened in the stern school of war, took over the peaceful strife of caring for their home, now twice as dear.

Hedengran was a deep thinker with not a little spirit of prophecy. His sermons were profound and brought the listeners deeply into the truths of the Word of God, if one took the trouble to pay attention. His theological writings about the last times, about atonement, and about the Bible as divine truth testify to love and aptitude for theological knowledge.

All of this did not save him from opposition. A story is told about one man who was "in a sort of devilish frenzy" because he believed himself to be condemned because he believed it was his fault that Hedengran had become the pastor of the congregation. At business meetings storms would sometimes break out. There were many business meetings in those days, one year as many as eight, so there was ample opportunity to practice debate and to keep all kinds of irons hot. The minutes tell about one man who "at a public business meeting had, with clenched fist, defied and insulted the teacher of the congregation." The minutes of another meeting tell about one "who came to the meeting and publicly read an insulting writing." Hedengran wrote an article about the difficulties at business meetings and read it to the congregation:

> I have tried to maintain order and decency, though often in vain, and I must sincerely say that of all business meetings I have attended, either in Sweden or America, I have never experienced such a noise, disorder, and misbehavior as here at our business meetings. It would, therefore, be a good thing if this congregation would begin to learn how a business meeting or other meeting should be conducted; because although each and all have the right to speak whatever is right, they should not, therefore, all speak at once or one interrupt the other.

1904

We will gladly admit that the congregation has learned quite much in this respect.

Hedengran no doubt had a strong tendency to feel depressed and often felt his calling to be quite difficult. At one occasion he said:

> If you find me to be unfit to be your teacher, by all means tell me so straight to my face; I'm willing to turn over the shepherd's staff to someone better and more capable than I am whenever you so wish. You need not torture me. Because of my feebleness I already feel inclined to lay down my heavy calling.

It was probably certain conditions that were the cause of such remarks. They may also have been the result of a temporary despondency and Hedengran's tendency to dwell much on life's shady side. He had high ideals in regard to Christendom and the Christians; ideals one seldom finds realized except in times of persecution and martyrdom—precisely the kind of times he expected would soon come. In his farewell address to the congregation his words, however, acquire a more satisfied tone than in the former quotation. There he said:

> This time of nearly fourteen years has certainly been a time of suffering, sorrow and strife, yet the Lord by his great grace has removed one burden after the other and, after storm and unrest, has let the sun shine. The protecting hand of the Lord has been extended over this congregation so the winds of error have not been permitted to remove more than a few. Thank you, dear congregation, for the moments when we have rejoiced together, for every favor shown to me, for every intercessory prayer sent up to God for me.

The message ended with the following characteristic prayer:

> O may the light of truth never grow dim in this congregation! God grant that all, both young and old, may walk in the light of truth, as children of light! May we all be wise and prepare ourselves for the coming stormy and unhappy days, which are certainly not far away, in order that we, in the power of Christ, may triumph over all and finish the race well and so, according to the promise, receive the crown that fadeth not away.

1904

Pastor Hedengran still lived for seven years after his resignation. Constantly sick during this time, it was only a very few times he was able to preach. The fact that during this time he received his support from the congregation is something for which we feel a justified satisfaction. October 31, 1880, this faithful shepherd of the congregation entered the rest of the people of God. Mrs. Hedengran lived many more years and passed away in the home of her son-in-law, J. P. Nord, February 22, 1897. Both of them are buried in the congregation's cemetery.

As successor of Hedengran, calls were extended to J. Aslund, C. A. Evald, C. P. Rydholm, and O. Olson, all of whom answered in the negative.

In July 1874, a call was extended to J. J. Frodeen, at that time a teacher at the school of St. Ansgar [Gustavus Adolphus College]. He accepted the call and following his ordination took charge of the congregation in the summer of 1875.

Frodeen's time of service, so far the longest, was characterized by zealous and thorough work in several areas. Two large churches were built, the chapel was purchased, and the parsonage remodeled. It was no easy task to get the building of the new church going. As early as 1877 a committee was appointed for the purpose of gathering money for a new church. But by March 1879, they had come no farther than to decide by a vote of 106 ballots to 90 to postpone the building of a church for five years. But the subject of building could not wait as long as that. In January of 1881, a subscription of $7,210 was presented and it was unanimously decided to proceed with the building of a new church immediately. It seems that they went about this business with real enthusiasm and an unusual unity. This work was conducted in a businesslike and systematic way.

1904

The work was placed under a supervision of a building committee consisting of Pastor Frodeen, A. Molin, C. J. Long, Peter Swenson (in Vibo), Gustaf Hultquist, J. J. Slattengren, J. Shaleen, J. E. Peterson, and David Sandberg. Pastor Frodeen served as chairman and J. E. Peterson as treasurer. The treasurer served for seven years. In 1888 when he submitted his final report and the congregation took over the account, unpaid subscriptions amounted to $1,306 and the indebtedness was only $141.86. It was left to the pastor of the congregation to take care of the debt—not a very big undertaking, but certainly not an enviable job.

The dimensions of the new church were set at 100 x 66 feet, not including the chancel and steeple, the same dimensions as our present church. It was at first decided to build a frame church, but after careful consideration of the opinion of knowledgeable men, the committee recommended that the church be built with bricks. As a result of this recommendation, it was almost unanimously decided to do so, a decision the congregation has certainly never had reason to regret.

When in October of 1883, the conference celebrated its 25th anniversary here, the church was so nearly finished that it could be used and in November of the same year it was dedicated for its holy purpose. The cost of the church building is figured at $25,000, of which $19,486 was cash and $5,513 in labor donated by members of the congregation.

About a year later, the church was beautifully painted in fresco and in June of 1888 a new bell was in its place in the steeple. At that time no one surmised that a catastrophe was only a few weeks distant. The terrible night of August 1 and 2, 1888, the church was set on fire by lightning. The rising sun of the next day illumined the smoking ruins of the devastated sanctuary. Is it any wonder that at the sight of this calamity the congregation felt depressed? This was also a memorable year in that there was quite generally a crop failure. Nevertheless, the congregation promptly went to work restoring the ruined church. Two weeks after the fire, on August 17, 1888, the following decision was made:

1904

> That the congregation, in the name of the Lord, go to work to restore the church with the aim of getting it enclosed and, if possible plastered, so it can be used through the winter.

A building committee was elected and in a comparatively short time the work was completed. The building was insured at $10,000 and the company paid $9,675.80. This sum must have been carefully used because when the church was again finished the debt was less than $2,000. There had still been no subscription list, but a mere ingathering for pews. In 1890, a new bell was purchased for $486 and the following year the present pipe organ was purchased for $2,200. The church was fresco-painted in 1894, and a few years later lovely ornamental windows were installed with the cost bbeing borne by the Ladies Aid of the congregation.

The same year as the church was completed, Pastor Frodeen tendered his resignation.

Various events of importance in regard to the inner history of the congregation were revealed and recorded during that time, but that time is still so close to our own that we cannot appropriately touch upon it. The years that have gone by under the guidance of the Lord may have somewhat changed our viewpoint.

As pastor to succeed Pastor Frodeen, the following were called: J. L. Haff, P. J. Sward, O. Olson, and J. F. Seedoff. Pastor Seedoff accepted a second call and moved to this place in the fall of 1890 and served the congregation until in September of 1896, when he was succeeded by the present pastor. We all remember this, and record it only for the sake of being complete. Pastor Seedoff's time of service is characterized mostly by activity in the purely spiritual realm of growth through the preaching of the Word.

I consider it inappropriate to give a close account of the activities of recent times, especially since my two immediate predecessors are present and will from their own memories and experiences relate what may be appropriate. The past 15 years have probably been a time of mostly inner development, whether for worse or better the future will reveal. It is plain that it has been in certain respects a time of spiritual groundbreaking; this is something our congregation has experienced in common with our whole denomination. It is certain that in comparison with the more modern types of Christians and congregation, we have much for which to thank God. Our confessions, our doctrinal books, and our pulpits are still protected.

Something should be stated further about the financial affairs of the congregation before we go on to other matters. At the outset, not much money was to be found here, but they got along quite well anyway, as they worked by the day and accepted grain as payment. The money that was needed was obtained by collections and subscriptions. Large sums were not needed. In 1857, Johannes Helin agreed to "keep

1904

fire in the church stove and see to it that no dogs came into the church"
for a salary of $2.75 per year. Several years went by before the salary of
the church janitor went up to $10.

In 1858, when Peter Shaleen was elected organist, his salary was
set at a freewill subscription and two collections. Six years later this was
reduced to two collections. Shaleen agreed to this reduction, apparently
to beat out a rival for the job, in which he was successful, but he was disappointed with the income and a change had to be made the following
year by which the salary was set at 25 cents a year per communicant "for
as long as Shaleen consents to serve as organist." But this time it was the
congregation that blundered and in 1866 the risky decision was repealed
and a definite salary of $100 was set. Two years later this was by request
raised to $150 and for this salary Shaleen afterwards served until his
death in February 1898. Without any break worth mentioning, he was
thus the congregation's organist for 42 years. He loved his service, was
faithful in his calling, and friendly in fellowship.

No large sums were needed for school teachers either in the early
days. In 1859 the school teacher received $4 per month "besides his
board and eight bushels of rye and corn." The school day was from 8
o'clock to 5, so he no doubt had to honestly earn his $4 and his grain.

1904

The congregation has also been in real estate business quite a bit.
Besides the two acres that were purchased for a church site, Pastor
Cederstam bought the 80 acres now owned by C. J. Long. But when
they became aware that this land was too distant to use as parsonage
land, it was offered for sale by auction several times, but in vain. Finally
they got rid of it and the 19 acres now occupied by P. Stendal and Jonas
Johnson were purchased. It seems that this real estate deal was made by
the trustees without authority of the congregation. The business was,
however, authorized by the congregation in the sense that the financial
record was accepted. Several years later, however, there were some who
tried to stir up trouble about it and both the congregation and the pastor were given severe rebukes about the business. Several years later

Pastor Hedengran purchased the 60 acres that now constitute the parsonage land and the cemetery. At that time the congregation disposed of its 29 acres and took over this land. Therewith the congregation's land speculation was terminated, probably forever.

The first parsonage was a two-story building of hewn timber situated on the church property. The question soon arose if it would not be better that it were moved to the 29 acres. There was quite a hot strife about this, too. It fell to the lot of E. Norelius to cleverly give a happy solution to this question; he suggested a waiting period of five years. This, however, had the inconvenience of the pastor being without a barn for the time being, although there had been business meetings giving quite explicit directions about such a barn.

When the present parsonage land was purchased, the matter of moving was also decided. The parsonage was sold for $300 and Pastor Hedengran built a house of his own on the site of the present organist's house. Upon Hedengran's resignation the older part of the present parsonage was built. An addition to this house was built in the latter part of Pastor Frodeen's time of service here, giving the building its present form.

1904

In 1884 the church building used by the Mission Friends was purchased for $600 and is now used as a chapel. Five years ago the congregation erected a suitable organist and school teacher residence. The property of the congregation has now a value of nearly $40,000.

The early times, when not much money was needed, was nevertheless the time that the congregation was the greatest troubled with debt. Thus in 1859 it had to mortgage its property and pay two percent interest monthly. There was a terrible trouble with unpaid church dues and unfulfilled promises of donated labor. The delinquents were threatened in every way and still it was hard to collect. The main reason for the many delinquencies was that for each project there was a separate treasury. If one was less interested in some project or didn't like the person involved, one deliberately failed to contribute and thereby had the satisfaction of indicating one's dissatisfaction. In order to remedy this situation a so-called finance committee was formed. Gradually all expenses were brought under an orderly per-communicant system. For the past several decades there has been no great trouble with debts and lists of non-payment. Financially, the congregation is in good circumstances and good working order.

In regard to the more spiritual development of the congregation, we consider the Christian church school to be of great importance. We can see plainly from the minutes that the congregation has been much concerned about this. We have already mentioned that E. Norelius conducted a school here the same year the congregation was organized.

The following year a Sunday school was started and Collin, Mobeck, and Bystrom were designated as leaders. As far as I have been able to discover, Sunday school has been conducted at some time of the year each year since that time. In 1859, the congregation chose its first permanent school teacher, Johan Peterson, better known as "School-Johan." He was to conduct school six months a year, dividing his time between four different places. But it was decided that before beginning:

1904

> The school teacher must appear before Pastor Hedengran to be examined as to his knowledge in spelling in order to be able to instruct in the Swedish language.

He must have done well in the examination, as he served for several years until he had to resign because of failing health. The following persons have, in the order they are listed, served as regular teachers under the congregation: Johan Peterson, J. A. Skoglund, P. A. Wigren, S. N. Carlman, L. Hokenson, and P. R. Melin. Carlman has had the longest time of service— nine years. During his time of service, Mrs. Carolina Sellman served as assistant teacher. P. R. Melin is the first one to also serve as organist. Besides the regular teachers there have often, especially in recent years, been several assistant teachers. The cost of such schools is now paid entirely from the treasury of the congregation. From 12 to 16 weeks of school are now held annually. Strangely, it now seems that there is a shortage of children to enroll in school. It can be seen from the statistics that it is different now from in former times. For instance, in 1886, 91 infants were baptized, while the number during the past decade has been between 40 and 50.

In this connection, we also want to mention how the congregation at various times has made decisions that indicate great thoughts about schools. At the annual meeting of 1872, the following resolution was passed:

> That a school house be built, where such of the children in the congregation as the Lord has gifted with outstanding abilities, which ought not be plowed under in the furrow, could be prepared for a continued development and maturity at our higher institutions of learning and thus be used in the service of the Lord.

1904

It was decided that the building was to be erected on the parsonage land, approximately where the picnic pavilion now stands. But the whole matter depended upon the possibility of getting a freewill subscription. There is no report of the result. Twenty years later, or 1892, the thinking was as follows:

> Carried, that a committee consisting of Pastor F. J. Seedoff, G. Hultquist, and J. J. Slattengren formulate and present to the congregation a motion to build and maintain a school for the young people of the congregation.

The following year the committee reported that such a school is needed; therefore, the proposition ought not to be permitted to lapse but that further preparations be made in order that the project may be started with that much greater certainty when the time comes. Eleven years have gone by since that time. It would have been proper that this 50th anniversary had been celebrated with a jubilee school-fund of $25,000. The need for a Christian high school is now greater than ever. When are the great ideas going to be realized? Here is something great and inspiring for the congregation to grab hold of and fill its future history.

But we do not now have time to dream about the future. We would like to briefly touch upon the activities of the Church Council. The minutes of the Church Council contain much of the history of the inner condition of the congregation and show how the work of caring for souls was conducted. It can easily be seen that not much of the details of this activity should be presented—that would involve the revealing of 50 years of the confessional of the congregation. From beginning to end these minutes contain serious witness and confessions of sin, such as drunkenness, immorality, wrath, quarrels, malicious slander, sinful amusements, secret societies, spiritual error, denial of Christ, and such. We may as well confess today that grievous sins have occurred and still occur. Mournful though it be to read through the minutes of the Church Council, a veritable book of sighs, there are, however, statements that bring about happier feelings; feelings of thanksgiving that the evil which has been committed within the congregation has been seriously disapproved and punished and that many wrongdoers have accepted reproof and punishment and have turned away from their life in sin. As far as I can understand, the congregation has always had a Church Council which has held to the right Christian principles, though it may not always have been able to put them into practice. The following quotation from the report of the Church Council in 1890, is no doubt well founded:

1904

> While I cannot maintain that everything that should have been done has been done, or that what has been done has been done as it could or should have been done, I nevertheless rejoice that no right principle has been sacrificed, and it is possible for the congregation and its Church Council, if they so desire, to keep on in the right direction in accordance with its high and holy calling.

One condition, which has often made it difficult for the Church Council to apply Christian principles, has been the fact that the council has lacked the support of the other church members. On this very topic we read in one report:

> Conditions in the congregation are not promising for the future,
> as I fear that the congregation to a great extent is indifferent in
> regard to such things as work to bring about destruction. While
> it is a virtue to be tolerant, such tolerance can become a very
> harmful mischief and a cloak for laziness.

If one believes that the Church Council, in the course of the years has been intolerant, one should read through its minutes. At least in certain instances, more would have been accomplished if one would have been more firm and decisive than was the case. Many of those for whom there was the greatest charity became in a marked degree children of grief; and the evil which has been quietly ignored has eventually come forth with increased strength.

No small part of the concerns of the council has necessarily been the collecting of debts and ingatherings for denominational causes. For a number of years before 1875, at each annual meeting there was a renewal of the resolution, "that the deacons in their respective districts raise money for the poor in Paxton and for the school in Carver." These troublesome financial campaigns gradually evolved into "the 25-cent fee," which since 1879 has been paid out of the general treasury of the congregation. The fact that the Church Council has had to, and still must, concern itself with the collecting of church dues, has no doubt sometimes been felt to be unrealistic. But looking at this matter more closely, we see that the practice of some members to neglect their duty toward the congregation is an actual crime that deserves to be handled by the Church Council. Not a few members have in the course of the years revealed their heart's attitude toward the congregation by their response to the dues required of them. From this point of view the church dues can be a blessing—although also a rock of offense.

One can also see from the minutes that the meetings of the Church Council have been serious moments, times of much prayer when cries from the depths have ascended to the Lord for the welfare of the congregation and its individual souls. In the course of the seri-

1904

ous discussions and the confidential conversations that have taken place, men have learned much from one another and the pastor of the congregation has had opportunity to air his troubles before his fellow-men. What a help for a pastor, to have sincere Christian brothers as his Church Council!

A record of such as have served as deacons indicates that several have served quite a few years. Mr. G. Hultquist has served the longest—25 years. The degree of faithfulness with which they all have served will be revealed on the great day of recompense when the Lord will "have called his servants home." As far as we can see, the congregation has reason to be thankful for those who in past times have served on the Church Council.

In regard to the attitude of the congregation toward doctrine, order of worship, etc., it has from the start been concerned about Evangelical Lutheran doctrine and Swedish Lutheran services. When Hakan Svedberg in 1855 was elected to lead the worship whenever no Evangelical Lutheran pastor was present, it was also decided that Luther's sermons ought to be read and the service conducted according to the Swedish order of worship. It was further decided:

1904

> That pastors or laymen of other denominations than the Evangelical Lutheran Synod of Northern Illinois not be permitted speak or preach until the regular service be concluded.

There is no record of any decision to unite with the Synod of Northern Illinois, but it was just natural that the congregation came to be considered as belonging there. The formation of the Augustana Synod was however hailed with joy, and the congregation decided twice—probably in order to be perfectly sure—to withdraw from the synod of Northern Illinois and unite with the Augustana Synod. In 1861 the congregation sent its first delegate to synod. Otto Wallmark was this delegate. The congregation pledged to pay traveling expenses —the meeting was in Galesburg—and also to reimburse Wallmark for loss of time with a bushel of rye per day.

The regular contributions of the congregation toward the synodical and conference schools, as far as the records show, indicate a sum of $15,702.78, or about 86 cents per day for 50 years. Little was done for missions in the early times. At any rate nothing is mentioned about this in the early minutes. Mr. Hultquist has given the information that a missionary society existed between the years of 1870 and 1876, which in the course of those years raised a total of $426.20. Since 1881, when reports began to be kept of contributions toward missions and other good causes, the following amounts of money have been collected and paid out: For missions $7,997.20; for the orphanage $2,407.13; for Bethesda Hospital $870.80; for other charities $3,450.18; all together, $15,151.51 or 83 cents per day for 50 years.

The congregation has thus desired to take part in the common work and has surely, by the grace of God, itself reaped great blessings thereby. The feeling of being a part of the denomination has also been strengthened by means of quite many conference and synod meetings

1904

held here, which have prepared for our people a wealth of spiritual growth at the same time as there has been opportunity to observe various churchly conditions. This may also very well have contributed a great deal to the circumstance that our people in this area have been spared from any considerable church split.

The congregation considers it an honor that the now so large Minnesota Conference was organized here in 1858. We also rejoice over the fact that the congregation has had opportunity to be closely acquainted with the "founders" of the denomination. The man who organized our congregation, E. Carlsson, as well as the honorable founder of our denomination, T. N. Hasselquist, made several encouraging visits here in the early years. In 1860 Hasselquist was here for the third time. We can read in detail about this visit in Hasselquist's biography of E. Norelius. We permit ourselves to quote a bit from this. After describing the lake and the location of the church, it reads thus:

The congregation here is growing steadily, so the fairly large church cannot always seat all who come to hear the Word, which is blessed and has power to make the soul blessed. Pastor Cederstam has here done preparatory work, both in regard to a church building and an orderly congregation. The sowing is often done in tears, but the harvest is then usually all the richer. That is the way it has been here.

Later on in his dissertation he writes as follows:

I was fascinated to see that the countrymen here were not ashamed to give a Swedish appearance to much in their church; when something is good and appropriate, so it is, even if it does hark back to the old Sweden. Some people are so indifferent to their own background that they want everything in their church to be like the neighboring American churches, that is, Reformed. Such people are soon ready to Americanize the doctrine, too. Indifference and looseness in one respect will bring the same attitude in the other.

I am not able to say much about the spiritual life in the congregation. That is something which cannot be recorded in earthly minutes. When the books are opened above, these hidden facts will be revealed. We do know that at least one fervent awakening has been, by the grace of God, the experience of the congregation. That was in 1859 and 1860. It was a quiet, deep, and quite ongoing work of the Spirit which took place at that time. It became a strict and somewhat legalistic type of Christianity. There are probably still not a few persons in the congregation who regard this time of visitation as the beginning of a new life and a serious concern about their soul's salvation.

1904

This situation is mentioned in the story by Hasselquist, from which a quotation has been made. After describing how the congregation for two whole days, almost until in the evening, had been generally present to hear the Word of God and how on the following day a large number of people had gone along to Taylors Falls to hear more, he writes:

It is plain that the Lord dwells among these people and is constantly busy gathering to himself lost sons and daughters. Pastor Hedengran told us about joyous instances of this, and I had several occasions to notice it myself.

Will we experience such a spiritual springtime again? May God grant it! We feel a need of it each time death removes from our midst one of those who are "old, yet fruitful and fresh." While we gratefully remember that the Lord in all ages in the church gives new birth to souls, we still cherish the hope that "the voice of the turtle is heard in the land" as in the springtime.

We need praying men and women who are willing to replace the mantle of Christian fathers and mothers, and enter into the service of the Lord and his church and bring it forward to victory over both old and new enemies.

1904

With gratitude for the past and with a hopeful look forward to the triumph of God's kingdom on earth and upward to the church triumphant in glory in heaven, may we in the name of the Lord, celebrate this jubilee festival!

Herewith we conclude this history of the congregation. Perhaps it is inappropriate that an occasional dark picture has been included but the intention has been to tell the truth.

> Now unto him that is able to do exceeding abundantly above all that we ask or think, according to the power that worketh in us, unto him be glory in the church by Christ Jesus throughout all ages, world without end. Amen.

Dr. E. Norelius

Chisago Lake Lutheran Church, 1854
Speech • Thursday, May 12, 1904

4

1904

A FESTIVE CANTATA was sung by the church choir following Pastor Eckman's history. The music had been composed for the occasion by the church organist, P. R. Melin. The solo parts were sung by P. R. Melin, Mrs. F. G. Lorens, and Pastor Ph. G. Thelander. The words by Pastor E. Schold were part of a festive composition, which he read at the 40th anniversary of the Conference at this place in October 1898. [The portion that was sung was in Swedish; the text of the cantata was not translated into English.]

After the cantata, Dr. E. Norelius spoke. His speech is recorded in part only. Dr. E. Norelius is a man who is well acquainted with our congregations and the history of our denomination. He is especially well acquainted with Chisago Lake. This was his first field of labor in Minnesota and ever since that time he has had close connections with the development here. He now came forward and gave an interesting talk about memories and told a great deal about events of which he had been an "eye-witness" in former times. Unfortunately, we are not in a position to record more than the introductory remarks of this speech. We refer the reader to Norelius' historical writings, where there is much material from his pen touching upon the early history of this area. As an introduction to his speech, Dr. Norelius spoke as follows:

THE KINGDOM OF GOD does not come with outward manifestations, but it does come and has come to Chisago Lake in the way the Lord has himself decreed.

1904

Before Jesus parted from his disciples on the day of the Ascension of Christ, he told them: "Ye shall be witnesses unto me both in Jerusalem and in all Judea, and in Samaria, and unto the uttermost part of the earth."

The disciples had imagined that he would immediately set up the kingdom of God for Israel and they asked him about this as he was about to leave them. But this could not now take place, because Israel had rejected their Messiah and for long ages forfeited their right to be the people or instrument by which the kingdom of God might soon with power spread over the earth and be victorious. Now it must take place in a more tedious and less sensational way, namely, by the simple witness of the apostles that Jesus is Christ, the promised Messiah, given because of our sins and raised for our justification, the mediator between God and man, the judge of the living and the dead! They were to begin this testimony in Jerusalem, the most ungodly and infamous place on earth, and then go on into other parts of Judea and into Samaria and later into all the earth. In that way, through the apostolic witness, the kingdom of God, in its preparatory phase, has come to Chisago Lake and our other congregations in this country. It took nearly a thousand years before this testimony reached our old Fatherland and it took more than 1850 years before the testimony began to be heard on the shores of Chisago Lake. The history of this colony tells how it came to this place. I do not want to undertake to relate this history in detail, as I have already done so several times, both in speech and in writing. I only want to say that here, too, the kingdom of God has not come with outward manifestations. On the contrary, it has come in a very simple and ordinary way but has nevertheless demonstrated its power.

In my remarks I want to speak about:

1. **The humble beginning of this congregation during its first 10 or 12 years.**

2. **The evident power of the gospel even here during this time of beginning.**

1904

From this point and on, the speaker called attention to many characteristics of the people and the congregation in the early days. In regard to temporal life there was great poverty. The people were not familiar with self-government and free-will offerings.

Some had the idea that here the pastors were not real pastors, but since it was impossible to get pastors from Sweden, one had to be satisfied with what was available and the people learned to love their teachers, who labored among them with great outward sacrifice. Illustrations of this were presented from the lives of Cederstam, Hedengran, and P. Carlson. The speaker said:

The people were faithful to the confessions of the church; they brought their Christianity along from Sweden, such as it was, but the great majority of those who eventually constituted the congregation were really not religious.

It can, however, be seen that the gospel changed much and many

in that many experienced a true conversion, a greater clarity in the faith
has come about, people have learned more self-government and personal responsibility and have become accustomed to free-will offerings
for church and charity, both within the congregation and throughout
the denomination.

Following the speech by Dr. Norelius, the church choir sang
"Hymn of Praise" by Schultz, followed by prayer and the benediction
and the congregation singing stanzas 6 and 7 of Swedish Psalm
No. 1.

1904

Pastor F. M. Eckman

Graveside Meditation · Thursday, May 12, 1904

Although the afternoon program lasted considerably longer than planned, quite many took part in the little memorial service that took place immediately after the close of the afternoon service. A procession, led by the pastors who were present, walked to the cemetery to the grave of Pastor Hedengran and that of his wife. The desire was to receive some memories and also to lay down a perishable memorial wreath here on "God's Acre." When the group had assembled in the stillness of the early evening beside these two graves, the pastor of the church spoke as follows:

WE HAVE ASSEMBLED HERE to gratefully dedicate a moment to the memory of the beloved teacher of the congregation Pastor Carl August Hedengran, who here rests in the grave. The word of God exhorts us: "Remember them which have the rule over you, who have spoken unto you the word of God: whose faith follow, considering the end of their conversation." Many from this congregation who are still here on earth, have lasting impressions of this departed teacher's words and fellowship. Though he is dead, he still speaks. For nearly a quarter of a century his body has been moldering in this grave. His soul, we believe, is enjoying blessedness with God while he awaits the moment when this mortal body shall be clothed with immortality. That moment is coming. The voice of the Son of God shall at some time be heard here, too, and at the sound of that voice the grave shall open, the dead body shall arise and shall glorified ascend to meet the Lord in the air. Good and faithful servant, with you we await that blessed moment! As a feeble expression of our gratitude and a token of our common hope, on this day of jubilee, the congregation lays down this memorial bouquet, an anchor, the emblem of Christian hope.

Hedengran gravestone

1904

> Thereupon were uttered the following words in memory of Mrs. Hedengran:

IT HAS BEEN GRANTED to the wife of Pastor Hedengran, Katarina, to follow him into the eternal realm. She too has found her final earthly resting place by the side of her spouse. Today we want to remember her too. The woman usually has an outwardly less prominent place in life, but the Lord has called her to an equal participation in grace and the hope of eternal life. It is with joy that today we lay down on the grave of Mrs. Hedengran this simple wreath as an expression of our love and gratitude.

At this moment and in this place our thoughts go to the home above. May we meet there, saved from death and destruction.

Homeland, homeland, rest eternal, after earthly storm and strife;
Homeland, homeland, with Our Father we await eternal life;
So with joy go forward, brothers, for the promise stands secure,
And 'tis not in vain we struggle, knowing that we shall endure.

The pastors who were present now read some appropriate Bible passages. Pastor Frodeen also spoke some words of memorial. Dr. Norelius quoted as his scripture passage: "Blessed are they that hear the word of God and keep it." "How do we know," he inquired, "that Hedengran is blessed?" Answer: "Because he heard the word of God and kept it." Thereupon the speaker cited some characteristics of the life of Pastor Hedengran, showing especially how conscientious he was even in the least matters.

The group read "Our Father" and the benediction and sang a stanza of a hymn:

Keep me prepared, O Jesus Christ, to await
Thy glorious coming when at last Thou shalt bring
Out of the vale of tears,
From earthly suffering
Thy bride to Thyself in the bright hall of joy.!

1904

While the tones of the melodious song, "Quiet Shadows," sung by a men's chorus, sounded across the graves, the flock dispersed. According to what was later commented, this little festive moment on the cemetery brought much joy. May the day be faithfully remembered and be a blessing!

Pastor J. J. Frodeen

Chisago Lake Lutheran Church, 1875–1890
Memorial Speech · Friday, May 13, 1904

THE SECOND DAY OF FESTIVITY, Friday, May 13, was a cloudy morning and a light drizzle was falling; nevertheless, the church was quite well filled at 10:00 A.M. On this day the festivities opened with the singing of stanzas 1 and 2 of Swedish Psalm No. 117. (Words of hymn indicated.)

Pastor Ph. G. Thelander of Escanaba, Michigan, led in scripture and prayer. After a song by the male chorus of the congregation, Pastor J. J. Frodeen of Spring Garden, a former teacher of the congregation, gave a heartfelt memorial talk. We present the following abridgement:

Honorable Chisago Lake Congregation!

Not unto us, O Lord, not unto us, but unto Thy name be glory; for Thy mercy, and for Thy truth's sake.

O praise the Lord, all ye nations; for his merciful kindness is great toward us: and the truth of the Lord endureth forever. Praise ye the Lord.

MAY THESE WORDS from Psalms 115 and 117 give direction to our thoughts and express the feelings of our hearts this day of memory and jubilee. The grace of our God has been mighty upon us, however weak and feeble we may have been, and the truth of the Lord of which we read that it lasts eternally, has not deserted us. Thanks to God, we may, and do, have occasion to remember especially the truth of the Lord at this festivity. The program for this day promises a "memorial speech" and I have been furthermore informed that I am expected from my store of memories to present such remarks as may be useful and edifying, and preferably touch upon the time when it was my duty and privilege to serve this congregation.

Although it is true, it still seems strange, that that time constitutes nearly a third of the existence of the congregation—from Christmas 1873 until May 1890; however, as regular pastor only from the latter part of the month of June 1875. This time has been characterized, as I have seen from someone from this area, as a "busy time" in the history of the congregation. I would consider characterizing that period of time in that way myself, but looking at the part I took in the work, we can do nothing better than to thank God for graciously helping and prospering his and our work.

1904

Until the year of 1874, the Chisago Lake congregation included Chisago City and area around Green Lake. When such as lived in the area, having quite a long distance to church, agreed upon organizing a congregation of their own, this was not at once ratified by the original congregation, but a protest was instituted against the recognition of the new congregation and its reception into the membership of the synod. At the meeting of the synod in Vasa in 1875, Pastor Jonas Auslund, who was at that time the pastor of the church in Saint Paul, and I, the pastor of this congregation, who was ordained at said meeting of synod, were appointed to endeavor to bring about a reconciliation and thus remove the hindrance to the congregation in Chisago City being received into the fellowship of the synod. Today we gratefully remember that the two committeemen succeeded in this endeavor to the satisfaction of both parties and there has been a good understanding between the two congregations ever after.

Several years later when still another daughter congregation came into being, it took place without opposition from the mother church, as far as I can remember. To the glory of the grace and truth of God, we remember today that the total and the communicant membership of this congregation nevertheless increased meaningfully during this time, the latter from 820 to nearly 1,400. For several years preceding this time the congregation did not own a parsonage; the former pastor had, according to agreement, himself had a house built on land belonging to the congregation. A parsonage was built in 1875, and about 10 years later an addition was built on, making it such as it now is.

Many of you remember the first children's Christmas festival, celebrated in this congregation's old church at the Christmas of 1875. Under the leadership of my wife, the children had practiced a few songs, most of them in Swedish but a few in English, and no doubt some of you remember how the children recited and sang to their heart's content. That was something new for the children and appealed to their hearts, however simple. The old church was filled to capacity by old and young. A few weeks later the children in one family became ill with diphtheria and two of them died. During the time of illness the older one, who had been along at the program practice and was greatly enthused with the singing, kept singing, "Oh, it will be blessed when we never part again." We hope that these and others are now in paradise where there is no more parting, illness, or death.

1904

We well remember how the need of a larger church became more and more obvious. The congregation was, nevertheless, for some time dubious about undertaking the building of a new church —it seemed not to have confidence in its own abilities. The members of the Church Council began more and more to see that a new church was not only desirable, but necessary. After considerable discussion, and also prayer for the guidance and blessing of God, the council became unanimous in promoting a subscription for the building of a new church according to the plans of the pastor of the congregation. Those who were to pledge money for the erection of a church would do so on the condition that the congregation within three years were to decide to build a new and serviceable church, and that the pledge be payable in three installments—one third as soon as an official decision to build was passed, one third when the foundation was laid, and one third when the church was "enclosed." The pastor was given authority on behalf of the council to present this plan to the congregation following a service and also to call for and accept pledges. Herewith the pastor went to work and himself pledged $200. The proposition was well received. By the gracious help and blessing of God, a new and roomy church was built, serviceable and complete, even in regard to painting and heating.

1904

It was dedicated when the Minnesota Conference met here for its 25th anniversary in the fall of 1883. We could also consider it all as almost paid. How happy we were then! I cannot sincerely say that we thanked God as humbly and wholeheartedly as we should have done. I remember the members of the congregation often remarking when speaking of the heating of this church in the winter time that "coming into the church now is like coming into paradise."

The congregation already had salvaged from the old church a bell, which was quite good, although not large. It had been purchased for $50 from the owner of an old steam boat. This was placed in the new steeple but was soon replaced by a larger one—weighing 2,000 pounds. The people were not generally satisfied with the sound of the new bell—some seemed to be critical—but it was loud and melodious. The old pipe organ, which was not large but of good quality, was naturally also moved and set up on the balcony of the new church. With all this we felt we had come a long way. Thus we lived into the month of July 1888.

We had guests in the parsonage, dear friends from Fish Lake, Pastor Fremling with wife and other company. I remember the first of August of that year—a beautiful but warm day—we were at a point by the lake northwest of the church. Seen from this spot, the church appeared especially imposing, and several in the group expressed their admiration, and I felt almost envious of those who traveled that way to church. We went home; our dear friends also left for their home toward evening and soon we had, not a silent night—as already in the early part of the night it became cloudy and soon the thunder was not only rumbling, but sounded off with almost deafening roar upon roar and the lightning flashed continuously.

The lightning struck not only trees, which in some instances were split and hurled far away but—oh, woe—in the church steeple, which was ignited, with the result that the whole church was soon in flames. In spite of all that human power and wisdom could do, everything that could burn burned and everything the could melt melted with the exception of the pulpit, a very few pews, and the chandeliers, which a few spectators were able to remove. A brave and resourceful young man dared to run up in the steeple after it had been struck and by striking a few strokes on the bell give an alarm. During this time, and almost throughout the night, the rain was falling in streams, a fortunate event, as it prevented nearby houses from being set on fire by falling brands.

At any rate, all that was left of our lovely church in the morning were portions of the walls, now scorched and darkened, only the ruins of brick and mortar and a lot of ashes. Oh, we saw a great, but terrible sight that night! Our church had never been so well lit up. But that which brought about such bright illumination also brought destruction. So we were given a very serious reminder and visible proof that all our works, the houses we build, including churches, and everything earthly is perishable and at best serves us only as long as we are here.

1904

God help us to make use of this world as if we were not using it. Let us not forget that this should and must be the attitude of the children of God.

Because of our inexperience, we came near to missing out of at least a considerable part of our comparatively small insurance, but finally managed to collect almost the entire amount. Thereby it was possible to begin the restoration of the church the same fall. The work was left to the same master builder and mason as supervised the building of the original church, that is Mr. Jonas Norell as supervisor of the whole project and Mr. Louis Johnson as contractor for the masonry. Certainly there are many who with me remember how, for lack of a large enough building, we gathered outdoors for services in the wooded park next to the parsonage, with the preacher standing underneath a tree and the old and faithful song leader and organist under the same or another one as he led the singing. The congregation stood, or sat on temporary seats as best they could. We cannot but praise the truth and grace of God, and also remember how God provided for the congregation so it would not be entirely without a meeting place under those conditions.

1904

We remember how previous to my arrival and for several years afterwards the so-called "Waldenstrom doctrine" on redemption was promoted and sadly enough, the minds of some of the folks here were receptive to it. The saddest thing about it was the fact that these persons were the ones for whom we had the best hope of being sincere, serious, and dedicated fellow Christians and zealous and faithful members of the congregation. According to their own profession, they had come to a state of life and peace with God within our Lutheran church. To the praise of the truth of the Lord, we can state and remember that it was only a few families who for this reason separated or were dropped from the membership of the congregation. But I do have painful memories, as do many of you, from that time and strife. I received characteristic and explicit writings at the time (and still have such on file) from former friends. It was only by the special grace of God that the result was only a slight loss to our congregation.

There were several circumstances and conditions, which I cannot go into now because of the shortage of time, which contributed to prepare a fertile soil for such a sowing. At any rate the "Mission Friends" had, even before our congregation built its new church, built "the chapel" as a so-called Mission House on the plot of land almost right in front of our church. They had been able to buy this lot from its former owner who was not exactly friendly toward our congregation. While working on the house, the Friends said: "When we get our Mission House completed, your church (meaning the old one) will be big enough for a long time to come." However, it turned out that they never got their house completely finished, much less paid for, and for that reason when this temple was completed, the Friends were in need of money and anxious to sell. The terms being reasonable and the house, situated as it was, having the potential of being useful in several respects, yes, even "filling a need," which soon was realized, the congregation decided to buy it.

1904

This building, although being made of wood and being so near at hand served as our place of worship. It was, nevertheless, sad to see and know that there was not room enough, even when it was crowded, for all who wished to be along. It can be said to the honor of the members of this congregation that they were faithful in attendance at services. I do not want to say if that is equally true of the younger members of the congregation since these demoralizing Sunday excursions have become so commonplace. I thought I noticed a difference and feared that the result would be damaging.

I think we remember with what satisfaction we began to conduct services in our restored church. That was in the winter of 1889. It was then sufficiently done, but lacked the appealing fresco painting as well as the colorful windows and other things which now adorn the interior. There was also silence both from the steeple and the balcony, since both the bell and the organ were totally destroyed in the fire. Congressman Snyder donated a so-called "reed" organ to the congregation and for some time it served for leading the congregational singing. It was not long before a new bell, which I think is more generally satisfactory, sent out from the steeple its sound of calling and urging to worship.

The congregation took another step during this time, which no doubt all now perceive and admit to have been a step in the right direction and which we now recall with thankfulness. I refer to the decision made, not without serious opposition, to pay from the general treasury of the congregation, year by year, our obligation toward the support of our higher institutions of learning. As far as I know, the congregation has acted according to this decision since the time when the synod decided that the conferences should be responsible for this ingathering. That was in 1882. Some of the members were firmly against complying with this decision, even to the extent of refusing to pay their church dues on account of the congregation abiding by this decision.

1904

It is a joy to recall today that only one head of a family for this reason withdrew from the membership of the congregation and another was dropped for other reasons as well. When the church burned and the congregation incurred debt through reconstruction—there was also a poor harvest that year—the trustees decided, against my advice, that the congregation should appeal to the conference for a cancellation of the sum it owed for this cause, about $250, thus less than one year's assessment. For this action, the congregation sadly, and in my opinion unjustly, had to bear much criticism both privately and publicly in newspapers. The congregation failed to get any cancellation and it is to its honor that it soon paid up in full. I have the satisfaction of knowing that the congregations I have served have become accustomed to fulfilling their obligations to the denomination. The annual statistics will bear this out.

Much could be said about the struggle against sin and misery, which struggle must constantly be waged, and how God has graciously stood by us as a congregation, but we shall close with these words: "The name of the Lord be glorified for the sake of his grace and truth." Also the words of the apostle to the congregation:

> Therefore, my beloved brethren, be ye steadfast, unmovable, always abounding in the work of the Lord, forasmuch as ye know that your labor is not in vain in the Lord.

1904

Pastor John Fredrik Seedoff

Chisago Lake Lutheran Church, 1890–1896
Memorial Speech · Friday, May 13, 1904

7
___
1904

THE CHURCH CHOIR then sang the beautiful song "Comfort My People," the music by Francke, following Pastor Frodeen's message. Next, another former teacher of the congregation, Pastor J. F. Seedoff, of Rockford, Illinois, gave the following interesting memorial speech:

SINCE I HAVE BEEN ASKED to say something about the seven years I had the privilege of serving as pastor of this congregation, I naturally want to comply with such a modest request, but I must still admit I do so with a certain feeling of confusion as to what might be appropriate to say. The outward results of the work of the congregation during my time of office may be found in the minutes and account books of the congregation, but it is not my duty now to present that information. Every congregation has an unwritten history which is preserved as precious memories by such as have for a longer or shorter time been involved in the work and have followed it with a vital interest. It is always very interesting and often very instructive to learn to know about the activities of a congregation in the light of personal experiences, and this is particularly true when it involves as long a time as half a century.

My duty on this occasion, if I have rightly understood it, is only to briefly present something from the history of the congregation during the time I served as pastor here, but mainly from the "unwritten history." This period of time is the years of 1890–1896.

In the early spring of 1890, I was surprised to receive a call from the congregation at Chisago Lake to become its pastor. I say *surprised* because I knew nothing about it until I received the call. I did know that my very dear friend and schoolmate, J. L. Haff of Stillwater, had had a call from the congregation before I did, and therefore I immediately suspected that he had something to do with it, since I had no acquaintances here and had never been inside the boundaries of

1904

Minnesota. How the large Chisago Lake congregation could ever thus venture to "buy the pig in the sack" is something I have never been able to understand, unless there was a feeling of disappointment at having received negative answers from three of the more outstanding men in our denomination.

My first visit at Chisago Lake was in the early part of June. It is an appealing sight for anyone to behold the landscape and smiling lakes of this community in summer garb, but especially so for one who has spent his childhood in similar scenery. As far as the call is concerned, I can sincerely say that it was my first desire that the will of the Lord be done and I tried to look away from the outward benefits that might come with the acceptance of the call. Circumstances, which I need not mention here, led me to the assurance that I ought to accept the call.

The time between my acceptance of the call and my moving to Chisago Lake became a time of trouble and suffering for me. First my wife became ill with typhoid fever and before she was able to leave her bed, I was ill and was bedridden until less than a month before we were to move. It was with great difficulty we made the move and by the time we arrived at Chisago Lake, I was better prepared to be laid in the grave than to preach my introductory sermon. Several weeks did go by before I was able to preach my first sermon. I would not here mention anything about this, since it only concerns me personally and not that it shows better than anything else the circumstances under which I received my first impressions of the Chisago Lake congregation. The words and deeds of love that this congregation showed me and my wife, both during the time of our illness in Kansas and our coming to this place, will among all precious memories stand forth as one of the most precious to which our thoughts can return.

For every pastor it is a joy to see that he is welcomed to his congregation; to see himself loved is more. In this respect I may say that I believe that the congregation that proves that it loves its pastor, both at the time of his coming and during the time he works in the congregation, thereby best serves its own interest. When lack of love disheartens and weakens the one who is called to be the leader against the forces of wickedness, no great blessing and progress is to be expected.

1904

We arrived at Chisago Lake in the early days of October, but my health was not restored to the extent that I was able to serve until shortly before Christmas.

Among the duties that required my attention during the first part of my stay here were preparations for the meeting of the Augustana Synod, which would meet here in June 1891. The congregation had invited the synod at its meeting of the previous year to meet at Chisago Lake, which invitation the synod accepted. Thereby the Chisago Lake congregation got an outstanding opportunity to show its ability to entertain strangers. I believe the judgment of most of the visitors was that the congregation did a good job and I can understand that the members of the congregation liked their guests, because when my successor was to be chosen, almost everyone at the meeting had a candidate to suggest and in each case this was one of the pastors who had been a guest here at the meeting of the synod.

In respect to the number of people in attendance, this synod meeting was the largest in the history of the Augustana Synod. The work required for hosting such a meeting is certainly not small, and, of course, the expense was large, and yet I am convinced that such meetings, because of their influence in bringing about and preserving a feeling of unity, are worth all of what they cost.

One job, which I would like to consider as a preparation for the synod meeting, was the installation of a pipe organ. Since the church was destroyed by fire in 1888, the congregation had no pipe organ. It was always difficult to lead the singing at services in the large church with a reed organ, but had it not been for the synod meeting, it is doubtful if a pipe organ would have been installed this soon.

At the annual meeting of 1891, former Minnesota Secretary of State, Mr Albert Berg, made a motion that a pipe organ be installed at

1904

a cost of about $2,500 and that the work be completed in time for the meeting of the synod in June. It is not to be wondered that the more conservative farmers became quite serious, both because of the very considerable cost and the short time allotted. But when Mr. Berg promised that he would alone take the responsibility of raising the money, it was decided to go ahead at once. No later than May 15, the organ stood in its present place, ready for use and paid for as nearly as $300. But we should also remember that it was not only members of the congregation, but other Swedes and also Americans, Germans, and Irishmen—yes, I was about to say Jews and heathen—who had been accosted by Mr. Berg and did not easily escape until they had contributed something toward the new organ.

I have since often thought of this incident as an example of what can be done in our congregations if we go about the job with strength and enthusiasm, even if it does really seem quite difficult. Often in our church work we make the mistake of discussing and wondering instead of going to work at once, and the result is very often that while we merely talk, other persons or denominations accomplish what we should have done. This is especially true in regard to the mission of the church, internal as well as external.

In this connection, I should like to mention a little episode from the time I was serving the congregation, which I believe by the grace of God turned out for the good of the congregation.

When I took over the care of this congregation, everything was outwardly in the best of order. My predecessor had, for 15 years, worked faithfully in the congregation and it had been granted to him to see the congregation at Chisago Lake develop in the most encouraging way until it became one of the largest in the synod. The church records, the financial system, the church school, and everything was in the best of order. And how thankful every pastor should be when he can take over the work of a congregation under such circumstances!

Although everything seemed to be so complete that one could almost be tempted to think that there was nothing left to do but to preach once a week and perform the necessary duties, I was still soon convinced that there remained much work to be done. Pastor P. Sjoblom, at that time president of the conference, who besides many other good qualifications also had the gift of being able to tell people the truth so they understood it, when that was needed, informed me and one of the older members that we at Chisago Lake were pretty feeble about contributing to missions and a deep-going improvement in this respect would be both necessary and welcome to the conference. I tried to defend myself by saying that I had been the pastor of this congregation only a few months and thus could not be held responsible for this condition, and my friend, Mr. Hultquist, was left to defend himself as best he could. For the time being I could do nothing but put my fist in my pocket and keep quiet, but I decided that as far as possible the condition should be changed.

As is probably customary in most congregations, one collection a

1904

month was taken for missions, which in the course of a year amounted to 10 cents per communicant. But Uncle Sjoblom did not think this was enough, but that it was a disgrace for such a large congregation not to contribute more. For two years I tried to help the situation by taking up a special offering for missions at the weekly fall meetings in the various districts. This worked out quite well and the contributions for missions rose considerably, but it was my desire that the congregation as soon as possible make some kind of arrangement whereby the support of missions could be made more stable in its operation.

I suggested to the Church Council that we arrange a festivity for the 4th of July and donate the income to missions. The motion passed and a committee was appointed to take charge of the festivity. So far, so good. But then some of the members of the congregation started an agitation against the project and positively maintained that there would not be a general interest in such a festivity if the money was to be "given away," as they expressed it. I then realized that here we had

1904   some old ice to break and that losing now would mean to lose in the future. I therefore stood solidly behind our decision that the proposed celebration was to be a missionary festival regardless of whether it be a success or a failure and that every dollar received should be used for missions or charity. I must give credit to those who opposed this festivity because as they saw their mistake in regard to the wishes of the congregation and its ability to serve the holy cause of missions, they gave up like men and did what they could for the project.

We later had such a mission festivity each year and it became easy for the congregation to turn in a decent donation for this important branch of the work of the kingdom of God. That which was now done was a good beginning and we now have cause to rejoice at the continuation of the good work and that the congregation today at its jubilee celebration stands as a worthy example to other congregations in our denomination. The minutes of the past year show a contribution of $500 from the congregation at Chisago Lake. Well done!

At the time of my service here, the Minnesota Conference was also busy paying its debts and an allotment was made upon all its congregations in proportion to its number of communicant members. According to this allotment, our congregation was set down for the considerable sum of $2,000. I remember very well the business meeting at which the congregation decided to pay this sum. The Church Council feared this matter so much that it questioned whether it would even be advisable to bring it up at the meeting. One feared there would be a terrible storm of protest against such a taxation, but the storm did not come. The matter was taken up and handled peacefully and the fellows were in the best of humor.

Folks asked me, "If we pay these $2,000, can we be sure we are then done with it?" I, of course, could not promise that in the future the congregation would escape all expenses for schools and charitable institutions, but I did promise that there would be no further taxation for this particular debt as long as I would be here. This promise certainly did not amount to much, but it was all I could or would promise. Of course, I could not surmise that this problem, which I then considered to be so great, would soon be overshadowed by one much greater. Only a few years later the congregation would, under the leadership of my successor, gather the sum of $3,000 for the same purpose. But the congregation has during this time become rich in good deeds. May God be praised for it all!

1904

I have not said this with intent to flatter, it is only a feeble remembrance of work well done, and at the same time as we joyfully remember that the congregation has done much for the sake of the kingdom of the Lord, both within and outside its own boundaries, it still has not done all it might have done. We hope that by the grace of God greater things than these will be done to the glory of the name of the Lord and great blessing to his kingdom.

Ten years ago, or in 1894, the congregation celebrated its 40th anniversary. Several members of the congregation and one pastor who served the congregation in its early years, have since that time been permitted to leave the work and the struggle here. In every respect that was a beautiful holiday. For that celebration the congregation had the church fresco-painted and installed a new pulpit and new altar, and made some minor improvements at a cost of about a thousand dollars.

Many a time during the years that have passed since I was the pastor of this congregation, I have in my mind gone through the small part of the history of the congregation that I was permitted to help with writing. For me personally, the call to and the work in the Chisago Lake congregation had the greatest significance. Here I became acquainted with church work in a large rural congregation, which I count as a great gain. Many lovely memories from the church and the homes here, from fellowship with the sick and dying, are preserved in faithful remembrance.

When one deals with many people, one cannot expect to escape all bitter experiences. Not until we reach the redeemed congregation above shall all disharmony cease. We also know that the more the Lord's work goes forward in any place, the more will the power of evil rise up in opposition. Sin in general, but also particular sins and vices, stand in the way for the Lord's cause. We must not fear and give up hope when we experience such, but withstand evil to the uttermost, knowing that triumph is certain in the name of the Lord and the reward for faithfulness is great.

Looking back upon the time I spent at Chisago Lake, I see many reasons for thankfulness to the Lord for special experiences of grace. Both I and my wife thrived here; we "felt at home." Here we had many experiences that cannot be forgotten. Four of our children were born here and at this altar they were, through Holy Baptism, received into fellowship with Jesus. For that reason, I have always loved to visit here occasionally. The brotherly hospitality I have always enjoyed in your parsonage with the loving friends there has enhanced my visits and made them into real moments of rest.

1904

But we have here no abiding city. For every Christian, but perhaps especially for a pastor under our circumstances, it is best to, as much as possible, not permit oneself to become too much bound to outward and temporary things, because first thing we know we must leave all and enter into new circumstances. My call away from Chisago Lake was for me almost as big a surprise as my call to service there. He, who in his lifetime became the occasion for me to come here, by his death became the occasion for my leaving. How strange are not the Lord's ways! So a farewell, a moving, and it all seems like a dream. It is my earnest prayer to God that he would give to your faithful teacher much grace and strength to lead and feed the flock of Christ among you, so that at the great jubilee at home with God there may be a large flock from the congregation at Chisago Lake.

Following this speech, Pastor P. Carlson of Omaha was to have taken part in the program, but he was unable to be present. Pastor Carlson did not serve this congregation as a permanent pastor, but often made preaching visits here in the early times and "Carlson in Carver" still lives in grateful memory among the older members of the congregation. His spot in the program of the day was filled by another elderly clergyman, Pastor P. J. Eckman, the father of the present pastor of the congregation. As a memorial scripture passage, he quoted John 8:31-32: "If ye continue in my work, then are ye my disciples indeed; and ye shall know the truth, and the truth shall make you free."

It was emphasized that it is a great advantage to have the Word of God, but

1904

Pr. P. J. Eckman

we must use it rightly and regularly and dwell in it. Our power depends upon this, yes, even our existence in the future as individuals and a congregation. There is a great deal of striving after false freedom, but our goal should be freedom in the truth. "If the Son therefore shall make you free, ye shall be free indeed." Following this exhortation the church choir sang David's Psalm 145, music by B. P. Melin

1904

Pastor Johannes Lundquist

Chisago District Chairman, Chisago City, Minn.
Sermon · Friday, May 13, 1904

8
1904

THE AFTERNOON PROGRAM was arranged so as to give special attention to the thought of the congregation being the mother congregation of the two daughter congregations in Chisago City and Almelund.

The two daughters had received a special invitation to be present and take part in this occasion. This invitation was joyfully received and quite many were present as a result of it. This gave occasion for a beautiful expression of the Christian understanding and common work and aspirations that respect for one another and do not try to damage each other or in a carnal way encroach upon one another's boundaries.

May the good will which has so far characterized the relations between our congregations in this area ever remain. For the promotion of this attitude, the common festivity of the afternoon

was surely conducive and was one of the most beautiful parts of
the jubilee celebration of Chisago Lake congregation.

The festivity opened at 2:00 P.M. with the singing of verses
1-3 of Swedish Psalm No. 274. Following prayer, the chairman of
the Chisago District, Pastor Johannes Lundquist, the pastor of
the Chisago City congregation, delivered a stirring presentation
of which we record this, his own, condensation:

THE ELDER UNTO THE ELECT LADY and her children, whom I love in
the truth; and not I only, but also all they that have known the truth,
for the truth's sake, which dwelleth in us, and shall be with us for ever.

Best wishes to the elect lady (Chisago Lake congregation) on her
"50 Years Jubilee!" On behalf of the daughter congregation in Chisago
City, with respect and love I convey these well-wishes, and at the same
time I express the thankfulness of the daughter for the honor of being
invited to share in this jubilee festival today.

1904

Best wishes to you, for you are the elect lady, yourself a daughter
of the Apostolic church, which was brought to the community of our
forefathers by means of an Ansgar, whom we saw on the pages of history as he appeared in Tiundaland on the shore of Lake Malaren,
Sweden, as he proclaimed the doctrine of the "White Christ," A.D. 830.

Best wishes to you, for you are the elect lady, a daughter of the
Lutheran church, which pure doctrine was first made known in
Sweden by the son of a blacksmith in Orebro, Master Olaus Petri,
when in A.D. 1519, he was returning to his homeland from Wittenberg,
Germany, where as a disciple of the great reformer, Dr. Martin Luther,
he witnessed Luther affixing to the door of the Castle Church, on
October 31, 1517, the ninety-five theses against the errors of the
Roman Catholic church, which had put the light of the truth under the
bushel of the dominion of the pope. This pure doctrine, which was
accepted at the meeting in Upsala in February 1593, consisted of the
three ancient symbols and the Augsburg Confession, from which con-

fessions all present at the meeting unanimously agreed they would not revert, but rather be prepared to risk their lives and their blood. Then the chairman, the venerable Nicolaus Bothniensis, exclaimed, "Now Sweden is one man and we all have one God."

You need not be ashamed of your ancestry, elect lady, if you say you are a daughter of this man. And if you are not ashamed of your ancestry, you will at this jubilee want to thank the Lord for the blessings he brought by bringing the Lutheran doctrine into the community of our pioneer fathers. Let us never, as long as we live on earth, cease to love Sweden and its language, not cease to teach it to the coming generation. Let us never cease to thank God for the good deeds of the fathers and founders within our dear Augustana Synod and for what they brought along from their past. Let us never sell this birthright for the porridge of false unionism which so many in our time cook according to an English cookbook, yes, sad to say, also according to a Swedish one, and serve it in a so-called Lutheran bowl.

Through the Reformation our ancestors had found the lost truth, and the truth made them free, that is, free from Roman error. That was a freedom more meaningful than the freedom of the United States from the oppression of England. But darkness covered the land of our fathers again, and not the least that portion from which most of the pioneers of the Chisago Lake colony came, namely Småland. There was a darkness of ungodliness both among teachers and hearers, which reigned until the Lord again raised up instruments to scatter the darkness. Among them was Petter Lorentz Sellergren, son of the blacksmith in Jönköping, one of the first men of the movement, assistant pastor in Helleberga on the eastern slope of Uppvidinge plateau in Småland.

In 1814, he suddenly arose out of a moral hibernation in drunkenness to the greatest of zeal in his calling for a period of 30 years. A missionary within the boundaries of three bishopricks, he is remembered as a church father. Sinners seeking after salvation went on

1904

pilgrimage as far as 10 miles (about 70 English miles) to get an answer
to life's most important question: "What shall I do that I may be saved?"

Among those who were deeply impressed by this pastor and soul-
carer from Småland was the honorable Augustana veteran, doctor of
theology, Erland Carlsson, who 50 years ago yesterday organized this
congregation at Chisago Lake, himself by the wonderful divine providence another Sellergren to the Swedes on this side of the West Sea.
In this connection I would like to just mention one of the fathers in
this congregation who arrived here the same year as it was organized:
Gustaf Collin from Elmeboda, Småland, a genuine follower of
Sellergren. It was touching to hear him speak about his experiences
from the time he visited Sellergren.

So, best wishes to you, for you are the elect lady because of the
good benefits you have experienced as a result of one of the most richly blest movements the Swedish church has experienced during the
past century.

1904   Hold that fast which thou hast, that no man take thy crown.
As an elect lady you have been able to bear daughters and be a mother
congregation, not only of Chisago City and Immanuel congregation of
Almelund, but of the entire Chisago District of the Minnesota
Conference. The daughter congregation which, so to speak, lies closest
to the mother's breast, is Chisago City (which means, large and beautiful city), which was organized at a meeting called to be held Sunday,
February 8, 1874. On February 20 of the same year deacons were elected, on March 13 trustees, and on May 14, 30 years ago tomorrow, the
constitution recommended by the Augustana Synod was accepted and
a motion passed to request membership in the Minnesota Conference
and the Augustana Synod. The number of communicant members was
then 113, of whom 37 had been members of the mother congregation,
and the residents were 219.

A church was built and a parsonage acquired in 1876. The church
was remodeled and a pipe organ installed in the year 1898, at a total

cost of $4,000. The congregation received a teacher of its own in 1880 when theological student, Er. J. Werner, from Augustana College and Theological Seminary in Rock Island, Illinois, accepted a call and took office after his ordination in the early part of July. He served the congregation until in 1886, when the present pastor, Johannes Lundquist, was on March 25 chosen as the teacher of the congregation and took office in the beginning of September the same year. After 30 years (that is to say, this year), the congregation consists of 566 communicants and 830 residents.

Three of the persons who came to Chisago Lake in 1853 belong to the Chisago City congregation at the time of this jubilee celebration: Peter Gustaf Gustafson, born in Långasjö parish, Småland, September 3, 1816; Magnus Anderson born in Östra Thorsås, Småland, May 26, 1872; Mrs. Gustafa Strand, born in Östra Thorsås, Småland, 1836.

In spite of all divisions, the congregation spiritually stands founded on the truth and the Lutheran Confessions and holds fast to its constitution; so we can say to the elect lady on her 50th anniversary that the daughter congregation, Chisago City, has not fallen before the spirit of the time, which is the spirit of antichrist and that financially we get along well and do not want to be slack in paying our allotted contributions to the denomination.

1904

Now may the truth remain with the elect lady and her children and be with us forever. And now, finally: "Peace be within thy walls, and prosperity within they palaces. They shall prosper that love thee!"

∾

The church choir from Chisago City sang the 84th Psalm of David, music by Wennerberg.

Pastor J. Emil Carlson

Serving a daughter congregation
Speech of Encouragement · Friday, May 13, 1904

9

1904

IT IS A JOY TO BE PRESENT at these holidays not only for myself, but for the daughter congregation in Almelund. It rejoices with you today and sings the praise of God. That is as it ought to be. We express thanks for the invitation to be present.

The duty given to me is to present a speech of encouragement. I would like to tell something about the daughter congregation and its activity. May it be considered as encouragement to the extent that it may.

Remembering the guidance of God, both with our fathers and ourselves and rightly understanding that guidance, tends to encouragement and tunes the heart to songs of praise. It is said about the people of Israel, "They saw the great hand which led them and they sang his praise." They were led by the hand of God. They experienced how wonderfully and lovingly he guided them both day and night. Yes, he carried them as a man carries his son, all the way they had to go until they came to the land that was prepared for them. And they needed such guidance. And under such guidance they could confidently go forward, knowing that no enemy could overcome them, no trouble come from which that hand could not rescue. As they both saw and experienced the faithful guidance of God, his help and protection, they were happy and sang his praises. And they had great cause to do so.

But it is not only the people of Israel who have seen or been the object of the faithful and and loving guidance of God, but other people as well. Our fathers and we have been carried by him as a man carries his son. We firmly believe that it is by the guidance of the Lord we have come to this land, for God has decreed times and boundaries for people to live, and he has graciously helped us and lovingly blessed us.

The Lord has given us a great task to perform in this country. We should clearly understand this task and joyfully perform it. We should boldly proclaim the pure Word of God and Luther's faith and doctrine. If we are faithful to our calling and willing to do the Lord's work, we shall continue to see and experience the Lord's abundant blessing upon our work. We shall go from victory to victory and our hearts shall be tuned to sing his praises for what he has done and will do.

1904

Celebrating people, as you look back upon the past 50 years, you can plainly see that the Lord has been with you and has richly blessed you. When you came, you were poor; now you are well situated. You have this beautiful temple, today in holiday garb, where you may gather around the Word of God and be strengthened in your most holy faith. Give glory to the Lord for it all and sing his praises. And that not only today, but every day. The joy of the Lord shall be your strength. A doubting and depressed heart does not have much power to conquer either the world or itself. "A sad heart has not a nimble tongue." You have no less reason to sing the praises of the Lord than had the people of Israel, but greater.

As you see your children—the daughter congregations—among you, that too should bring you joy. And they rejoice with you today and sing the praises of the Lord:

The children's as the father's voice shall arise to God above calling down his loving goodness upon us and upon all.

I would like to briefly mention one thing and another about the daughter congregation, as you call it. It was not in a spirit of selfishness or ill will that they left home, they who constituted the beginning of the Immanuel congregation, but it was needed for the welfare of themselves, their children, and their environment. For people who have had a churchly background, the land itself cannot satisfy even if it does produce a rich reward for the work of the farmer. The majority of those who first settled around Almelund united with the Chisago Lake congregation. They came from a Christian country and for them Christianity was a precious inheritance, which they had brought along and wanted to preserve and wanted their children to have as their most precious treasure. For the present time they did not even think of organizing a congregation of their own, nor could they have done so; they were too few. They did not want to be without the fellowship of a congregation. Joyfully they united with this congregation and faithfully attended its services although the road was both long and troublesome.

1904

No doubt they wished that the church were nearer at hand. There were some with a clearer eye to the future who saw that this wish would be realized in the near future. And the spot where the church now stands was called the church hill long before there was even any talk about organizing a congregation.

They plainly perceived that there was an urgent need of a congregation, partly for their own sake and partly for the sake of the community. More and more people were moving into the area and most of them remained outside the membership of the congregation with the excuse that it was so far to Chisago Lake. So the sectarians were working to get them into their hands.

It was decided to organize a congregation. A petition was sent to the Chisago Lake congregation requesting permission to do so. There was some opposition, but permission was finally granted. A business meeting was announced to be held in the Carl Shander home on January 31, 1887, for the purpose of organizing a congregation. Pastor J. J. Frodeen was the chairman, John Lindquist the secretary. The minutes of the meeting read, in part, as follows:

> The chairman announced the purpose of the meeting, namely to establish and organize a congregation, which proceeding the congregation at Chisago Lake had, by request, authorized.

It was hoped that the business of the church might be better ordered and the spiritual needs better supplied. Forty-five persons requested membership and most of them had previously belonged to Chisago Lake congregation. At this meeting it was also decided to build a church. John Malm and John Hassel offered to donate land for a church site and a cemetery. This offer was gratefully accepted because it was a suitable spot—the church hill previously mentioned. The church was built in the course of the summer. This work required work and sacrifice, but the generosity was great and the work went forward

1904   rapidly. There was joy in having a church in which to gather around the Word of God.

Student Carl Edman was called—at that time a student at Augustana College and now the pastor of the Taylors Falls congregation—to teach school and to preach. To their joy, he came. The services were held, sometimes outdoors in a grove, and the people gathered with joy to hear the message of salvation. In the first report of the Church Council, it is stated that 69 communicants had united with the congregation and that the total population was 239. Further on we read:

> Which one of us would have imagined that we would so soon have this beautiful temple so nearly completed that we now could gather there to celebrate the beautiful service of the Lord.

When we consider how wonderfully God has helped us and made the people willing to take part and sacrifice, for the sacrifice has been great, we are happy and thankful to both God and man.

The congregation has increased each year. It now includes 422 communicants and 672 souls. It has property worth about $8,000. During these years it has paid out $18,400. Quite a sizable sum for such poor people.

The sectarians have made great efforts to coax them into their slippery byways, and they have succeeded in capturing a few. Had not the congregation been here, they would surely have succeeded better in their destructive work. There are many living in our area who still remain outside of the congregation. The future will reveal whether such can be won or not.

This is what I would like to present on behalf of the daughter congregation to briefly show what it has done and the necessity of having a congregation here. The motives behind the activity can be better judged after 17 years than when they first came into being, especially as one looks at the results.

The daughter congregation wishes the mother congregation the abounding grace and blessing of God.

Finally, a few words to the children of both the mother and daughter congregations. What do we owe the congregation to which we belong? To love her and work for her progress and development. Do we love our church? Are our growing children possessed by the sincere and childlike trust in God that characterized our fathers? Will the hand of God that guided our fathers be outstretched over us in grace and faithfulness? We cannot escape the hand of God. If it is not stretched out over us in grace as he desires, it will be in judgment.

We have examples of this in the history of the children of Israel. In the place where the glory of the Lord used to shine, where the Savior and his apostles walked and preached, how does it look now? Jerusalem is trodden under foot by the heathen. Why? They rejected the hand that was ready to lead them in grace and love, and the result was the candlestick was removed, the kingdom of God was taken away from them. What about these beautiful temples that our fathers erected with

1904

hard labor under the guidance of God and where now the Word of God is preached and praises to the Lord are sung—will coming generations there sing to the Lord?

We are not able to look into the future, but the present looks foreboding. True fear of God is waning in our time. People are not ashamed to jeer at and insult Christ and his Word. Such as do so are honored and such as do not agree are considered to be stupid. That which brings about carnal enjoyment is considered to be great, but that which belongs to the unseen world is considered to be as nothing.

In the same measure as this spirit of the times becomes prominent, the church will suffer oppression. However, the church of Christ cannot be destroyed. Jesus says, "Be of good cheer; I have overcome the world." In the eyes of the world the church does not look bright, but… "As poor, yet making many rich, as having nothing, and yet possessing all things" (2 Cor. 6:10) for she possesses Christ, who was and is and shall be. He knows very well how to preserve her through the coming tempests. His church must grow and triumph through storm and strife, and all the assaults of the enemy will only serve to increase the brightness of his triumph and to show the world how wise and firm are the pillars on which it rests. "Fear not, little flock, for it is your Father's good pleasure to give you the kingdom."

1904

Celebrating people! Humble yourselves under the mighty hand of God. Let that hand guide you and no enemy shall be able to prevail over you. Cherish the inheritance which is yours. May these days of festivity encourage us to more eagerly run the course toward heaven. Homeward and upward, let that be the motto of each of us, and we too shall triumph in the name of Jesus Christ.

Pastor Jonas Magny

A son of Chisago Lake congregation
Sermon · Friday, May 13, 1904

He gave some, apostles; and some, prophets; and some, evangelists; and some, pastors and teachers; for the perfecting of the saints, for the work of the ministry, for the edifying of the body of Christ: till we all come in the unity of the faith, and of the knowledge of the Son of God, unto a perfect man, unto the measure of the stature of the fullness of Christ: that we henceforth be no more children, tossed to and fro, and carried about with every wind of doctrine, by the sleight of men, and cunning craftiness, whereby they lie in wait to deceive; but speaking the truth in love, may grow up into him in all things, which is the head, even Christ: from whom the whole body fitly joined together and compacted by that which every joint supplieth, according to the effectual working in the measure of every part, maketh increase of the body unto the edifying of itself in love (Ephesians 4:11-16 KJV).

IF ANYONE OR ANYTHING IS TO GROW, life is required, and when it is
a matter of the growth of a congregation, life and power must be found
in it, because a dead person or body, while it can be outwardly adorned,
cannot grow. If there is no Christian life in a congregation, it can develop only in that which is evil, and such a development can only serve to
keep it in a state of death, as it is then "dead in trespasses and sins." As
we are now about to speak about the growth of a congregation, and the
development of a local congregation, such as this large Chisago Lake
congregation, it must be that there is life and power, even if this might
be feeble.

A sure sign of life in a congregation is the need for nourishment.
It requires food, and this food should be suitable and nourishing for
such spiritual life as is to be found. According to the development of
spiritual life, steady food is needed. The food should certainly be tasty,
but the taste should not always be decisive; it must be nourishing. The
nourishment must be sound and tend toward "the growth of the body
into a perfect man." Thus will the congregation outgrow its state of
infancy and become capable of proving the spirits and distinguishing
between good and evil. Then it will not be driven about by every doctrinal weather, nor will the gamble of delusion or the sly plots of false
teaching lure it away from divine truth. It will accept all spiritual gifts
from Christ, the chief shepherd. It knows that it is he who has set "some
to be apostles, some prophets, some evangelists, some pastors and
teachers." It realizes that the congregation cannot endure and develop
without the office of the pastor. This office has been instituted for the
perfection of the saints and necessary guidance in the work, "for the
work of ministry, for the edifying of the body of Christ."

We said that the church needs spiritual nourishment and wise
guidance. It will not insist upon the outward glamour of elocution. It
will not be charmed by many words, well put together. It will not go to
church merely for temporary enjoyment, but in order to have something to take along home. "It needs a pastor who can preach to the sat-

isfaction of intelligent people." From this we learn that in order to attain a steady and sound development, the following is required:

1. A faithful pastor, grounded in the Word of God and rightly dividing the word of truth.

2. In the second place, it is required that the congregation permits itself to be led into unity in the faith and the knowledge of the Son of God. There must be unity, and the first thing all the faithful must have together is faith in Christ. He must be the foundation of the faith of all. Our own power must be rejected and all self-righteousness condemned. There must also be a common knowledge about Christ. This knowledge should involve all of Christ—what he is as a person and his work, redemption. Through this knowledge the Christian becomes established in faith, for the better he can grasp Christ, the better can he quietly rest in him. This knowledge not only touches upon who Christ is as a person and his once for all accomplished work of redemption, but also what Christ is doing to bring his church to completion. By means of this knowledge the hope of prosperity in the work is strengthened, and the temporary strifes and difficulties in the work do not weaken but rather inspire renewed zeal for the work.

3. To hold to the truth. The knowledge about Christ will be attacked, and in order to grow it must be grasped as the divine word of truth. The knowledge that has been acquired then becomes a precious truth. Truth without love or correct doctrine without love makes man hard, but love, united with truth, sets the congregation into a proper activity so it can grow in all respects into Christ, so one becomes more and more into his likeness. On the other hand, there is a love that is not founded on the truth, but is false and tears down instead of building up. It seeks peace at the expense of truth and therefore cannot resist evil. A congregation motivated by this false love does not resist false doctrine, but contrary to the Word of God tolerates even rank ungodliness. It might speak up against such as belong to other denominations

—————
1904

in the event that they try to entice away its members, but gladly toler-
ate members whose opinions are totally contrary to the Christian religion, such as the secret societies and similar groups. It takes more
account of outward growth than of preserving the truth, and thereby
has within itself divisive elements. Therefore, it cannot attain unity "in
faith and in the knowledge of the Son of God" and the outward body
of the congregation must sooner or later fall apart, for "a house divided
against itself cannot stand," says our Savior.

**4. Our text presents as the fourth condition for growth; it must be
united in its work.** Our Savior likens the congregation to a body. The
body consists of many members and they are all active. Each member
has something specific to accomplish and no specific member interferes
with the task of any other, and yet each individual member works for
the welfare of the whole body.

We notice further that although each member performs only the
activity that has been allotted to it, it must be "fitly joined together and
compacted by that which every joint supplieth." If therefore any one
member were alone, it could not accomplish anything. It would have no
strength, no guidance, and no purpose for its activity. We see clearly
from this that there must be unity in the work of the congregation. No
activity may be neglected, but everything must work for the welfare of
the congregation and be recognized by the congregation as being its
own work.

The pastor not only works for the good of the congregation, but
what he does is the work of the congregation. When the pastor
instructs the children of the congregation in confirmation instruction
or otherwise, the congregation is fulfilling the command of its Lord to
teach them to observe all that he has commanded. The same principle
applies when the teacher instructs his class, when the organist leads the
singing at the worship service, and so forth. What the council, the
trustees, the women's organization, yes, every individual member
accomplishes should not only tend to promote the welfare of the con-

gregation, but be conceded as being a part of the work of the congregation. In that way, says the apostle in our text, "It maketh increase of the body unto the edifying of itself in love."

Thus we can say about the Chisago Lake congregation: It maintains public worship; it instructs its children; it takes care of the poor, the sick, and such as are in need; it exercises church discipline and does not permit false teaching in the congregation, nor that ungodliness become the rule. It removes itself from everything that may promote evil, such as dance halls, saloons, theaters, and so forth.

The congregation is a Christian congregation and the whole community a Christian community. It promotes the welfare of the whole denomination and carries on a missionary project that has been richly blessed. Every father and mother is concerned about rearing their children to become good church members, and each child and young person works for the upbuilding of the congregation. When one goes to church, to Sunday school, to prayer meetings, to meetings of the women's organization, and so forth, one is not just concerned about one's own enjoyment, but for the edification of all. The pastor is then not the only one to bear the burdens, nor is it the Church Council or the trustees; everyone takes part. The pastor need not then become a detective to ferret out where evil is to be found nor need he be a policeman to put a stop to it and the council will not be regarded as a power that encroaches upon the personal liberty of the members of the congregation. All work as one man, each one in his place and in his calling.

1904

You might say that these are but illusions; we say it is the true situation and such necessary conditions for the proper development of a congregation that if but one of these conditions is lacking, the congregation will not develop properly. You cannot expect any progress without life and power.

1. If there be not life and power, it cannot possibly grow.
2. If there be unity only in faith and understanding, it cannot grow, not grow normally.

PASTOR JONAS MAGNY • SERMON

3. Unless love be founded on the truth, it cannot reject evil and simultaneously promote good.

4. If there be not a right order and unity in the work, the work will not promote its own growth and edification.

But if you, congregation, have these characteristics, your future is assured and you will be a city set on a hill and a wholesome salt preserving from decay.

⟜

1904

Pastor J. Theo. Kjellgren

Serving a neighboring congregation
Sermon · Friday, May 13, 1904

Because thou has kept the word of my patience, I also will keep these from the hour of temptation, which shall come upon all the world, to try them that dwell upon the earth. Behold, I come quickly: hold that fast which thou hast, that no man take thy crown. Him that overcometh will I make a pillar in the temple of my God, and he shall go no more out: and I will write upon him the name of my God, and the name of the city of my God, which is new Jerusalem, which cometh down out of heaven from my God: and I will write upon him my new name (Rev. 3:10-12 KJV).

CELEBRATING CONGREGATION! The great shepherd of the flock and our soul's bishop speaks these words which we have read from the third chapter of the book of Revelation to a faithfully striving and laboring congregation, the one in Philadelphia, Asia Minor. It was probably not yet 50 years old at that time, but certainly not far from it. The Holy and True One had nothing to remark against this congregation but instead it receives the best word of commendation, the richest promises, and the most loving warnings.

To what extent the circumstances in this congregation and the one at Chisago Lake can be compared and be said to be similar, and thus the words of the Lord to the church in Philadelphia can simply be applied to the church here, we shall not judge: God sees the similarity or the difference best. But we have no doubt that the words the Lord spoke to the congregation in Philadelphia can be regarded as words of promise and exhortation to you, too. Since all of the Word of God concerns us, so does this portion. Let these words of promise and exhortation now become the climax of our devotions at this time of festivity.

1. "Because thou hast kept my patience," etc. (verse 10). The congregation in Philadelphia had held faithfully to the word of the Lord, and for that it received praise; for this it receives the comforting promise, "I will keep thee." The concept of being kept in the Lord's word of patience does not merely involve that the Word of God is kept pure in the pulpit, in the confessions of faith, and understanding of his word, but also that in daily life one obediently bows before the will of the Lord in all respects. One sets the word of the Lord over and above the thoughts and ideas of oneself and all other people, and lets the truth be truth, and lets the truth teach, correct, and admonish oneself. Then one needs and uses the Word of God daily. One not only goes to church each Sunday and hears the sermon, but one goes to the very spring of water daily, examines the scriptures, brings one's needs to God in prayer and becomes established in grace. It is thus a Christian keeps the word of the Lord, hides it in the heart, lives thereby, and becomes blessed therein.

And to such as keep his word, the Lord promises his faithful almighty protection. "If you hold fast to me, I shall hold fast to you," says the Lord through the prophet. And in the verse preceding our text we read:

1904

I will make them to come and worship before thy feet, and to know that I have loved thee (verse 9). I also will keep thee from the hour of temptation, which shall come upon all the world, to try them that dwell upon the earth (verse 10).

Times of trial have occurred at many times and in many places here on earth, but here we see that a special time of trial will come and extend over all the world.

At that time, wherever one goes there will be only poverty and oppression, restriction, and difficulty. Those who are faithful to the Lord will then experience in the fullest measure that they are in a strange land where only danger and enemies surround them, but they will also experience the powerful protection of the Lord." I shall protect you," says the Lord, the almighty.

When thou passest through the waters, I will be with thee; and through the rivers, they shall not overflow thee: when thou walkest through the fire, thou shalt not be burned; neither shall the flame kindle upon thee (Isaiah 43:2 KJV).

1904

To preserve and adhere to the word of the Lord, to obediently listen to what the Spirit says to the churches, to trust in the Lord alone amid all outward and inner distress, that has the promise of protection. What security for God's feeble flock! What comfort for every striving congregation and for every individual Christian!

But if we forsake the word of Christ as the Son of God and the Son of Man as our atonement and mediator, as our crucified and risen Savior, who "died for our sins and was raised for our sanctification," then we have no foundation for our faith, no power in our life, no ground for our hope. The future and eternity lie before us in darkness and night, with not a ray of light to meet us.

2. **For our further strengthening amid trials and troubles in this life, the Lord gives us this encouraging promise:** "Behold, I come quickly: hold fast which thou hast, that no man take they crown" (verse 11). It is just a matter of a short little time and the Lord will come. Think

of that often, O striving congregation. Comfort yourself with this thought in the days of trouble: My Jesus is soon coming; my salvation draws nigh. Hold on to this promise. Keep what you have until Jesus comes, and you will receive the entire fullness of all that he has acquired for you. You already have a great deal. You possess him and all his springs of blessedness through faith. You have the forgiveness of sin, righteousness, and peace. You have an inheritance, rich and everlasting, in heaven. You have access to all the goodness of God through prayer in the name of Jesus—keep what you have, O precious congregation.

Keep faith and a good conscience, keep the word of the Lord and a childlike obedience to it! Don't strive for the vain glitter of time; don't follow the charming but empty coaxings of the world. Don't sell your right to citizenship in heaven for any real or imaginary earthly benefits, for the world shall pass away with its lusts. Rather, let anything else be lost than that you should lose Jesus and, with him, all the treasures of heaven. Keep what you have; risk life and goods and honor—every-

1904 thing, for the imperishable crown of righteousness, which awaits every faithful disciple of Jesus. Some day your eyes shall behold the king in his glory, and you shall be like him and forever enjoy his blessed fellowship. Great is the glory which awaits the bride of Christ at his coming; therefore, never let go of the goal, but keep up the strife.

3. It is a matter of overcoming (verse 12). Only he who stands firm to the end will be blessed. Either you will overcome the world and its evil, or the world and its evil will overcome you. The strife is hard and serious, the enemies many and mighty. However, they are forces that have been overcome. Our Savior has overcome the world, the devil, and death. He accomplished that by his humiliation and death upon the cross. Through him we, too, shall overcome, and for us as well it will be through humiliation, defeat, and death. If we but experience weakness, sin, and poverty in ourselves, Christ will be mighty and perfect, and his power is mighty in the weak. Through faith in him we, too, shall overcome, and that only for the sake of the blood of the Lamb and for the sake of the testimony of the Word and that we don't love our own life unto death.

No one receives the crown unless he has striven lawfully, so keep on in wakefulness, prayer, and strife, in faith, hope, and love. But don't trust in your own strength, don't make flesh your defense, congregation of God, for then you will soon be lost. Do not trust in earthly wealth, wisdom, or might; they cannot help. Do not turn one step away from the truth because of the urging of the world and unbelief. Let the ungodly and the hypocrites rage, persecute, and threaten; they will not be able to do anything against you.

> Who is he that will harm you, if ye be followers of that which is good? But and if ye suffer for righteousness' sake, happy are ye: and be not afraid of their terror, neither be troubled (1 Peter 3:13-14 KJV).

But rest upon the Lord with all your heart. Fear and love him and trust in him above all things and then you will overcome in the power of him who has overcome all your enemies.

1904

> He that overcometh will I make a pillar in the temple of my God, and he shall go no more out: and I will write upon him the name of my God, and the name of the city of my God, which is the new Jerusalem, which cometh down out of heaven from my God: and I will write upon him my new name (verse 12).

Blessed words of promise! "A pillar in the temple of my God." God's temples here on earth have such pillars as, so to speak, support a part of the building. We often speak about pillars in the church or the denomination and thereby we mean such persons as have been consistently known for their zeal, faithfulness, and perseverance. In past times people have looked up to this congregation as being a supporting pillar both within the conference and the synod. Truly it is a great honor to be regarded by God as a pillar in his kingdom.

He that overcometh shall nevermore go outside of the house of God—no absence, no more parting, no more pain, no more tears. The old has passed away, all things are made new. "I shall dwell in the house of the Lord forever." It is well worthwhile to strive, to suffer, to keep the patience of the Word of God and keep that which one has received from God. The triumphant reward is glorious and imperishable. Even our old name, reminding us of the "old man" and the sin in this world, shall be removed and we shall be given a new name, a divine and blessed name which will continually remind us of our high and glorious condition. "Bless the Lord, O my soul, and all that is within me, bless his holy name!"

4. **"He that hath an ear, let him hear what the Spirit saith unto the churches" (verse 13).** Congregation of God, continue to turn your ear and your heart to listen to what the Spirit speaks to you. He still speaks to the churches. Listen to the word from the mouth of your teacher; he is speaking to you in the place of Christ, the heavenly king. Listen to the words of calling, warning, admonition, and comfort. Listen to the voice of the Spirit in your heart, read the Word of God, watch, and pray. Know that man does not live by bread alone but by every word that proceeds from his lips. Be awake and look around, watch the signs of the times, and you will to some extent know what time it is. Keep your ear and heart open for all that the Spirit of God has spoken and speaks, but keep them closed toward all strange voices.

1904

Look upward and homeward; await your bridegroom. He will soon come. Be prepared and preserve your raiment; keep that which thou hast that none may take your crown.

A great work has been accomplished within this congregation; the task that lies before us is also great. Be faithful to the Lord and his Word:

> Because no word is given
> As firm as God's own word,
> And nothing been accomplished
> Apart from his command.
> Rejoice in hope, for

All things come to him who has found the Way,
To him who finds all blessedness in Christ.
O God, is it not true, not a mere myth?
Thou hast spoken, and Thou canst not lie.

"Persevere in the strife, in labor and suffering," as the apostle Paul says. "Be ye steadfast, unmovable, always abounding in the work of the Lord, forasmuch as ye know that your labor is not in vain in the Lord" (1 Cor. 15:58 KJV).

Ye shall overcome for the sake of the blood of the Lamb, be crowned with the indestructible crown of righteousness and remain in God's heavenly temple eternally. May it so be, for the sake of Jesus Christ! Amen.

1904

Pastor Ph. G. Thelander

*Secretary of the Minnesota Conference of
the Augustana Synod, 1899–1901
Communion Address • Sunday, May 15, 1904*

I, if I be lifted up from the earth, I will draw all men unto me
(John 12:32 KJV).

IT IS OUR PRECIOUS SAVIOR, Jesus Christ, who speaks these words
immediately before his going to the Father. The eternal counsel of the
Father and our need had drawn him hither to become one of us. He
came to earth solely for the purpose of drawing us all away from the
power of sin, death, and the devil and to the Father's home and bosom
where he himself is at home. The preceding part of the church year has
through its Gospel texts shown us how Jesus has loosed us from our
prison "not with gold or silver, but with his holy and precious blood and
with his innocent suffering and death."

On Good Friday we saw how Jesus paid all of our debt as he suffered, the righteous for the unrighteous, a punishment which had otherwise been that of us all. By his obedience unto death, an obedience which endured every test, he obtained for us an eternal righteousness, innocence, and blessedness.

The great event of Easter, the Father's great Amen to the words of Jesus, "It is finished," reveals to us that the sin of humanity was removed, the debt paid, and the trespass atoned for and an eternal righteousness obtained for us all.

Ascension Day showed us how we poor sinners have, in Christ, been transformed into the heavenly realm at the right side of the Father on high. It is from that place he is now active in drawing us all to himself. He is that firm point, from which the calling takes place.

Subject: Our risen Savior's calling of the redeemed children on earth to actual participation in his salvation.

This calling does not take place with omnipotence, but in truth. Only

1904 one compulsion may be used through the holy means of grace. There is a difference between the calling of small children and of adults. A little child is received into the bosom by a tender hand, because it does not think of resistance, but instinctively feels the loving heart behind the touch of the hand.

Beloved communion children! Thus we were all through baptism received into the arms of eternal salvation and transported into the heavenly realm in Christ Jesus. Did any of you remain there? God forbid that there should be any among you young ones who today are for the first time to meet Jesus in his supper, who cannot say, "I still rest like a child in the arms of love wherein I was laid in baptism." But in these times it would seem that such a case would be a real exception. In regard to the majority we must before God deplore that he or she at an early age wandered away, away in sin and the world. But how do you feel there? You youngster, you old one? Are you really satisfied? Don't you carry judgment in your heart? I know very well that there are many who try to deny this. But you must admit that every time the church bell summons to worship, to you who stay away it sounds like a judgment alarm; every time death strikes its mark nearby you it resounds like a drummer's call; every time sickness becomes your guest, the trumpet of judgment rings in your ears; every time the Lord by his holy law in your conscience or the preaching of the Word set your sins before your face and said, "Thou shalt fear and love God, not take his name in vain, hallow his day, and so forth," it was as if a finger were writing on the wall of your heart: "Thou hast been weighed and found wanting."

Verily, you cannot escape judgment, no matter how hard you may try. And I well know that you do try many a time. Perhaps you deaden the voice of judgment by sport and dance, trashy reading, or maybe with a drink, when you feel ill at ease, or by a restless devotion to your regular work.

Perhaps you may also try to bribe the voice of judgment by means of certain times of devotion or church attendance and for a time endure admonition and so consider yourself to have atoned for your sin to some extent. or you may try to bribe the voice of judgment by temporarily refraining from certain sins, especially when you plan to go forward to receive the Lord's Supper where you then hope to get your debt of sin erased, yet without any desire for liberation from sin—or through certain offerings of labor or money for the benefit of the church or public welfare.

1904

Beloved communion children! Let me tell you: you may try, and to some degree succeed, in suppressing the voice of judgment as did Pharaoh or bribe it like Saul or Eli. Some day, however, the voice of the unbribable judge shall thunder in your ear, "Depart, ye cursed," and you shall recognize yourself, for it was the voice of cursing you constantly heard in your conscience; it was with cursing you filled your miserable life, and if you try again to bribe your conscience here at the communion table, Jesus will deny you all comfort and fill your heart with terror.

Oh, that you would take to heart that even this inner judgment constitutes the beginning of the call of Jesus. He wanted to make it bitter for you in the service of sin and the world in order to create a longing for the liberty which has already been won. He wanted to make you very unhappy and miserable in the faraway land in order to bring to remembrance the lost home that was yours through the grace of baptism. Will you not then listen to the voice of your childhood Savior and permit him through the Word and his voice in the Word to bind you with those threads which together form the strong cord by which he desires to draw yourself to him?

He says, "I will draw all men unto me." He does that through his Holy Spirit who comes to you in the Word. For what is the main subject of the Word? Is it not Christ? For the Holy Spirit takes of that which is his in order to proclaim it to you. Thus he sets Jesus before you. Look only at him! Does he look hard or repulsive? Behold him in his holy life, which was entirely given in loving service to raise up and help men. Behold him in Gethsemane, bowed under the weight of your sins and willingly taking the cup which was given him by the hand of the Father! Behold him on the cross, with tortured body and a heart pierced by the poisoned arrow of evil, yet with the glow of love just as warm in his heart, love to the Father who had forsaken him and to us, his executioners, for whom he prays and lovingly comforts, raises, and soothes the condemned criminal by his side. Behold him, in his resurrection, and ascension, still working exclusively for your salvation! Is he so unworthy of your love and adoration? He has a holy right to own you. Behold also yourself among these dark figures, who hitherto have wounded his heart with your contempt and your insults, even as Jerusalem spurned and blasphemed him, like the priests who spit on him, by profanity denied him, even as did Peter!

Oh, beloved young communion guests, has he so met you during your time of instruction for confirmation that you would consider it a disgrace to be with him and adhere to his Word? Do you feel that the

1904

world is so charming and glorious, that for its sake you would deny and forsake him? Will he have to complain about you: Why will ye die, O house of Israel, when I have, and in myself am, eternal life?

You would not come to me that you might have life and abundance! And you older folks, look at these, your own children! Do you remember the moment when you yourselves received the Lord's Supper for the first time? Do you remember how you felt when you brought these children to baptism? Do you want to bring sorrow to your Savior and be the cause of the downfall of your children and the children of your friends? When you some day stand at the gate of death, do you want to hear your conscience say, "Why do you want to die? Where are the children I committed into your care?" Oh, don't you feel the calling of Jesus? Don't you see him at this festive board? Behold the cross, placed here, with Jesus extending his arms toward you, O sinners, and proclaiming, "Come unto me, all ye."

Oh, do none of you hear in the depth of your heart a feeble sigh, a wailing voice, "I will arise and go unto my father?" Oh, it is the Holy Spirit who has put this sigh into your heart. Let yourself go! The urge may never come again. Let it be your experience that "he stood up and came unto his father."

1904

And how did he come? He walked again, though in the opposite direction, the path he walked away from home, walked the path with a genuine repentance for sin, and what did he find? Yes, a father with open arms, the message of forgiveness and righteousness, restoration into all the benefits of childhood. That is how Jesus meets you when you return. No longer need you excuse or forgive yourself. The arms are open. It is finished; your sins were removed on the cross; your righteousness was sealed in the resurrection of Jesus; you may hide your face and weep by the heart of the compassionate one.

He will meet you here at the altar railing, when you, drawn by his Spirit, the Spirit of grace and love, in an honest spirit of confession of sin return to the Father. Then Jesus meets you and says in the absolution,

"Your sins are forgiven; my body, given for you, my blood, shed for you."

Thus has the calling become blessedly accomplished. You may, and you can, come; you may, and you can, bow before the heart of Jesus. And you who have already found peace and rest there but are still strangers and guests in an evil world: through trouble and trial Jesus is drawing you closer to his heart. You, too, have many steps yet to walk in true repentance, in renewed faith and faithfulness. You, too, would look in vain for anything in yourselves with which to comfort your-selves. Jesus is calling you, too, through the power of the blood back to the cross, the sinner's throne of grace. There is rest, there is forgiveness, righteousness, peace, renewed strength and blessedness. Rejoice! Jesus still draws all to himself at communion. He is the forgiveness of sin, life, and blessedness.

> O pilgrim, worn and weary,
> Come here and rest and pray;
> Before the loving Savior,
> Your heavy burden lay;
> Then go and bring the message
> To others joyfully;
> The way that leads to heaven
> Goes straight through Calvary.

1904

Pastor Axel F. Almer

13

A son of Chisago Lake congregation
Vesper Sermon • Sunday, May 15, 1904

Dear Brethren!

> The end of all things is at hand: be ye therefore sober, and watch unto prayer. And above all things have fervent charity among yourselves: for charity shall cover the multitude of sins. Use hospitality one to another without grudging. As every man hath received the gift, even so minister the same one to another, as good stewards of the manifold grace of God. If any man speak, let him speak as the oracles of God; if any man minister, let him do it as of the ability which God giveth: that God in all things may be glorified through Jesus Christ, to whom be praise and dominion for ever and ever. Amen (1 Peter 4:7-11 KJV).

THE LAST DAYS HAD THEIR BEGINNING with the coming of Jesus into the world. Therefore all New Testament time is called "the last days." It is the last or final period of time before the great day of the Lord, just as Saturday is the last or final day of the week. Even at the beginning of this period of time it could therefore properly be said, "The end of all things is at hand," just as in the morning hour of the day of the week it can be said, "The day of rest is at hand."

These words have therefore resounded very seriously throughout all of New Testament time. They resound even more seriously to us, who are living in the latter days of this period of time. It is getting to be near evening and the day, the last times, is approaching: "The end of all things is at hand."

The congregation has celebrated its 50th birthday. The main events of the 50 years of history of the congregation have been present-ed. Whoever wants to do so will, in this presentation find many sub-jects for serious, educational, and inspiring contemplation. But who is going to tell that which has not been written, and cannot be written? How much of that nature falls within the frame of 50 years! The his-tory of souls who have celebrated divine worship in the sanctuary of this congregation, such vivid records they might contain! But such a history will not be written on earth. That which has taken place is, however, not banished into forgetfulness.

1904

> Never returning are days that are gone,
> Surely that fact is decreed,
> But how we use them will ever be known,
> God is recording each deed.
>
> *Hymn translation by E. Gustav Johnson, 1946*

Will we be granted another 50 years as a group of people and a congregation? We don't know. But we do know that 50 years from now many of us will not be alive. We will then have left this world and gone to the judgment of God, who will render to every man according to his deeds, whether they be good or evil. "The end of all things is at hand."

Who can say how near the day of the Lord is? It is not for us to know times or seasons which the Father has set according to his own authority. But we know that the last day of the latter times is rapidly approaching. And so the bride, the congregation, sings:

> Come quickly, O Lord Jesus!
> Make haste, we long for Thee!
> Come Thou to still the tempest
> And bid the darkness flee.
> Soon let thy church, dear Savior,
> Its consummation know,
> The bride in wedding garments
> Before the bridegroom glow.

"Watch therefore, for ye know neither the day nor the hour wherein the Son of man cometh."

1. The end of all things is at hand. Glorify in us, O Jesus, thy saving love. "Be ye therefore sober, and watch unto prayer" is the admonition of the apostle in our text. What is prayer? Prayer is man's answer to the call of the spirit of God and his works of grace, the innermost expression of man's Christianity and faith, the outstretched hand whereby he requests and receives the gifts of God. Prayer is all the power in all the works of man and the innermost substance in all his thankofferings to his God. This prayer life, which implies a true faith, involves not only particular expressions of the life of faith, but all expressions of faith as a whole. As the blood circulates to every part of the human body, so the spirit of prayer is active in every expression of a true life of faith. The believing soul has fellowship with God in prayer and fellowship with the whole flock of the saved in heaven and on earth. In prayer one's longing for God and for fellowship with him and his holy ones finds its most beautiful expression. But without love there is no longing, and without longing no true prayer.

How our Savior did pray! In the days of his flesh he prayed with strong cries and tears to him who could save from death. His whole life was a life of prayer and herein was contained all of his saving love, his love to do the Father's will, to his Father's house and fellowship with

1904

him, and his love to fallen man.

We have our earthly home. We love this home, we love it more than anything else that earth has to offer. A purer joy than that which a Christian home bestows is not to be found on earth. "There's no place like home; Oh, there's no place like home." We gladly join in this beautiful confession.

But heaven is, nevertheless, our true home. The best home on earth is one where all are of one mind in Christ Jesus, where all are built up in their most holy faith, where love rules and where regularly all experience something of the words of Jesus: "Where two or three are gathered in my name, there am I in their midst." But how few are such homes; they can be quickly counted even in such a large congregation as this one. And how quickly they are rent asunder by sin or death!

> Never the soul found you,
> Home, in the darksome vale.
> 'Twas Jesus who struggled and won;
> Jesus has ransomed you.

1904

The people of God have in all ages felt themselves to be guests and strangers on earth, and their earnest longing has been directed to that better and abiding home in fellowship with God. Do you feel attached to this home? Is this where you have your treasure, your heart's fellowship, and your peace? Do you have daily need of fellowship in prayer with God in heaven? Do you earnestly long for these moments, when you can pour out your heart before him, as a child before his father? Or are you still living in sin, a stranger to God and fellowship with him?

> Where art thou? Where art thou? Art thou still at ease,
> Out there in sin and transgression?
> Are you still spurning your heavenly Friend,
> Growing still deeper involved with the world,
> The world, so far from the Lord?

God has also prepared for us a true home on earth, and that

home is his church and congregation. The believing soul is bound to the congregation of Christ with unbreakable bonds. Here it finds a city of rest and a city of refuge through the days of trouble and strife, and entrance room to heaven itself. For of every individual congregation of God, this is true. How dreadful is this place! This is none other but the house of God, and this is the gate of heaven. Jesus loved his Father's house on earth, the temple and the synagogue; thus the believing soul also loves his congregation, which is his Father's house.

> How amiable are thy tabernacles, O Lord of hosts!
> My soul longeth, yea, even fainteth for the courts of the Lord:
> my heart and my flesh crieth out for the living God.

Such are the feelings and thoughts of every true child of God. In the congregation of God, in the house of the Lord, that life of prayer of which the apostle speaks in our text appears in its most beautiful form. We need to hold on to this truth in these latter days when fellowship with God is not considered to be necessarily connected with the congregation on earth.

1904

If you love God, have a longing for heaven and for the unspeakable peace of the elect, then you will also love the congregation, you will have a longing for its services of worship, its moments of prayer and devotion, and for personal fellowship with the heavenly Father in the word and in prayer. This is the right kind of longing for home and love of home. It will not get lost in empty religious ceremonies, nor in waves of emotion or obsessions, which may have the appearance of Christianity but lack its power; it will bear fruit, thirtyfold, sixtyfold, and a hundredfold. In this way we are made capable of receiving our fellow men with love.

> And above all things have fervent love among yourselves: for love shall cover the multitude of sins. Use hospitality one to another without grudging. As every man has received the gift, even so minister the same one to another, a good stewards of the manifold grace of God.

PASTOR A. F. ALMER • VESPER SERMON

God alone is love. By fellowship with him we acquire true love, and without such love we have nothing to give to our fellow men that can be called love.

It is important to be careful about this, for in the last times the love of many shall get cold and lawlessness shall become rampant, because people will forsake and refuse love for the saving truth, for God's gracious revelation in Christ and his congregation on earth. We have already gone quite a distance in this direction. Troubles are increasing with every year that passes. One kingdom sets itself up against another, one group of people against another, brother against brother. But while this is taking place everyone talks about mutual love, and a type of love is coming into being and spreading which, to the degree in which it prevails, make people indifferent toward saving truth. The word of the Lord tells us what this all means:

> For this cause God shall send them strong delusion, that they should believe a lie; that they all might be damned who believed not the truth, but had pleasure in unrighteousness (2 Thes. 2:11-12).

1904

On the walls of the great community buildings of our time, these words are written *Mene, mene, tekel, upharsin,* numbered, weighed, divided. But who has time to pay attention to that? "Be watchful," so says the Lord, "And strengthen the things which remain, that are ready to die." And to you who know the name of the Lord, comes this admonition: "Watch and pray that ye enter not into temptation." A time of testing is coming over all the world.

> For the time has come for judgment to begin upon the house of God, and if it begins with us, what shall be the end of those who do not believe the gospel of God?

But to such as remain in the truth he says:

> Because you have kept the word of my patience, I shall keep you from the time of trial which is coming upon the whole world to try them which dwell upon the earth. Lo, I am coming soon; keep that which thou hast that no man may take they crown.

Thanks be to God for this promise! By this promise we will, as followers of Jesus, be at peace and patiently await the help of the Lord.

> So even I shall conquer
> In the name of Jesus Christ,
> Yes, even I, so weak and frail,
> Some day shall reach the harbor
> In heaven's gloryland.
> So even I shall conquer,
> In the name of Jesus Christ.

Awaken and glorify in us, O Jesus, thy saving love, a true love for
our right home, for fellowship with others in thee, for our fellow men
in all the world, for brothers and sisters in the faith.

2. Accomplish through us, O Jesus, thy saving will. The will of God
is that men may be saved and come to the knowledge of the truth. But
how are they to become partakers of the saving grace? Through faith.
But faith cometh by hearing, and hearing by the Word of God. This
places serious responsibilities upon the followers of Jesus. It becomes a
matter of faithfully adhering to the Word of God and abiding in it and,
as much as possible, making it known to other people. That is why it
also says in our text:

1904

> If any man speak, let him speak as the oracles of God; if any man
> minister, let him do it as of the ability which God giveth; that
> God in all things may be glorified through Jesus Christ, to whom
> be praise and dominion for ever and ever. Amen.

Everyone who proclaims the Word has the duty to speak as the
Word of God speaks. For him in the first place, it is a matter of being
certain of what the Lord says, what the Bible teaches, for we have no
other word of the Lord than the words of the Bible. Later he must with
all boldness speak this Word, whether people will listen to it or not.
The Lord says:

> Children of men, all my words that I speak to you, take them to
> your heart and hear them with your ears and go to the prisoners,

the children of your people, and speak to them and say to them: thus saith the Lord, whether they will hear it or not.

But the admonition "if any man speak, let him speak as the oracles of God" is not meant only for such as proclaim the Word; it concerns every Christian. Day by day, and under all circumstances, their speech should be such that it is not a variance with the word of the Lord.

> Let no corrupt communication proceed out of your mouth, but that which is good to the use of edifying, that it may minister grace unto the hearers.

But, oh, how little this admonition is heeded! Shallow and unholy speech flows like a destructive deluge over daily business and social life. The unholy tongue "defileth the whole body, and setteth on fire the course of nature; and it is set on fire of hell." Christ says that a time shall come when love shall grow cold, because lawlessness will have taken the upper hand. What is it that will bring about this time? We answer: Spoken and printed words in which the Spirit and mind of Christ have been erased.

1904

The closer we come toward the end of these latter days, the more seriously do we need to heed this admonition and take it to heart: "If any man speak, let him speak as the oracles of God." For false spirits will come, speaking much about the Word of God, but little or nothing as the Word of God. Scorners will come forth who find delight in mocking and insulting because "for them the word of the Lord is derision." But they will certainly not come like ravening wolves but like angels of light, like speakers and defenders of the truth. The Savior says these words and they are certainly not empty words:

> For there shall arise false Christs and false prophets and shall shew great signs and wonders; insomuch that if it were possible, they shall deceive the very elect.

But he who trusts in the Lord shall not be put to shame. The

Lord is nevertheless king and he shelters his own on the day of calamity and protects them in their humble abode. In former times the reading of the Bible was forbidden; in our days men try to rob the public of their Bible by minimizing its value and reputation, and thus there are many who have no Bible. For many others it has not yet gone as far as that. They have their Bibles, but they neglect or misuse them to their own harm. How about you? What is the status of the Bible in your home? Is Christ and his Word that central point around which the innermost life of the heart revolves? Can you boldly declare:

> The Lord is my light and my salvation; whom shall I fear?
> The Lord is the strength of my life; of whom shall I be afraid?

Does not the Savior say, "He that believeth in me, though he were dead, yet shall he live; and whosoever liveth and believeth in me shall never die"?

> O word of power, word of life,
> For blessedness upon our earth,
> From God, the Lord, this gift was given.
> In it all truth and life abides;
> The way to heaven it provides,
> For God, the Lord, has spoken.

1904

Faithfulness to the Lord and his Word; that is the first step in the doing of the will of God. But thereupon follows faithful service.

> As every man hath received the gift, even so minister the same one
> to another, as good stewards of the manifold grace of God. If any
> man minister, let him do it as of the ability which God giveth.

This service, which is spoken about here, pertains to the spiritual welfare of our fellow men, as well as their temporal welfare. The first congregation was a missionary congregation. The words of Jesus, "Make disciples of all nations," was a living power in the life of the Christians, a power which forced the congregation forward from city to city, from nation to nation, with the message of salvation in Christ.

This congregation was also extremely active in regard to helping with supplying the physical needs of the people. Those who were relatively better supplied shared their means "with the needs of the saints." Besides all this, there were in every place servants, deacons and deaconesses, who primarily were dedicated to the work of caring for the sick, the poor, strangers, and such. To all such this charge was given: "As every man hath received the gift, even so minister the same one to another." The following words applied to the remaining members of the church: "As good stewards of the manifold grace of God, if any man minister, let him do it as of the ability which God giveth."

"Christ died for us. Much more then, being now justified by his blood, we shall be saved from wrath through him." You were born and reared in a Christian congregation and all the benefits of Christianity have surrounded you from childhood. What is the value of all this? Would you be willing to trade off all this for the darkness in which, for instance, the heathen lives? No, not for all the gold in the world. The good gifts you have received from Christ are worth more than all the treasures in the world. You know that, yet you will have nothing to do with Christ. You live as if no God existed, as if you had nothing for which to thank him.

1904

> Would you sell heaven's splendor for the earth?
> Or barter life for death, or gems for dust?
> What of the choice? Oh, think thereon in time,
> That you may not too late regret your choice!

And you, who believe in the Son of God and have found life and peace in him, you who can make this confession:

> I have a home, a blessed home,
> E're since the blessed time
> When crushed by sin, in Jesus blood
> I found my anchor firm.

What do you think of the love which God has bestowed upon you? You can but confess, "I have obtained mercy." God has given me all this by grace alone and his paternal goodness, without any merit or worthiness of my own. Can you keep quiet about what you have heard and experienced? Can you remain idle and turn a deaf ear to the exhortation of the Lord? "As good stewards of the manifold grace of God, if any man minister, let him do it as of the ability which God giveth." What is the answer in your heart? We have a big field at our very door within our own congregation, a field which requires much love, prayer, labor, and sacrifice. We have another big field among the suffering, the deprived, and the lost. We have yet another field in the large heathen world where hundreds of millions still sit in the shadow of darkness and death. Oh, the Lord is still calling and beseeching: "My son, my daughter, go today and work in my vineyard."

When we now seriously think about what we have done to serve God in the person of our fellow men, we feel that our sins of indifference and omission are horribly great. We have had the Word of God, pure and clear, in our midst and with great zeal we have watched over it, that it might continue thus. We say that in our own favor. But in this respect we have in many cases—I don't say in every case—been satisfied. We confess this with shame and humility.

1904

And now, Lord, have mercy upon us, that thy will may be done among us, as in heaven, so on earth. Give us a genuine faith, a right faithfulness, a firm hope in thy mercy, and a willing obedience to thy commandments. Help all thy children to remain faithful to thy Word and to patiently await thy gracious help. Be with us, as thou hast been with our fathers that the good work which they started among us may, by thy power, continue and be completed at the day of Jesus Christ.

We are weak; thou art our strength. We are surrounded by powerful enemies; deliver us from evil. We are on our way to meet a mighty persecution; preserve us in fellowship with thyself and grant that on us may be fulfilled thy promise: "Thou shalt tread upon the lion and adder; the young lion and the dragon shalt thou trample under feet."

Give us, Lord, a revival from thee, which may spread from heart to heart, from home to home, from town to town, until our whole congregation may celebrate a Pentecost and be arrayed with new power from on high. To that end, pour out upon thy servants the Holy Ghost and grant that they may boldly speak thy Word, and the name of Jesus Christ. And finally, when the day shall close, take us by grace for Jesus' sake, to thyself in the kingdom of glory. Hear us, God and grant our petition, in Jesus' name.

> All things shall come to him who found the Way,
> To him who here in Christ has found his peace.
> Oh, God, 'tis true and not imagination!
> Thou hast so said and thou canst speak no lie.
>
> Some day God's people in white raiment
> With palms of triumph stand before the Lamb,
> When God himself will all console his children
> And with his hand wipe every tear away.
>
> Awaken, Jesus, this thought within my heart,
> Whene'er the way becomes too troublesome!
> It lovingly shall soothe each bitter feeling
> And, from the tears, bring forth a happy smile. Amen.

1904

50th Anniversary Sermons

Thursday, May 12, 1904

A.M.   Ascension Day sermon by Dr. J. Fremling
Speech of welcome by Pastor F. M. Eckman

P.M.   History of Chisago Lake congregation by Pastor Eckman
Speech by Dr. E. Norelius, recorded in part only
Meditations at the graves of Pastor Hedengran and
       Mrs. Hedengran by Pastor Eckman

Friday, May 13, 1904

A.M.   Sermon by Pastor J. J. Frodeen
Sermon by Pastor J. F. Seedoff and brief talk by
       Pastor P. J. Eckman, the father of Pastor F. M. Eckman

P.M.   Sermon by Pastor Johannes Lundquist, Chisago City, Minn.
Sermon by Pastor J. E. Carlson, Almelund, Minn.
Sermon by Pastor J. Magny, Volga, Wis.,
       a son of Chisago Lake congregation
Sermon by Pastor J. Theo Kjellgren, Scandia, Minn.

1904

Sunday, May 15, 1904

A.M.   Communion address by Pastor Ph. G. Thelander
(Sermon by Pastor P. J. Seedoff not recorded)

P.M.   (Sermon by Dr. Gustav Andreen not recorded)
Vesper sermon by Pastor Axel F. Almer, Forest Lake, Minn.,
       a son of Chisago Lake congregation

50th Anniversary Speakers
and where they were serving in 1904

Dr. Johan Fremling, D.D.
  President of the Minnesota Conference of the Augustana Synod
  Pastor at West Union, Carver, Minn.

Pastor Frans M. Eckman
  Chisago Lake Lutheran, Center City, Minn.

Dr. Eric Norelius
  President of the Augustana Synod
  Vasa Lutheran, near Welch, Minn.
  Zion Lutheran, Goodhue, Minn.

Pastor Johan J. Frodeen
  Spring Garden Lutheran, near Cannon Falls, Minn.

1904

Pastor Johan F. Seedoff
  First Lutheran, Rockford, Ill.

Pastor Peter J. Eckman
  Wadstena (Vadstena) Lutheran in or near Storden, Minn.
  Residence in St. James, Minn.

Pastor Johannes Lundquist
  Swedish Lutheran (now Zion), Chisago City, Minn.

Pastor J. Emil Carlson
  Immanuel Lutheran, Almelund, Minn.

Pastor Jonas Magny *(son of Chisago Lake congregation)*
  Balsam Lutheran, Amery, Wis.
  Immanuel Lutheran, Clayton, Wis
  Residence in Volga, Wis.

Pastor Johan Theodor Kjellgren
   Elim Lutheran, New Scandia, Minn.

Pastor Philip G. Thelander
   Bethany Lutheran, Escanaba, Mich.
   Bethany Lutheran, Perkins, Mich.
   Swedish Lutheran, Ford River, Mich.

Dr. Gustav Andreen
   Professor at Augustana Seminary, Rock Island, Ill.

Pastor Axel F. Almer (son of Chisago Lake congregation)
   Swedish Lutheran (now Faith), Forest Lake, Minn.

Dr. J. Fremling, D.D.   Pr. F. M. Eckman   Dr. E. Norelius

Pr. J. J. Frodeen   Pr. J. F. Seedoff   Pr. P. J. Eckman

50th ANNIVERSARY SPEAKERS

Pr. J. Lundquist

Pr. J. Emil Carlson

Pr. Jonas Magny

Pr. J. T. Kjellgren

Pr. P. G. Thelander

Dr. Gustav Andreen

Pr. A. F. Almer

Interior of church in 1904 at 50th anniversary

Chisago Lake Church, Erected 1882

CHISAGO LAKE EVANGELICAL LUTHERAN CHURCH

Part Two

The First 100 Years

1854–1954

❧

EMEROY JOHNSON

Emeroy Johnson (b. Sepember 18, 1899; d.
December 20, 1986) is a son of Chisago Lake
Church. He is the author of many articles and
books on Swedish-American history and church
history, including *Chisago Lake Evangelical Lutheran
Church, 1854–1954*, a 100-year history of the congregation. Part Two, "The First 100 Years," is an
edited version of this book.

Preface to Part Two

EMEROY JOHNSON WAS BORN on September 18, 1899, the third child of Solomon and Elizabeth Johnson. The family lived in the home that Elizabeth's father built around 1890. Emeroy attended the little one-room school in the community in which he lived.

Lindstrom–Center City High School was constructed in 1916 and he was in the first graduating class. He graduated from Gustavus Adolphus College, Saint Peter, Minnesota, in 1925 and from Augustana Lutheran Seminary, Rock Island, Illinois, in 1928. He was ordained upon receiving a call from a congregation in Missoula, Montana, and then served several congregation in Minnesota.

In 1934, Emeroy translated into English the autobiography of Eric Norelius, which the Reverend Norelius had written in Swedish in 1916. In 1946, Dr. Emil Swenson, president of the Lutheran Minnesota Conference of the Augustana Synod, stated in his annual report to the conference that plans were being made to publish a history of the early years of the conference for the 90th anniversary to be observed in 1948.

The Reverend Emeroy Johnson was asked to write this history and as a result he authored the book *A Church Is Planted*, which was published in 1948. A sequel to this book is *God Gave the Growth*. He was also the author of *Eric Norelius: Pioneer Midwest Pastor and Churchman*, a biography of Eric Norelius, which was published in 1954.

In 1939, Chisago Lake Lutheran Church, under the leadership of Pastor J. Henry Bergren, voted to have a history written. Emeroy Johnson was asked to write this history of his home church and he agreed to do so. The history he wrote at that time was not published, but he revised his manuscript and completed it for the 100th anniversary of the congregation in 1954. This book has been edited and reprinted as Part Two of this publication.

After Emeroy Johnson's retirement, he served as archivist at Gustavus Adolphus College. He passed away in December 1986 at the age of 87.

EUNICE JOHNSON ANDERSON

Preface to First Edition, 1954

IT IS AN INTENSELY INTERESTING experience to study the story of
one's own spiritual background and to examine that soil in which one's
own roots have developed. The writer of this volume was a member of
the Chisago Lake congregation from the day of his baptism in 1899
until shortly after his ordination to the ministry in 1928. Mother had
come to the community with her parents in the early 1870s, and father
came in 1886. The old family home is still maintained, and the Chisago
Lake Church still is the "old home church." Memories of childhood and
youth are still cherished and frequently recalled to mind. As the years
go by one begins to realize how deeply one's life is rooted in the soil of
one's home community and church. For these reasons the writer considers it a privilege to have been entrusted with the responsibility of
editing this volume.

The project was begun in 1939, when, at Pastor J. Henry
Bergren's suggestion the congregation voted to have a history written.

No history of the congregation had been published in English prior to that time, except a brief summary in *The Beginnings and Progress of Minnesota Conference* in 1929.

The source materials were mostly in Swedish, including the minutes of the congregational meetings since the organization of the church in 1854, the minutes of the church board and of several of the organizations of the church.

Eric Norelius has given us somewhat detailed accounts of the early history of Chisago Lake in *De Svenska Lutherska Församlingarnas och Svenskarnes Historia i Amerika, Volume I,* pages 540-601, and in his *Tal Hållit vid Minnesotakonferensens 25-års Fest* (a historical address delivered in the Chisago Lake church 1883 and published 1898). These were based partly on his own experience and personal records, partly on letters written by pioneers at Chisago Lake, and partly on a manuscript history written by Pastor C. A. Hedengran in 1867. (This manuscript is in the archives of Augustana College, Rock Island, Illinois.)

At the 50th anniversary of the congregation in 1904 Pastor F. M. Eckman wrote a history of Chisago Lake, which was included in the *Minnesskrift* published by the congregation.

In 1908 Eckman edited a historical volume on the occasion of the 50th anniversary of the Minnesota Conference. Chisago Lake occupies a prominent place in the book.

Dr. Emil Lund's *Minnesotakonferensens och dens Forsamlingars Historic,* published 1924, also tells the story of Chisago Lake (Volume I, pages 341-352) .

The history written by the present writer in 1939 was not published, but a brief summary of it was published for the 95th anniversary of the congregation in 1949. Further research has been made in the years since then, and the manuscript written in 1939 has been completely revised and brought down to date. In this revision various new sources have been used, particularly manuscript letters and other materials found in the archives of Augustana College, Rock Island, Illinois,

Gustavus Adolphus College, Saint Peter, Minnesota, and a few items in the possession of the writer. Most of the photographs used as illustrations in this book have been collected by the present pastor of Chisago Lake Church, the Reverend J. Walton Kempe, under whose leadership the congregation is celebrating its centennial with special festive services on all the Sundays of the month of May 1954

It is the hope of the writer that this history may serve the present generation and future generations or members of Chisago Lake, to acquaint them with the story of their church, how it was founded, what obstacles have been met and overcome, what religious principles have permeated the pastors and the people of this congregation. Above all, it is the writer's hope that a knowledge of our past history may so enlighten and inspire us that we will become more appreciative of our church, more faithful to our God, more willing to serve our fellowmen in humility and love.

EMEROY JOHNSON

Chisago Lake Church, Erected 1888

Per Anderson

Minnesota's First Lutheran Layman

THE CHISAGO LAKE Evangelical Lutheran Church, Center City, Minnesota, is the second oldest congregation of the Lutheran faith in Minnesota, having been organized on May 12, 1854.

As a group of believers joining together for informal worship without any pastoral leadership but with laymen conducting services, performing baptisms, burying the dead, it dates back to 1851 and is thus the earliest group of Lutherans in the state of Minnesota. These early settlers were Swedish immigrants who had crossed the Atlantic to make their homes in the "land of opportunity." A famous Swedish writer, Fredrika Bremer, had visited Minnesota in 1850 and had then predicted, in her *Homes of the New World*, that Minnesota would some day be a

> glorious new Scandinavia.... Here the Swede would again find
> his clear, romantic lakes, The plains of Scania rich in corn, and

---

Per Anderson is the real-life person on whom the fictional character Karl Oskar is based. This statue of Karl Oskar and Kristina Nilsson shows them *looking back, missing the familiar; looking forward, anticipating the new.*

the valleys of Norrland.... The climate, the situation, the character of the scenery agrees with our people better than any other of
the American states, and none of them appears to me to have a
greater or a more beautiful future before them than Minnesota.

Miss Bremer wrote down those impressions on October 25,
1850. On that very day a Swedish sailing vessel, the Odin, was nearing
the shores of America, bringing to this land some of the first settlers at
Chicago Lake, the vanguard of a hundred thousand Swedish settlers
who would come to fulfill Miss Bremen's prophecy of a "Scandinavia in
Minnesota."

Per Anderson, familiarly known in his home community as "Joris
Pelle," had sold his farm in Helsingland, Sweden, and had decided to
emigrate to the United States. Others in the community followed his
example, until there were more than 100 in a party that sailed from the
port of Gävle in August 1850. After 11 weeks on the ocean with days
of storm and days of calm, the group—minus nine who had died during the voyage—landed in New York on October 31.

1850

It had been their purpose and plan to stay together in America,
establish a new colony, and organize a congregation. Before they left
Sweden they had conferred about calling a pastor. They had sought to
secure Pastor A. Wiberg of Stockholm as their spiritual leader in
America. He had declined but had recommended Pastor G. Palmquist.
The group had agreed to this suggestion and Palmquist had promised
to come the following year.

No definite plans had been made as to a place for their colony. As
soon as the group reached New York, one after the other dropped out,
The first was Anderson's hired girl, Britta, who had been scolded
because she whiled away time on board ship with the sailors as her
companions. Others left the group in Chicago and elsewhere along the
route. It seemed that the plan for a new colony was being frustrated.
But Per Anderson was not to be dissuaded. While he spent the winter
in Moline, Illinois, he received a letter from an old friend of his, Ulrik

Nordberg. This letter set Anderson's thoughts winging toward Minnesota.

Nordberg had emigrated to America with a Swedish religious group known as the "Erik Jansonists." Janson was a religious fanatic who separated from the Church of Sweden and with some 2,000 followers settled at Bishop Hill, Illinois. They attempted to maintain a sort of social-religious community where no one was to own private property. Ulrik Nordberg became dissatisfied with this experiment and went on a journey to Minnesota Territory in the fall of 1850. Coming up the Mississippi and Saint Croix Rivers to Taylors Falls he explored the unsettled, thickly wooded regions a few miles west, discovering Chisago Lake, then known to the Chippewa Indians as "Ki-chi-saga." One lone white man by the name of Van Raensler lived in a hermit cabin on a little island in the lake (where Park Island Hotel was built many years later).

Nordberg was pleased with the region and wrote to Per Anderson in Moline, sending along a crude map indicating how to reach the place. The description of the place given by Nordberg of a beautiful lake with many bays and inlets, wooded shores and islands, plenty of fish and game, possibilities for farming when the land was cleared, appealed to Per Anderson. He determined to move to Minnesota, and as soon as river navigation opened in the spring he and his family with two other families and several hired men, set out on the up-river journey. The other families were the Per Bergs and the Peter Wicklunds. On the boat they met another Swedish family, the Anders Swensons, who had immigrated to America via New Orleans. They had had the unfortunate experience of losing all their baggage at Saint Louis. Fortunately, however, the famous Swedish singer Jenny Lind was giving a concert in St. Louis the same day. When she heard of the plight of her countrymen she gave the Swenson family 50 dollars.

The four Swedish families with their hired men landed at Stillwater, which at that time was the head of steam navigation on the

1851

Saint Croix. There they built two crude flatboats, and with the power of the men themselves propelling the boats, the voyage to Taylors Falls was completed on April 23. Women and children stayed in the village a few days while the men made a trail through the forest to Chisago Lake.

The Wicklund family stayed near Taylors Falls. The others in the party settled on the shore of Chisago Lake. As closely as can now be determined, the Anderson family built their log cabin home about half a mile east of where the Chisago Lake church now stands, approximately at the northeast corner of the old cemetery. South Chisago Lake extended almost up to that point in those days. The Berg family settled on land now included in the parsonage property. The Swensons took over Nordberg's claim, which was the narrow ridge of land that later became the site of the village of Center City. (Nordberg did not stay long in the community after other settlers arrived.)

The land was unsurveyed, and the settlers were squatters on government property. This was a common practice all along the frontier. When the land was offered for sale, each farmer could buy 160 acres at $1.25 per acre.

1852

Other settlers arrived at Chisago Lake during the summer, and 10 farms were begun. Nine of the farmers were Swedish immigrants, one was an American. Another 10 or 12 families arrived at Chisago Lake in 1852, with more in 1853. They generally chose land along the wooded bays and inlets of the lake, and on the shores of smaller lakes nearby. The lakes furnished their water supply before wells were dug. Fishing was good, providing an excellent addition to the diet. With the oncoming wave of immigration the land farther from the lakes was soon occupied. Within five or six years nearly all the government land in the region had been claimed by settlers, almost all of them Swedish people. In 1856 the population was estimated to be about 500.

It was a difficult and often a discouraging task to begin farming in a heavily wooded area. Most of the work was done by manpower.

Only Per Anderson, of the early settlers, had a horse, and this faithful friend of the whole settlement was found dead one day in the woods.

Trees and brush had to be cut down and burned, and little patches of field and garden started between the stumps. But progress was made in spite of a rainy spring in 1852, which made land clearing a slow and soggy job. In the fall of that year Anderson mentioned in a letter to a friend that he had planted apple trees and that they had raised tomatoes, cucumbers, and other vegetables in their gardens. The usual field crops were potatoes, corn, oats, and wheat.

Per Anderson's group of immigrants included one young man whose purpose in coming to America was to study for the ministry. His name was Eric Norelius. Anderson had great confidence in the young Norelius, who was only 17 when he came to America. The two became intimate friends. When Anderson was founding a new Swedish colony in Minnesota, Eric Norelius was a student at a German Lutheran college and seminary, Capital University, in Columbus, Ohio. Letters written by Anderson to Norelius in 1851, 1852, and 1853 have been preserved and constitute an interesting source of information about the first few years of the Chisago Lake community.

1852

According to these letters it is clear that the settlers met for worship in the out-of-doors in 1851. The first service indoors was held on the First Sunday in Advent, November 30, 1851, in the newly finished Anderson home. Here also the settlers met to celebrate their first Christmas in Minnesota. Again on New Year's Day in 1852 they assembled for song and prayer, but on that day they decided to have no more services until the group increased in number.

Anderson was one of those who in Sweden had been deeply affected by the pietistic movement. This was also true of Eric Norelius. Anderson felt that his neighbors at Chisago Lake were in spiritual darkness, and he longed for the day when a pastor would come and a congregation would be established. "I long for the arrival of Palmquist as the bird waits for the coming of dawn," he wrote to Norelius on

PER ANDERSON

March 21, 1852. Pastor Palmquist came to America, and was on his way to Chisago Lake in the summer of 1852. He and a companion came by river steamer to Stillwater. There was no steamboat service up to Taylors Falls, and they feared a 30-mile hike across country. Consequently Palmquist never reached Chisago Lake. But the greatest disappointment for Per Anderson was the news obtained on a visit to friends in Iowa, that Palmquist had given up the Lutheran faith and had become a Baptist.

It was Anderson's firm hope and desire that a Lutheran congregation should be established at Chisago Lake, but now that Palmquist had failed them there was no immediate prospect that the hopes could be fulfilled. Not until 1854 did a Lutheran pastor come to visit the Swedes in Minnesota. In the meantime the settlers at Chisago Lake were visited by ministers of two other denominations, the Episcopal and the Methodist. But, chiefly, the settlers met for occasional devotional services, sometimes under the leadership of Anderson, sometimes with other men of the community in charge. Anderson wrote to Norelius suggesting that he discontinue his college studies in order to come and serve as pastor at Chisago Lake.

Anderson may rightly be called "Minnesota's first Lutheran layman." Though he was not immediately successful in getting a congregation established at Chisago Lake, his influence on the community was undoubtedly one of the prime factors in determining the religious character of the settlement.

The first native-born child in the community was a daughter of Mr. and Mrs. Per Anderson, born in November 1852. As there was no pastor to be had, the little girl was baptized by her father, and given the name Kristina.

During the winter of 1852–53 Anderson worked in a logging camp at Rice River, 60 miles northwest of Chisago Lake. He returned home on March 25, 1853, and from that day on there was hardly a day that he and his family had the house to themselves. Many new settlers

1852

were arriving, some from Illinois, immigrants who had come from Sweden a year or two earlier, others coming directly from Sweden. In June, Eric Norelius was going to New York to meet a company of Swedish immigrants, including his own parents, brothers, and sisters. Anderson wrote to Norelius and asked him to accompany this group to Chisago Lake. They did not come as early as expected, and on August 7 Anderson wrote to Norelius telling him that it would be difficult to provide lodging and food for more immigrants during the coming winter. So many new settlers had come during the spring and summer of 1853 that every available home was crowded, and food supplies were not any too plentiful. The Norelius party did not arrive in New York until November. They spent the winter in Illinois and some of them came to Chisago Lake the following spring.

One of the settlers who came to Chisago Lake in 1853 was Daniel Lindstrom, Per Anderson's half-brother. In 1854 he took possession of the land that later became the site of the village of Lindstrom, so named in honor of the first settler.

Among the many new arrivals in 1853 was one large group of immigrants from the province of Småland, people who in their home parish had been deeply influenced by a zealous and able pastor, Erland Carlsson. He was called to America to serve a newly organized Swedish Lutheran congregation in Chicago. When he left Sweden to accept this call a large number of his parishioners decided to emigrate with him. Many of these came to Chisago Lake in the summer of 1853 and became influential in the building up of the community and in the plans for organizing a Lutheran congregation.

Chisago Lake Wants a Lutheran Church

Gustaf Unonius, a Swedish Episcopalian minister in Chicago, was the first ordained pastor to visit the Chisago Lake colony. This was in the fall of 1852. Though he accomplished nothing in the way of establishing a congregation, the story of his visit is of interest and importance.

He was an able man and had he succeeded in
getting a call to Chisago Lake the story of this
congregation might have been a glowing chapter in the history of the Episcopal church in
America.

Unonius had emigrated from Sweden in
1841 together with a group of so-called "better
people," people from the ranks of the cultured
and professional classes who were generally
considered above the peasants and the labor-

Pr. Gustaf Unionus

ers. They settled at Pine Lake, about 30 miles from Milwaukee, near
the present village of Nashotah, Wisconsin. Unonius's descriptions of
his life on the frontier are colorful and interesting. But he did not stay
on his pioneer farm. He had been a student at Uppsala University.
Shortly after his arrival in America he decided to enter the ministry in
the Protestant Episcopal church, having become acquainted with a
great Episcopal leader, the Reverend James Lloyd Breck.

1852

Breck established a seminary at Nashotah, and Unonius studied
there three years. His ordination in 1845 is said to have been the first
ordination of an Episcopalian minister in Wisconsin. He served for a
time at Manitowoc, and in 1849 moved to Chicago, where he organized
a Swedish Episcopalian congregation called St. Ansgar's Church. He
was convinced that the Episcopal church in the United States was the
true counterpart of the Lutheran Church of Sweden, and he set himself forth as the only true representative of the Swedish church in
America. He even sought official support for this claim from
Archbishop Wingard of Sweden, but in this he failed.

Knowing that there were Swedish immigrants in Minnesota
Breck arranged for Unonius to visit the settlements in Saint Paul,
Scandia, and Chisago Lake. It was on September 17, 1852, that
Unonius conducted services at Chisago Lake.

Concerning this visit Per Anderson wrote to Eric Norelius:

We have today for the first time had the honor of having a pastor at Chisago Lake. Unonius from Chicago has been here and. had a communion service. It was indeed a festive occasion, but one thing was lacking, namely, the mystery of the gospel, which is above all human understanding. He preached the Word of God just fairly well and defended the sacraments fully according to our confession, but in every respect just like the state Church of Sweden... he gave us strict admonitions not to turn away from our confession, and warned particularly against Baptists and other sects; but he insisted that no unordained person had the right to perform any pastoral acts, as e. g., baptism. He referred us to English pastors of the Episcopal Church if there was any need for such services. For my part this has no importance, for I set more value on Christ's command and the Word of God than ordination and clerical garb, if the necessity arises; but many stumble at it, if we ourselves should do anything like this. Please write me a few words about this next time you write.

Unonius will surely hasten the settling of this region, and it seems that the population will increase considerably this fall. Five or six families are now on the way, and are expected today or tomorrow, and Unonius said he will send a large number here next spring. He has also made arrangements with the governor in St. Paul to have the adjacent land around this settlement held open for incoming Swedish people, and this was granted... He promised, or rather he offered to get us a pastor as soon as possible, and for this purpose he intends to go to Sweden next spring to bring ministers to this country. I could not oppose him, but I thought: Lord, wilt Thou send laborers into Thy vineyard; Thou knowest who is most useful.

1852

That Unonius had made agreement with the governor to have certain lands reserved for Swedes is very unlikely. Possibly he had called on Governor Ramsey in Saint Paul to ask about Swedish settlements in the territory, but the governor had no authority to designate certain lands for certain groups of people.

Later in the winter (1852–53) Pastor Unonius offered to come to

Chisago Lake and to serve as pastor of the people in the settlement. In a letter dated February 9, 1853 Per Anderson wrote to Norelius:

> I have had another letter from Unonius. He offers to come next fall to be our pastor. I have not replied yet, but I say openly that I, for my part, do not want him, although I know that most of the people around me think highly of him.

It does not seem that Unonius ever again visited Chisago Lake. In the fall of 1853 he went to Sweden. He came back to America in 1854, but in 1858 he returned to Sweden and remained there the rest of his days.

Though Unonius had very little influence on the religious life of the Chisago Lake community, it is likely that he guided and encouraged many Swedish immigrants to settle in Chisago Lake. He occupied a strategic place in Chicago as the only Swedish clergyman in the city at a time when hundreds of Swedish immigrants were coming to look for a place to live in America.

1853

The first Methodist minister to visit Chisago Lake was Carl Peter Agrelius. He had been a pastor in the Church of Sweden for a number of years. On his coming to America in 1851 he joined the Methodist church in New York. He later made his way west and came to Minnesota. The exact date of his first visit to Chisago Lake is not known, but it was some time before January 27, 1854, for on that date one of the settlers, Daniel Peterson wrote to Pastor Erland Carlsson at Chicago and said, in part:

> We have what we need for our bodily life, but for the spiritual life we need help. We gather every Sunday to read and sing, but we need more to edify our souls. We have had a minister here by the name of Agrelius. He proclaimed the Word of God acceptably, but we did not generally dare to take communion, since he has a different doctrine.

After a Lutheran congregation had been organized, in May 1854, Agrelius and other Methodist missionaries continued their efforts. The first Swedish Methodist "camp meeting" ever held in Minnesota was held at Chisago Lake in 1858. A small Methodist congregation existed for a time in Center City, but was moved to Lindstrom, becoming the nucleus for the present Methodist congregation there.

During the summer of 1854 a Baptist missionary, Frederik O. Nilsson, came to Chisago Lake to seek to win adherents to his faith. A few Swedish Baptists had come to Chisago Lake from Illinois, and in 1855 a Baptist congregation was organized by Nilsson. Among those who were won to the Baptist faith were the parents of Eric Norelius. Eric's brother, Anders, had previously joined the Baptist church in Illinois and became a Baptist preacher.

The Baptists moved away from Chisago Lake, being among the earliest settlers at Cambridge, where a large and flourishing Baptist congregation came into being.

Per Anderson, Daniel Peterson, and others who longed for the establishment of a Lutheran congregation at Chisago Lake, determined to seek the help of the Swedish Lutheran pastors in Illinois, of whom there were three at this time: L. P. Esbjorn at Andover, T. N. Hasselquist at Galesburg, and Erland Carlsson in Chicago. All these three men visited Chisago Lake in the pioneer period, but it was Carlsson who came first and organized the congregation in the spring of 1854.

1854

∾

PER ANDERSON

Pastor Erland Carlsson

A Congregation Is Organized

15
1854

THE PASTOR WHO LED in the organizing of the Chisago Lake Church was Erland Carlsson. He was then 32 years of age, unmarried, pastor of the Swedish Lutheran Immanuel congregation of Chicago. He had been in the ministry five years, having served a congregation in his native province of Småland, Sweden, four years prior to his emigration to America. At a time when many of the pastors of the state church of Sweden were guilty of neglecting their spiritual responsibilities towards their people, and even neglecting their own spiritual life, Erland Carlsson was one who preached the law and the gospel fully and clearly and sought his people for pastoral counseling with them. He had marked success in his parish and people flocked to hear him.

Among his friends who emigrated with him to America was Daniel Peterson, mentioned in the previous chapter. In the letter already referred to, written by Peterson on January 27, 1854, he pleaded with Carlsson to come for a visit:

We have what we need for the temporal life, but for the spiritual life we need help…. We are longing for Pastor Erl. Carlsson's coming in the spring. I hope you will come, pastor. We will pay the travelling expenses. I hope you will come and stay with me while you are caring for us here in the settlement.

Not only the Chisago Lake colonists, but also the Swedish Lutherans in Saint Paul were asking for a pastor at this time. A letter dated March 15, 1854, addressed to Pastor T. N. Hasselquist, reported that the Swedes in Saint Paul had formed a Lutheran congregation, and they asked for help and advice in regard to getting a pastor. They stated that the number of Swedes in Minnesota at that time was about 600: Chisago Lake was reported to have 200, Marine (Scandia) 100, Saint Paul 150, and various scattered places 150. This letter was signed by Frank Mobeck, C. J. Lindstrom, C. A. Hedengran, P. M. Anderson, and A. J. Ekman.

In response to the Macedonian call from Minnesota, the pastors in Illinois agreed that Carlsson should visit Minnesota in the spring and that Hasselquist should make a missionary journey to those settlements later.

1854

Leaving Chicago in the latter part of April, Carlsson came to Rock Island and then journeyed by Mississippi River steamer to Saint Paul, which at that time was a city of some 6,000 inhabitants. When he set foot at the levee at the foot of Jackson Street he was the first Lutheran minister to come to Minnesota. He stayed a few days in Saint Paul helping the Swedes to get a Lutheran congregation established. The letter written to him in March made mention of a congregation already established, but he found that the organization had not been perfected, and therefore a meeting was held on May 6 for the formal organization of the First Lutheran Church of Saint Paul.

Pastor Carlsson then continued his journey to Chisago Lake. His friends and former parishioners welcomed him heartily, as their hopes and wishes were at last fulfilled. Now they could have a Lutheran service. Now a Lutheran congregation would be organized. The organization meeting was held on Friday, May 12, after which Carlsson stayed in the community a few days, conducting services several times. On his return to Saint Paul he organized the Scandia congregation on May 19.

No list of charter members of the Chisago Lake Church is now in existence, and it seems that none was ever made. Dr. Erik Norelius, in his history of the Swedish Lutheran congregations, stated that there were about 100 communicant members when the congregation was organized. In the history written by Dr. F. M. Eckman at the time of the 50th anniversary of the congregation he gave the number of charter members as 57. Dr. Emil Lund, in his history of the Lutheran Minnesota Conference, quotes from a letter written by Erland Carlsson on July 10, 1854, to Dr. Peter Fjellstedt in Sweden, in which Pastor Carlsson said that there were about 200 persons in the Chisago Lake community at the time of his first visit there and that nearly all of them joined the congregation.

The oldest church register of the congregation dates from 1855, and was begun by Pastor P. A. Cederstam. There is no separate listing of charter members, but the records indicate the date when each person joined the congregation. In this book we find records showing that the following became members of the congregation on the day of its organization: Maria Carlsdotter; Mr. and Mrs. Anders Swenson and three children; Mr. and Mrs. Daniel Peterson and one child; Johannes Helin; Mr. and Mrs. Pehr Nilson Berg, their son Nils Berg and one child not confirmed; Daniel Nilsson; Mr. and Mrs. Hakan Larson Swedberg and one child; Matthias Swedberg; Swen Swedberg; Mattis Bengtson; Mr. and Mrs. Per Johnson Lund and one child; Mr. and Mrs. Anders Magnus Ahlstrom and three children; Mr. and Mrs. Daniel Larson Lindstrom; John Johnsson; Mr. and Mrs. Peter Johansson Wiberg and one child; Johannes Jonasson Lind; Mr. and Mrs. Sven Magnus Peterson and two children; Johanna Christina Peterson; Helena Nilsdotter; Mr. and Mrs. Carl Jonasson Lind; Mr, and Mrs. Clas

1854

Dahlhjelm; Mr. and Mrs. Carl Magnus Petterson; Mr. and Mrs. Magnus Jonasson and four children; Carl Swenson Ek; Anders Peter Nelson Glader and three children; Carl Gustaf Glader; Gustaf Adolph Glader; Mr. and Mrs. Nicolaus Jonasson; Mr. and Mrs. Carl Petter Nelson Dolk and one child; Maria Pettersdotter; Swen Magnuson; Mr. and Mrs. Lorentz Johansson and two children; Petter Johan Carlsson; Johan Smith. This list includes 51 communicants and 23 children.

At a congregational meeting held on November 27, 1856, it was decided that all those who were enrolled as members of the congregation when it was organized, and who had not yet given their name, birthplace, date of birth, and other information for the church register should be required to give such information before January 1, 1857, and that those who failed to do so should no longer be considered as members. It is probable that there were some who neglected to do this and therefore were not recorded. The name of Per Anderson is not found in the church register, but in the records at the Chisago County court

1854

house his name appears as one of the incorporators of the congregation. The articles of incorporation were recorded on December 6, 1855.

The original church register contains the names of 57 families and 21 individuals who had arrived in America prior to 1854. It also lists the names of 46 families and 33 individuals who came to America in 1854. Approximately 60 percent of these early settlers at Chisago Lake were from Kronobergs län in Småland, the district from which Erland Carlsson had come.

The secretary of the organization meeting was a former schoolmaster, John Håkanson. First church board members were: deacons— Håkan L. Swedberg, Per Anderson, and Carl Peterson; trustees—A. M. Dahlhjelm, Per Berg, and Anders Swenson. The organization meeting was held in Berg's new log haymow (or threshing floor).

Though Mr. Berg had promised to let the congregation have its meetings in his house it was decided to build a "meeting house" on a plot of ground already selected for that purpose, in Section 27, where

Per Berg's haymow (or threshing floor)
where Chisago Lake Church was organized

the owner, Anders F. Swenson, had promised to sell one to four acres
of land to the congregation at the government price.

Some of the men who were chosen as leaders of the new congregation are known to us from the writings of Dr. Norelius. He quotes a
letter by Dahlhjelm to Erland Carlsson, written in the early part of
1854, showing that he was then a lay preacher among the people at
Chisago Lake. He reported that he had been preaching "God's unadul-
terated Word" every Sunday and holiday for a year and a half. He had
also baptized five children and buried three. He also mentioned having
warned his neighbors against the false teachings of the Methodist pastor Agrelius. Dahlhjelm evidently was a man of strong opinions and a
great deal of self-confidence. He was not satisfied with the way
Carlsson organized the congregation and during the following summer
he attended services only once.

Per Berg has already been mentioned as being one of the original
settlers at Chisago Lake in 1851. His son, Albert Berg, born at Chisago
Lake in 1861, held various political offices, including that of secretary
of state of Minnesota.

Håkan Swedberg arrived from Sweden in 1853 and spent the
first winter in Chicago. While there he was a member of a class of

1854

adults who studied English under the tutelage of Erik Norelius. He came to Chisago Lake in 1854. In 1855 the congregation chose him to lead the services when no pastor was available. He was the lay delegate from Chisago Lake at the organization meeting of the Minnesota Conference in 1858. His stepson, Jonas Magny, became the first student to enroll in the school started by Norelius at Red Wing in 1862, which was the beginning of Gustavus Adolphus College. Magny was ordained in 1870 and served as pastor until his death in 1910.

Per Anderson was the leader of the first contingent of settlers at Chisago Lake. When he left Sweden he had money not only for his own and his family's journey, but he also helped many of his fellow-travellers, and still had several hundred dollars left when he arrived. Norelius said of him that he was too generous for his own good. Anderson was well read, could write and figure, and he had a good insight into the truths of the Bible and the doctrines of the Lutheran church. His letters, written to Norelius more than a century ago, are as legible today as the day they were written. He used an excellent grade of paper and ink though he lived in the most primitive surroundings. Norelius characterized him as a "poor farmer," one who cared more for forests and lakes, fish and game, lots of room and fresh air. In a few years he thought it was too crowded at Chisago Lake, and he moved to the Cambridge community. There he died

1854

Anderson gravestone

in September 1881, at the age of 64. The Cambridge Lutheran congregation has marked his grave with a suitable monument.

Of the other church officers, Anders Swenson and Carl Peterson, not much is known. Swenson was one of the early settlers, coming with

Per Anderson in 1851. He was from Östergötland. Peterson was from Småland.

Though Erland Carlsson stayed only a week at Chisago Lake, and, as far as we know, revisited the place only once, he left something of a permanent influence. His sermons were characterized by a warm, evangelistic fervor. His motto as a preacher was: "The law in its strictness, and the gospel in its glory." He took an interest in people. He was concerned about their spiritual welfare. Not all the Swedish immigrants who came to Chisago Lake had been touched by the spiritual awakenings occasioned by the pietistic movement in their homeland, but in general they were churchly minded and heard Carlsson gladly. His visit was not soon forgotten.

The building in which the congregation was organized has long since disappeared and its location has not been marked. It was built of rough-hewn logs, and stood a few rods east of the old cemetery near the county road. At that time a bay of south Chisago Lake extended almost that far up. The lake was much higher than it has been in recent years.

1854

The new "meeting house" was built in the summer of 1854, and was undoubtedly the first Lutheran house of worship in Minnesota. It was not large enough to accommodate even half of the people in the community. It was not intended to serve as a church, but was planned and equipped to serve as a school, and was evidently used both as a public school and a church for some time.

> The next three pages show scans of the minutes of the organizational meeting of Chisago Lake May 12, 1854, which were in Swedish. Following these pages are four pages with the English translation of these minutes.

PASTOR ERLAND CARLSSON

No 1.

Protokoll hållet wid allmänt samman-
träde af wid Chicago Lake Minnesota Trä-
Boende Svenskar, af Evangeliska Lutherska Bekän-
nelsen den 12 Maj. 1854.

De Svenskar, hvilka kommit att bosätta sig på
denna plats. Hade länge känt behofvet af ett ordnadt
Kyrkoskick, och som de nu hade ett besök, Af Lutherska
Pastorn Erl. Carlson från Chicago, blef ett almänt möte
utlyst att denna dag hållas i och för ordnandet af de kyrkli-
ga angelägenheterna och blefvo härvid följande beslut fattade:

1854

§1 Man öfverenskom att förena sig till en menighet under
     Namn, af den Svenska Evangeliska Lutherska Församlin-
     gen, wid Chicago Lake.

§2 Såsom almän Christlig och särskilt såsom Evangelisk
     Luthersk erkännas denna Församling ej allenast den Hel-
     liga Skrift såsom Guds Ord och till följe deraf såsom
     den enda tillräckliga och ofelbara norm en för menniskor-
     nas tro och lefverne utan antager tillika, utom de tre äldsta
     Symbola (det Apostoliska, Nicaenska och Athanasianska)
     den oförändrade Augsburgiska bekännelsen såsom en kort
     men trogen sammanfattning, af Christendomens
     hufvudläror.

§3 I afseende på medlemmars upptagande beslöts, Att

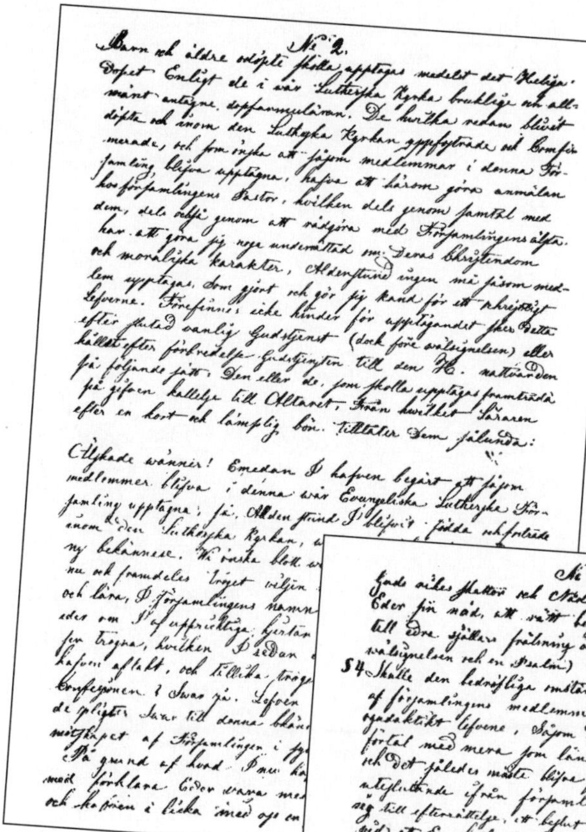

No. 2.

Barn och äldre odöpte skolla upptagas medelst det Heliga Dopet Enligt de i wår Lutherska Kyrka brukliga och allmänt antagne doppformulären. De hwilka redan blifvit döpta och inom den Lutherska Kyrkan uppfostrade och Confirmerade, och som önska att såsom medlemmar i denna Församling blifwa upptagna, hafwa att härom göra anmälan hos församlingens Pastor, hwilken dels genom samtal med dem, dels också genom att rådgöra med Församlingens äldsta har att göra sig noga underrättad om Deras Christendom och moraliska karakter, Aldenstund ingen må såsom medlem upptagas som gjort och gör sig känd för ett okristligt lefverne. Förefinnes icke hinder för upptagandet sker detta efter slutad vanlig Gudstjenst (dock före wälsignelsen) eller hållet efter förberedelse-Gudstjensten till den H. nattvarden på följande sätt: Den eller de, som skolla upptagas framträda på gifven kallelse till Altaret, från hwilket Läraren efter en kort och lämplig bön tilltalar Dem sålunda:

Älskade wänner! Emedan I hafven begärt att såsom medlemmar blifwa i denna wår Evangeliska Lutherska Församling upptagna; så, Aldenstund I blifvit födda och fostrade inom den Lutherska Kyrkan, w… ny bekännelse. Wi önska blott w… nu och framdeles troget wiljen … och lära, I församlingens namn … eder om I af uppriktiga hjertan … fen trogna, hwilken I sedan … hafven aflagt, och tillika troge … Confessionen? Swar ja. Lofven … de plikter Isar till denna bkän… mötskapet af Församlingen i sy… På grund af hvad I nu ha… med förklara Eder wara me… och hafven i läcka med oss en …

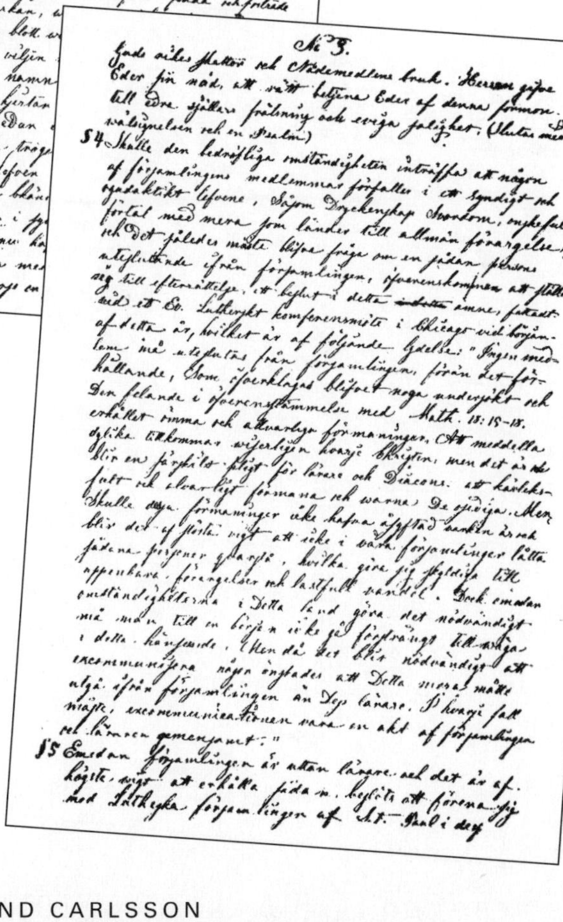

No. 3.

gade wikes skattör och Nådemedlens bruk. Herren gifve Eder sin nåd, att rätt betjena Eder af denna förmon till edra själars frälsning och ewiga salighet. (Slutas med wälsignelsen och en Psalm)

§4 Skulle den bedröfliga omständigheten inträffa att någon af församlingens medlemmar förfaller i ett syndigt och ogudaktigt lefwerne, såsom Dryckenskap, Swordom, okyskhet, förtal med mera som länder till allmän förargelse, och det således måste blifwa fråga om en sådan persons uteslutande ifrån församlingen, öfverenskommen att ställa sig till efterrättelse, ett beslut i detta ~~i detta~~ ämne, fattadt wid ett Ev. Lutherskt konferensmöte i Chicago vid början af detta år, hwilket är af följande lydelse: "Ingen medlem må uteslutas från församlingen, förrän det förhållande, som öfwerklagas blifwit noga undersökt och Den felande i öfwerensstämmelse med Math. 18: 15-18. erhållet ömma och allwarliga förmaningar. Att meddella dylika tillkommer wisserligen hwarje Christen; men det är dessutom en särskild plikt för lärare och Diacons, att kärleksfullt och allwarligt förmana och warna De syndiga. Men skulle dessa förmaningar icke hafwa åsyftad verkan är och blir det af största vigt att icke i våra församlingar lätta sådana personer qwarstå, hwilka göra sig skyldiga till uppenbara förargelser och lastfull wandel. Dock emedan omständigheterna i detta land göra det nödvändigt må man till en början icke gå försträngt tillwäga i detta hänseende. Men då det blir nödvändigt att excommunicera någon ungtades att detta moras måtte utgå ifrån församlingen än dess lärare. I hwarje fall måste, excommunicationen wara en akt af församlingen och lärarnes gemensamt."

§5 Emedan församlingen är utan lärare och det är af högsta wigt att erhålla sådan, beslöts att förena sig med Lutherska församlingen af St. Paul i dess

1854

PASTOR ERLAND CARLSSON

1854

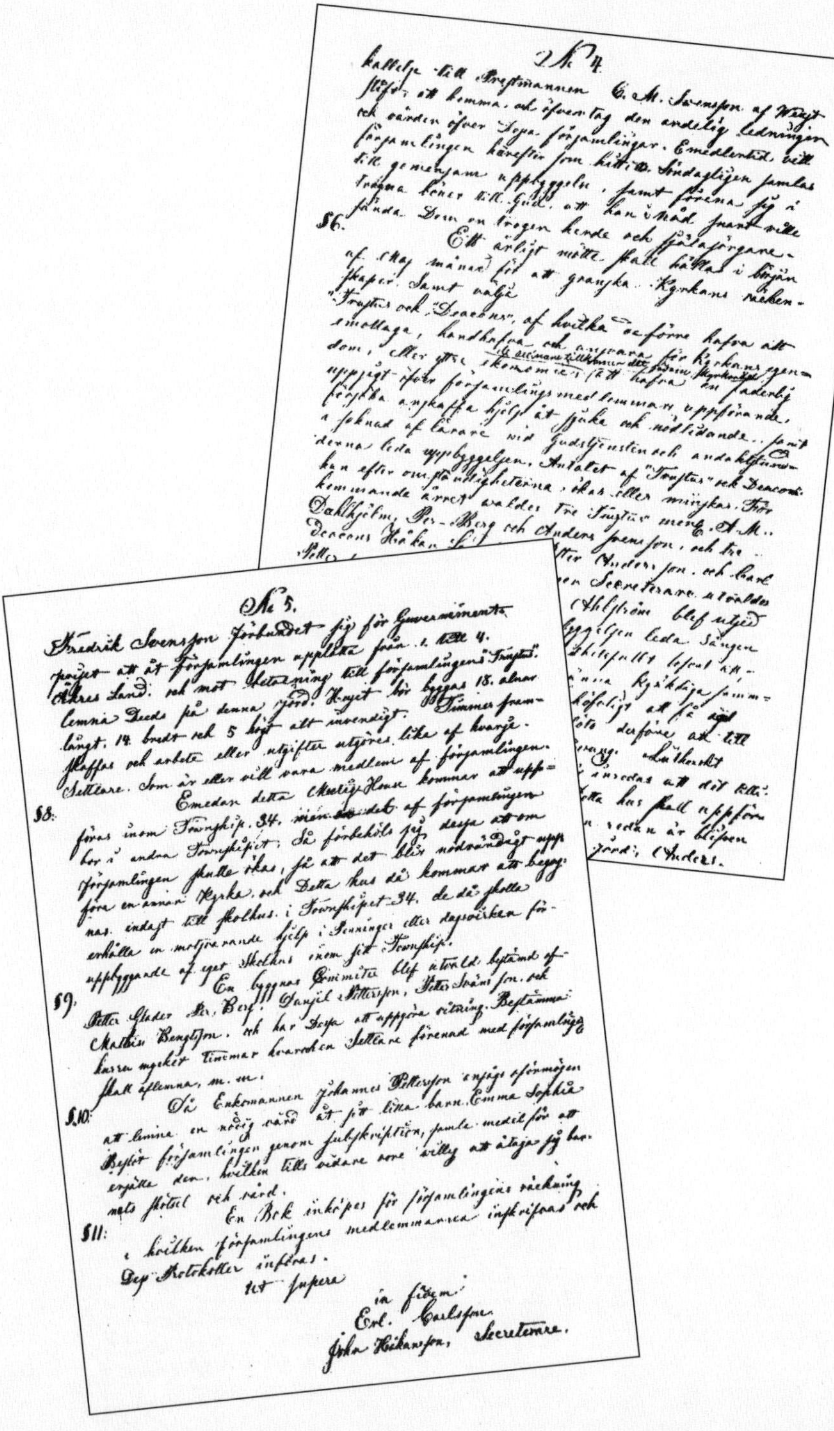

Translation of Minutes of Organization Meeting
Chisago Lake • May 12, 1854

(From Augustana Historical Society Publications, Vol. XI, Pages 50-52)

Minutes kept at a general meeting of Swedes
of Evangelical Lutheran confession living at
Chisago Lake, Minnesota Ter., May 12, 1854.

The Swedes who came to settle in this place have long felt the need of an organized church order, and as they had now received a visit from the Lutheran pastor Erl. Carls[s]on from Chicago, a general meeting was announced to be held this day for the purpose of setting in order the church affairs, and at this meeting the following resolutions were passed:

#1. Resolved that we unite in a congregation under the name of the Swedish Evangelical Lutheran congregation in Chisago Lake.

1854

#2. As in general Christian and in particular as Evangelical Lutheran this congregation acknowledges not only the Holy Scriptures as God's Word and therefore as the only sufficient and infallible norm for the faith and life of mankind, but also accepts, besides the three oldest symbols, (the Apostolic, Nicene, and Athanasian) the unaltered Augsburg Confession as a short but faithful summary of the chief Christian doctrines.

#3. In regard to the reception of members it was resolved, that: Children or unbaptized older persons are received according to the rubrics and forms in our Swedish Lutheran Church handbook. On the other hand when anyone, who has already been baptized and confirmed, wishes to unite as a member with this congregation, he is to notify the pastor of the congregation of his wish, who, partly by private conference, partly by counselling with the congregation's elders* shall make himself thoroughly familiar with the person's Christianity and his moral character; for no one, who engages in and shows himself to be living in an unchristian and sinful man-

*Which here means deacons.

PASTOR ERLAND CARLSSON

ner, may be received as a member of the congregation. If no objections are found to his reception it may occur at an ordinary service, or also at the service preparatory to the reception of the Holy Communion, in the following manner: He or they, who are to be received as members, come forward to the altar when called, and after a short prayer are addressed as follows: Beloved friends, as you have asked to be received as members of this congregation, therefore as you have been born and brought up in the Lutheran Church, we will not require of you a new confession. We wish simply to know if also in this country you will hold fast to our old, unchangeable faith and doctrine. In the name of this congregation, therefore, I ask you, if you with honest hearts will remain faithful to that confession which you have already made before the Lord's altar, and in accordance with the same will be faithful to the Augsburg Confession? Answer: Yes.

Do you also promise to accept in honesty those duties to which this confession in general and membership in the congregation in particular obligates you? Answer: Yes.

In consequence of what you have now declared I hereby declare you to be members of this our Evangelical Lutheran congregation, and to have as such, in the same free access to the treasures of God's kingdom and the use of the means of grace. The Lord grant you His grace that you may zealously and faithfully use these privileges to the saving of your souls and eternal blessedness. Amen. (Close with the benediction and a verse.)

1854

#4. Should it happen that the grievous circumstances arise, that any of the members of the congregation fall into a sinful and ungodly life, such as drunkenness, profanity, quarrelsomeness, malicious slander, or others, which lead to general offense and the grief of God's congregation, and therefore the question is raised whether such a person is to be excluded from the congregation, it was agreed to follow a resolution on the same question, adopted by the Conference in Chicago, Jan. 4-9, 1854. This resolution reads as follows: "No one may be excluded from the congregation before the conduct with which he is charged has been fully investigated and the erring one has been sympathetically and earnestly warned and admonished, privately and openly in accordance with Matthew 18:15-18. To administer these admonitions truly is one of the rights of every Christian; but it is and remains a special duty for the pastor and deacons to warn and admonish the evildoer in love and seriousness. But if this does not accomplish the expected purpose, it is of the highest importance that such persons are not allowed to remain in the congregation, who are evidently guilty of mischief and a profligate life. Yet under the conditions that exist in this country it becomes necessary that at the beginning one should proceed cautiously. But when it becomes necessary to excommunicate anyone it is desirable that this might proceed more from the congregation than from the pastor. In every case the excommunication must be a common act of both congregation and pastor."

#5. As the congregation is without a pastor and as it is of the greatest importance that it should have one, it was moved that we unite with the Lutheran congregation in St. Paul in its call to Pastor C. M. Swensson of Wexiö diocese, to come and assume the spiritual leadership and care of these congregations. Meanwhile the congregation will continue as before to gather on Sundays for our common edification, and to unite in faithful prayers to God that He in mercy may soon send us a faithful shepherd and "carer for our souls."

#6. A yearly meeting shall be held in the beginning of the month of May to examine the accounts of the church and to elect "Trustees" and "Deacons," of which the former are to receive, have in charge and be responsible for the church's property, or the outer economic [affairs]. The latter shall constitute a church council to exercise a fatherly oversight over the members of the congregation, to endeavor to secure help for the sick and suffering, and in the absence of a pastor to lead the devotions at services and prayer meetings. The number of "trustees" and "deacons" can be determined by circumstances and may be larger or smaller. For the coming year three trustees were elected, namely A. M. Dahlhjelm, Per Berg, and Anders Swenson, and three deacons: Håkan Larson, Petter Anderson, and Carl Petterson. As secretary of the congregation Joh. Hakanson was elected, and A. M. Ahlström was elected to lead the singing at the devotions.

1854

#7. While Mr. Berg kindly offered the use of his house for the general church gatherings it was yet felt that it was necessary that a house belonging to the congregation and intended for this purpose be secured, and therefore it was resolved to erect an Evangelical Lutheran Meeting House by next summer, which house is to be so arranged that it can also be used as a school house. This house shall be erected on Section 27 at the place which has already been selected, and the owner of this ground, Anders Fredrik Swensson, has obligated himself to sell to the congregation from 1 to 4 acres of land at the government price, and on receipt of the money to deliver a deed for this ground to the "trustees." The house shall be built 18 yards long, 14 wide and 5 high, all inside [measurements]. Timber is to be prepared and work or contributions to be given alike by every settler, who is or expects to be a member of the congregation.

#8. As this Meeting House is to be erected in township 34, but part of the congregation lives in another township, therefore it is stipulated by those (in the other township) that if the congregation shall increase, so that it becomes necessary to erect another church, and this house then will be used as a schoolhouse in township 34, they then shall receive corresponding help in money or days work in building their own school house in their township.

#9. A building committee consisting of Petter Glader, Per Berg, Daniel Petterson, Petter Swensson and Mathis Bengtson was elected, and these are to draw a plan, decide how much timber each settler connected with the congregation is to furnish, etc., etc.

#10. As it was considered that widower Johannes Petterson is unable to give the necessary care to his little child, Emma Sophia, it was resolved that the congregation by subscription gather money in order to pay some person who until further notice will be willing to assume the care and keeping of the child.

#11. That a book be purchased for the church accounts, in which the names of the members of the congregation and its minutes are to be entered.

1854

> As above,
> In faith,
>
> [Signed]   Erl. Carlsson
>
> John Hakanson, Secretary

Read and approved at a general meeting May 13, 1854, witness on behalf of the congregation

> Daniel Petterson
>
> [Signed]   Lars Petter Skjolin
>
> Petter Gustaf Gustafson

Eric Norelius

Pioneer Preacher

THE NEW CONGREGATION at Chisago Lake desired to have a pastor as soon as possible. No ordained minister could be secured immediately, but student Eric Norelius arrived a week after Carlsson had left. He stayed through the summer of 1854, being the first stationed Lutheran preacher in Minnesota. He was also the pioneer church school teacher. He was then 20 years old.

Born at Hassela, in the province of Helsingland, Sweden, Eric Norelius had spent most of his childhood and youth as a farm boy, living in the out-of-doors a large part of the time. His parents were industrious and thrifty, but were unable to provide for the education of their son when he felt the call of God to enter the ministry. After a year of studies in the high school of Hudiksvall in 1849 and 1850 he found it necessary to return home. All doors seemed to be closed against him.

It was then that "Joris Pelle" Anderson had determined to emigrate to the United States. Eric and his next older brother, Anders, decided to join the Anderson group. Coming to Andover, Illinois, in the late fall of 1850 Eric found Pastor Lars P. Esbjörn, who was able to give him good advice and help.

From 1851 to 1853 Eric Norelius studied at Capital University, Columbus, Ohio. Then, after a summer in New York and a winter in Chicago he came to Moline, Illinois, where his parents and some other relatives were wintering after their arrival in this country. They had decided to move to Minnesota, and Eric accompanied them. After a six-day journey on a river boat they reached Saint Paul, a young but lusty and growing city of 6,000 people. The Swedish Lutherans in the capital of Minnesota Territory invited him to conduct a service, and this he did. The meeting was held in a little schoolhouse on Jackson Street, on the evening of May 21.

1854

The boat left for Stillwater the next day and the Norelius party arrived there late in the evening. They spent the night on the boat landing under the open sky.

The lumberjacks had then come down from the camps farther north, and Norelius has given a vivid description of them:

> If one were to be well dressed and stylish in the St. Croix valley in those days one must wear a bright red wool shirt with a little embroidery in front, and no vest. A young man in such a costume, with a leather belt around his waist and a "plug hat" on his head, standing on a street corner or in some other public place, with hands on hips, or whittling a stick, and looking boldly around, was a gentleman of the approved type in those days.

From Stillwater to Taylors Falls they rode on the mail stage on May 23. The next day they walked through the woods to Chisago Lake, and found it a place of great natural beauty. Having lived nearly all his life in close communion with nature, the life of the pioneers appealed to Eric Norelius.

It was soon agreed that Norelius should stay and serve the congregation. On May 25, Ascension Day, he preached for the first time in Chisago Lake. On June 12 he started teaching school, the first school of any sort in the community.

Both Agrelius, the Methodist minister, and Nilsson, the Baptist preacher, gave Norelius competition throughout the summer. The first sermon he heard Agrelius preach was "beneath criticism," said Norelius later:

> The sum and substance of it all was to show how fortunate the Swedes were who came to America. Here they could "fear God" as much as they wanted to. It was dangerous to remain in Sweden, because of the "Russian bear." Russia bordered on Sweden north of the Baltic Sea, and by this route the "Russian bear" would come some fine day and give Sweden a bear hug, and then it would be best not to be there.

Agrelius came to the Lutheran services and would then announce his presence and give a speech. He offered his services in this way:

1854

> If you like the Methodist way you may have that, and if you want the Lutheran way you may have that. I know how it should be done. I was a minister in Sweden twenty-six years.

After he quit the Chisago Lake community he lived for a number of years at Big Lake in Washington County.

Nilsson, the Baptist man, stayed only a week in Chisago Lake in the summer of 1854. He returned the following year and organized a little congregation. Eric Norelius's brother Anders had become a Baptist in 1852, and their parents embraced the Baptist faith and left Chisago Lake in 1857, settling in Isanti County.

During the summer the Chisago Lake congregation considered the question of the location of the proposed church, but it was a difficult problem since the settlers were scattered at various places around the lakes, and no decision was reached. Many new settlers arrived from Sweden during the summer and the colony increased rapidly in numbers. Economic conditions improved gradually. The people learned to live within their means. In Taylors Falls the settlers could not buy a nickle's worth on credit. This compelled them to live in a plain style, to have as few needs as possible, and to cultivate their inventive ability. Each settler cut timber on his land to build his log house, and furniture also was homemade. Wooden plugs were often used instead of nails. Clothing was simple and plain. Wooden shoes were common. The grain was cut with a scythe and threshed with a flail. No one farmed with the expectation of making money, but only to make a living.

The surrounding country, especially towards the northwest, was still a little known region. Norelius explored the territory for some miles around, and discovered Sunrise Lake, the Sunrise River, and the Sunrise "prairies." East of Sunrise Lake, in the midst of thick forest, he found a lonely hermit's cabin. It was Van Raensler who had betaken himself away from his former haunts when settlers arrived at Chisago Lake.

1854

There were differing spiritual tendencies among the people, depending on the various preachers whom they had heard in Sweden. Norelius preached to the best of his ability, according to the evangelical emphasis that prevailed in some of the pietistic circles in Helsingland. Those who had a more legalistic view were not entirely satisfied. Håkan Swedberg, one of the deacons, wrote to Erland Carlsson:

> Eric Norelius continues to preach. As I am hard to please I am not fully satisfied with his sermons, but he is young and not accustomed to the work, and perhaps inexperienced in regard to what he should preach. God knows, not I.

Per Anderson, on the other hand, was pleased, and hoped that Norelius could soon be given a permanent call.

After his sermon on September 10, Norelius bade the congregation farewell. He was given $25 as salary for his summer's work. No doubt he felt that the experience he had gained was a far more valuable remuneration. After revisiting friends in Illinois he returned to Columbus, Ohio, for his third and final term at Capital University.

Though he did not become pastor of the Chisago Lake congregation after his ordination, his summer in the community had aroused great interest in and love for Minnesota. Two years later he settled in Goodhue County and gave 60 years of his life to building up the Lutheran church in this state and throughout the Northwest.

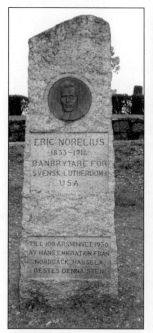

1854

Norelius gravestone in Hassela, Sweden

The altar painting at the church in Hassela depicts Eric Norelius, Per Anderson, and Daniel Lindstrom, emigrants to America

Attempts were made to secure a pastor from Sweden. At the organization meeting Pastor Carl M. Svensson of the Växiö diocese in Småland was called, but after a long period of hopeful waiting the congregation was disappointed in getting a negative reply.

The call to Pastor Svensson had been sent through Dr. Peter Fjellstedt, a leader in the missionary movement in Sweden, with the understanding that if Pastor Svensson declined, Dr. Fjellstedt would have authority to issue the call to someone else whom he considered suitable. On the basis of this authority he sent the call to a missionary pastor in India, G. E. Lundgren. Pastor Lundgren wrote a letter of acceptance but for some unknown reason returned to Sweden instead of coming to America.

Pastor T. N. Hasselquist of Galesburg, Illinois, came for a visit in the fall of 1854, staying from October 30 to November 1. He conducted services three times, including a communion service. Per Anderson wrote to Norelius:

> He spoke on Luke 15. He described the circumstances of the
> prodigal son, both when he left his father's house and when he
> came back in such a vivid manner and in the spirit of the Gospel
> so that the floor in our new schoolhouse could have softened. But
> I fear that not many hearts were touched by it.

A month later, however, it was apparent that hearts had been touched to such an extent that Hasselquist was called to serve as pastor in Chisago Lake, but Anderson would have preferred Norelius.

1855

Hasselquist did not accept the call, as he had an extensive parish in Illinois and felt that he should stay where he was.

In the spring of 1855 the Chisago Lake congregation sent an urgent plea to the Swedish Lutheran pastors in Illinois, asking that they should try to find someone who could be sent to Minnesota. This letter was read at a meeting of the Scandinavian Conference of the Synod of Northern Illinois in Chicago April 14. In response to this petition the Conference asked P. A. Cederstam to go to Minnesota.

Pastor P. A. Cederstam
1855–1858

PEHR ANDERSON CEDERSTAM had come to America in 1853 at the age of 23. He had been confirmed in the Church of Sweden by Pastor T. N. Hasselquist. As a child he had learned to love the Lord, but in his home there was no reading of the Bible or any prayer, and when the boy indicated that he intended to take Christianity seriously he was met with derision and scorn. At the time of his confirmation he had felt God's call to the ministry and during the following years this conviction was strengthened, with the result that he enrolled at a school in Kristianstad. He was about ready to begin his theological studies in 1853, but he had been thoroughly aroused by the fact that some ungodly ministers in the state church were allowed to continue unmolested while pious and zealous ones were sometimes persecuted by the authorities. With hatred in his heart for the ministers of the state church Cederstam left Sweden in May 1853.

Arriving in New York he soon became acquainted with the Swedish Methodist minister O. G. Hedstrom, and for a time was interested in the Methodist Church. Early in 1854 he was sent to Chicago as colporteur for the Methodists. Cederstam knew very little about Methodism, as they had no books in Swedish at that time, and Hedstrom had told him that the Methodists were really the same as the pietists in Sweden. In a state of religious uncertainty Cederstam came to Chicago and after much hesitation he went to Pastor Erland Carlsson for advice. He was received with brotherly kindness, and Carlsson urged him to go to see his confirmation pastor, Hasselquist in Galesburg.

The result was that Cederstam moved to Galesburg, intending to learn some trade. However, he soon became an active participant in the work of the church. In the fall of 1854, when Hasselquist visited Minnesota and later made a trip to New York, Cederstam preached in his place and thus was drawn into the work which he thought he had given up for ever. When the conference, in April 1855, asked him to go to Minnesota, he acceded to the request. On Pentecost, May 27, he preached at Chisago Lake for the first time.

1855

The new pastor was young and quite inexperienced, still not ordained, and the task laid upon him was no easy one. Though some of the members of the congregation were sincere and pious believers, this was by no means true of all, and even among the "good Christians" there were different views and opinions.

A church was needed as soon as possible, and before it could be built the location of the new church must be agreed upon. This problem almost caused a serious rift in the congregation, but Pastor Cederstam had the courage and wisdom and grace from above to guide the congregation through these trying times.

The first congregational meeting after Cederstam's arrival was held on July 4, 1855. The question of a church was considered and after much discussion and debate it was decided to accept a gift of land offered by Per Anderson and Daniel Rattig. This land was "at the northeast corner of P. Berg's fence." Two members protested, but the congregation voted to build in spite of this protest.

However, at a meeting on September 12 the same year it was decided to build the church "on the two acres purchased for $50 from F. Mobeck on the Nordberg peninsula." No explanation is given in the minutes for the change in plans.

In the history of the congregation by Dr. F. M. Eckman in 1904 the following account is given (Dr. Eckman quoted from a written report by Cederstam but he did not state whether it was a letter or a published aricle):

> When the congregation was organized by Pastor Carlsson a church site was selected about where the Methodist church now stands (this was about half way between Westlund's and the court house). Later in the summer another place had been chosen and a clearing made in the woods. This was on Peter Swenson's land east of the lake, not far from where A. Molin's place now is. At this place several bodies had been buried.

1855

> Such was the situation when I arrived at Chisago Lake. But there was no unanimity about the choice of this new place. At this time a poor American was staying in the settlement, and he and Per Anderson platted the land now owned by Peter Shaleen, and this was to become a big city. It was given the name Center City, since it was to be the central point in the settlement. Now it was evident that this was to be the location of the church. Lots were promised for it at the most beautiful place, a little to the east from where the parsonage now is located.

> It was decided to build the church here, but those who lived south and west of the lake protested, though they were in the minority. Then those south of the lake began to look for a church location on the land owned by P. Glader, and those who lived around "The Narrows" began to talk about building a church there. Those who lived at Little Lake reckoned that they could build a church. In vain we tried to reconcile their differences. Everything seemed hopeless. But they all said: If we can get a

donation of two acres of Mobeck's land we will all unite and build a church there.

I was very dejected and did not know what to do. One day it occurred to me to go to Mr. Mobeck and offer him $50.00 for two acres of land. I began to count my money, but I did not have much. Fortunately I had received a subscription for *Hemlandet*, so that, when I put everything together, my money and *Hemlandet's* money, it was just the required amount. I put the money in my pocket and went to see Mr. Mobeck, who then was living on his land. I want to mention here that Mr. Mobeck had become disgruntled and unyielding as a result of the criticism showered upon him because he had bought this land, which, as many believed, he knew the settlers had chosen for church, cemetery, and parsonage. He was willing to donate enough for a church lot, but the people wanted enough for a cemetery also. After discussing for a while the deplorable dissension in the congregation I said that I had come to buy land. I laid my money on the table. "See here," I said, "is fifty dollars in gold and silver. This money you will take, Mr. Mobeck, in payment for two acres of land for a church lot. Tomorrow you can go to the U.S. Land Office in Stillwater and buy forty acres of land nearby, and you will have more use of that."

1855

Mr. Mobeck did not believe that the congregation would agree to this. They did not want to buy land.

I replied, "I am the one who is buying the land, and it will be my loss if this does not succeed."

After some further discussion, and after Mrs. Mobeck had interceded for me, Mobeck said, "Well. if I can deal with you, pastor, and if I can decide on the south boundary of the two acres, then I will let it go."

Herewith he extended his hand to me, and Mrs. Mobeck put both her hands on ours, and wept tears of joy. After we had read the Word of God together and prayed, I went my way happy and satisfied.

I now hurried to "Uncle" Swedberg to tell what I had done. He laughed at me and said, "You are brave, pastor." But he thought that it was a shame to pay such a high price for that piece of land.

I replied, "If we can win unity by it, it is not too much."

"That is true, pastor," he said, and was satisfied.

The news spread rapidly in the settlement. Some thought it was absurd, some did not know what to think. The next Sunday, after the close of the service I said that I had heard with sorrow the news that they intended to build churches at several places in the settlement, and I pointed out, as well as I could, the inadvisability of this. And since I had heard that they all were in agreement about building on Mobeck's land they could now get two acres there if they so desired.

The reply was, "Yes, but what will that land cost?"

I replied, "The land is bought and paid for and will be turned over to the congregation if you will agree to this plan."

With this they were satisfied. No one voted against it.

1855

Then I added, "I have bought the land and paid for it. But you all know that I am poor, and I have done it for the sake of achieving unity. If anyone would be willing to contribute twenty-five or fifty cents, it would be welcome."

Everybody was satisfied with this, and we parted with joy over the fact that the struggle was at an end. Within a couple of weeks sixty dollars was donated to pay for the land.

From his account it will be seen that Pastor Cederstam deserves most of the credit for getting the church located where it is. It was an unusually attractive location when the lakes were high and the natural beauty of the place was in its primeval condition. And who is there today who would prefer any other location for the church? It seems that divine guidance and wisdom enabled Cederstam to take his bold step.

The choice of this location was of the greatest importance in that it served to unify the congregation. If Cederstam had blundered it is

PASTOR P. A. CEDERSTAM

quite likely that three or four small churches would have been built, and the community might easily have been split by dissension and perhaps would have become a fertile field for seeds of religious discord.

Later in the fall of 1855 the congregation was incorporated. At an election on December 5 Peter Anderson, Daniel Peterson, and Håkan Swedberg were elected trustees. The articles of incorporation were filed in the office of the Register of Deeds of Chisago County and were recorded in *Book A of Bonds and Mortgages*, pages 89 and 90, by Thomas Lucy.

Now that the church site had been selected and the congregation duly incorporated, the matter of building a church was soon decided upon. Mr. P. Glader was elected to take charge of the project. The church was to be 48 by 36, 18 feet high, with a vaulted ceiling. The members cut logs and prepared the heavy timbers for sills and joists. This material was valued at about $500, and they also subscribed $430 in cash. This amount was further increased, and labor to the value of about $400 was donated. The total cost of the church, including materials and labor donated, was $1,795.25. A bell was purchased for $50 from the owner of an old river boat,

1855

Frame church erected 1856

and served as church bell for many years.

The first Sunday school was organized on July 4, 1855, with

Gustaf Collin, F. Mobeck, and N. H. Bystrom in charge. The first con-
firmation class was instructed by Pastor Cederstam and was confirmed
by him on August 19, 1855. The members of this class were: Andrew
Anderson, Olof M. Linnell, Olof Norelius, Carl J. Strand, Carl J.
Peterson, Ola Jonson Winquist, Carl August Peterson, John Holcomb,
Lars Larson, Mary Van Custer, Christina Bengtson, Christina Nelson,
Mathilda Peterson, Anna Maria Glader, Malena Mattson, Lena C.
Linn, and Katarina Berg.

In general the church members lived an outwardly respectable
life, but church discipline was a very real problem in the young congregation. These people had been accustomed to the state church of
Sweden, where church discipline was enforced by the sheriff or his officers and the true conception of church discipline had been allowed to
lie dormant. Now they were members of a free church where they must
learn to discipline themselves. They must learn to respect their own
constitution, their church council, and the decisions they themselves
made at congregational meetings. In Sweden the church was government supported. Here they must support it themselves.

1855

In addition to his busy schedule at Chisago Lake, Pastor
Cederstam also made occasional visits to Taylors Falls, Scandia, Saint
Paul, Carver, and other Swedish settlements. In the summer of 1857 he
served as one of the delegates from Chisago County at the state constitutional convention, and his signature is on the original constitution of
Minnesota. He served as chairman of the committee that wrote the
article on elections.

Pastor Cederstam never had a permanent call to the Chisago
Lake Church, and this fact in itself made his work more difficult. On
September 9, 1856, he was given a call for one year more. In December
1857 he announced his intention of leaving the following spring, and
since no one said a word against this, he accepted a call to Scandian
Grove and Saint Peter.

There is no record as to salary paid Cederstam the first two years in Chisago Lake. From October 1, 1857, to April 1, 1858, he was to have one dollar per communicant. This would have been about $200 if everyone paid. But after he had moved to Scandian Grove he wrote to Hasselquist and mentioned that he had $300 coming from Chisago Lake. Financial panic had hit Minnesota at that time, and it is doubtful that he ever was paid in full.

There was no parsonage yet, and Cederstam had to provide his own lodgings. He lived most of the time at Daniel Peterson's (the farm now owned by Fred Nelson). He was not married when he came to Chisago Lake, but he married in 1856. He was ordained the same year.

After leaving Chisago Lake he continued to serve in various places in the Augustana Synod, part of the time as traveling missionary in the Minnesota Conference. During his ministry he organized 10 congregations and helped with the erection of 12 churches. He died in 1902 at Olsburg, Kansas.

Cradle of the Minnesota Conference

1856

Several attempts were made to secure a pastor after Cederstam's departure, but in vain, and the congregation remained vacant almost a year and a half. Services were conducted by Håkan Swedberg and others of the laymen, and occasional visits were made by the few pastors stationed in Minnesota, Norelius and Beckman in Goodhue County, Peter Carlson in Carver County, and Cederstam in Nicollet County.

These pastors all were ordained or licensed by the Synod of Northern Illinois, to which the Swedish Lutherans of Illinois also belonged. Some, particularly Norelius, felt dissatisfied because of the synod's loose attitude towards the Lutheran teachings. The Minnesota pastors also felt that they were treated in a stepmotherly fashion. Distance and difficulties of travel also caused inconvenience.

Scandinavians and Germans considered the possibility of a Minnesota Synod, and a meeting was held in Norelius's church in Red Wing July 4 and 5, 1858, for the purpose of forming such a synod.

After careful consideration, and in conformity with the wishes of the brethren in Illinois the Swedish pastors declined to join the Minnesota Synod. They petitioned instead for the right to organize a Minnesota Conference of the Synod of Northern Illinois, and this was granted.

The first plans called for a meeting to be held in East Union, Carver County, but this was changed to Chisago Lake, since the congregation was vacant and this would be an opportunity for a visit by the pastors. The date was set for October 6, but the delegates, delayed by bad weather and poor means of travel, did not arrive until noon on the 7th.

Eight voting members founded the Lutheran Minnesota Conference. The only ordained pastor was Eric Norelius. Three licensed pastors, Peter Beckman, Peter Carlson, and J. P. C. Boren, newly-arrived assistant to Norelius, were present. P. A. Cederstam had visited Chisago Lake a few days before the time set for the conference, but was unable to remain because of duties at home. Though absent, he was counted as a member of the conference.

The lay delegates were: Håkan Swedberg, Chisago Lake; Daniel Nelson, Scandia; F. C. Bjorklund, Rush City (no congregation had yet been organized there); and Ola Paulson, East Union.

1856

Norelius was 24 years old, Boren 34, Beckman and Carlson 35. Paulson was a young man, the other delegates were older.

The difficulties of pioneer travel are revealed in Norelius's description of his journey (given in an address at Chisago Lake on the occasion of the 25th anniversary of the Minnesota Conference). On the afternoon of October 4 he and Boren went to the boat landing in Red Wing. They waited until three o'clock in the morning for a river boat to take them up the Mississippi to Prescott, Wisconsin. Arriving at dawn, they went by stage to Hudson, then on foot to Stillwater, where they found lodging for the night. The next day they walked 18 miles in a soaking rain to "Islycke" (near junction of highways 95 and 97). They stayed overnight at the home of a Swedish family, and the next day they rode by oxcart to Glader's place on south Chisago Lake. Crossing the lake in

PASTOR P. A. CEDERSTAM

a rowboat they arrived at the church about noon on the 7th.

The new church had been built but the interior had not been finished. Loose planks were used for benches, and a temporary pulpit stood on the platform. In this church the Minnesota Conference was organized on October 8, 1858. Pastor Boren was chairman of the organization meeting, Pastor Norelius, secretary. Ola Paulson was elected treasurer. A constitution proposed by Norelius was adopted.

After the details of organizing the conference had been taken care of the discussion turned to the problem of vacant congregations, and first of all, Chisago Lake. Pastor Boren was asked to stay at least until the end of October, and if he could not stay longer Beckman and Carlson should take turns with Boren in making regular visits to Chisago Lake.

Special mention was made of the fact that the Chisago Lake congregation had contributed $25 to the fund for the Scandinavian professorship at Illinois State University. (This school was not a state institution, but the school of the Synod of Northern Illinois. L. P. Esbjorn was the Scandinavian professor.) This contribution was undoubtedly the first gift to Christian higher education by Lutherans in Minnesota.

1856

Divine services were held every afternoon during the conference meeting with many people in attendance. On Sunday two services besides Holy Communion attracted crowds from far and near. An offering on Sunday morning for the conference treasury totalled $5.09. Money was scarce as Minnesota had been in the grip of financial panic for more than a year. Cranberries were about the only commodity that could be sold for cash by the Chisago Lake people in 1858. They had succeeded in selling several hundred bushels at $1.75 per bushel.

Norelius later said concerning this first conference meeting:

I have been here at many gatherings and have seen much larger crowds than at that time, but never have I seen such seriousness, such interest, such enthusiasm as we saw then. It was not only that this was a new project, but spiritual breezes had begun to blow both here and in other congregations. A sacred, festive spirit, a deep earnestness permeated our meeting. At the same time we felt inspired with happiness and courage. We thought we had come a long way in our religious development when we could organize a Conference. We did not think about difficulties. Nothing seemed impossible.

The Chisago Lake congregation was glad to have the promise of regular visits by pastors, and on October 27 voted to remunerate them. Pastor Boren was allowed $25 for the time he had been there, and thereafter each pastor would receive $15 and a free will offering for each visit. Board and lodging would also be provided. Visits were made more or less regularly, but the congregation was less regular in making the promised payments. As late as in 1862 the congregation was struggling to raise money to pay the pastors who served in 1858 and 1859.

Because of poor roads and unreliable means of transportation, the journeys to Chisago Lake were no pleasure trips. Beckman and Boren each had about 90 miles to Chisago Lake, and Carlson almost as far. On these trips the itinerary would usually include Taylors Falls, Scandia, Stillwater, and Saint Paul. Each journey, even at the best, required about two weeks.

1858

An attempt had been made to call a pastor from Sweden. After vainly waiting a year for a reply the congregation decided, in April 1859, to call Hasselquist, but he declined again.

On August 25, 1859, the congregation called a layman from Carver County, Carl August Hedengran. He accepted and was ordained in 1860.

∾

Pastor C. A. Hedengran
1859–1873

CARL AUGUST HEDENGRAN, a layman from Carver County, was called by Chisago Lake on August 25, 1859. He accepted and was ordained in 1860.

Hedengran thus became the first pastor to have a regular call. His salary was to be: Free use of the "church land," consisting of 29 acres; $200 in cash; and from each farmer two bushels of grain, wheat, oats, rye, and corn, half a bushel of each kind. This would amount to a total of 200 bushels. It was further stipulated that the pastor should officiate at baptisms, funerals, and the churching of women without fee.

A parsonage was built, a two-story house of timbered logs. It stood near the church. A few years later this house was moved and a new parsonage was built on the farm which now was owned by the congregation, originally part of Per Berg's farm. The purchase of this land had put the congregation into debt, and during the severe depression years, 1857 to 1859, this debt constituted a rather serious problem. In January 1859 the congregation was faced with a threat of legal action on the part of Anders Johnson and was forced to give him a mortgage with interest at the rate of two percent per month. In spite of these and other difficulties the congregation came through the years of financial hardship without suffering a setback.

The Minnesota Conference also continued to grow. It did not long remain a part of the Synod of Northern Illinois. In the spring of 1860 the Swedish Lutherans seceded and organized the Augustana Synod. Chisago Lake sent no lay delegate to the organization meeting but had taken action favoring the step. Of the 35 congregations that formed the Augustana Synod, Chisago Lake, with 370 communicant members, was the largest.

Civil War and Reconstruction Era

1859

Pastor C. A. Hedengran was the spiritual leader of the flock from 1859 to 1873. It was his first and only parish. This was the period of the Civil War and the Reconstruction era, which was followed by several years of financial depression, a most trying time for our nation and for the church. Hedengran's training for the ministry was rather meager, and his health was none too good. His task at Chisago Lake was far from easy, but the congregation continued to increase in numbers and in spiritual strength and stability. It is not too much to say that it is the most remarkable period in the history of Chisago Lake.

Though Hedengran's formal training was very limited, he had a personal spiritual background that fitted him unusually well for dealing with the problems of individuals in times of stress. He had come through spiritual stress and strain that almost proved to be his undoing, but he had found what God can do for a man in the extremities of despair and fear.

Born in 1821 in Skane, Sweden, he lived in a home where true piety prevailed. The father especially prayed earnestly for his children. After Carl August was confirmed, however, he began to drift into a life of sin. He became an unbeliever, denying that the Bible is the Word of God, and openly showing contempt for his father's entreaties. He lived for the pleasures of this life, thinking there was no retribution after death.

News of the California gold rush in 1849 reached Sweden, and Hedengran felt lured by the prospects of ease amid plenty. He was now a married man, and he and his wife set out for America to dig gold. They never reached California, but stayed in Peoria, Illinois, where he worked at his trade as a wagonmaker. Then they moved to Saint Paul, and later to Carver County. During these first years in America illness and other adversities had forced him to think of his spiritual condition. He began to read the old Swedish "psalmbok," and Arndt's *True Christianity*. His Bible he had sold before he left Sweden, thinking he would never want to see it again. But there came a time when he was glad to have another.

1859

The Hedengran's had a three-year-old daughter whom they had neglected to baptize. Reading a warning against such neglect, but finding no pastor, he now baptized the girl himself, thinking it might relieve his anxious conscience. But his troubles did not end, for his soul was torn with grief over all his sinfulness. He cried out to the Lord for mercy and vowed to God that if God would save him, he would go and preach wherever God might call him to go.

Still he found no peace. His neighbors tried to comfort him, but in vain, as they failed to realize the depth of his anguish. It seemed as if he was on the verge of mental breakdown. At home he crawled on the floor like a worm. Once he went to look for his gun and would have ended his life, but fortunately he did not find the gun. His desperate struggles lasted two years, and only gradually did he come to a victorious faith that enabled him to say, "Now I can call God my gracious Father for the sake of Christ."

PASTOR C. A. HEDENGRAN

With fear and trembling he held to this faith, humbly witnessing of the grace of God.

Eric Norelius met him for the first time in May 1857, and described him thus:

> He was so afraid his peace of heart might be disturbed that he hardly dared to open his mouth in private conversation. However, he read the Bible and, the writings of Luther, and was growing in Christian knowledge and faith.

At Christmas time 1857, Peter Carlson came to Carver County as colporteur and stayed for a time to conduct services for these shepherdless pioneers. Now Hedengran began to testify publicly at prayer meetings, giving evidence of a deep and thorough grasp of Christian teachings. In 1858, after Carlson had become pastor at the Union settlement, the Hedengrans moved a few miles farther west, locating near a little lake. In the log house which they built for their home, Hedengran began to conduct services, with the knowledge and approval of the pastor and

1859 the congregation. This was the beginning of the West Union church.

In 1859, as already mentioned, the Chisago Lake congregation had no pastor. Peter Carlson made occasional visits, and about midsummer Hedengran accompanied Carlson on one of his journeys. When Carlson was to return home the people asked Hedengran to stay for a time. With a sense of obligation to help the congregation he stayed a few weeks, preaching on Sundays and holidays, with evident success, in spite of his lack of special training for the pastoral work.

The congregation met on August 25 to call a pastor, and of 81 votes cast, 80 were for Hedengran. He was granted a license by the Synod of Northern Illinois, and in October Hedengran, with his family, moved to Center City. In the spring of 1860 Hedengran was given three months' leave of absence to take some special studies under the tutelage of Pastor O. C. T. Andren in Moline, Illinois. At the organization meeting of the Augustana Synod in June 1860, Hedengran was ordained.

When the Civil War broke out Minnesota was the first state to respond to Lincoln's call for volunteers. As the war dragged on more men volunteered, and still others were drafted for the army. Fourteen percent of the 1860 population of Minnesota served in the Union armies. Chisago Lake families said farewell to many a brother and son, and fathers, too. Most of them, though not all, returned to their homes.

A group of the "boys in blue" from Chisago Lake, while stationed in the South, decided to send a gift to their congregation. Contributions totaled about $70, which was used to purchase a set of silver communion vessels.

During the war years Minnesota also experienced the frightful Sioux massacre of 1862. Though these ravages all occurred on the western frontier, and Chisago County was far from the scene of the battles, the people all over the state were aroused to action. The need of defense was felt even at Chisago Lake. Fortifications were hastily erected near the church, and in response to an appeal sent to Governor Ramsey the state furnished a three-foot long cannon and a supply of ammunition. The redskins never attacked Center City.

1860

In spite of wars and rumors of wars the population of Minnesota increased rapidly between 1860 and 1865. Congress passed the Homestead Law in 1862, giving free land to settlers. The war brought about an increasing demand for wheat and lumber, the two main products of Minnesota. The price of wheat went as high as $1.50. The National Banking Act of 1863 brought order into the financial system. Consequently the economic situation at Chisago Lake, as elsewhere in the state, improved greatly. New and comfortable homes replaced the pioneer log shacks. The roads were improved. Many farmers sold their oxen and bought horses. Better farm machinery came into use.

The church building likewise was improved. A bell was bought, new pews and pulpit were installed. An organ was purchased at a cost of $170. The church was dedicated by Hasselquist in 1862.

A post office had been established in Center City in 1858, the

Psalmodikon—First musical instrument used in the pioneer days

first postmaster being A. Nilson, who was succeeded by S. Hamilton. The third one was Peter Shaleen, who also was the church organist. The village had a store, a sawmill, a blacksmith shop, and a wagon shop, by the end of the Civil War period.

Prosperity did not save the congregation from trouble. There had been disagreements and dissension since Cederstam's pastorate. In 1856 the congregation had bought 80 acres for "parsonage land." Soon they decided to sell the 80, and a 29-acre tract was purchased instead, nearer the church. The original plan had been to have the cemetery around the church, and a few burials were made on the east side of the church. During the pastoral vacancy in 1858 a decision was made to build the parsonage near the church and use a part of the 29-acre tract for a cemetery. This caused great dissatisfaction, and cemeteries were started at three other places, on Glader's land south of the lake, on Lindstrom's land west of the lake, and on Pehrson's land on the east side of the lake. The portion of the 29 acres intended for a cemetery proved to be unsuitable, and another plot of four acres was bought a little nearer to the church.

The strife about these matters broke out anew at a meeting in 1860. Not only was there a question about where the cemetery and the parsonage should be, but the trustees were accused of having bought the 29 acres without authority from the congregation. Two men accused the trustees of misappropriating funds of the congregation, but they were unable to prove their charges. When summoned to

1860

appear before the Church Council, one of them voluntarily withdrew from the congregation, the other one was expelled.

Nevertheless, others took up the battle again in 1866. After a heated argument at a meeting of the congregation it was decided that cemetery and parsonage should stay where they were. Those who were demanding a change secured 70 signatures to a petition for another meeting. When this meeting was held Eric Norelius was present and served as chairman. After listening to the wrangling and the personal insults for a while Norelius suggested that the question should be tabled for five years, when there might be a chance to settle it in a friendly way. This suggestion was adopted, and the raging storm gradually abated.

The first parsonage was built on the church lot, but was soon sold and a new one was built on the parsonage land. The cemetery was not moved back to the church lot, but remained below the hill.

Another episode in the history of dissension is an example of how certain problems of the mind and the soul were misunderstood at that time. In the fall of 1863 an elderly couple accused a neighbor woman of being a thief, but the couple was unable to furnish any proof. The Church Council sought to bring about reconciliation and after a time they seemed to have been successful. Then the old folks began to accuse the neighbor woman of practicing witchcraft. Under their front steps they had found the means of her sorcery, a bundle of old rags.

1863

The unfortunate old couple, evidently victims of some mental aberration, instead of being sent to an institution where they might have received proper care, were summoned before the Church Council and were voted out of the congregation. The people now took sides for a showdown. Hedengran wrote to the president of the synod, Pastor Hasselquist. He and most of the pastors of the Minnesota Conference came to Chisago Lake to settle the matter, and after some investigation sustained the action of the Church Council, and praised the deacons for their decision in the case. The old couple was never reinstated.

Hedengran was inclined to be sad and often looked at the dark side of the picture. The unseemly outbursts at congregational meetings, and even threats of violence, caused him great sorrow. At one time he read this statement to the congregation:

> I have tried to maintain order and decorum, though often in vain, and I must honestly say that of all the congregational meetings I have attended, in Sweden or in America, I have never seen any that were worse than our meetings in noise, disorder and confusion. It would be well, therefore, if this congregation would begin to learn how to conduct a congregational meeting; for, although every one has the right to speak, they should not all speak at the same time, or one person interrupt another while that one has the floor.
>
> If you find that I am unfit to be your pastor, tell me so openly. I am willing to leave my position to someone who is better and more capable than I, whenever you desire it. You need not torture me. Because of my weaknesses I am already inclined to withdraw from my burdensome calling.

1864 This was in 1862, three years after he began his ministry in Chisago Lake. But he stayed many years after this, busy not only with the ever increasing duties of a large, widely scattered parish, but also serving Scandia at intervals when there was no pastor; organizing congregations in Taylors Falls, 1860, and in Cambridge, 1864; writing letters to friends and fellow workers; and several articles for publication.

Hedengran was one of those who most strongly urged Eric Norelius to start a school for youth of the conference in 1862, and a young man from Chisago Lake, Jonas Magny, stepson of Håkan Swedberg, was the first student to enroll at the school in Red Wing, which later developed into Gustavus Adolphus College, Saint Peter.

Pastor Hedengran was one of the first to urge Norelius to establish an orphan home in Minnesota. He wrote to Norelius on September 15, 1864:

> Swedberg is a very sick man. I have given him communion. He handed me $5.00 with a request that I give it to some Christian

cause. I decided to give it to a future Children's Home in Minnesota, in case there is a possibility of such a Home. Perhaps it would be worthwhile to talk about it at the next conference?

I have thought about you a great deal, since we have no one else among the Swedish brethren to whom we can entrust this matter. If this comes up for consideration, it seems to me that it would be best that you take it, as Passavant or Francke, on your own responsibility, trusting in God. If it is to be established under the control of the Conference there will be strife and many difficulties. You could not have it as you want it. It would not be so encouraging, but would be a heavy burden and a trial and test of faith. But if God would bless it, the joy would be just as great. Now the time seems to be right, for there probably will be no lack of fatherless children when the War ends.

The Vasa Children's Home became a reality in the fall of 1865, and Hedengran was faithful in helping to raise money. During the first year Chisago Lake contributed $116.50, besides a gift of $5 from "little John Swenson's savings bank." More contributions were sent in succeeding years.

1867

In 1867 Carolina Magny of Chisago Lake gave heed to the urgent pleas of Norelius and Hedengran to go and help with the work at the Vasa Home. She became the second matron, serving until 1880.

Hedengran also worked for an independent synod in Minnesota, but in this he was not successful.

The population of Chisago County increased from 1,729 in 1860 to 4,309 in 1870. The 1870 census showed 2,164 foreign-born in the county, of whom 1,670 were Swedes. Chisago Lake township was solidly Swedish. The congregation had increased to more than 400 communicants in 1867, and in 1873 when Hedengran retired, there were more than 800. The church had been too small almost as soon as it was built. In 1869 an addition was built at a cost of $923.05. This church was one of the first in the Minnesota Conference to have a pipe organ. The organ was purchased in 1871, at a cost of $1,200, and was installed just before the synodical convention which was held in Chisago Lake that year. Peter Shaleen, who had been "song leader" since 1856, became the first organist, a position he held until 1898.

Peter Shaleen

Three times during Hedengran's pastorate Chisago Lake served as hosts to the Minnesota Conference: In February 1860; October 1863; and January 1867. The conference was still small in numbers and the delegation at the three meetings totalled, respectively, 10, 14, and 17.

Parochial Swedish school was begun a month after Hedengran came to Chisago Lake. Johan Peterson—later known as "Skol-Johan"—was chosen to be the teacher, at a salary of $4 per month, plus eight bushels of rye and corn, and free board. He was to have school in four places, a total of six months. The school day was from eight o'clock until five. Skol-Johan continued to serve as teacher for several years, giving instruction in Christianity and in Swedish.

1867

Pastor Hedengran's salary was $200 in cash, and approximately 200 bushels of grain per year until 1866, when the congregation voted to pay him $550 cash salary. Church dues were then set as follows: $2.50 per year for each farmer; $2.00 for a man who is not a farmer; and $1.00 for each woman member of the congregation.

That which constituted Pastor Hedengran's chief contribution to the church was not growth in membership, improvement of the church property, establishing the church school, and organizing the people for more effective service, but rather his earnest efforts at soul-winning through his public preaching and especially his conscientious private counseling. He was known as an extremely conscientious man in all details of his life.

During this time Pastor Hasselquist wrote, after a visit to Chisago Lake, that the people sat for two whole days listening to the preaching of the Word, and on the following day, when he went to Taylors Falls to conduct services, a large number of the people from Chisago Lake went with him to hear more. Hasselquist stated as his opinion: "It is evident that the Lord dwells among this people and is busy gathering unto Himself prodigal sons and daughters."

Though Hedengran's ministry had often been difficult and discouraging he felt that the Lord had richly blessed him and the congregation. In his farewell to the congregation he said:

> This period of almost fourteen years has certainly been filled with suffering, sorrows, and struggles, but the Lord has most graciously lifted one burden after another, and after dark and stormy days He has let the sun shine again. The Lord's protecting hand has been stretched forth over this congregation, so that only a few have been drawn away by the winds of error ... I thank you, my beloved congregation, for the hours when we have rejoiced together, for every kindness that has been bestowed on me, for every prayer that has been sent up to God for me.

1873

He had often been ill. In 1873 his friends had despaired of his life. He retired from service, but recovered his health and lived seven years more. The congregation provided a place for him and his wife to live, and an annual pension of $300. His death occurred on October 31, 1880. His remains are resting in the Chisago Lake cemetery. Mrs. Hedengran died on February 22, 1897. She also is buried in the Chisago Lake cemetery.

There had been occasions at business meetings of the congregation when Pastor Hedengran had seen the hard, knotted fists of angry men close to his face. To be given a home and a pension upon retirement was an indication of the remarkable change that had taken place through the years. Civil War and Reconstruction in the nation had had their counterpart in the congregation at Chisago Lake. Perhaps it would be too much to say that Hedengran was the Lincoln who "saved the Union." Hedengran would have said that God's Spirit had reconstruct-

PASTOR C. A. HEDENGRAN

ed human hearts and lives, and bestowed God's grace on his church.

When the parish was looking for a successor to Hedengran calls were issued to Jonas Auslund of Saint Paul, C. A. Evald of Minneapolis, C. P. Rydholm of Burlington, Iowa, and Olof Olsson of Lindsborg, Kansas. Each one of them in turn declined.

Once again the congregation called a man who was not ordained, Professor J. J. Frodeen of Saint Ansgar's Academy at East Union.

❧

1873

Pastor J. J. Frodeen
1875–1890

JOHAN JOHANNESON FRODEEN was a native of Fröderyd, Småland, the parish where Lina Sandell's father was pastor and where the great poet herself began her career of singing and writing. The Frodeen family emigrated to America in 1857, when the son Johan was nine. They settled in Illinois, and in a few years Johan enrolled at Augustana College, which then was located in Paxton. After four years of study he was called to the Minnesota Conference school to serve as assistant professor. From 1872 to 1874 he was head of the institution. Upon receiving the call to Chisago Lake he took a year's training at Augustana Seminary and was ordained in 1875, after which he moved to Center City.

The stream of immigration had slowed down considerably in 1872 and 1873 because of a financial panic which affected the entire nation. Then the stream not only resumed its flow, but became a flood.

The period 1875 to 1890 was the period of the greatest immigration from Sweden to America, and these were the years of Frodeen's pastorate in the Chisago Lake Church. In 1880 the population of Chisago County had risen to 7,982, of whom 3,122 were natives of Sweden. By 1890 the figures were: population, 10,359; born in Sweden, 3,955.

Even before Hedengran's pastorate the Chisago Lake community had ceased to be a frontier and had become a well settled region. Though it was somewhat isolated because of poor roads, hundreds of Swedish immigrants found their way each year to this, the most Swedish community in the United States. In 1870 the Lake Superior and Mississippi Railroad (later part of the Northern Pacific) was built to connect Saint Paul and Duluth. This brought Center City within 10 miles of a railroad. In 1884 the branch line from Wyoming to Taylors Falls was completed, giving railroad service to Chisago City, Lindstrom, Center City, and Shafer. Truly this was the dawn of a new day, bringing still more settlers and giving village life a great boost.

1875

As the community grew and developed it was evident that the people could not all belong to one congregation. The first daughter church had been organized in Taylors Falls in 1860 under Hedengran's leadership.

The second one was organized in Chisago City on February 8, 1874, during the time of vacancy in Chisago Lake after Hedengran's retirement. No pastor was present at the organization. An active layman of the Chisago Lake Church, Otto Wallmark, who lived in Chisago City, was the leader of the movement. Charter members of the Zion congregation, Chisago City, numbered 113 communicants and 106 children. The Chisago Lake Church did not give its approval to this action until the following year, when all difficulties were ironed out after Frodeen had come to Center City.

The Immanuel Church of Almelund, the third daughter of Chisago Lake, was organized by Pastor Frodeen on January 31, 1887. There were 45 charter members. Pastor Frodeen also organized the

Trinity congregation in North Branch in 1887.

In spite of the fact that these new congregations took some members from the mother church, the Chisago Lake congregation continued to grow, from 820 communicants to 1,320 during the 15 years of Frodeen's pastorate. It should also be noted that many people who came to Chisago Lake and joined the congregation later moved to newer settlements in the great Northwest. Chisago Lake has been a mother church to many, giving sons and daughters to scores of Augustana congregations in Minnesota, Wisconsin, the Dakotas, and other states.

Building and Rebuilding

Two church buildings were erected in Center City during Pastor Frodeen's period of service. The church in use when he came was the old frame building erected in 1856 and since then remodeled twice. But with a congregation of a thousand members it was inadequate. Shortly after Pastor Frodeen's arrival discussions were started relative to the building of a new church. In 1877 a committee was elected to raise money for this project, but two years later the congregation voted, 106 to 90, that the proposition of building a church should be postponed for five years. In spite of this decision the question was soon raised again. In January 1881 subscriptions totalling $7,210 had been scured, and the congregation decided to proceed immediately with plans for a new church. A building committee was elected, consisting of Pastor Frodeen, A. Molin, C. J. Long, Peter Swenson (in Vibo), Gustaf Hultquist, J. J. Slattengren, J. Shaleen, J. E. Peterson, and David Sandberg.

1877

The size of the church was to be 100 by 66, besides the apse and the narthex. First plans called for a frame building, but after further consideration the committee recommended the use of brick, and to this the congregation agreed. The brick was purchased at Carver, 150 thousand at $16.50 per thousand, and 150 thousand at $6 per thousand.

1882

Church erected 1882; destroyed by fire 1888

The cost of the church when completed was estimated at $25,000, of which $19,486 was paid in cash, and the rest in donated labor. The church was ready for use in the fall of 1883, and in October the Minnesota Conference met there to celebrate its 25th anniversary amid great festivities. In these first 25 years of its history the conference had grown from 5 pastors and 13 congregations to 80 pastors and 200 congregations. Pastor Eric Norelius gave the main historical address at the anniversary, an address which later was printed in book form.

The steamboat bell which had hung in the old church steeple, was hung in the new one.

Interior of church erected in 1882

1884

In 1884 the interior of the church was decorated. In June 1888 a new bell, costing $520 and weighing a ton, was placed in the tall steeple that towered above the village and the surrounding community. The inscription on the bell was:

> *For Ev. Luth. Forsamlingen*
> *vid Chisago Lake 1888*
> *Kom, O folk, hor och lar*
> *Vagen som till livet bar*
>
> *(For the Ev. Lutheran Congregation at Chisago Lake, 1888.*
> *Come, O people, hear and learn the way that leads to life.)*

A few weeks later the tall steeple and the whole beautiful structure lay in ruins. In the early morning hours of August 2 lightning

PASTOR J. J. FRODEEN

struck the church and set it on fire. Some brave young man was one of the first to arrive at the scene and clambered up to ring the bell, summoning a great many of the church members. But little could be saved of the equipment and nothing could be done to save the building. When day dawned, the imposing temple was nothing but a smoldering mass of ruins.

Dismay and grief filled the hearts of the church members, but they did not despair. On August 17, just a fortnight after the fire, the congregation met and adopted this resolution:

> That the congregation proceed in the Name of the Lord to rebuild the church, with the purpose of getting it enclosed and, if possible, plastered this fall, so it can be used during the winter.

1888

The work proceeded rapidly, under the supervision of the same building and mason contractors as when the church was originally built, Jonas Norell and Louis Johnson. A total of $9,675.90 was received from the fire insurance companies, and no subscriptions were necessary except an ingathering for new pews. When the church was finished the congregation's debt was only $2,000. In 1890 a new bell was purchased for $486, and a pipe organ the following year, at a cost of $2,200, gathered largely through the efforts of Albert Berg, Secretary of State of Minnesota, a son of the Bergs who had come to Chisago Lake with the first group of settlers in 1851.

In addition to the great task of building and rebuilding the church, the congregation also improved its property in other respects. A little frame church, which had been erected by the "Mission Friends" directly across the street from the front of the Lutheran church, was purchased by the congregation in 1884 for $600 to be used as a chapel. It also served as the church in 1888 after the fire until the new one was built. Some of the services were held in the church park. The congregation also built a new parsonage shortly after Frodeen arrived in 1875.

It is evident from the records of the congregation that Pastor Frodeen undertook to be thorough and zealous in his work. Church discipline was to be strictly maintained, and good order was to be enforced. In the report of 1880—the first one that appears in the minutes—the pastor called attention to two specific evils that needed correction. He warned against drunkenness. He complained about disorder at church services.

> Members come into church late and some leave before the close of the service. Some never come in but spend the time visiting outside the church.

The balcony and the stairways leading to it seem to have constituted a special problem. In 1876 the congregation had voted to build a solid wall across the balcony to separate men from women, and men were forbidden to ascend the stairs leading to the women's section.

Laws and warnings did not bring an immediate end to the problems. In 1885 it was solemnly decreed by the congregation that no one should be allowed to walk on the church lot during services. The following year drastic steps were taken to eliminate disorder at the main entrance. The doors were to be closed during the reading of the Confession of sins, then opened again until after the singing of the pulpit hymn, then closed until the benediction had been pronounced. But these rules were relaxed, and even well into the twentieth century many people had the habit of leaving the church service as soon as the offering had been received. It was considered shameful to leave earlier.

1888

Families were generally larger then than now. Seven or eight children in a family was common, and many families had 10 or 12. In 1886 there were 91 children baptized. At various times in this decade the congregation was concerned with the matter of maintaining a midwife in the community. In 1884 it was decided to tear down the old church and use some of the materials to build a home for a midwife. Mrs. Helena Magnuson was elected to serve in this capacity, and a committee chosen to solicit for her wages, "not less than $2200.00 nor more than $250.00." In 1885 she received $218 and she was rehired. Two years later the Chisago City congregation sent a delegation to confer with Chisago Lake about the possibility of having the two congregations jointly support a midwife, with the suggestion that she live between the two towns, in Lindstrom. The congregation elected a committee—of nine men!—to study the proposition.

A dance hall on the island near the railroad station (Park Island) caused a serious problem of church discipline in 1888. The hall had been there for several years but ownership of it was so secret that the Church Council did not know whom to summon. At last one of the owners revealed the secret. Seven of the 12 owners were church members. Those residing in the community were summoned but failed to respond until the third summons. Only one promised to cease from his connection with the dance hall.

Other cases of discipline during Frodeen's pastorate brought about the exclusion of members on grounds of adultery, operating a saloon, attending dances, and for adherence to doctrines differing from the Lutheran Confessions.

1888

The "Mission Friends," followers of P. P. Waldenstrom in Sweden, had a few adherents in the Chisago Lake community, including some members of the Lutheran church. In 1878 the Church Council summoned the man who undoubtedly was the leader of that group. He was questioned as to his beliefs about the doctrine of the atonement, but he failed to give clear and definite answers. He was suspended, but the Church Council was cautious and conducted several hearings, postponed the case several times in hope that the man would at last decide to return to his former faith. The question put to him was this:

> Has Christ by his active and passive obedience made complete satisfaction for our sins and the sins of the world, and do we for Christ's sake receive the forgiveness of sins and justification by faith?

When he continually refused to give a definite answer he was finally excluded from the congregation on November 6, 1879, but not excommunicated.

The Mission Friends, after they had sold their little chapel to the Lutherans, built a small "meeting house" near the District 14 school-house, four miles north of Center City. In this building regular servic-es were conducted for a number of years and occasionally until 1918. Neither the building nor the congregation is now in existence.

During Frodeen's pastorate the "lodge question" appears for the first time in the history of the congregation. In 1889 a man who applied for membership was told he would have to withdraw from a lodge to which he belonged. This he promised to do, but the following year he had already forgotten this promise. Several others in the congregation were given notice to sever their connections with lodges or leave the church. Before the matter was settled Pastor Frodeen resigned, and this delicate and difficult problem was left to his successor.

In the summer of 1889 Frodeen received a call to become finan-cial solicitor for Gustavus Adolphus College, and he resigned with the intention of accepting this call. But he did not become solicitor for the college. At the annual meeting on January 10, 1890 he gave his last annual report and therein he expressed his feelings about leaving. He had then received and accepted a call to the Spring Garden Church near Cannon Falls. There he served until 1905, after which he went to Canada as a home missionary, stationed at Wetaskiwin, Alberta. He died on October 17, 1912. Because of the distance and the difficulties of communication it was almost a month before his friends in Minnesota heard of his death. He lies buried in Wetaskiwin. Mrs. Frodeen is buried at Spring Garden. A son, Arthur, who drowned in north Chisago Lake on June 11, 1904, is also buried at Spring Garden.

1890

The obituary of Pastor Frodeen, written by Dr. J. Telleen for *Korsbaneret 1914*, gives some glimpses of the character of the man who served Chisago Lake during the busy years 1875 to 1890:

> He was zealous for good order, but his churchliness was not of
> the type that consisted entirely of outward observances, customs,

PASTOR J. J. FRODEEN

rules, and forms ... In these matters he knew how to distinguish between essentials and nonessentials ... He had a sensitive, alert conscience that did not let him speak or act without restraint. By nature he was severe, but he curbed it, and never defended it. He was strict with others, but still more strict with himself ... For many a person Frodeen undoubtedly seemed to be a man of contradictions. He appeared both shallow and deep, both narrow and broadminded in his views ... But he was fully convinced and constantly set forth that only the gospel of the cross can give victory unto the truth and bring about gain for time and eternity .... His preaching was a powerful tes-timony concerning Christ and Him crucified.

An example of his "strictness" may be seen in his reply to the confirmation class of 1884 when the class asked if they might have a processional into the new sanctuary on confirmation day. He firmly said No, because he feared the boys and girls might think more of the marching than of the confirmation vows.

1890

Frodeen also sought to be strict with the congregation in the matter of paying its obligations to the conference and the synod. Only once did the Trustees petition for a reduction. This was in 1888, when the church burned, and which was also a year of poor crops. The conference granted no reduction, and others roundly criticized Chisago Lake for even suggesting it. The entire amount was paid.

∾

Pastor J. F. Seedoff
1890–1896

20
1890

JOHAN FREDRIK SEEDOFF, a native of Sweden, had studied five years at the Fjellstedt School in Uppsala before coming to America in 1882. Completing his education for the ministry at Augustana College and Theological Seminary he was ordained in 1888 on a call to Topeka, Kansas.

When Chisago Lake was looking for a successor to Frodeen, calls were issued to Olof Olsson, Joel L. Haff, and P. J. Sward. All these calls were declined. On March 13, 1890 J. F. Seedoff was called, but he declined. A second call, issued on April 30, was accepted. Before the time came for him to move to Center City both Pastor and Mrs. Seedoff suffered serious illness. They moved in October, but Pastor Seedoff was unable to conduct the services until shortly before Christmas.

He found the congregation numbering more than 1,300 communicants and about 700 children, the largest congregation in the Minnesota Conference, and the third largest in the Augustana Synod. The congregation had a new, commodious church, which, however, was not completely furnished and equipped. It was valued at $24,000, and the debt was $1,175.

A Period of Growth

The first half of the 1890s was a time of great economic unrest in our nation, the year 1893 marking the beginning of the "Cleveland depression." The country was plunged into financial hardship for several years. Yet this was a period of gradual growth and improvement in Chisago Lake, particularly with reference to the congregation's interest in the missions and benevolences of the church. The pastor who served during this period was J. F. Seedoff.

1891

The Augustana Synod had been invited to meet at Chisago Lake in 1891. To prepare for this convention became Seedoff's first large task. When the new church was built after the fire in 1888 a reed organ was obtained as a gift from Congressman Snyder. To secure a new pipe organ in time for the synodical convention became an urgent necessity, and with Mr. Albert Berg as chief solicitor money was secured from members and friends. The organ was installed at a cost of $2,200.

It was also a time of improvement in many homes as the members of the congregation prepared to entertain guests. Many a farmer bought a new surrey or top buggy. They could not take the delegates to and from church in their old lumber wagons.

The Synod of 1891 was of considerable historical significance. P. J. Sward was elected president of the Augustana Synod to succeed S. P. A. Lindahl. Dr. Olof Olsson was elected president of Augustana College and Theological Seminary to succeed T. N. Hasselquist. And one day a few women sat on the church lawn listening to Mrs. Emmy

Evald, a daughter of Erland Carlsson, as she unfolded her hopes and plans for a Women's Missionary Society in the Augustana Synod. Inspired by the response to her idea that was first broached at Chisago Lake, Mrs. Evald took the lead in organizing the W. M. S. the next year when the Augustana Synod met in Lindsborg, Kansas.

Shortly after Seedoff's coming to Center City the conference president, Peter Sjöblom, told him in very plain language that Chisago Lake was not doing enough for the support of missions and Christian higher education. In spite of some strong opposition Seedoff persuaded the congregation to do better. In his annual report to the congregation in 1892 he stated that the contributions to benevolences during 1891 were larger than for any previous year in the congregation's history. They were: for missions, $313.36; for other benevolences, $134.20. At this time the congregation pledged itself to pay $2,000 toward the retirement of the conference's debts. One of the methods inaugurated under Seedoff's leadership to raise money for missions was the annual Fourth of July picnic. The first such event, in 1892, brought in $400. Opposition gradually subsided. In 1895 the congregation gave $764.06 to benevolences.

1892

The Swedish school, conducted in district schoolhouses at many places in the congregation, flourished in this period. A total of $16^{1}/_{2}$ months of school was held in 1892, with 262 children enrolled. The Sunday school had 150 pupils, in 19 classes, besides two Bible classes. The congregation entertained hopes at this time of building its own Christian high school. A committee was elected in 1892 to study this matter, but though a need for such a school was felt, the matter was postponed and never came to be realized.

No drastic disciplinary problems arose during Seedoff's pastorate. There were occasional instances of members being summoned before the deacons on charges of drunkenness, marital infidelity, quarreling, etc. The minutes of the Church Council are frequently amplified to describe the discussions and the prayers, even the thoughts and feelings and sighs of the deacons as they pondered over the spiritual welfare of the congregation. A typical paragraph is this one from 1891:

> And now this meeting was closed with an earnest prayer to God that He would spare our congregation from every kind of sin, and pour out His Holy Spirit in rich measure over the congregation and that many precious souls might be won for His heavenly kingdom.

But with all due respect for the genuine piety and godliness of those men, one gets the impression now and then that certain disciplinary actions have a little flavor of self-important and officious meddling.

1894

A group of unidentified pastors in front of the church, 1894

Aside from the synodical convention of 1891 the greatest festivity of this period was the 40th anniversary of the congregation, observed in May 1894. Several of the charter members were still living, and many others who remembered the pioneer days. They had seen the congregation grow to a parish of almost 1,500 communicants and 800 children, now worshiping in one of the largest and most beautiful rural churches in the state. In preparation for the anniversary the church had been decorated, and new altar and pulpit had been installed.

Pastor Seedoff was instrumental in the organizing of the Young People's Society, which years later became the Luther League. Organized in 1892 with 68 members, the Young People's Society had as its first officers: Pastor Seedoff, president; L. Hokenson, vice president; Burney Slattengren, secretary; Mary Andrews, treasurer. Meetings were held twice a month at the chapel. The dues were 50 cents at the time of joining, and 25 cents every three months. A fine of 10 cents was assessed for absence from meetings, and 25 cents for refusing to be on the program when asked to take part. During the first year of its history the society had on its programs two speeches, six lectures, 24 declamations, nine readings, seven debates, five choir numbers, and six solos.

1894

The only time in its history that the congregation has been involved in litigation was in 1893–94. The Center City school district had chosen as a site for a new school a plot of ground just east of the parsonage. The congregation offered instead to sell an acre and a half south of the road which leads past the parsonage. But the district was not satisfied and instituted condemnation proceedings. The court awarded the land desired by the district for a school site. The congregation intended to appeal to the supreme court but delayed in filing notice of appeal and found that they had acted too late. Twenty-five years later, after Center City and Lindstrom had built their consolidated school the old Center City school was abandoned and the land reverted to the congregation.

Pr. & Mrs. Seedoff and children

On April 12, 1896, Pastor Seedoff announced his resignation, and on April 21 the congregation voted unanimously not to accept his resignation. But he could not be persuaded to stay. In September he preached his farewell sermon. He had accepted a call to First Lutheran Church, Rockford, Illinois, where he served as pastor until his retirement in 1927. He died on July 27, 1939. Mrs. Seedoff and three children had preceded him in death. Five children survived him.

Dr. F. M. Eckman
1896–1913

PASTOR FRANS M. ECKMAN, who succeeded Pastor Seedoff at Chisago Lake, witnessed a transition period during his 17-year pastorate. Changes that affected the nation and the world had their effect also on the Chisago Lake community. The great stream of immigration from Sweden subsided and practically ceased. New methods of transportation and communication began to change people's ways of living and thinking. The coming of electricity brought benefits that the pioneers had never imagined. The automobile made its appearance, and Eckman drove a car as early as 1910.

The Reverend F. M. Eckman was the first American-born pastor to serve the Chisago Lake Church. He was born near Cokato, Minnesota, in 1867. His father was a pioneer farmer and lay preacher who later became an ordained pastor of the Augustana Synod.

Eckman attended Gustavus Adolphus College in the 1880s before a complete college course was offered, finishing at Augustana College in 1889. In addition to his seminary training at Augustana he also studied at Uppsala University in Sweden 1892–94. He was ordained in 1894 on a call to Brainerd. On May 7, 1896, the Chisago Lake congregation called him and he accepted, beginning his duties on October 1, two weeks after his predecessor had moved. The salary stipulated in the call was $1,000 per year, the same as it had been during Seedoff's pastorate. It remained at that figure until the last year of Eckman's period of service. At first it was paid semi-annually, but in later years monthly.

Into the Twentieth Century

When Pastor Eckman came the congregation had 1,431 communicants and 781 children. The highest point in membership was reached in 1905, when there were 1,495 communicants and 816 children. For several years the membership was at or near those figures.

1901

Some members of the congregation joined the English Lutheran Church in Lindstrom, which was organized by the Synod of the Northwest in 1901. This did not represent any serious split, but the entry of another synod into the territory of the Chisago Lake Church was looked upon with disfavor. In 1903 it was decided to build a chapel in Lindstrom, to be used for school and for services. A committee secured subscriptions totalling $1,107, but the project was reconsidered and voted down. Dr. Eric Norelius, in his history of the Augustana Synod, intimates that it was a mistake that this synod did not organize a congregation in Lindstrom. Dr. Norelius had a vision

Picnic flyer

The Chisago Lake parsonage

and an understanding of the need of English work long before the
other leaders in the synod seemed to grasp this problem.

Several building projects were considered during the Eckman
period, but only two of major importance were brought to reality. A
home for the organist was built in 1899, and a new parsonage (the present one) in 1907. Minor building projects were a pavilion in the church
park, where the Hillside Cemetery now is located, and an addition to
the old chapel. The project of building a high school for the congregation was discussed in 1901, but nothing was done to bring this about.

The building committee for the parsonage, elected in 1906, were
William Carlson, Charles Lindstrom, J. Lindquist, C. J. Long, J. N.
Westlund, A. B. Holm, and J. Frid. The house was built in 1907 at a
cost of $5,888, and when completed there was a debt of $3,440. Pastor
Eckman and his family moved into the new home on November 2,
1907. Since the Eckmans lived there, seven other pastors have had it as
their residence.

Peter Shaleen, the faithful old organist who had served since
1856, died on February 17, 1898. Peter R. Melin of Ashland,
Wisconsin, was called as his successor, to serve as organist, choir direc-

1907

tor, and parochial school teacher, at a salary of $500 per year and house. The house built in 1899 as an organist's residence stood on the south side of the road leading past the parsonage, a few rods east of the cemetery. There the Melin family lived until 1909, when Mr. Melin resigned. Emil Anderson of Joliet, Illinois, became his successor.

During P. R. Melin's tenure the Swedish school reached its peak in enrollment and began to decline. In 1900 there were 300 children enrolled. In 1908 the enrollment was as follows: District 2, 21; District 3, Center City, 37; District 3, Shafer, 35; District 4, 40; District 5, 22; District 6, 36; District 7, 27; District 8, 36; total, 254.

As long as P. R. Melin played the organ it was pumped by hand. The possibility of using a gasoline engine to run the blower was investigated in 1903, but it was found that it would be too expensive and would increase fire insurance rates. An electric blower was installed in 1912, paid for by the Young People's Society. The last organ pumper was Jonas Johnson.

1911

The clock in the church tower was installed in 1907. Concrete steps at the church entrance and a sidewalk to the street were built in 1911, replacing the old wooden steps and walk.

The congregation still continued to use the Swedish language exclusively all through the Eckman period, except for the Young People's Society, which used both Swedish and English. As yet there were no English classes in Sunday school. Confirmation instruction was in Swedish. During his years at Chisago Lake Pastor Eckman baptized approximately 650 children and confirmed more than 700 catechumens.

At the first annual meeting presided over by Pastor Eckman in 1897, he sounded a warning that those who were guilty of drunkenness and those who joined lodges should expect to have the constitutional provisions enforced. These warnings were repeated the next year, with special mention of the custom of serving liquor when threshing was finished on the farms.

Several lodge members were summoned by the Church Council,

but only a few were persuaded to yield. About 15 were dismissed from the congregation, some on their own request, some by action of the Church Council. In no case was there hurried action.

The liquor problem was also attacked more definitely than ever before. In 1897 the deacons were authorized to circulate petitions for legislative action on the county option law. At various times resolutions favoring such a law were adopted by the congregation. It was considered a great victory for the drys in the community when Lindstrom voted out the saloons in 1910. But no county option law was enacted until in 1915, after Pastor Eckman had left Center City. Following enactment of the law Chisago County went dry by a vote of 1,730 to 610, and remained in the dry column until repeal of the 18th amendment in 1933.

The Reverend Eckman was actively interested in the general work of the church and did a great deal to arouse the interest of the congregation in the China mission work, which had its beginnings when Dr. A. W. Edwins was sent to China in 1905. The China Mission Society was at first a voluntary group, not officially sponsored or sup- **1911** ported by the synod. At a meeting of this society held in Chisago Lake February 13 and 14, 1905, Pastor Edwins's acceptance of his call was announced, resulting in great rejoicing and thanksgiving.

Pastor Eckman also took great interest in the deaconess cause. The Minnesota Conference established Bethesda Deaconess Institute in Saint Paul, and Eckman's influence is reflected in the fact that seven young women from Chisago Lake entered the service of this institution. One of them, Sister Eleanora Slattengren, became an outstanding leader in the work serving for 16 years as directing sister of the Deaconess Institute and of Bethesda Hospital, later serving for more than a quarter of a century as matron of Bethesda Old People's Home at Chisago City.

Eleanor Slattengren

PASTOR F. M. ECKMAN

Sister Esther Porter, another Chisago Lake girl, served as teacher at the Deaconess Institute.

Pastor Eckman was one of those most active in the establishment of the Home at Chisago City, which had its beginning in 1904, the first institution of its kind owned by the Minnesota Conference.

Prior to Eckman's pastorate only one man from Chisago Lake had entered the ministry, Jonas Magny, who was ordained in 1870. During the years of Eckman's service four sons of the congregation were ordained. The first native-born Chisago Lake boy to enter the ministry was Caleb E. Shaleen, who now lives in retirement at Center City and assists occasionally in pastoral duties. He was born November 25, 1874, received his college degree at Gustavus Adolphus in 1897, and was graduated from Augustana Seminary in 1900, and ordained on a call to Clarkfield,

Pr. Jonas Magny

1912

Minnesota. He has served at Clarkfield, 1900–1906; Akron, Ohio, 1906–1911; Langford, South Dakota, 1911–1921; Centuria, Wisconsin, 1921–1929; Langford, South Dakota, 1929–1947.

S. D. Hawkins was born at Chisago Lake in 1863, but in his early childhood the family moved to Vasa. He was ordained in 1906 and served a number of parishes, mostly in the Minnesota Conference, until his death, which occurred on June 7, 1928.

Pr. Caleb E. Shaleen

Two brothers who were born in Sweden but came with their parents to Chisago Lake in 1883 were ordained to the ministry. These were A. F. Almer, ordained 1897, and N. A. Almer, ordained 1901. A. F. Almer has served Zion, Rock Island, Illinois, 1897–1899; Forest Lake, 1899–1906; at Bethesda Deaconess Home, St.

Fourth of July picnic in church park

Pr. A. F. Almer

Paul, 1906–1916; New London–Spicer, 1916–1924; chaplain at Bethesda Hospital, St. Paul, 1924–1927; chaplain at Immanuel Deaconess Institute, Omaha, Nebraska, 1927–1944. He is retired and lives in Omaha.

N. A. Almer was ordained in 1901 and has served the following congregations: Bertrand, Nebraska, 1901–1907; Isanti, 1908–1911; Forest Lake, 1911–1915; Isle–Opstead–Malmo, 1915–1917; Prince– ton, 1917–1932; and Bock, 1932–1938. The Reverend N. A. Almer retired from active service January 1, 1939 and resided in Princeton until his death on April 10, 1952.

1912

Pr. N. A. Almer

Five children were born to the Eckmans during their years of residence at Center City. Among the vivid memories now cherished by them is the first family car, a 1908 Ford Runabout with a little cheesebox set in back outside of the protection of the top, and sometimes referred to as the place for the poor relatives to ride. Pastor Eckman purchased this car from Mr. Dahl in Chisago City in 1910. The only other automobiles in Center City at that time

PASTOR F. M. ECKMAN

were owned by F. G. Lorens, J. N. Westlund, and Dr. A. N. Gunz.

The sandy country roads were difficult to negotiate. It was almost always necessary that someone help with a little push to enable the car to make the grade up the parsonage driveway.

Dr. Philip Eckman of Duluth recalls one particularly amusing incident that happened a few days after his father had bought the car. While waiting for the evening mail as was customary, the conversation in the post office of course concerned the car, and Eckman apparently did a little bragging about how easy it was to learn how to drive it. As he stepped

1912

into it to go home, he made a wide U-turn in the road in front of the post office. The turning radius was unfortunately inadequate, and a telephone pole stopped the progress of the

Pr. & Mrs. Eckman, Edith, Ragnar, Philip

bright red car that was so "easy to drive." Eckman could think of nothing better than to shout "Whoa!" He never had any more accidents, but his embarrassment on that occasion must have been great.

The first out-of-town trip was to mission meeting in Forest Lake. Such a trip had always been half a day's drive. Eckman was up early. Philip went along for the ride. He still remembers the surprised look on his father's face when they arrived in Forest Lake to find people just beginning to stir out of their beds.

The golden jubilee of the Chisago Lake congregation was observed while the community was still enjoying the golden era of the horse and buggy, or the surrey with the fringe on top.

Ascension Day, May 12, 1904, marked the beginning of the celebration of the 50th anniversary. The festivities continued until the following Sunday, the 15th. Two former pastors, J. J. Frodeen and J. F. Seedoff, appeared on the program; also Dr. Eric Norelius, president of the Augustana Synod, Dr. J. Fremling, president of the Minnesota Conference, Dr. Gustav Andreen, president of Augustana College and Theological Seminary, and others. A 115-page book was published after the festivities, containing the sermons and addresses, including a history of the congregation written by Pastor Eckman. A number of interesting illustrations were also included. Five hundred copies were printed at a cost of $483.95. The book was sold at $1.00 and the entire edition was soon sold out.

In October 1898, the Minnesota Conference observed its 40th anniversary in Center City. Among pioneer pastors in attendance were Eric Norelius, P. A. Cederstam, and Peter Beckman. *A Conference Album* was published, with Eckman as editor. The 50th anniversary of the Minnesota Conference was a celebration of grand proportions, being held October 7 to 11, 1908, in Saint Paul, Minneapolis, and Center City. Again Eckman was chosen to edit a history of the conference, an illustrated volume of 254 pages.

1913

In January 1913 Eckman resigned, having accepted a call to Moorhead, Minnesota. There he served until 1926, when he moved to Carlton. After 11 years of. service in that parish he retired and settled in Duluth, where all his four sons are engaged in professional practice, two as attorneys and two as doctors. Pastor Eckman received the honorary degree of doctor of divinity in 1931.

After his retirement he was called on frequently to serve vacant congregations temporarily. In the fall of 1939 Dr. and Mrs. Eckman spent a few months in Center City and Dr. Eckman had charge of his former parish during the vacancy that then existed. Dr. Eckman died on September 27, 1947.

When the congregation was looking for a pastor to succeed Dr. F. M. Eckman, the Church Council nominated Dr. John E. Oslund of Marshfield, Oregon, and a call was issued on February 6, 1913. The call was accepted and the Oslunds arrived in July.

1913

Pastor J. Edward Oslund
1913–1917

22
1913

PASTOR JOHN EDWARD OSLUND was born in 1873 near Cokato, Minnesota, a few miles from the birthplace of Eckman, though not in the same parish. In youth Oslund worked at various occupations and attained proficiency as an engineer. But he felt the call of God to the ministry and enrolled at Gustavus Adolphus College, where he received his A. B. degree in 1903. Three years later he graduated from Augustana Theological Seminary. (He took part of his theological course at Maywood Seminary in Chicago.) He had served in Idaho, Washington, and Oregon before coming to Chisago Lake.

Dr. Oslund's pastorate was comparatively short, only four years. This period was characterized by some significant improvements in the church property, notably the erection of a new chapel to replace the old one, which had been used since 1884. The congregation elected a committee in 1915 to study the proposition of enlarging the old chapel. This committee consisted of Solomon Peterson, F. G. Johnson, C. J. West, A. B. Holm, and J. N. Westlund. The following year the Young People's Society pledged $1,250 for a new chapel, and the committee recommended that a new one be built, rather than to remodel the old one. The congregation agreed to this, but limited the cost to $3,000.

The new chapel was built on the southeast corner of the church lot, and was constructed of brick similar to that used for the church. It had an auditorium seating close to 400, and a basement equipped with kitchen facilities and a large dining room. It served as a parish center for 25 years, until destroyed by fire in 1941.

In the same year that the chapel was built—1916—the choir petitioned the congregation for permission to gather funds for a new pipe organ. The petition was granted. A few months later, on June 15, 1916, at a special business meeting of the congregation it was reported

1916   that the Carnegie Corporation had promised to donate $2,400 for a new organ provided the congregation would give a similar amount. The offer was accepted and purchase of the organ was authorized.

In spite of the recommendation of an architect that the organ be placed in the front of the church, the congregation decided that it should be on the balcony, as formerly.

Electric lights were installed in the parsonage and in the organist's residence in 1913, and in 1914 in the church. The church ceiling was covered with steel plates, and the church was redecorated the same year.

The Board of Trustees reported the valuation of the church property at $55,710.90 in 1917, an increase of $18,000 since 1913. The congregation also increased somewhat in membership during these years.

A petition from 52 Shafer residents was presented to the congregation in 1913, asking that services and Sunday school be conducted

there. This was approved by the congregation, and the following year
C. J. Wiberg, Sunday school superintendent in Shafer, reported that 78
children had been enrolled, and that 60 of these had never attended
Sunday school before. In 1914 the enrollment dropped to 56. In 1915
it was 67, in 1916 down again to 51. During these years the Sunday
school enrollment in Center City was: 1914, 132; 1915, 140; 1916, 139.

The Swedish summer school was still maintained, though enrollment was gradually going down. In 1914 Swedish school was held in
eight districts, a total of $15\frac{1}{2}$ months, with total enrollment of 198
pupils. In 1915 there were 15 months of school in eight places, with
181 pupils. In 1916 there were $13\frac{1}{2}$ months of school in eight places,
with 151 children enrolled. Most of the children were instructed for
confirmation in Swedish, but beginning as early as with the class of
1914 there were occasional requests for confirmation in English.

A "Confirmation League," organized in 1916 by the young people
confirmed by Dr. Oslund, conducted its meetings and programs almost
entirely in the Swedish language, but the Young People's Society used
English as its "official language" at this time.

1917

The congregation observed its 60th anniversary in 1914, with
Pastors Seedoff and Eckman in attendance, and also the patriarch, Dr.
Eric Norelius, then past 80 years of age. He had seen tremendous
changes take place in Chisago Lake since his first visit in 1854.

The Minnesota Conference met at Chisago Lake in 1917. It was
the 10th time that this congregation had been host to the conference.

Three months later Dr. Oslund resigned to accept a call to
Moscow, Idaho. At a meeting on August 17 a motion was adopted by
a vote of 188 to 41 asking him to withdraw his resignation.
Nevertheless he held to his decision and left Center City in September.
He served in Moscow until 1920, after which he moved to Cannon
Falls, Minnesota. He served there until 1927, when he was called to the

PASTOR J. EDWARD OSLUND

neighboring congregation at Vasa, which became his last field of service. He retired in 1948 and moved to Red Wing, where he died on April 24, 1950.

Before Oslund's term of service at Chisago Lake had ended, the United States had become involved in the first World War. A new and different era had dawned for this nation, and every community was soon to feel the effects.

The pastor who succeeded Dr. J. Edward Oslund was Pastor Oscar Sandahl.

❧

1917

Pastor Oscar Sandahl
1917–1927

PASTOR OSCAR SANDAHL was born in Sweden in 1874 and had come to America together with his parents in 1888. They settled in Stillwater, Minnesota, and the young man was confirmed in Trinity Lutheran Church by Pastor Joel Haff. He became an active worker in the congregation in his youth, but felt the call of God to a more definite service for the church as a pastor. He received his college training at Gustavus Adolphus and the theological course at Augustana Seminary. He was ordained in 1908 and served at Marquette, Michigan, and Wahoo, Nebraska, before coming to Center City. He began his service at Chisago Lake Church on Advent Sunday in 1917.

The young men of the nation were being called to the colors. Eighty-three members of the Chisago Lake congregation served in the armed forces. Three of them died while in service.

The largest number of draftees to leave the community at one time was the contingent of 118 men from all parts of the county who left by special train from Center City on February 24, 1918. They assembled on the previous day at the county seat. On Sunday, the 24th, they attended morning worship in the Chisago Lake Church and heard a special service. In the afternoon a farewell program was given in the church with Henry N. Benson, Saint Peter, then a state senator, as the main speaker. It was an impressive and never-to-be-forgotten day for those who were leaving to serve their country in war, and also for the hundreds of relatives and friends who said farewell to the men that winter day.

Three young women from the congregation served as Red Cross nurses in the war. The congregation gave about $4,000 for the National War Service conducted by the National Lutheran Commission and the Lutheran Brotherhood of America.

After the Armistice was signed on November 11, 1918, the men
1918 soon began to return home, and the next Memorial Day, May 30, 1919, became the occasion for a great festive welcome at Center City. Six thousand people gathered for the festivities, and 245 Chisago County veterans were in attendance. The programs were held at the church and at the church park and cemetery, with Pastor Sandahl taking a leading part.

The "war prosperity" of the 1920s was both a blessing and a curse. Many farmers were enabled to build new barns and new dwelling houses in the years immediately after the close of the war. But there were some who overextended themselves, thinking the prosperous times would continue. The "farmers' depression" began in 1921 and some who had bought land or made improvements with borrowed money were caught unprepared.

The aftermath of war was a moral laxity that left its imprint on the nation, and Chisago Lake was not wholly spared from this blight. Worldliness and secularism led to religious indifference on the part of some. But there were factors that helped to make church work easier.

A portion of the cemetery

Good roads and good automobiles solved the transportation problem, and church attendance improved greatly. The English language was gradually taking the place of Swedish, making the church services more interesting and attractive to the younger generation. The Swedish parochial schools declined, as was to be expected, but this was to a large extent compensated by a greater attention to the work of the Sunday school and the training of the children in church worship. English was introduced into the Sunday school during the war years, and by 1920 there were seven English classes with 66 pupils. In 1925 English services were being held every Sunday, a 30-minute service before the regular Swedish morning worship. Gradually attendance at the English services increased while the Swedish were less well attended.

1925

During Oslund's pastorate services were held in a hall in Shafer every other Sunday afternoon. Sandahl continued this schedule and also held services in Lindstrom on the alternate Sunday afternoons. Erection of a chapel in Shafer seemed a definite prospect in 1920 when a committee reported that subscriptions totalling $2,010.50 had been secured for that purpose. The following year a Shafer landowner,

Charles Lindstrom, offered to donate a lot for a chapel site and the congregation voted to build a chapel in Shafer. No decision was made as to plans for the building, or when construction should begin, and the chapel was never built. In 1924 the Shafer people hired a bus to transport their Sunday school children to the church, and the need of a chapel in Shafer was eliminated.

The only building project of major importance during Oscar Sandahl's pastorate was the purchase of a new home for the organist in place of the one built east of the village in 1899. The new one was in the village, a few blocks from the church.

Emil Anderson had served as organist, choir director, and occasionally as Swedish school teacher from 1909 to 1918, after which Carl S. Malmstrom held the position for seven years. He was succeeded in 1925 by J. A. Wallin.

1925

A new altar was installed in the church shortly after Sandahl took over his duties, and vestments in the liturgical colors were procured. The individual communion cups were introduced. The clerical robe was not adopted by Sandahl as long as he served in Chisago Lake. He wore the traditional long black clerical coat, and the white tabs, as his predecessors in the congregation had done for half a century.

Two new organizations made their appearance in 1918, the Brotherhood and the Women's Missionary Society. The first report of the W.M.S. shows that there were 80 members. A cemetery association was organized at about this time to take care of the upkeep and the beautifying of the cemetery.

During the "prosperous '20s" the congregation responded generously to several appeals for funds for the general work of the Church. An increasing interest in missions was reported by Pastor Sandahl at the annual meeting in 1920, and during that year the congregation's mission treasurer received $6,709.36. In addition, the congregation gave $3,496 to the Augustana Pension Fund in 1920. Nearly $12,000 was contributed in a special appeal for Gustavus Adolphus College in

1922. Pastor Sandahl personally took the leadership in this appeal for funds for the college.

Previous to World War I it was rare that any member of the Chisago Lake Church went to college. The Chisago Lake High School graduated its first class in 1917, and soon after this the interest in higher education began to increase. More and more of the graduates went to college, university, nurses' training schools, or teachers' colleges. In the school year 1923–24 there were 12 members of the Chisago Lake congregation enrolled at Gustavus. Two members of the congre-

Dr. Emeroy Johnson

gation, Emeroy Johnson and Harold Peterson, began their preparation for the ministry while Sandahl was their pastor. The former was ordained in 1928, the latter in 1929. (Paul Melin, born at Center City in 1900, but who moved away in 1909, was ordained in 1927.)

1927

Pr. Harold Peterson

Dr. Johnson is at present serving as pastor of Scandian Grove Lutheran Church, Saint Peter, and secretary of the Minnesota Conference. The Reverend Peterson is the chaplain at Moose Lake State Hospital. The Reverend Melin is pastor at Salem, South Dakota.

Pr. Paul Melin

Miss Minnie Johnson (now Mrs. Simon Johansson) left in 1921 to enter the service of the Swedish Alliance Mission in India.

Oscar Sandahl took a leading part in the work of the charities of the Minnesota Conference. From 1922 to 1924 he was a member of the Board of Tabitha Society, which supervised Bethesda Hospital, Bethesda Invalid Home, and Bethesda Old People's Home. When all the charities of the conference were merged under the Board of Christian Service in 1924, Sandahl was the convener of the first meeting, and was re-elected to the Board for successive terms until 1944.

Pr. & Mrs. Sandahl and daughters

Pastor Sandahl resigned from Chisago Lake in 1927 to accept a call to Bethel Church, Minneapolis. After six years of service in that congregation he moved in 1933 to the Spring Garden Church near Cannon Falls. He retired in 1944 and he and Mrs. Sandahl then made their home in Cannon Falls. He died on February 6, 1950.

1927

No successor to Oscar Sandhal was secured at the time he left, though three calls were issued to Emil Swenson, Albert Loreen, and C. A. Eckstrom, respectively. Dr. J. A. Krantz was called as temporary pastor and served for one year.

❧

Dr. Axel N. Nelson
1928–1939

THE REVEREND AXEL N. NELSON of Chicago accepted a call in 1928 and began his work at Chisago Lake on Sunday, September 2.

Pastor Nelson, a native of Sweden, was born in 1887 and came to America in 1902. He was a graduate of Augustana College and Theological Seminary, and he was ordained in 1914. He served Concordia Lutheran Church, Chicago, Illinois; Bethany, La Porte, Indiana; and Bethesda, Chicago, before coming to Center City.

His years in Chisago Lake proved to be a time of transition and change in various ways. It was largely a period of financial depression, which caused changes in attitudes and ways of thinking, and also in ways of living and working. Since pioneer days the community had seen many of its young people go to the cities to find employment. This trend increased in a marked manner in the 1930s, and was especially noticeable with regard to the young women. In 1940 Chisago County had 189 men to every 100 women. This created problems both sociologically and religiously.

A Time of Transition and Change

In 1928, with Dr. Krantz in charge, ambitious plans were set in motion for a long look at the past, the celebration of the 75th anniversary in 1929. The Minnesota Conference was invited to hold its convention in Center City May 7 to 14, 1929. The conference was asked to cooperate in the erection of a suitable monument to perpetuate the remembrance of the beginnings of the congregation and the Minnesota Conference. A memorial booklet was to be published. The king and the archbishop of Sweden were to be invited to send representatives or personal greetings. Dignitaries of the church and the state in this country also were to be invited.

It is interesting to note that at the same meeting of the congregation a committee was authorized to dispose of the church stables, and

1928

Church stables and cemetery

$300 was appropriated to be used, if necessary, to pay for razing them. Thus passed the horse and buggy era.

Older members of the congregation can still recall, perhaps with pleasure and nostalgic feelings, the days when frisky horses crunched the snow under their hoofs as sleigh bells jingled in the frosty air. Cutters and bob sleighs glided noiselessly in long rows down the church hill, some turning north towards Little Lake, Furuby, and Vibo, others heading east to Shafer and Franconia; still others headed south from the church, and west towards Lindstrom. Horses were eager to go after standing still for two hours or more, prancing because they knew this was the homeward trip. Most of them had left home about nine in the morning, and many would not be home until half past one or two in the afternoon. In summer the roads were often dusty, and with eight or ten buggies in a row the people at the end of the line were sure to get their Sunday clothes gray with dust.

It was not all romance in those good old days of sleigh bells or surreys. To come to church with a team of horses and to find a deep snowdrift blocking the stable door, or the bottom of the door frozen fast in ice after a spring thaw was hardly conducive to worship. Walking several miles to church was not uncommon, even in winter. In pioneer times mothers with babes in arms sometimes walked four or five miles to early Christmas morning services (*Julotta*).

1928

Another item of interest at the annual meeting in 1928 was the decision to enlarge the cemetery. A committee elected the previous year reported that at a cost of $2,500 an area 100 feet wide on the east side of the cemetery could be filled and made suitable for use as a burial ground. This plan was adopted. Between 1900 and 1939 almost 1,000 members of the congregation passed on to "that bourne from which no traveler returns."

Pastor Nelson's first year at Chisago Lake was an extremely busy one. Besides proceeding with the plans already made for observance of the 75th anniversary, the congregation decided to make extensive changes in the church, particularly the removal of the pipe organ from the balcony to the front of the church. Pledges totalling about $5,000 for the remodeling project had been received from the Brotherhood, the Ladies Aid, and the Luther League.

When work was begun on this project other changes were found to be necessary. A new heating plant was installed at a cost of $2,600 and the church was redecorated at a cost of $1,629. The total cost of all improvements, including a statue of Christ (Hoffman's), was $12,861.44. At the end of the year 1929 a total of $7,626.99 had been received, leaving a debt of $5,234.45.

Besides these heavy expenditures for the renovation and remodeling of the church the congregation assumed half the cost of the massive monument erected on the church grounds in commemoration of the organization of the church and of the conference. The congregation's share was $1,000.

1929

In response to the invitation extended to the Church of Sweden to participate in the festivities Bishop Hjalmar Danell, with his wife, came to Center City. This visit cost the congregation $500. The total disbursements from the church treasury in 1929 were $29,982.88, the highest of any year in the congregation's history thus far. The total debt of the congregation at the end of 1929 was $11,000.

Diamond Jubilee Festivities

The diamond jubilee festivities, held in connection with the Minnesota Conference meeting, May 7 to 14, 1929, were without doubt the greatest of all celebrations held in the Chisago Lake community, and one of the greatest ever held anywhere in the Augustana Synod. On Sunday, May 12, the exact anniversary date, the jubilee reached its climax with an estimated 12 thousand persons in attendance. The monument, erected jointly by the congregation and the Minnesota Conference, was unveiled by Bishop Danell in an impressive ceremony. Other speakers included Dr. P. A. Mattson, conference president; Dr. G. A. Brandelle, president of the Augustana Synod; Theodore Christianson, governor of Minnesota; Dr. J. A. Aasgaard, president of the Norwegian Lutheran Church (ELC) ; Nils Leon Jaenson, Swedish consul in Minneapolis; and state senator Victor E. Lawson. By means of a public address system the program could be heard by the immense crowd.

The monument erected on the church lawn is in the form of an obelisk, 32 feet high. The base is six feet square. The die which carries the inscription is made of black Swedish granite quarried in Småland, the province from which many of the Chisago Lake pioneers came. The monument has the following inscriptions:
On the north side:

> *Till minne av stiftandet av Sv. Ev. Luth. Chisago Lake Forsamlingen den 12 maj, 1854. Upprest av tacksamma attlingar. (Forsamlingen ,stiftades en half mil oster harifran.)* **Translation:** In commemoration of the organization of the Swedish Evangelical Lutheran Chisago Lake congregation on May 12, 1854. Erected by grateful descendants. (The congregation was organized half a mile east of this place.)

1929

Monument

On the east side:

> *Thy kingdom, Lord, is an everlasting kingdom, and Thy dominion endureth throughout all generations. Psalm 145:13.*

On the west side:

> *This monument is erected to the memory of the pioneers, who here organized the Lutheran Minnesota Conference. Pastors: P. Carlson, E. Norelius, P. Beckman, J. P. C. Boren. Laymen: Daniel Nelson, Hakan Swedberg, Frans C. Bjorklund.*

PASTOR AXEL N. NELSON

On the south side:

> *Din spira, Jesus, strackes ut sa langt som dagen hinner; Ditt rike ,star till*
> *tidens slut, det star da allt forsvinner.* Translation: Thy scepter, Jesus,
> shall extend as far as day prevaileth; Thy glorious kingdom, with-
> out end, shall stand when all else faileth.

This monument, noble in plan, in appearance, in workmanship, is
a worthy expression of honor and esteem for the pioneers who laid the
foundations of the Chisago Lake congregation and the Lutheran
Minnesota Conference. However, it is a matter of regret that the name
of one of the laymen who helped to organize the conference, Ola
Paulson, has been omitted. It is unfortunate also that P. A. Cederstam
was not mentioned as the first resident pastor.

1929

A small part of the crowd in May 1929

Until 1931 Swedish services were conducted every Sunday
forenoon. For several years previous to that time double services were
held, first English, then Swedish. At the annual meeting in 1931 a new
schedule was adopted: Swedish on the first and third Sundays of each
month, and English on the second, fourth, and fifth Sundays. This
order was followed for eight years.

The pastor's annual report was given in Swedish until 1936. The
first time that the minutes of the annual meeting appeared entirely in
English was in 1937. The congregation was then 83 years old. The great

majority of the members were native-born Americans, mostly of the third and fourth generation, some even of the fifth and sixth.

During Nelson's pastorate the congregation adopted the pledge system in place of the church "dues" system, which had been in use for 75 years. When Hedengran was called in 1859, part of his salary was to be grain, two bushels from each farmer. In 1866 dues were set as follows: $2.50 per year for each farmer; $2.00 for a man who is not a farmer; and $1.00 for each woman member of the congregation. As the years went by the system became quite rigid. From 1887 a finance committee had the duty of determining what each member of the church should pay. That they were thorough and conscientious is evident from the records of their meetings. The congregation adopted a sliding scale of dues. The finance committee's job was to classify the members according to ability to pay.

The change from this system to the pledge system, involving the every-member canvass and the use of weekly envelopes, was decided on in 1929, to be effective on January 1, 1930. Average receipts for the last nine years under the old dues system (1921–1929) was $6,930.83. The average for the first 10 years under the pledge system (1930–1939) was $8,572.22, though the latter was the depression period.

1937

On February 15, 1937, Pastor (now Dr.) Nelson announced that illness made it necessary for him to take a prolonged rest. He offered to resign immediately if the Church Board so desired, or that he be given a leave of absence in order to rest and recuperate. The board decided on the latter alternative and granted Dr. Nelson a six-month leave. Pastor C. E. Slatt of Chisago City was engaged to serve as acting pastor. Dr. Nelson was allowed $100 per month during his absence. After six months his health was restored sufficiently to enable him to resume his duties as pastor of the congregation. He continued to serve as pastor of the Chisago Lake Church until May 24, 1939, when he left to become superintendent of the Augustana Inner Mission in Chicago. He died on February 14, 1947.

PASTOR AXEL N. NELSON

The Years of the Second World War

When Hitler's troops marched into Poland on September 1, 1939, Americans tried to believe that the conflict would not become a second world war. But such hopes were futile. Not many months had gone by before every community in the United States was bidding farewell to young men drafted for the defense of their country. Pearl Harbor Day, December 7, 1941, sent America into action in the greatest conflict of all history.

More than 100 members of the Chisago Lake congregation went out to the far-flung battlefields of World War II. They did not all return home.

The pastors of the congregation during this period were the Reverend J. Henry Bergren and the Reverend (now Dr.) Gilbert T. Monson.

1939

Following the resignation of Dr. Axel N. Nelson in 1939 there was a vacancy of about six months' duration. The congregation was served temporarily by Dr. Carl Christenson from May to September, and Dr. F. M. Eckman from September to November.

The Reverend John Henry Bergren accepted a call issued to him in August 1939, and he began his service at Chisago Lake on November 15.

Pastor J. Henry Bergren
1939–1941

THE REVEREND JOHN HENRY BERGREN was a native of Sweden, but had come to America at the age of three. He graduated from Gustavus Adolphus College in 1926 and from Augustana Seminary in 1929. He was ordained on a call to Swedlanda Lutheran Church, Hector, Minnesota. In 1932 he moved to Saint Cloud, where he was serving when called to Center City. Pastor Bergren was installed on December 10 by the conference president, Dr. Emil Swenson.

The English language had gained the ascendancy over the Swedish at church services. On the first Sunday of each month double services were held, English at 10:15 A.M., Swedish at 11. On the other Sundays only one morning service was held: on the third Sunday of each month it was in Swedish, on all other Sundays in English. In 1940 double services were held the first and third Sundays, with only English on other Sundays. Attendance at Swedish morning worship services had dwindled to such a point that in 1944 that it was decided to eliminate them, and to have devotional services in Swedish on two Sunday afternoons each month. This schedule was dropped in 1945, and since that time Swedish services have been held only occasionally.

Attendance at services had declined in the depression years. Reasons for this decline were undoubtedly many and varied. Financial hardship may have been a factor in some instances, but as an excuse rather than as a reason. In the 1940s there was a slight improvement, though figures indicate that less than half of the members were at church on an average Sunday morning. The average reported in 1940 was 532; in 1942 it was 633.

The constitution authorized by the Augustana Synod in 1939 was adopted on first reading in 1940 by Chisago Lake, but it was not finally ratified until 1943.

1941

The Reverend J. Henry Bergren's pastorate was short, a little less than two years. He announced his resignation on January 4, 1941, to be effective September 15. He had received a call to become a teacher at Lutheran Bible Institute in Minneapolis. While serving as pastor at Chisago Lake he had accepted a number of invitations to speak at Bible camps and conferences in Minnesota and other states. He served on the L.B.I. faculty 10 years; then he accepted a call to First Lutheran Church, Litchfield, Minnesota.

Before he left Chisago Lake the congregation was unexpectedly faced with a major building project. Fire destroyed the chapel on Jauaary 7, 1941. At the annual meeting held a few days later the question of rebuilding the chapel or making a full basement under the church was considered, and a committee was elected to study the matter further. On March 28, at a special meeting, the congregation approved the plans submitted for a church basement, and construction was begun in June. Work proceeded rapidly and the new church parlors were ready for dedication on November 30. The total cost was $18,378.55. The debt, when the project was finished, was $9,000.

Pastor Bergren continued to serve until October 12, 1941 His successor arrived a few days later.

The Reverend Reuben Ford had been called to succeed the Reverend Bergren, but he declined.

The Reverend Gilbert T. Monson of Oakland, California, was called on July 2, 1941. He accepted the call and began his duties at Chisago Lake on October 18.

1941

Pastor Gilbert T. Monson
1941–1944

26
1941

THE REVEREND GILBERT T. MONSON was born in Nebraska. He graduated from Gustavus Adolphus College in 1926, and from Augustana Theological Seminary in 1929. He served at Great Falls, Montana, Bertrand, Nebraska, and Oakland, California, before coming to Center City to begin his duties on October 18, 1941.

It was only a few weeks after his coming to Chisago Lake that the United States was forced into World War II by the Japanese attack on Pearl Harbor. By the end of 1942 the Chisago Lake congregation had sent 49 of its members into the armed forces, including one young woman in the Army Nurses' Corps. One young man, Kenneth Haroldson, was reported missing in action. Later the War Department confirmed that he had lost his life in the fall of Bataan.

Two more men were reported missing in action in 1944, Earl Stromquist and Clifford Broberg. Lieutenant Darrel B. Johnson was killed in action and buried at sea January 17, 1945.

A total of 123 members of the congregation served in the armed forces during the war. Two paid the supreme sacrifice. Stromquist and Broberg returned home safe and sound.

Death took no holiday in the Chisago Lake community. The old cemetery, including the area added in 1928, was rapidly being occupied, as 20 to 30 graves were dug each year. It was necessary to begin preparations for a new burial ground, and the congregation decided that the hillside across the road from the cemetery, which had served as a church park for half a century and where many a Midsummer picnic had been held, should be cleared and graded for use as a cemetery. This work was begun in 1944, the year of the congregation's 90th anniversary.

The anniversary was celebrated with three days of festive services, from May 12 to 14, 1944. Speakers included the conference president, Dr. Emil Swenson, and all the former pastors who were still living, Dr. Eckman, Dr. Oslund, the Reverend Sandahl, Dr. Nelson, and the Reverend Bergren. Though looking backward on a history of nine

1944

decades, the program was arranged to emphasize the present and the future opportunities and responsibilities of the congregation.

A few days prior to the observance of the anniversary Pastor Monson had announced his resignation. He had been called by the Augustana Lutheran Church to be president of a newly established institution, the Church's Canadian Seminary at Saskatoon, Saskatchewan. He left Center City in July. He gave six years of service to the task of preparing theological students to serve the Augustana Church in Canada. Since 1951 he has been pastor in Kansas City, Missouri. He received the degree of doctor of divinity in 1951.

During the Reverend Monson's pastorate one of the sons of the congregation, Clifford C. Peterson, was ordained to the ministry. A graduate of Augsburg College,

Pr. Clifford Peterson

Minneapolis, he completed his theological course at Augustana Seminary and was ordained in 1943 on a call to Gladstone, Michigan, where he is still serving. He is a brother of the Reverend Harold E. Peterson.

Miss Mildred Hasselquist, a daughter of the congregation, but recently transferred to Trinity Lutheran Church, Minneapolis, accepted a call from the World Mission Prayer League to go as a missionary to Nepal, a country closed to the Christian gospel. She, together with other missionaries, reached the border of the country, remained for seven years in the hope of entering, but was able to establish only an outpost for further Christian work. After her return to America she became the wife of the Reverend Luverne Tengbom, who at present is serving as pastor in Calgary, Alberta, Canada.

Mr. Philip Lindblom, a son of the congregation, while serving in the army, was assigned as chaplain's assistant, and after his discharge from the army devoted himself to full time work in the Augustana Lutheran Church as a lay preacher. His first assignment in 1947 was in the Isanti parish. He then served several years in the Harris–Fish Lake parish, after which he was transferred to Bark River, Michigan.

1945

Completing the First Century

World War II ended in the summer of 1945, but brought only an uneasy peace which soon congealed into a cold war between Communism and the West. Drafting of young men continued. In 1950 came the Korean War, which ended in a frowning truce in 1953. The year 1954 finds the world in tense uncertainty, dreading the terrible possibilities of atomic warfare.

Chisago Lake, seemingly as peaceful a community as could be found anywhere, experienced the effects of the war and of an uncertain peace. One young man from Chisago Lake, Stuart Lindahl, was killed in action in the Korean War. The far-reaching effects of hot and cold war may not be apparent to our present generation, but it is clear to all what some of these effects are. World War II brought about the greatest dislocation and migration of people in the history of the world. In some nations the movement of population was forced, as millions became refugees or slaves. In the United States it was a voluntary migration. It is said that 20 million people moved from one state or region to another. Even old conservative communities, such as Chisago Lake, were affected to a great extent.

As a result of factors that have always been present, but greatly accelerated by the conditions prevailing in the 1930s and 1940s, rural areas have declined in population, while cities have been growing. In many instances it is not only a decline of the rural population, but a great change in the kind of people on the farms. The Chisago Lake area, once solidly Lutheran, has seen many people of other denominations moving in. Fifty years ago, even 25 years ago, it would have seemed inconceivable that a Roman Catholic parish would come into existence in the midst of this strongly established Lutheran community. A change has come, and Saint Bridget's Church of Lindstrom was organized in 1950 with some 35 families as charter members.

1945

The pastoral leadership of this changing and challenging era in Chisago Lake has been in the hands of the Reverend J. Walton Kempe, who was called on June 12, 1945, and arrived to assume his duties on October 16.

Pastor J. Walton Kempe
1945–1954

THE REVEREND J. WALTON KEMPE, a native of Iowa, completed his college training at Augustana College in 1914, and his theological course at Augustana Seminary. He was ordained in 1916 and had served congregations in Creston, Iowa; Des Moines, Iowa; and Astoria, Oregon, before coming to Center City. He was called by Chisago Lake on June 12, 1945, and arrived to assume his duties on October 16. This was a challenging and changing era in Chisago Lake.

Though Swedish may still be heard (mixed with English) occasionally in some homes, the old language of the pioneers had disappeared from the church services by the end of World War II. The name of the congregation, however, still was the "Swedish Evangelical Lutheran Chisago Lake Church." In 1948 final action was taken to change the name to "Chisago Lake Evangelical Lutheran Church." The long process of transition to an American church was completed.

In that same year—1948—the congregation was host to the Minnesota Conference at its 90th anniversary convention, May 3 to 7. Among the speakers at this convention was the governor of Minnesota, Luther W. Youngdahl.

1949   Parsonage Christmas tree, 1948   Chistmas stockings, 1948

The 95th anniversary of the congregation was observed in 1949, with Minnesota Conference president, Dr. Emil Swenson; the vice president, Dr. Paul Andreen; the editor of *The Lutheran Companion*, Dr. E. E. Ryden; and two former pastors, J. Henry Bergren and Gilbert T. Monson, as speakers. A brief historical sketch written by the Reverend Emeroy Johnson was published.

At the time when the congregation voted to call the Reverend Kempe, a resolution was adopted authorizing the board and the new pastor to secure the services of a parish worker whenever they deemed it advisable. The first one to be engaged for the position was Miss Bernice Mattson, who served from February to August 1946. She was succeeded by Miss Anita Egge, who served one year. Miss Mildred I. Nelson held the position from August 1947 to July 1949, and Miss Joyce Rundquist from July 1949 to December 1952.

A monthly parish paper, *Reflections*, was begun in 1947, and it continues regularly to furnish items of news about the congregation and its organizations, as well as the district, the conference, and the church.

A number of improvements have been made in the church, the major project being the complete rebuilding of the pipe organ in 1953, at a cost of $8,400. A dedication concert was given by the eminent organist, Claire Coci of New York on November 15, and dedication of the organ took place on November 22 with Dr. Emil Swenson officiating. On the same day Dr. Swenson also dedicated the Chisago Lake Hillside Cemetery.

Consideration has been given to the project of building a parish education building and also the matter of a new parsonage to be built in the village. No decisions have been reached conerning either of these two projects.

After 15 years of service as organist Miss Agda Wennerberg retired from this position on January 1, 1953. Mr. Faylon W. Geist of Buena Vista College, Storm Lake, Iowa, became the new organist and choir director.

1953

Faylon W. Geist at the organ

PASTOR J. WALTON KEMPE

The congregation at worship

1954

One of the daughters of the congregation, Miss Marian Hawkinson, volunteered her services as missionary and was called and commissioned for the new Augustana field in Japan in 1952.

A son of the congregation, Vernel Lundeen, graduated from Gustavus Adolphus College in 1950. He completies his theological studies at Augustana Seminary in 1954 and will be ordained to the ministry in June on a call to Clarkfield, Minnesota.

The poetic gift has not been entirely lacking in the Chisago Lake congregation. William Johnson has been a frequent contributor of sacred poetry to *The Lutheran Companion* and several other periodicals over a period of 20 years. In 1948 he published a book of poems under the title *Wild Flowers*. One of his poems, entitled "Calvary," has been accepted for publication in the forthcoming Lutheran hymnal sponsored by seven Lutheran church

Pr. Vernel Lundeen

bodies of the National Lutheran Council.

"And what more shall I say? For time would fail me to tell" of all who in some way have contributed to the advancement of the kingdom by their faithful use of God-given talents, by their time and strength and money throughout these hundred years since the congregation was established. Many hundreds of men and women have served as church school teachers. Others have been

William Johnson

deacons, trustees, custodians, choir members, officers of organizations, committee members, every-member canvassers, Scout leaders, solicitors for special projects. Many have carried their load of concern for the church in quiet ways, unseen and unrecognized by human eyes. "More things have been wrought by prayer" in Chisago Lake as elsewhere, "than this world dreams of." God knows of many a widow's mite, and also many a widow's might through the power of intercessory prayer.

1954

The Chisago Lake congregation has been a spiritual force through 100 years. Several thousand persons have come under the Christian influence of this church. How many have been made wise unto salvation, how many have found the peace of Christ, will never be recorded in books here on earth. May there be many names of the past, many of the present and of the future, written in the Book of Life.

PASTOR J. WALTON KEMPE

Pastors Who Served

Chisago Lake Evangelical Lutheran Church
the First 100 Years

Erland Carlsson (organizer of congregation) 1854

Eric Norelius (student, served three months) 1854

Pehr Anderson Cederstam 1855–1858

Carl August Hedengran 1859–1873

Johan Johansson Frodeen 1875–1890

John Fredrik Seedoff 1890–1896

Frank Magnus Eckman 1896–1913

John Edward Oslund 1913–1917

Oscar Sandahl 1917–1927

Axel N. Nelson 1928–1939

John Henry Bergren 1939–1941

Gilbert T. Monson 1941–1944

J. Walton Kempe 1945–1954

Pr. Erland Carlsson

Eric Norelius

Pr. P. A. Cederstam

Pr. C. A. Hedengran

Pr. J. J. Frodeen

Pr. J. F. Seedoff

Dr. F. M. Eckman

Dr. J. E. Oslund

Pr. Oscar Sandahl

PASTORS WHO SERVED

Pr. Axel N. Nelson   Pr. J. H. Bergren   Pr. G. T. Monson

Pr. J. W. Kempe

The Year of Jubilee

This year of jubilee,
Chisago Lake, sing praise!
With gladsome melody
Your grateful anthems raise!
Throughout a hundred years, each day
The Lord has led you on His way.

His wondrous deeds retell,
Performed in days o f Old,
How He has guided well
And graciously His fold,
That souls need not depart and stray,
But find His good and perfect way.

Gird for the coming days!
Follow where Christ would lead,
Ready in all your ways
His loving voice to heed,
Then shall this church a stronghold be
For God each passing century.

WILLIAM JOHNSON

Chisago Lake Evangelical Lutheran congregation at worship. Photo taken for the 140th anniversary and 1994 directory by Debra Barott Wiler.

Part Three

The Next 50 Years

1954–2004

∽

EUNICE JOHNSON ANDERSON

Eunice Johnson Anderson (b. March 28, 1927), is a lifelong member of Chisago Lake Church. She served the congregation as treasurer for 12 years, as secretary for the pastors from 1985 to 1992, and as church librarian for more than 20 years. She attended Gustavus Adolphus College and is a niece of the brothers William and Emeroy Johnson. She is the author of Part Three, "The Next 50 Years," which is based on annual reports and monthly newsletters.

Preface to Part Three

WILLIAM JOHNSON, TRANSLATOR for Part One of this book, and Emeroy Johnson, author of Part Two of this book, were brothers, and they were my uncles. I recall that the last time Dr. Emeroy Johnson visited in my home, he asked the question, "Who will continue to write the history of this area and of Chisago Lake Lutheran Church after I am gone?" Several people have written books about this area, but the history of Chisago Lake Lutheran Church since 1954 was yet to be written.

While Dr. Dale Peterson was pastor of this congregation, he, too, asked the question, "Who will write this history of this church since 1954?" Perhaps Emeroy had planted a seed in my heart that had grown over the years so that when the historical committee of the congregation asked me if I would be willing to continue the history of the congregation in preparation for the 150th anniversary of the congregation in 2004, I agreed to do so.

The materials that I have used to gather information for the history of this congregation since 1954 were the annual reports of the congregation and the monthly newsletters of the church. Occasionally I have also used Church Council minutes. It has been my intent to record facts as I have found them and not depend upon memory.

When I began in 1997, I contacted each senior pastor to offer them the opportunity to submit information about their backgrounds and to give suggestions as to what they felt was important during the years of their ministry. I chose not to interview others, as I felt that their memory was probably not any more reliable than mine.

Writing about the last 10 or 15 years was difficult since it was so recent; it was more like current events. Yet it was important that there be something about these years to complete the manuscript.

This has been a very interesting project and I thank all those who have read and re-read what I have written. Those who have served as pastors of Chisago Lake Lutheran Church since 1954 have all had the opportunity to edit this material. They are: Pastors Burdette Benson (now deceased), James Almquist, Robert Knutson, Russell Peterson, Dale Peterson, and Lawrence Lystig. Special thanks to my daughter, Barbara Wikelius, for her editing and to John Wind, our congregation's youth director, and Harriet Ryberg, for their comments, and to Carolyn Lystig, who edited and designed this book and helped it reach publication.

Several things have been obvious to me as I have researched material for this book. First, the building itself. What sacrifice was made by the early pioneers who built this beautiful sanctuary! Their homes were humble, without the amenities we take for granted today, yet they wanted to build the very best to honor their Lord. And then the constant upkeep that a building like this requires. Through generation after generation the devotion and dedication has been here to keep it in good condition.

Second, the people who have been called to pastor this congregation. Each one has been a true servant of the Lord, doing his best to keep the faith of our fathers—to stay true to the Lutheran heritage that the early pioneers treasured. In every instance, God has supplied the right leader for the time. At all times the Word has been preached and the sacraments administered rightly. Thanks be to God for the people he has provided to lead this congregation for soon 150 years.

Third, the conflicts this congregation has weathered. Even before the first church was built, the members of the congregation disagreed on the best location. A strong pastor took matters into his own hands and bought the land he felt God had led him to purchase for his people. Over and over again we see evidence of dissension and conflict; yet, God has always been here and kept this congregation strong. Perhaps conflict causes us to turn back to God who alone can bring peace.

Fourth, the stewardship of this congregation has always had its ups and downs. Recently I heard a speaker say, "I don't know how it works, but when a congregation gets involved in God's mission (outreach and benevolence) first, God gets involved with the congregation." When our benevolence giving has been the highest, the congregation has been the strongest.

It is my desire that we can learn from our history what vision God wants us to have for the future. "Where there is no vision, the people perish" (Proverbs 29:18). It is my prayer that the Holy Spirit will fill the hearts of the members of this congregation so that each one may know God's love and grace and serve God wherever God calls. To God be the glory.

EUNICE JOHNSON ANDERSON

Chisago Lake Church, 2003

CHISAGO LAKE EVANGELICAL LUTHERAN CHURCH

Centennial Anniversary

28

THE SPRING OF 1954 was a time of jubilation and celebration as Chisago Lake Lutheran Church observed its centennial. In preparation for the Jubilee events, the pipe organ had been rebuilt and a new console purchased for the sum of $8,400. Twenty of the stained-glass windows had been reset and storm glass installed for $2,600. A great deal of effort was expended in planning the centennial celebration so that all might be done in good order and to the glory of God. The theme chosen for the anniversary was "A Mighty Fortress is our God." Former pastors, former members, and church leaders from the synod and from the conference came to join in the festivities.

The celebration began on Sunday, April 25, at the morning worship. Pastor J. W. Kempe preached the keynote sermon and the music was based on the anniversary theme. In

Pastor J. W. Kempe

257

Dr. Emil Swanson

the evening, the choir presented *A Requiem Mass* by Mozart. The *Requiem* was dedicated to the memory of all members of the church who had faithfully worked during these first 100 years to perpetuate the Chisago Lake Lutheran Church and had passed on to the church triumphant.

On Sunday, May 2, the guest preacher was Dr. Emil Swenson, president of the Lutheran Minnesota Conference. On the following Sunday, May 9, the guest preacher was Dr. Oscar A. Benson, president of the Augustana Lutheran Church. On this, the actual Anniversary Sunday, there was also an evening service with the address was given by Dr. Edgar M. Carlson, president of Gustavus Adolphus College in St. Peter, Minnesota.

1954

May 16 was Confirmation Sunday. At the morning worship service 27 young people participated in the rite of confirmation. The theme for the day was "The Next 100 Years."

Dr. Oscar Benson

The guest preacher was Pastor J. Henry Bergren, a former pastor who was serving a congregation in Litchfield, Minnesota.

May 23 was Communion Sunday with Dr. E. E. Ryden, editor of *The Lutheran Companion*, as guest preacher. At 3:00 P.M. that afternoon there was a confirmand reunion, which was well attended and gave opportunity for fellowship with confirmation classmates from former years. Dr. Gilbert T. Monson from Kansas City, Missouri, a former pastor

Pr. J. Henry Bergren

of the congregation, was the guest speaker.

Special messages came to Chisago Lake Lutheran Church on this historic centennial celebration from King Gustav of Sweden, Archbishop Yungve Brilloth of Uppsala, Sweden, President Dwight D. Eisenhower, Governor C. Elmer Anderson and other dignitaries from both Sweden and the United States. Pastors of the other churches in the community participated in the events as did

Dr. Gilbert T. Monson

sons of the congregation who were pastors of other congregations.

Pastor Kempe Resigns

On May 30, 1954, just a few days after the completion of the centennial celebration, Pastor Kempe submitted his resignation to the Church

Pr. & Mrs. Kempe

Council and the congregation to be effective August 1. His resignation stated that this was too large a congregation for "one pastor of advanced age" and that a younger pastor was needed. Pastor Kempe accepted a call to become associate pastor at Gloria Dei Lutheran Church in Saint Paul.

1954

At the annual meeting of the congregation on January 14, 1954, Pastor Kempe included in his annual report the following:

> I want to remind the members of the congregation that the most important work of the pastor is preparation and giving of sermons. There are those who do not realize that study and preparation are essential, consequently their attitude is that time spent

in his study by the pastor is wasted.... I, also, want to express appreciation to all members who have given a helping hand, and who have shown real encouragement in Mrs. Kempe's and my work in the parish this last year. It appears that a much friendlier spirit, with much less criticism toward our suggestions and endeavors, now prevail in our parish. At least the obstructionists have been less vocal than any year in our ministry here. 1953 has been a very pleasant year for us. We thank you for kindnesses shown, forbearance in our mistakes, forgiveness in sins committed.

These words indicate that the Kempes had found their years of ministry here difficult. Pastor Kempe may have felt inadequate in working with the youth, but in June of 1953, 24 young people from the Chisago Lake congregation attended the National Youth Conference in Boston. This was no doubt the largest group of young people from this congregation ever to attend an event like this. Much planning and fund raising was necessary to make this possible. It would not have been posssible without Pastor Kempe's support.

1954

Calling a New Pastor

A special meeting of the congregation was called for Thursday evening, July 15, 1954, at 8:15 P.M. to vote on issuing a call to a new pastor. The Church Council had unanimously nominated Wymore M. Goldberg of McPherson, Kansas, to succeed Pastor Kempe. This nomination was seconded and unanimously carried. There was a total of 123 votes cast, with 116 voting yes and 7 voting no.

Pastor Goldberg was issued a call to become the pastor at Chisago Lake Lutheran Church at a salary of $5,500 per year, plus the use of the parsonage, and also to defray moving expenses. Pastor Goldberg acknowledged receipt of the call and asked for the congregation's prayers as he made his decision. He also visited Center City and preached at the church on the evening of July 1. Pastor Goldberg later declined the call.

Pastor Clarence W. Peterson, pastor of Zion Lutheran Church in Chisago City, was appointed vice-chairman of the congregation until a new pastor would assume the duties of the church. During the first few weeks of the vacancy, guest pastors helped with the Sunday worship services. The first of these was Pastor

Pr. C. W. Peterson

Russell E. Nelson, a missionary to Hong Kong who was home on furlough. Our congregation had been helping to support this missionary family for several years and it was a special joy to have him lead the worship service. One Sunday Mr. John Erickson and his seeing-eye dog, Chief, led the worship. Mr. Erickson represented Braille evangelism. Another Sunday Pastor Daniel Cederberg of Staffanstorp, Sweden, was the preacher.

Pr. Russell E. Nelson

1954

As the weeks went by, it became evident that Chisago Lake Church needed an interim pastor and Pastor Hugo Thorene, a retired pastor, was asked to fill this position beginning October 1. This he agreed to do.

The council continued to work with the conference president in searching for a new pastor. A special service was scheduled for the evening of October 27, when Pastor Carl P. Everett of Chicago, Illinois, would preach. This was to be an opportunity for him to meet the congregation and for the congregation to become acquainted with him prior to issuing him a call. However, the service was canceled because of Pastor Everett's illness and a call was not issued.

Pr. Hugo Thorene

At a meeting of the congregation on April 28, 1953, the issue of what to do with the parsonage was discussed. The following item was on the agenda:

> To authorize the Board of Trustees to dispose of the present parsonage property, if something should develop whereby it could be replaced for a reasonable consideration.

As the congregation looked for a new pastor, the matter of the parsonage was brought up. Some members thought that the parsonage was a deterrent in securing a new pastor. Perhaps this was the time to sell the parsonage.

Pastor W. Burdette Benson, pastor of Augustana Lutheran Church of Cumberland, Wisconsin, was recommended as a candidate for pastor. A service was scheduled for Tuesday evening, January 25, for him to come as guest speaker. A special meeting of the congregation was called for February 13, 1955, after the Sunday worship service, for the purpose of extending a call to Pastor Benson. There were 277 votes, with 276 voting yes and 1 voting no. The call was similar to the previous one with a salary of $5,500 per year, free use of the parsonage, and moving expenses. Included in the call were details about vacation time and other items.

The Bensons had a family of four children, so the decision about selling the parsonage was delayed pending a reply to the call. If the call were accepted, perhaps the family would like to live in the parsonage. On Easter Sunday the good news was announced that Pastor Benson had accepted the call to be the pastor and that he would begin his work at Chisago Lake congregation on July 1, 1955. God had answered the prayers for a permanent pastor. The family was indeed willing to live in the parsonage and was appreciative of such a spacious home. Plans were made to clean and redecorate the parsonage in preparation for the Benson family's move.

In the spring of 1955, Miss Alma Hasselquist was hired as a full-time church secretary. A detailed job description was drawn up for her and published in the church newsletter, *Reflections*, so that the congregation would have a clear idea of the responsibilities of her position. During Pastor Kempe's years at Chisago Lake, parish workers had been hired to assist the pastor. The duties of a parish worker included calling on members or prospective members, working with the Bible school, bringing a message to a Ladies Aid meeting, and assisting the pastor in other

Alma Hasselquist

kinds of ministry. Miss Hasselquist's duties were to be those of a secretary and office administrator. The publication in the newsletter reminded the congregation that:

> This work should be the work of a secretary only—not a dumping ground for unwanted chores of others, not an easy way out for program committees, not a quick way to select a Sunday School superintendent, not a dependable way of electing an organization officer. The duties recommended are a full-time position in themselves and the burdening of a staff-member with too many "extras" leads to discouragement, and also takes away from the congregation the responsibilities they need to keep them alive as church members.

1955

Her salary was $3,000 per year with two weeks of paid vacation. Plans were also made for providing office space for her.

∾

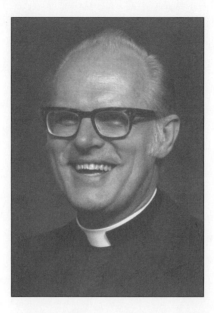

Pastor W. Burdette Benson
1955–1969

PASTOR W. BURDETTE BENSON was born in Honan province in Central China, the oldest child of Pastor and Mrs. Nels Benson who served as missionaries there. When Burdette was in the third grade, the Communist Armies came into Central China and all Americans were asked to leave. They were brought to Shanghai until they could get ship's passage to the States. The Benson family came to the Midwest and Burdette graduated from high school in Hinckley, Minnesota; from Gustavus Adolphus College in St. Peter, Minnesota; and later from Augustana Theological Seminary in Rock Island, Illinois.

On June 9, 1944, Burdette was commissioned as a missionary to China, and two days later on June 11 was ordained as a pastor in the Augustana Lutheran Church at First Lutheran Church in Saint Paul. On June 14, he married Elaine Allerson at Lafayette, Minnesota, and by July 1 they were both enrolled in Chinese Language School at the

University of California at Berkeley. During their two years at school, they became parents of their first son, Bruce.

On September 30, 1946, the Benson family was among about 900 missionaries who boarded the troop transport ship, Marine Lynx, for the trip to China. They docked in Shanghai in mid-October. Headquarters for many of the missionaries was the Lutheran Center operated by the Lutheran World Federation (LWF). Pastor Benson was asked to work for LWF to help Christian workers as they came to Shanghai from the United States, Canada, or Europe. One of his duties was to schedule flights for the Saint Paul, an LWF-owned plane, which was used to transport missionaries in and out of China as needed. Even at that time, missionaries were being forced to leave Manchuria in far North China because of Communist occupation there. It was in mid-April 1947 that the Bensons were able to return to Honan. Pastor Nels Benson had also returned to China and was with the family. The Bensons taught Chinese Bible in the mission school and English Bible in seven non-mission schools in the city of Hsuchang.

1955

The Bensons experienced some perilous times as the Communists moved into Central China. In December 1947, they lived through shelling and even had the Communist "liberators" enter their own home. On the day before Christmas Eve, the Benson family fled the city in a two-wheeled cart, leaving Pastor Nels Benson behind, and arrived in Yuchow just five minutes before the gate closed for the night. The next day they rode in a coal truck to Chengchow where there was an airport and where several days later the Saint Paul landed and flew them to Shanghai. One month later their daughter Carolyn was born in Shanghai.

Pastor Benson was needed at the Lutheran Center again and also preached at the Lutheran Church of Shanghai. By the end of March 1948, Grandpa Benson also arrived in Shanghai, having narrowly missed being captured by the Communist soldiers as he hid under a blanket in an ox cart. It took one year for the Red army to move south and then Shanghai, too, was threatened. The American Consul-General ordered all women and children to leave, and Elaine and the children were evacuated on an American ship that was provided. Pastor Burdette and his father, Pastor Nels Benson, remained in Shanghai and assisted in moving the LWF offices to Hong Kong. They arrived back in the states in the spring of 1949. (Information taken from *His Life By His Wife, a short story of the life of W. Burdette Benson* by Elaine Allerson Benson, 1984.)

In October 1949, the Bensons were called to the Augustana parish in Cumberland, Wisconsin, and they served there until they accepted the call to Chisago Lake in 1955. During their six years in Wisconsin, they welcomed two more children into the family, Theodore in July 1952 and Gracia in December 1954.

Pastor Benson assumed his responsibilities as pastor at Chisago Lake Lutheran Church on July 1, 1955. Installation services were scheduled for that evening with Dr. Emil Swenson, president of the Minnesota Conference in attendance.

1955

At the time Pastor Benson arrived, the congregation was struggling with a debt, due in part to extra expenses for the Centennial Celebration, but also due to poor stewardship habits and an excess of non-resident members. The Augustana Synod had a practice of assessing each congregation according to its membership. Oftentimes members would move away and become established in a new community but leave their church membership in their "home" church. In 1955 the records showed 164 non-resident members. One of the first concerns for Pastor Benson was to help the congregation with a membership audit and an "Every Member Visit" stewardship approach. The Every Member Visit program was a structured program that had proven successful in other congregations. This kind of stewardship program was continued in the congregation for several years with a gradual increase in financial support.

PASTOR W. BURDETTE BENSON

One of the most pressing problems the congregation faced was lack of space. There was no private office for the pastor at the church. He shared an office with the secretary. This was not a good situation for either of them. There were more than 200 children enrolled in Sunday school, and classes were held in the sanctuary pews, in the choir loft, in the balcony, and in the nursery. The space problem was again brought into focus when at the annual meeting on January 17, 1956, the congregation voted to invite the Minnesota Conference to hold its Centennial Convention in 1958 at Chisago Lake Lutheran Church, the church that had hosted the organizational meeting of the Conference in 1858.

A Piece of Church Property Sold

When the Board of Trustees was considering selling the parsonage property, Mr. and Mrs. Louis Anderson had indicated an interest in purchasing the property. After the Bensons had accepted the call and were willing to live in the parsonage, the sale of the property was no longer an option. The Andersons then asked if the congregation would be willing to sell the one-and-a-half acre plot at the east end of the church property where the Center City public school had formerly been located. The first school had been located nearer to what is now known as Pioneer Lake on the corner of what is now the intersection of County Highway 9 and 310th Street. In October of 1893, School District No. 13 purchased the one-and-a-half acre plot at the east end of the church property from the church for $204.25. A school was built there, which served the community until the new Lindstrom–Center City school was built between the two villages in 1916. The property reverted back to the church in 1920 and the building was demolished in 1924.

The Board of Trustees agreed to recommend to the congregation the sale of the 200 feet at the east end of the property but wanted to

1956

sell the land the entire length of the property, which amounted to 6.16 acres. At the annual meeting on January 17, 1956, the congregation approved the sale of the East 200 feet of the Southwest Quarter of the Southwest Quarter of Section Twenty-six, Township Thirty-four, Range Twenty. It was purchased by the Andersons for $4 per foot, a total of $800.

Organist Change

On February 14, 1956, the Board of Administration received a letter of resignation from the organist, Faylon Geist, effective June 1, 1956. Mr. Geist had served as organist of the congregation for three and one-half years. During this time the organ had been rebuilt and the choir had been strengthened. The congregation asked him to reconsider, but the resignation was accepted at the March board meeting. There were opportunities for him and his wife in Hamburg, Iowa, where Mrs. Geist's mother lived and they felt that this was the right time for them to make a move.

1956

Advertisements for someone to fill this vacancy were placed in *The Lutheran Companion* and in *The Diapason*, a musicians' magazine. Responses were received from Maine to California, 28 in all. The position was offered to and accepted by Mr. Glen Lovestrand, an Augustana Lutheran from Ivanhoe, Minnesota, who was completing his master of music degree at the University of Redlands in Redlands, California. He was highly recommended and could assume his duties on July 1, 1956.

Mr. Lovestrand fit in easily as a staff person and began his plans for the new choir year. The district Reformation service was scheduled to be held at Chisago Lake, which included a mass choir from all the district churches. The senior choir would prepare for a Christmas choral service and the carol choir would present a Christmas cantata written for children's choir. During his tenure, he also started a boys'

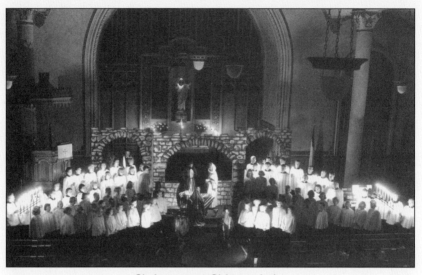

Christmas at Chisago Lake

choir. A robe committee was making plans to buy new choir robes to replace the ones that had been handmade in 1929. The new robes were two-piece garments with a black cassock and a white surplice. Fifty robes were ordered at a cost of $16.50 each. These were to be paid for by donations from two of the women's organizations, The Willing Workers and The Loyal Helpers, as well as from some memorial gifts.

There were organizations in the church for everyone. Each was self-supporting and had its own treasury. The auditor's report for 1957 lists seventeen separate organizational units. Among these were: Augustana Churchmen, Ladies Aid, Women's Missionary Society, Willing Workers (a group of ladies in Center City), Loyal Helpers (a group of ladies in Lindstrom), Mary and Martha Circle (young mothers who met in the evening), Young Women's Missionary Society, Junior Missionary Society, and Luther League, in addition to the Sunday school and the choir.

The Ladies Aid met once each month. They sponsored the nursery, the Memorial Day dinner, the annual Pioneer Service (a Swedish service), and quarterly birthday socials. The birthday socials were an opportunity for every member of the congregation to be recognized as "special" once each year. A special table was set for each of the three months in the quarter, appropriately decorated, and there was a cake provided for each table. Children were seated at their own small tables. Programs at these events were always planned with special care to provide family entertainment.

Congregation Name Change

The Chisago Lake community was settled by immigrants from Sweden. Therefore, it was not surprising that the name they gave their church was "The Swedish Evangelical Lutheran Church of Chisago Lake." As the twentieth century began the community was still Swedish, but after the two world wars this began to change. By the 1950s the community had grown to include many other nationalities. The time had come to modernize the church name.

A special meeting of the congregation was called for Easter Sunday, April 21, 1957, following the service, to vote on the following resolution:

1957

> IT IS HEREBY RESOLVED that the Board of Trustees of the Swedish Evangelical Lutheran Church of Chisago Lake be, and they hereby are, expressly authorized to amend the Articles of Incorporation so that this religious organization have as its corporate name and be henceforth known as Chisago Lake Evangelical Lutheran Church of Center City.

There were 507 votes cast with unanimous approval for the resolution. So began a new era in the Chisago Lake congregation.

Another special meeting of the congregation was called for Friday evening, July 12, 1957, to amend the rules and regulations governing the care and maintenance of the church cemetery to include the Hillside Cemetery. These rules and regulations included care of cemetery lots, planting of trees and shrubs, use of flowers, and types of markers and monuments permitted.

Minnesota Synod Centennial

In 1958 Minnesota celebrated its centennial. It was also one hundred years since the Minnesota Synod was organized at Chisago Lake. The invitation to the Minnesota Synod of the Augustana Lutheran Church to hold their centennial convention at Chisago Lake in April 1958 was accepted. There would be 500 delegates attending this meeting. The planning for housing, feeding, and meeting the needs of all these people was a huge undertaking for any congregation. It was especially challenging in an old church with very limited space. Planning began early and help was given by neighboring congregations.

The choir, under the leadership of its director Glen Lovestrand, began the project of establishing a permanent archive to keep valuables pertaining to the history of the congregation. Many items were collected including the original altar cross, communion ware, and psalmodikon. Many books and Christian writings, some dating from

1958

Communion at Chisago Lake

the early 1700s, were found and assembled. There was a complete set of the annual reports of the Augustana Synod from its organization to the current time. There were photos of the church as it looked when it was constructed as well as changes that had been made over the years. A home for this archive was found on the balcony level of the church building.

The choir was also getting familiar with the new *Service Book and Hymnal* (the red hymnal), which was to be introduced at the centennial convention. The new *Service Book and Hymnal* had been thirteen years in the making. Eight Lutheran church bodies were involved in bringing it to life. More than four million Lutherans in about 11,000 congregations would be using this book in their churches. This was a stepping stone towards bringing the Lutheran churches together. The people at Chisago Lake were excited to find in the new hymnal a hymn written by one of their own members, William Johnson. Hymn 80, "Deep Were His Wounds," a poem of William's, had been set to music by Leland B. Sateren, choral director at Augsburg College in Minneapolis.

1958

Another area that needed modernizing was the kitchen. New stainless steel sinks were installed and the room was cleaned and painted. A great deal of planning was done to prepare for the serving of two meals each day for four days for 500 persons.

A public address system was installed in the church, and although not completed, was ready for use.

The April issue of the church paper, *Reflections*, gives an account of plans for the convention. It reads, in part, as follows:

> Prominent members of the Conference who will participate in the special services at the convention include: Governor Orville Freeman; Dr. Oscar A. Benson, President of the Church; Dr. Leonard Kendall, President of the Conference; Dr. Emil Swenson, President Emeritus of the Conference; Dr. A.W. Arthur, Vice President; all of Minneapolis; and Dr. Emeroy Johnson of St. Peter, Conference Secretary. Representing the Church of Sweden will be Pastor Gosta Soderberg of Hassela,

Sweden, the native community of two founders of the Conference, Dr. Eric Norelius and Mr. Per Anderson.

A historic tour will be conducted on the opening day of the Conference, April 29th, at 9:45 A.M., when delegates will visit the landing place of the first Swedish settlers in Chisago County at Taylors Falls and the community of Scandia where a monument to the first Swedish settlers has been erected.

Preceding the centennial worship service that evening will be a centennial procession from the Center City Courthouse to the Chisago Lake Lutheran Church.

The worship service will see the introduction of the new standard Lutheran liturgy which has been developed for all congregations affiliated with the eight church bodies comprising the National Lutheran Council. Pastor Thomas W. Wersell, newly elected Director of Stewardship Education and Finance for the Minnesota Conference will be installed at the service at which Dr. Benson and Governor Freeman will speak.

1958

A memorial and thanksgiving service will be held Wednesday, April 30, at 8:00 P.M., conducted by Pastor Evald Olsenius of Red Wing and Dr. Emeroy Johnson.

The Historical service at 8:00 P.M., on Thursday, May 1, will feature Dr. Emil Swenson and Pastor Gosta Soderberg. The convention will conclude Friday, May 2, with a service of consecration lead by Dr. C. O. Granlund of Minneapolis.

Reports to the convention will be made by Dr. Leonard Kendall, President; Dr. Edgar Carlson, President of Gustavus Adolphus College, St. Peter, Minnesota; Dr. Christopher Hoff of St. Paul, Treasurer; Mr. Kenneth Holmquist of Minneapolis, Superintendent of Hospitals for the Board of Christian Service; Mr. Morton V. Bjorkquist of St. Paul, Superintendent of Services to Children and Aged; Pastor Thomas W. Wersell of Minneapolis, Director of Stewardship Education and Finance; and Mr. Ed Wang, Minneapolis, Executive Secretary-Treasurer of the Augustana Pension and Aid fund, who will also represent the Augustana church in an address.

These plans were carried out, and the convention was a memorable occasion for the Chisago Lake congregation.

Changes, Improvements, Modernization

The Ladies Aid received some monies for the work they did in preparing the meals for the convention. From these funds they gave $1,800 to be used for installing an electric ringer for the church bell. Up to this time, the bell was rung by pulling a rope by hand. The bell was rung on many occasions, e.g.: 6:00 P.M. on Saturday evening, announcing the time for the Angelus and preparing for the Sabbath; on Sunday morning issuing a call to worship; at 10:00 A.M. the morning after a member died, giving as many rings as the number of years the member had lived; and tolling as the funeral procession left the church following a funeral. To ring the bell, the sexton would need to climb the stairs to the bell tower. Knowing the proper way to ring the bell was a real art because the bell was very heavy.

1958

From the time the Chisago Lake congregation had an organ, a house had been provided for the organist. The first organist's house was located east of the church about one-fourth of a mile on the south side of the road. That house was sold many years ago but is still in use today. For many years the organist's house was located one block from the church, on the back street, on the southeast corner of what is now the intersection of Centre Street and Mobeck Ave. There was discussion about the feasibility of owning this house, and at the annual meeting on January 23, 1958, there was a vote on a resolution to sell this home. The resolution failed with 64 voting yes and 80 voting no.

Another resolution voted on at this meeting was to appoint a committee to be in charge of all the cemeteries. The Glader Cemetery on the south side of South Center Lake had been cared for by a special committee and the other cemeteries had been the responsibility of the Board of Trustees. The resolution read as follows:

RESOLVED that the Glader Cemetery Committee be discontinued with this annual meeting and that a special Cemetery Committee be appointed by the Board of Trustees to administer all cemeteries of the church and that this Committee consist of five persons—two Trustees and three members at large, all responsible to the Board of Trustees.

This resolution passed with 137 voting yes and 5 voting no.

It had been the practice to list all members in the back of the annual report each year and the amount of their contributions for the year. In 1957 it was decided to discontinue this practice and in 1958 the annual report listed the members with their telephone numbers.

At the 1957 Synod Convention action was taken to unify the women's organizations of the church. The Women's Missionary Society was requested to expand its program of work to include all the women of the local congregation, and to change its name to the Augustana Lutheran Church Women. The purpose of this organization was:

1959

> To advance the Kingdom of God by uniting the women of the
> congregations of the Augustana Lutheran Church in a program
> of fellowship in membership, education and service.

At its meeting on February 12, 1959, the women of the congregation voted to adopt the ALCW plan. This would mean a big change for the women of Chisago Lake. Twelve units were started for small group Bible study and service projects. The units met monthly and the ALCW also held monthly meetings. Units were named for locations mentioned in the Bible such as Nazareth, Cana, and Bethel. The Moriah unit chose the library as its project and under its direction the library was improved in many ways.

At the annual meeting on January 22, 1959, the decision was made to proceed with the electrification of the clock and bell. The I. T. Verdin Company of Cincinnati, Ohio, dismantled the clock and brought it to their factory to rebuild it. In examining the tower, it became evident that some structural work would need to be done in order for it to support the new mechanism. A steel beam was installed and old timbers replaced. The cost of the steeple repair was $2,056. The cost of electrifying the clock was $2,334.40. The contract with the I. T. Verdin Company called for a down payment of $1,800, the exact amount already donated by the women's organization. The new ALCW offered to assume the responsibility of paying the balance of $534.40, which would be due in twelve months with no interest.

The completion of the work on the steeple meant that work could begin on re-roofing the church building. The contract for this project was with the Marvin Johnson Roofing Company of Lindstrom for a cost of $5,900. The roof was completely covered with plywood sheets and new shingles. At the completion of this project, the congregation owed $3,082.97. This was covered with a bank loan of $2,000 and a loan from the memorial fund of $1,000.

On March 9, 1960, the Board of Administration of the congregation received a written resignation from the organist, Glen Lovestrand. He had accepted a position in the music department at Gustavus Adolphus College while Dr. Paul Allwardt had a one year's leave of absence. Mr. Lovestrand had served at Chisago Lake for four years and had provided inspirational leadership in art and music for the congregation. His resignation was effective at the end of May.

1960

A replacement for Mr. Lovestrand was found quickly and on May 20, 1960, a contract was signed with Mr. Roger Crary. Mr. Crary had a bachelor of science degree from the University of Minnesota with a major in music education (vocal) and a minor in history. His master of arts degree was also from the University of Minnesota with a major in music history and literature and a minor in applied music (organ) and history. He had also studied voice and played the piano. He would begin his ministry at Chisago Lake on July 1. Since Mr. Crary was not interested in living in the organist's house, the house was rented out.

PASTOR W. BURDETTE BENSON

During the previous years there had been a great deal of discussion about a merger between the Augustana Lutheran Church (1860), the United Lutheran Church of America (1918), the American Evangelical Lutheran Church (1872), and the Suomi Synod (1890). At the Minnesota Conference Convention in Litchfield in April 1961, a vote was taken on this issue. With the approval of this merger by all concerned church bodies, the constituting convention would be held in Detroit from June 28—July 1, 1962. The merger was approved by the conference at this convention and eventually by all those involved in the merger. Synods were organized in the fall of 1962 and by January 1963 the Lutheran Church in America was in operation.

The Chisago Lake congregation had been divided into nine districts since its earliest beginnings. Originally they were called *roten*, which is Swedish for routes. At the annual meeting in January 1961, a realignment of these districts was approved. Two plans were presented to the congregation. Plan A was adopted. This plan divided the congregation into six areas. Two deacons and two trustees were to be elected from each area for a board of 24 people. This plan went into effect at the annual meeting in 1962.

1960

Historical Monument Dedicated

Mr. Carroll Westlund, owner of Westlund Monument Works of Center City and a member of the congregation, offered to donate a monument marking the approximate site of Per Berg's haymow where the church was organized in 1854. Mr. Westlund was closing his company, which had been serving the community for more than sixty years and this was to be the last monument made. On Sunday morning, July 30, 1961, this monument was dedicated.

A special unveiling ceremony was held at 9:30 A.M. followed by the worship service at 10:15. Two sons of the congregation present to assist in this ceremony were Dr. Emeroy Johnson, pastor of Scandian Grove Lutheran Church near Saint Peter, Minnesota, and Pastor Harold E.

Dedication of monument July 30, 1961

Peterson, chaplain at the State Hospital in Moose Lake, Minnesota. At that time no one could know that the site would become a popular tourist stop for bus loads of Swedish visitors and other groups.

Needs for a Larger Facility

1961

The children born between 1945 and 1960 were to become the "Baby

The Benson Family

Boomer" generation. In the early 1960s these children were growing up. Many families had four or five children in this age group. This included the Benson family, which had added Rebecca in January 1957. The primary concern of the many families in the congregation who were raising their children during these years was providing them with a good foundation in Christian values and helping them to know Jesus Christ as their personal friend and Savior.

PASTOR W. BURDETTE BENSON

This meant that the Sunday school was large—the church school superintendent's report for 1959 indicates an enrollment of 269 with 58 teachers. It was not unusual to have 30 students in the confirmation class. About 200 children attended vacation Bible school. The Junior Mission Society, the Luther League, and the Young Women's Missionary Society were all active organizations. The Churchmen sponsored the Boy Scout troop and the Cub Scouts, which were large and active. Many of the parents and children were involved in 4-H clubs. The annual banquet for the Chisago County 4-H clubs was served for many years by the ALCW as a money-raising project. With all these activities for the youth, it was very evident that more space was needed for Sunday school classes and large gatherings such as banquets.

One of the burdens that Pastor Benson continued to carry was for the financial health of the congregation. When he arrived in 1955 the congregation was carrying a debt, and over the years this debt increased rather than decreased. The financial statement for December 31, 1961, shows an indebtedness of $19,988.36—just a few dollars under $20,000. How could the congregation provide the space needed for the future when it could not pay its current debt and operating expenses?

1961

Part of this debt was due to the synod. The amount each church was requested to contribute to the synod was determined by the membership. This meant that non-resident members and inactive members became a burden to the active resident members. The congregation was in a dilemma as to how this financial problem could be solved without excluding anyone from membership in the congregation who desired it.

In his report at the annual meeting on January 18, 1962, Pastor Benson asked:

> How long are we going to wait to provide for the spiritual needs
> of our growing population of children? What regard do we have
> for the children who tomorrow will be our church, school and
> state leaders?

And the church school superintendent in his report asked:

As a parent or as interested members of this congregation, have you visited your Church School lately? You should! This is what you would find: Classes meeting in every conceivable place. For example: in the church office, in the Pastor's study, in Mr. Crary's office and the entry way, in the kitchen, on the platform, and in the choir loft and under the coat racks, and on the balcony where nearly 60 young people meet each Sunday morning.

Lack of space, privacy, or quiet, means a serious handicap for many of our teachers. We recommend that the church give serious thought to the alleviation of some of these disadvantages.

At this same meeting a resolution regarding the indebtedness was passed. It read:

Our present indebtedness be gradually diminished by the use of special envelopes for debt reduction, pledges to be made over a 3-year period, beginning with the EMV (Every Member Visit) in 1962, with the exception that the loan of $2,000 from the Chisago County State Bank and the loan of $1,000 from the Memorial Fund be paid in the year 1962.

1962

By the annual meeting held a year later on January 17, 1963, the situation had changed. For one thing, the merger was going into effect and the congregation would no longer be the Augustana Synod, but would now be a part of the Lutheran Church in America. Therefore, at this meeting a resolution was presented to amend the action taken at the annual meeting in 1962. The resolution, which was adopted, read in part:

WHEREAS, our Church Board, out of concern that we enter merger without dragging past financial obligations into it, acted at its December 11, 1962, meeting to request of Minnesota Conference forgiveness of the unremitted balance on our apportionment for 1960 and 1961…and

WHEREAS, a communication dated January 8, 1963, was received from what is now Minnesota Synod Headquarters, containing the following paragraph: "As far as we are concerned therefore, the unremitted balances from Chisago Lake Church for 1960 ($7,000.00), and 1961 ($1,685.68), are forgiven..."

NOW, THEREFORE, BE IT RESOLVED that action effective for three years taken at our 1962 annual meeting be totally amended for action from this meeting on by substituting the following: "That present indebtednesses incurred by Chisago Lake congregation be recognized and provided for by the use of special envelopes included in the offering boxes, receipts from which shall be divided equally—50% to be applied on Our Christian College Advance and 50% to be applied on the note for $1,000, held by our Cemetery Committee at Chisago County State Bank, Center City, Minn."

Also at this meeting the following resolution was adopted:

Instead of the usual allocation, we ask the Minnesota Synod for the privilege of handling our benevolence program for church and synod on the following basis:

1962

A. The first 20% of paid pledges to Minnesota Synod.

B. The next 10% of paid pledges to Chisago Lake Lutheran Church for its building fund.

C. All other undesignated receipts to Chisago Lake Lutheran Church for its local needs, subject to the provisions that in the event there remain further undesignated receipts after payment of the above, they shall go to the Minnesota Synod.

D. Upon conforming to the above payment plan, no further obligations to Minnesota Synod shall exist.

Three other important resolutions were adopted at this meeting:

A. A resolution to set up a committee to study the need for a Parish Education Building

B. A resolution to adopt the constitution of the Lutheran Church in America

C. A resolution to sell the organist house, with the net proceeds thereof deposited in the building fund of the church.

With the debt to the synod forgiven, new enthusiasm was given for eliminating the rest of the church debt and getting on with a building fund for a future education building. Much of this enthusiasm was generated by Mr. John Galowitz, who had joined Chisago Lake Lutheran Church with his wife and son in 1960. Mr. Galowitz not only set a fine example of Christian stewardship in his own life, but he was a motivational speaker and had a talent for spreading his enthusiasm to others. Under his leadership "Operation DRUM" was started to "drum up" money for debt reduction. The Churchmen sponsored an Operation Drum Banquet, which enabled them to give $1,740 toward the debt. Other organizations were inspired to have other fund-raisers, and individuals also made their contributions. The financial report at the end of 1963 shows no liabilities and a building fund balance of $6,489.07.

Hazel Tkach Becomes Music Director

On March 12, 1963, the church board received a letter of resignation from Mr. Crary, the church organist, effective July 1. He had served the congregation well for three years, and had continued the carol and cathedral choirs as well as the senior choir. He did not wish to continue with the ALCW Chorus, but this continued under the leadership of Mrs. Louis Anderson and Mrs. Marlyn Abrahamson. During the time he served this congregation he had married, and the young couple felt that this was the right time for them to move on.

1963

A music committee, chaired by Mrs. Elliott Hawkinson, was appointed to study the music needs of the congregation and to search for an organist who would fill these needs. Contacts were made with the Twin Cities Choir Masters' Association and the Minnesota Chapter of The American Guild of Organists. From the applications received, Mrs. Hazel D. Tkach was chosen to be the music director and organist. She began her duties on September 1, 1963. During the summer months, guest organists from the community served.

PASTOR W. BURDETTE BENSON

When Mrs. Tkach accepted the position, she indicated that she would like to live in the organist's house, so it was taken off the market. Instead, the house was improved and redecorated.

Mrs. Tkach held the music director and organist position until July 1, 1966, except for a few months during 1964–1965 when she left to take a position at St. Andrews Episcopal Church in Minneapolis. During the months she was absent, Mr. Paul Carlson, a graduate student at the University of Minnesota, was hired as organist and Mr. Russell Griswold, a member of the church and a music teacher in the Stillwater school district, served as senior choir director.

Under Mrs. Tkach's direction, the senior choir grew to 60 members. She also started a motet choir, which was composed of 16 high school students from within the senior choir. The cathedral choir was composed of 16 junior high girls, and the carol choir had 36 members of elementary school age.

1963

The highlight for the senior choir was presenting the cantata *Adoramus Te* by Joseph Clokey during the Lenten season of 1964. This cantata was presented both at the First Lutheran Church in Amery, Wisconsin, and at Chisago Lake.

At the annual meeting in January 1964, the Church Council suggested that Mrs. Elmer Bloom be contacted about the purchase of her property, which was adjacent to the south side of the parking lot. The purpose for this house would be to provide space for Sunday school classes. In April the council decided to purchase the property and a special meeting of the congregation was called for May 10, to approve of this purchase. At this same meeting the council was authorized to try again to sell the organist house.

The organist's house was sold to Donald Lent for $7,750 and the Bloom house was purchased for $7,250. Also at this time, the church purchased six small pieces of property east of the church, which had been forfeited to the State of Minnesota because of non-payment of taxes. Undoubtedly these had been owned by men who kept their horses on an allocated space of land in the church's horse barns at an earli-er time. Cost of these bits of land was $55. After these property trans-actions and closing costs had been paid, there was a balance of $464.71, which was designated for the building fund.

When Mrs. Tkach returned to resume her duties at Chisago Lake, the Bloom house was redecorated and this became her home. The Sunday school students returned to the crowded conditions in the sanctuary.

Some interesting statistics from January 1, 1964, show that the total church membership was 1,193, of which 903 adults and 290 chil-dren. The Sunday school report shows nearly 300 children in Sunday school with 50 teachers. Average attendance at worship services during 1963 was 396.

Steeple Repair

The steeple had not been re-roofed at the time the church roof was replaced. At the annual meeting in 1964, the council was authorized to proceed with this project and the painting of the exterior of the church. Pearson Bros. of North Branch was hired to take responsibility for this work, working with Mr. Genz, a steeplejack from Shakopee. The shin-gles on the steeple were replaced to harmonize with the roof, and all the exterior trim and woodwork on the church was repaired and painted. The four faces of the tower clock were also refashioned from metal to replace the old wood.

1964

The Boy Scout troop, under supervision of Louis Anderson, scoutmaster, assisted with this project by putting the numerals on the clock faces with scotchlight tape. After the clock faces were replaced it was noticed that one of the XIIs was a XIII. Whether this was an hon-est mistake or a prank was not known, but the face was removed and some black paint used to cover up the unwanted I. (These faces were the same until 1998.)

PASTOR W. BURDETTE BENSON

Constitution and Committee Changes

The new LCA constitution was adopted at a special meeting in November 1963, to go into effect at the annual meeting in January 1964. This involved changing the composition of the church board (or council) from 12 deacons and 12 trustees, a total of 24, to a 12-member council working with constitutionally fixed committees. Committees would be appointed by the Church Council with at least one council member on each committee. These committees included social ministry, finance, stewardship, evangelism, Christian education, worship and music, and church property. Other committees at Chisago Lake included: publication and public relations, memorial, cemetery, and building planning.

110th Anniversary

1964

The 110th anniversary of Chisago Lake Lutheran Church was in 1964. A decision was made to have special events throughout the year in observance of this anniversary. Throughout the year, the church newsletter, *Reflections*, featured articles about each of the pastors who had served the congregation.

In January, the concert orchestra of the 3M Company and the 40-voice choir of the First Lutheran Church in St. Paul presented *The Childhood of Jesus* by the composer Hector Berlioz. Featured in this concert were four distinguished soloists. On Palm Sunday, the Chisago Lake Choir presented *The Adoramus Te Cantata* by

Pastor Benson leading worship

Joseph Clokey. On May 3, the Swedish Cultural Society of Minneapolis presented a program of singing and speaking.

A confirmation reunion was held on June 21 with Pastor J. Walton Kempe as guest speaker. A Pioneer Day Swedish communion service was held in September with Dr. Emeroy Johnson leading worship. In November Pastor Clifford Peterson spoke at the annual Churchmen's banquet. Dr. Johnson and Pastor Peterson were sons of the congregation.

Historical Committee Established

When Mr. Lovestrand was the church organist, he had helped to establish an archive center for the congregation. Because of the historic significance of Chisago Lake Lutheran Church, many items were given to this center, and its importance continued to grow. At the annual meeting in January 1965, a resolution was passed that the following article be added to the constitution of the congregation:

1965

> There shall be an Historical Committee for the care and propagation of the archives of the congregation. It shall preserve photographs, articles, documents, artifacts and other items it deems of historical value to the congregation, and shall display items of historical interest to the congregation and its visitors.

Since that time the historical committee has continued to be an active committee and many items of historical value have been added to the archives. Hundreds of tourists come every year to enjoy the display of artifacts, books, and documents housed in the archive room.

Building Committee Established

The Building Planning Committee worked diligently during the year of 1964. Their plans showed that we needed an education building, a music center, adequate space for the office and administration department, a small chapel, a library, and a large parking area. At the 1965 annual meeting a resolution was passed to change the name of this committee to the Parish Building Committee and to authorize the committee to add members as needed and to secure the assistance of an architect. Mr. Robert Koehn served as chairman of this committee.

Also at this meeting, the council was authorized to proceed with plans for the redecorating of the sanctuary, including updating the lighting.

L.Y.E. Ministry in Sweden

In 1965, Pastor Benson was invited by a Lutheran Youth Encounter Gospel Team of college-age youth to accompany them for one month of a three-month tour they were making in Sweden in the fall of the year. After much prayerful consideration of this invitation, Pastor Benson decided to accept this invitation and to use this time as his vacation. The congregation decided to take an offering to finance a two-week trip for both Pastor B. (as he was lovingly called by all the youth and many of the adults) and Mrs. Benson to Northern Europe and Scandinavia prior to his beginning the tour with the L.Y.E. group. Together they were able to visit England, The Netherlands, Germany, Denmark, Sweden, and Norway.

1965

A musical highlight of 1965 was a hymn festival held on November 28, with Paul Manz as the guest organist. Senior choirs and youth choirs from four other churches joined together in the Chisago Lake sanctuary for this inspiring evening of singing and organ music.

Mrs. Benson remembers that it was during the pastor's absence the parsonage garage burned. No one was ever able to determine for certain what caused the fire, but the car was in the garage and it exploded and burned also. This garage was located east of the present one and had a storage shed in the rear, which served as a wood shed and where the screen windows and storm windows were stored. These were also destroyed. By the time the fire department arrived on the scene, their main concern was to save the house. The heat from the fire was so hot that it blistered the paint on the northeast corner of the house.

The financial records for 1966 show that the new garage was built for a cost of $1,583.69. At this time the new driveway was made for the parsonage coming in on the north side of the cemetery. This made it possible to have easier access to the parsonage in the event of icy roads when the hill to the south would become impassable. The parsonage was painted on the exterior, and new screen and storm windows were purchased.

Building Plans Progress

At the annual meeting in January 1966, the building committee proposed a time schedule for the construction of an education building. The plan called for an architect to be selected in the spring with approval of the master plan and preliminary design scheduled for January 1967. Construction could then begin in the middle of the year. The committee received authorization to interview architects and the firm chosen was Armstrong, Schlichting, Torseth, and Skold, Inc. Mr. Torseth was very familiar with the community because he owned a cabin on the north shore of North Center Lake and worshiped with the congregation often during the summer months. He would be the firm representative who would work with and for the congregation.

1966

In Pastor Benson's report at the annual meeting, he again expressed his concern for the need of additional staff to carry on the work in such a large congregation. His suggestion was that this could be an older pastor who could serve in visiting shut-ins and older members while also assisting with preaching and the administration of the sacraments. Or, it could be a business administrator who could also assist with youth work. A third idea would be to have a theological intern. No action was taken on any of these proposals.

PASTOR W. BURDETTE BENSON

In May of 1966 Mrs. Tkach resigned from her position as music director and organist, effective July 1. Mr. James Iverson, a member of the congregation assumed the position as music director when she left, and Mr John Rebischke of Little Falls, a graduate of Gustavus Adolphus College, was secured to act as organist for the month of July. He continued on in this position until August 1, 1967, when Mrs. Kathleen DeBolt was hired as a permanent organist.

With the tuck-pointing of the brick on the church during the summer of 1966, the exterior of the building was in good condition, but the interior was sadly in need of repair. The old coal-burning furnace was sending specks of black dirt throughout the sanctuary. The ceiling was dirty and the paint was peeling in the narthex. There were cracks in the sanctuary walls and the lighting system was inadequate. The interior decorating committee met with the building committee and with the architect and representatives from a heating company. It was decided not to do any major redecorating until after the vote on the new building.

1966

Preliminary plans for the new building were ready on schedule and a special meeting of the congregation was called for February 2, 1967, to discuss and vote on the building plan. Financial records for December 31, 1966, show a balance in the building fund of $36,605.17. It had been decided that in order to undertake a building program of the size needed, the vote should pass by a two-thirds majority of those voting. A total of 237 votes were cast and it was defeated by less than 10 of the two-thirds majority needed to proceed with the plans.

For those who had worked on the building committee and the many members who were excited about the building program, this defeat was a great disappointment. Soon after this, a petition signed by more than ten percent of the confirmed members in good standing was presented to the Church Council asking for another vote. Instead of calling another meeting for the purpose of voting, a survey was taken to determine why the vote did not pass. The number one reason given for the defeat was that the cost was too high. Cost of the entire plan was estimated to be $310,000. If the building of the chapel were postponed, the cost would be about $250,000. Others felt that we should repair the church first before we started a building program. A few did not like the design and location of the planned addition. There was also disagreement on hiring someone to conduct a fund-raising campaign for the building project.

New Heating Plant

The most important item that needed to be addressed at this point was the condition of the furnace. Several furnace companies were contacted and many meetings were held to ascertain what could be done both for the short-term and long-term benefit of the building. The final decision was to contract with Milton Erickson and Son for a gas-oil system that would be large enough to heat both the present facility and a new building when it was built. To comply with the guarantee for the new heating system, it was also necessary to insulate the church attic.

1968

Another need was for more parking space. It was decided to use as much of the Bloom property as possible for additional parking and also to purchase the space across the street on the north side of the church from Mr. Carroll Westlund for $1,000.

Special Congregational Meeting

In response to the petition received by the Church Council asking for another vote on the building project, the building planning committee was asked to prepare for a congregational meeting on May 21, 1968. Six informational meetings were held prior to the May 21 meeting. These meetings were not well attended, but those who did attend were very interested and good discussion took place with some misinformation being cleared up.

PASTOR W. BURDETTE BENSON

The result of the vote at the May 21 meeting was favorable, but still did not meet the two-thirds majority. The recommendation to have the Lutheran Layman's Movement organize and manage a fund-raising to make the building construction possible was defeated with 98 voting yes and 224 voting no.

Since the use of LLM to assist in the raising of funds for the building project was voted down, the finance committee suggested an every-member visit in the fall, but it was decided not to include this with the regular stewardship drive because the Church Council felt the con-gregation was not ready at this time. Instead it was decided to "sell bricks"—a voluntary opportunity for donations and pledges to the building fund. A display was put up at the back of the church showing a brick building, and as donations came in the bricks were colored in to show the progress of the fund. Bricks sold for $100 each. The architect was paid for his work to date and the building project was "put on hold."

1968   Sanctuary Redecorated

An interior decorating committee was authorized at the annual meet-ing in January 1965. This committee met faithfully under the leader-ship of Kermit Christensen, chairman, to determine what the priorities were that needed attention. They worked with the building committee and the property committee in getting the sanctuary insulated and the new heating system installed.

The redecorating of the sanctuary, which was done in 1968, was extensive. The east, west, and north walls of the sanctuary were re-plas-tered with a complete underlay of metal lath and then painted. The ceiling and the woodwork were washed and then painted. This work was done by A Shelgren & Son, Inc. The work took several weeks and worship services were held in the midst of the scaffolding.

The light fixtures were also replaced. Mr. Daniel O'Neil, a part-ner in Nakashian-O'Neil in St. Paul, together with artists at New Metal Crafts in Chicago designed the chandelier light fixtures. These fixtures were designed to resemble the original fixtures with candles and were made with materials from Sweden, Germany, and Belgium. The molds for the fixtures were destroyed after the work was completed and you will not see similar fixtures any other place. They are unique. The new fixtures required new wiring and control panels along with some other outdoor lights. The entire project cost $20,331.19. This did not include the refinishing of the floor and the carpeting, which was done later.

Pastor Benson Resigns

On June 10, 1969, the Church Council received a letter of resignation from Pastor Burdette Benson specifying that August 31 would be the family's last Sunday at Chisago Lake. He was accepting a call to Swedlanda Lutheran Church in rural Hector, Minnesota. With three children still in school, the family wanted to move before the school term began in September. They had been here for fourteen years. To the younger children this had always been home and the two older children had graduated from high school here and had formed many last-

1969

ing friendships. On April 6, 1968, Bruce had married Carol Hovland at Chisago Lake, and later when Carrie was married, she too chose to be married in this church.

Pastor Benson's influence was felt far beyond the local con-

April 6, 1968

gregation. For several years he served on the Board of World Missions of the Augustana Church. When the merger occurred and the congre-

PASTOR W. BURDETTE BENSON

gation became part of the LCA, his service on this board ceased. He served on the Board of Trustees at Gustavus Adolphus College at the time Christ Chapel was built. He also served on the Luther Point Bible Camp Board for many years.

In reading through annual reports and newsletters from the years the Benson family was here a number of observations can be made. First, the entire family was involved in ministering to this congregation. Elaine Benson was a teacher. Occasionally she was called on to be a substitute at the high school, but always she used her teaching skills in the church. She helped with vacation Bible school and taught Sunday school and/or confirmation. She was an active member of the LCW and took her turn as chairman. She served on committees and entertained at the parsonage for youth activities, for LCW Teas, for unit meetings, and committee meetings. She opened the parsonage for Sunday school classes when there was no space in the church.

1969

Bruce Benson, 1972

Bruce was a leader in the Luther League and was the first president of the Sequoia 4-H Club, which was organized in Center City during the 1960s. He played basketball at school and played his guitar for the youth at church. Bruce graduated from Chi Hi in 1964 and from Augsburg College in 1968. From February 1 to June 1 of 1966, Bruce attended Talladega College in Alabama where he was the only white student. There he played on the varsity basketball team. He went on to seminary and now serves as chaplain at St. Olaf College, Northfield, Minn.

All the children sang in the choir for their age, were involved in other youth activities and attended Bible camp, leadership schools, youth conventions, etc.

During "the Benson years" there was a strong emphasis on Global Missions at Chisago Lake. There were many reasons for this. First, the

Bensons had been missionaries to China, and Pastor Benson had been born in China. They knew many other missionaries who would find their way to Center City and were always given the opportunity to tell about their work in Sunday school, at LCW, at a birthday social, or by preaching on a Sunday.

Tengbom family, 1956

Mildred Hasselquist Tengbom, a daughter of this congregation, and her family were serving on the mission field in Tanzania. Both her sister Alma and her brother Paul visited them in Africa and brought home pictures and greetings from them. They also sent letters to the congregation and visited when they were home on furlough.

Marian Hawkinson

1969

Marian Hawkinson, another daughter of the congregation, was serving as a missionary in Japan. She too sent letters and spent much of her furlough time with family and friends at Chisago Lake. At Christmas time in 1969, Marian married Masaharu Ano at a ceremony in her home church.

The congregation always had several young men in military service. Their service took them to many places in the world and, of course, these were the Vietnam War years. Some young people served in the Peace Corp.

Before the time of the reorganization of the women's groups, Chisago Lake had a strong Women's Missionary Society and these women continued to exert a strong mission emphasis in the congregation. The pastor's report of 1968 indicates that the congregation was visited by missionaries from New Guinea, Tanzania, Japan, and India. Also that year funds were raised for the suffering in Biafra.

There has been mention before of the large number of children in the congregation during the 1960s and the emphasis on youth programs. The congregation sponsored the Boy Scout program and many boys were served through this organization. Men of the congregation served on the Scout committee and were scout leaders; women served as den mothers.

The Luther League met at least twice each month. Many children attended Bible camp each summer. Each year some of the youth went to leadership school, to youth conventions, and to Lutheran Youth Encounter events.

For many years it was the custom for the congregation to go to Luther Point Bible Camp on the second Sunday of September. Worship was held in the chapel, a potluck dinner was served in the cafeteria, and the afternoon was spent in games for the children, a soft-

1969 ball game, and swimming if the weather was warm enough. This was a time to acquaint children with the camp and a wonderful opportunity for fellowship with other members of the congregation.

For ten of these years, from 1958 to 1968, Mr. Arnold Carlson served as the Sunday school superintendent. Enrollment was large and space was limited. He was a faithful leader and dedicated to providing the best possible for the children. A large staff of faithful teachers and a diligent education committee supported him. Mr. Carlson was also a lay pastor and would often conduct the service in the absence of the pastor.

There were a number of funding appeals during this time. There was O.C.C.A. (Our Christian College Advance) in the early 1960s, and also a special fund for the building of the Gustavus Adolphus College chapel. At about the same time, funds were raised to help build the chapel at Luther Point Bible Camp. The Minnesota Synod had a capital-funds program, U.N.I.T.E. (Undergird Northwestern In Theological Education) for the seminary. This congregation was asked to serve as a pattern church and had the direction of the Lutheran Layman's Movement in setting up this two-year program. In the late 1960s there was G.A.L.A. (Gustavus Adolphus Leadership Appeal) and an LCA funding appeal known as "ACT."

Another observation addresses the number of musical programs each year. The Chisago Lake Choir had special concerts at Easter and/or Christmas. There were L.Y.E. groups that came with their programs. There were organ concerts and guest vocal soloists. There were piano recitals to dedicate new pianos. There were college choirs that gave concerts in the sanctuary. Music was a high priority for the congregation.

An interesting sidelight from 1968 was the presence of Nils Hasselmo in the community. He was conducting a Swedish language study in Chisago and Washington Counties. He conducted a survey of the members of Chisago Lake Church as well as visiting in the homes of some for personal interviews. After the completion of his study he sent a report to the congregation of his findings with thanks for their help with his project. Many years later when he became president of the University of Minnesota he still remembered people from the congregation and would occasionally attend worship here.

1969

Fun at the Parsonage

This accounting of the years the Benson family occupied the parsonage would not be complete without some glimpses into life in the parsonage. One of the hobbies the Benson family had was cooking maple syrup. Each spring as the sap began rising in the trees the entire family became involved with this "sweet" proj-

The Parsonage in the Winter

PASTOR W. BURDETTE BENSON

ect. There were many maple trees on the parsonage property that could be tapped. There were plenty of fallen trees in the woods to stoke the fire. Everyone took their turn at feeding the fire and skimming the vat. The canning was Elaine's task.

With five children in the family there were many birthday parties, slumber parties, and 4-H meetings. Mrs. Benson was a seamstress and sewed many of the children's clothes. She not only taught her own girls to sew, but she helped other girls with their 4-H projects. She also created beautiful red draperies for the parsonage living room.

1969

The Benson Family:
Bruce, Pr. Benson, Rebecca, Gracia, Theodore, Elaine, and Carolyn

There were piano lessons to practice and the older children played other instruments; Carrie played the violin. The children's friends were always welcome and there was often an extra plate set at the table. Family devotions were a part of every evening meal and guests were always included. Many of the children's friends experienced family devotions around their table. No one who was a member of the Sequoia 4-H club will forget the Halloween parties in the attic and bobbing for apples in a tub in the center of the kitchen floor.

Of course the children had a dog. Pastor Benson remembers a funeral in the Hillside Cemetery when the dog escaped from the house and sang with him as he sang a stanza of a hymn during the committal service. How embarrassing!

Pastor Benson served the church in rural Hector until his retirement. He and Elaine then moved to a home in the country near Le Sueur, Minnesota. Here they enjoyed entertaining family and friends and pursuing their many hobbies. When Pastor Benson's health began to fail, they moved to a townhouse in Northfield, Minnesota. It was here that Pastor Benson died on January 24, 1999. He is buried in the cemetery at Scandian Grove Lutheran Church in rural Saint Peter.

Calling a New Pastor

Upon Pastor Benson's departure, September 1, 1969, Pastor Frank Johnson of Faith Lutheran Church in Forest Lake was appointed vice-pastor at Chisago Lake. Assisting him were Pastor Antti Lepisto, who was able to stay at the parsonage, and a lay pastor, Arnold W. Carlson, who conducted the Sunday worship services.

1969

During the time the congregation was without a resident pastor, a number of committee projects were "put on hold." One of these was the securing of an assistant pastor. The worship and music committee had begun the study necessary before hiring an assistant pastor, but this now needed to wait until there was a full-time pastor.

The building committee no longer was functioning, but the voluntary contributions and pledges continued to come in. The treasurer's report shows that as of January 1, 1970, there was $48,351.97 in the building fund and $17,950 had been received in pledges.

The interior decorating committee was making plans to change the steps in front of the altar, to refinish the pews and the floor, and to install new carpeting. These items were all postponed.

PASTOR W. BURDETTE BENSON

Interesting statistics from December 31, 1969, show a total membership of 1,083 members, with 876 adults and 207 children. Average Sunday morning attendance during 1969 was 350.

On Sunday, December 28, 1969, a special meeting of the congregation was held after the morning worship service for the purpose of issuing a call to Pastor James A. Almquist from North Emanuel Lutheran Church in Saint Paul. Pastor Melvin A. Hammarberg, synod president, was present to act as chairman of this meeting. Because of a heavy snowfall during the night, only 150 voting members were present, but these members cast a unanimous ballot for Pastor Almquist.

The Church Council recommended that should Pastor Almquist accept the call his financial package would be free use of the parsonage with all utilities and:

Salary	$7,700.00
Car expense	1,200.00
Misc. expense account	250.00
Pension fund in full	1,155.00
Social Security in full	554.40

1969

Pastor Almquist accepted the call to Chisago Lake and arrived in March 1970. Prior to his coming, Pastor Lepisto was asked to vacate the parsonage so that it could be redecorated for the Almquists.

At the annual meeting in 1969, a resolution was adopted to change the fiscal business year to run from October 1 through September 30. This change was made because it seemed that there was often extremely cold weather at annual meeting time in January. This required a constitution change and needed to be voted on again at the January 1970 meeting. At the January meeting it was decided to hold the next annual meeting October 22, 1970 at 8:00 P.M., which meant that the year would be shortened to nine months. The resolution was adopted.

For several summers—June through the church school outing in September—the congregation had conducted two worship services on Sundays at 8:15 and 10:45 A.M. with Sunday school at 9:30. More and more people were traveling and taking weekend trips during the summer. It was difficult to find teachers for the summer months and Sunday school attendance was very poor. At the January 1970 annual meeting the schedule was altered to conduct Sunday school in June only and not to conduct a Sunday school during July, August, and through the September outing. This resolution was adopted unanimously.

Another resolution that was passed at the 1969 annual meeting concerned the discussion to establish a seminary scholarship fund in the amount of $500 to encourage young people to prepare for the holy ministry. This was referred to the Christian education committee for discussion, which led to a resolution proposed at the January 1970 annual meeting that read as follows:

> Be it resolved that Chisago Lake Ev. Lutheran Church establish a scholarship fund of $500.00 a year for each student of the Chisago Lake Church entering the seminary to study for the ministry of the L.C.A.
>
> Be it further resolved that the amount of $500.00 be set aside annually from the general fund. In the event there should be no student enrolled in the seminary, the fund will be limited to $1,500.00 until used and then re-activated.
>
> Application and approval of applicants would be handled by the Church Council.

This resolution was unanimously approved.

During the absence of a resident pastor, it became difficult to find ordained clergy to distribute the Sacrament of Holy Communion. At the 1964 National Convention of the L.C.A., a recommendation had been adopted to allow qualified laymen to assist an ordained minister in the communion service. At the January 1970 annual meeting the congregation approved unanimously a resolution to adopt this practice at Chisago Lake.

Pastor Almquist had attended a Church Council meeting prior to the annual meeting and approved of these resolutions.

1969

∽

Pastor James Almquist
1970–1980

PASTOR JAMES ALMQUIST was born in Omaha, Nebraska, the son of Pastor and Mrs. Arthur Almquist. He graduated from Bethany College in Lindsborg, Kansas, in 1949, and from Augustana Seminary in Rock Island, Illinois, in 1953. He was ordained into the Augustana Lutheran Church in Rockefeller Chapel, Chicago, Illinois.

James Almquist was married to Violet Steinkamp in December 1952, and they had one daughter, Deborah Ann, who was born in December 1953. Pastor Almquist served at Bethany Lutheran Church in Norway, Michigan, from 1953 to 1957 and at North Emanuel Lutheran Church in Saint Paul from 1957 to 1970.

Pastor Almquist arrived with his family in March. The installation service for him was held on Palm Sunday, March 22, 1970, at 8:00 P.M. Dr. Melvin Hammarberg, synod president, conducted the service.

By decision of the Church Council, the summer worship schedule was amended so the services were held at 8:00 and 10:30 A.M. with church school at 9:30 A.M. during the month of June.

Beginning on July 5, a fellowship hour would be held between services so that members could get to know each other better and visitors could be welcomed. LCW Units were in charge of coffee.

The outing at Luther Point was held on the second Sunday of September with an 8:00 A.M. service at the church and the service at Luther Point at 11:00. This gave the opportunity for those who did not wish to travel to Luther Point to attend a service. At the end of the summer, so many members had expressed an appreciation for two services that the council decided to continue with the 8:00 and 10:30 services in the fall. Sunday church school was scheduled for 9:15. In choosing the 10:30 A.M. from the 11:00 A.M. hour, the congregation recognized the need to have worship early enough so those who attended from Hazelden could get back in time for their noon-hour lunch.

The Fifth Biennial Convention of the Lutheran Church in America was held in the Minneapolis Auditorium June 25 to July 2, 1970. It was a unique opportunity for congregations in and near the **1970** Twin Cities. On Sunday, June 28, Dr. Reuben Swanson, president of the Nebraska Synod was guest preacher at Chisago Lake. Also spending the day with this congregation were 15 synod delegates. These delegates were from North Carolina, Pennsylvania, Michigan, and Canada. They came for the worship service and joined the congregation at a potluck dinner following the service. In the afternoon they had an opportunity for some sightseeing in the area and also for visiting in the homes of some of the members.

Pastor Almquist's first annual meeting at Chisago Lake was held on October 22, 1970. He had been in the congregation about eight months. He stated in his annual report that during these months he tried to assess the situation at Chisago Lake to determine the direction to go and the tasks that needed doing. He begins his report with "The Manifesto," an LCA "Call of God to the Church in Each Place." Since this is a brief statement of the purpose of the church, it seems fitting that we include it here.

This is God's world: the object of God's love,
the arena of man's achievement, and the scene of
man's struggles.

This is God's time: exciting and full of hope,
confusing, and plagued with anxiety.

The Church is God's people: the new humanity in
Christ, called into being, sustained and empowered
by the Holy Spirit.

God's people are sent into the world to speak His
Word and to be his agents of reconciliation.

As his people we confess that we are hesitant in
our faith, timid in our ventures, and halting in
our obedience.

Yet the Church continues to be God's own people,
the community of faith and love and servant-hood.
Centered in Jesus Christ, this community is
continually renewed as it relives his life, death,
and resurrection in worship and mission.

1970

Faithfulness in our day requires that the congregation
come to a clearer understanding of what it means to be
the Church in each place and welcome today's world as
the given setting for its mission.

The report then continues with a challenge to the congregation
to be willing to change to meet the needs of the 70s in "our place."

New Building Task Force Appointed

At the October 1970 meeting the Church Council was authorized to
appoint a building task force to analyze the present and long range
need and desire of the congregation. Although the previous plan for an
addition to the church had not passed, the need for additional space
was still a top priority. Those appointed were Marcus Brottem,

Glenden Berglund, Arnold Carlson, Mark Grandstrand, Richard Mueller, Fred Sass, Arnold Johnson, and Robert Koehn.

This committee reviewed the plan which had been put before the congregation in 1968 and went on to determine if and how the needs of the congregation had changed and what kind of a facility could meet these needs. A questionnaire was sent out to every member of the congregation to determine the amount of interest still existing for a building program. There were 289 questionnaires returned with 190 in favor of building, 78 not in favor, and 21 undecided. This indicated that 65 percent of those who responded were in favor of building a Sunday church school and administrative facility.

Intern Added to Staff

The former worship and music committee had recommended that we proceed with hiring some assistance for the pastor. This could be a visitation pastor, an intern, or an assistant pastor. At the October 1970 meeting the Church Council was authorized to continue to explore the possibility of sharing a person with another congregation, or possibly with Hazelden. As a result of this study, Mr. Ed Long joined the staff as an intern on September 1, 1971. Mr. Long worked with the youth program, and the Bloom House became a place for the youth to meet.

1970

"Kichi-Saga" New Name for Newsletter

In January 1971, the church newsletter took on a new look. It was renamed *Kichi-Saga*. This name was taken from the old Indian name given to this area, which meant the tale of big waters. The change in name indicated that the newsletter would not so much reflect on what had already happened, but would emphasize the coming events— would tell the tale of what was to occur by the big waters. Mrs. Lester Johnson (Lois) was the editor.

Moon Property Purchased

On Sunday, February 7, 1971, a special meeting of the congregation was held to vote on the purchase of the Keith A. Moon property, formerly known as the Johnson property, which joined the church property of the Bloom House and was now for sale. The ballot read:

> Shall the Church Council of the Chisago Lake Evangelical Lutheran Church, Center City, Minnesota, be authorized to purchase the Keith A. Moon property in Center City, Minnesota, as described in the Notice of Special Meeting and to borrow the sum of not to exceed $17,500 at 8% interest per annum for that purpose?

Of the 234 ballots cast, 222 voted yes, 11 voted no, and 1 was blank. As a result of this vote, the Moon property was purchased and the congregation assumed a mortgage on the property for $17,000.

After the Moon House was purchased, it was rewired and new carpeting was installed. The furnace was rebuilt and a used range and refrigerator were purchased for the kitchen.

1971

Pre-Lent Every Member Visit

The congregation had participated in every member stewardship visits during the fall for several years, but in 1971 the evangelism committee led the congregation in a pre-Lent every member visit. The purpose of the visit was to bring information about the Lenten services and Lenten devotional materials to each home and to invite and encourage members to participate in the opportunities available to deepen and strengthen their faith. Lenten luncheon services were planned for noon on Wednesdays during the season in addition to the 7:30 P.M. services. The members of the LCW served the luncheons. Services were in the form of a dialogue with men who were involved with the passion of our Lord—Judas, Peter, Caiaphas, Pilate, and Dismas.

First Communion and Confirmation

At the 1970 convention of the Lutheran Church in America, a report was adopted that proposed changes in the age that children would receive their first communion and also in the kind of instructional program that should be used for confirmation. The report defined confirmation as:

> A pastoral and educational ministry of the church which helps the baptized child through Word and Sacrament to identify more deeply with the Christian community and participate more fully in its mission.

It further suggested that children be admitted to communion at about the fifth grade and that confirmation instruction continue over a longer period of time until about the tenth grade.

This report was adopted at Chisago Lake at the 1971 annual meeting and steps were taken to make the necessary changes in the Christian education program. The resolution included:

1971

> That the congregation offer a program of intensive instruction as a part of the confirmation ministry to children and youth, beginning at grade five and continuing until the youth is able to confess his own Christian faith and to assume greater responsibility for ministry and mission through the congregation, community and world.

As this program was put into place, there was no longer a "confirmation class." Students were to indicate when they felt ready to confess their Christian faith and to become an adult member of the congregation. For some students this was a very meaningful experience. For others it was overwhelming and they never reached the point of being "confirmed." They continued to be baptized members of the congregation far into adulthood. Students being confirmed individually missed the fellowship and camaraderie of being in a class. In a short time, students were getting together and asking to be confirmed on the same Sunday, thereby creating their own class. After a trial period, this program was discontinued.

First Holy Communion for fifth graders was a meaningful experience for them and worked well. It was begun in 1973 and has continued to be the normal practice at Chisago Lake. Instruction takes place during Lent and students partake of their first Holy Communion on Maundy Thursday.

Sanctuary Decorating Completed

By October 1971, the interior decorating fund had grown to $12,577. The committee recommended that this fund be used to finish the work in the sanctuary. The recommendation was approved and the following work was done:

1. Uncarpeted floor areas were refinished.
2. The pews were refinished and re-spaced.
3. The floor registers were removed and the openings covered.
4. The steps to the altar area were widened.
5. The choir area was changed.
6. New carpeting was installed.

1971

When the old carpeting was removed, an envelope was found with a copy of the March 1948 *Reflections*, a copy of the program from the 90th annual convention of the Lutheran Minnesota Conference of the Augustana Synod, a list of the members of the carpeting committee, and an invoice. The old carpeting had been there for 24 years. This work was completed before the LCW District Assembly in the spring of 1972.

Reminders that Death Can Come Suddenly

On Good Friday in 1972, the custodian, Herbert Valleen, prepared the sanctuary for the day's services and draped the outdoor cross with a black cloth. He went home for lunch and a time of rest. As he rested, the Lord called him home and he died peacefully in his sleep. It was a shock to his family and his church family, but a wonderful reminder of what Good Friday and Easter are all about. Herb and his wife, Nettie, had served the congregation faithfully for nine years.

The Viet Nam War continued to go on and at any given time from 10 to 15 young men and women were serving in the armed forces. Many of them served in Viet Nam. On June 20, 1972, the sad news reached the community that Earl Frederickson, 22 years of age, had been killed accidentally while serving in the United States Navy. This was a time of sadness for his family, his friends, and his church family. It was a reminder to remember to pray for the safety of our young people and to thank God that most of them did return home safely.

Groundbreaking for Parmly Residence

The Chisago Lutheran Home was a part of the Board of Social Ministry of the Minnesota Synod. It was with joy and thanksgiving that this home received $1,000,000 from the estate of Margaret S. Parmly. The facility was old and badly in need of replacement, which could now become a reality. Groundbreaking ceremonies were held on

1972

July 16, 1972, for the new facility, the Margaret S. Parmly Residence, named after its benefactor. Dr. Melvin Hammarberg, president of the Minnesota Synod, officiated. Pastor Almquist, who was a member of the Synod Board of Social Ministry, had a special interest in this event. Miss Ruth Parmly, a daughter of Mrs. Margaret Parmly, was also present at the ceremony.

Dr. M. Hammarberg

Later, when Pastor Almquist became chairman of the Board of Parmly, long-range planning was done, which resulted in the building of 60 units at the Lakeview Apartments and 63 apartments and 46 townhouses at Point Pleasant Heights.

"To Burn Again"

The building task force completed its work, so a building committee was appointed: Arnold Carlson, James Froberg, Marjorie Hawkinson, Mark Wikelius, Shirley Carlson, Grace Carlson, Richard Gustafson, and LeeVerne Peterson, with Pastor Almquist as an ex-officio member. This newly appointed committee met twice each month in 1972 to develop a statement of purpose for the congregation and a program for long-range planning to fill its need for space. They also authorized a topographical property study by Hult and Associates of Forest Lake, Minnesota, which would be used by an architect in making decisions regarding the building site.

A brochure of information was prepared with the assistance of Robert A. Hawkinson, a graduate of the University of Minnesota with a degree in landscape architecture and a member of the congregation. The first page of this brochure, entitled "To Burn Again," reads as follows:

> On Pentecost a fire started to burn
> The fire was The Spirit in the hearts of men
> This fire burned within the men who
>   established this church
> It ignited their spirits to build and rebuild
> The fire was spread as men: Studied,
>   Shared, and Served
>   LOVE…of God, to men, is the force
>   of the fire
> Is there a fire burning now?"

1972

The brochure presented a vision for the future. It provided for sufficient parking space, for a future Swedish cultural heritage type of museum, for sports activities, and for retirement housing, as well as for the immediately needed education and administration building. The historical committee felt that if they were to continue with plans for the museum, it would be necessary to purchase the Peterson-Swenson property along Pioneer Lake.

Property Purchased

A special congregational meeting was held after the worship service on Sunday, October 8, 1972, for the purpose of voting on the purchase of the Viola Peterson property, also known as the Peterson-Swenson property. The resolution read in part:

> BE IT RESOLVED that the Church Council of the Chisago Lake Evangelical Lutheran Church, Center City, Minnesota, be and are hereby authorized to purchase said property for the sum of $15,000.

> BE IT FURTHER RESOLVED that said Church Council is hereby authorized to borrow the sum of not to exceed $15,000 if necessary, with interest thereon not to exceed 8% per annum, to purchase said premises and to execute the proper instruments to accomplish any necessary loans in connection therewith."

Blank ballots were distributed with instructions to write "yes" or "no" on the ballot. The result of the vote was 92 voting yes, 69 voting no, and two ballots that were blank. The property was purchased.

The finance report presented to the congregation at the annual meeting on October 29, 1972, shows that the congregation ended their fiscal year in the black, but that they were $6,000 behind on the synod apportionment. Since the synod fiscal year ended December 31, there were three months left in which to meet this commitment.

Hospitality and Friendship

As Pastor Almquist became acquainted with the congregation, he felt that it was important for the people in the congregation to get better acquainted with each other. During the summer of 1970, soon after his arrival, a fellowship hour was started between services on Sunday mornings, which provided an opportunity to have friendly conversation over a cup of coffee. Sunday potluck dinners were held often. Lenten luncheons were held on Wednesdays during Lent. There was a

1972

women's banquet in the spring and a men's banquet in the fall, sponsored by the LCW.

Hospitality involves more than eating events, and in 1972 the greeter program was started under the direction of Don Bungum. This Sunday morning welcome to Chisago Lake Lutheran Church was greatly appreciated by both members and visitors and has continued to be a part of the congregation's worship service.

A clothing bank was started offering used clothing to needy members of the community through the Chisago County Welfare Department. The Bloom House was used for this purpose and an LCW circle was in charge. This was a forerunner of the Family Resource Center.

On August 1, 1971, a picnic and carnival was held on the parsonage lawn. This event was reported to *The Lutheran* magazine by Mildred Tengbom and featured in an issue. The picnic became an annual event and provided fun and entertainment for all ages. In 1972, all were encouraged to dress in "gay nineties" fashions. Some found garments packed in trunks since the "gay nineties" era. Others sewed new dresses from "gay nineties" patterns.

1972

Picnic on the parsonage lawn

The Thanksgiving Eve "pie-fests" started in 1972. Having pie and coffee after the Thanksgiving Eve worship has become a tradition at Chisago Lake.

In September 1972, Michael Wittkamper joined the staff as an intern pastor when Ed Long and his wife Suzann returned to the seminary. Michael and his wife Eldrie resided in the Moon house and Eldrie had a teaching position in the local school district.

Sweden's Princess Christina
Comes to Chisago Lake

A special event for the Chisago Lake Area was the visit of some Swedish dignitaries in October 1972. On October 25, Sweden's Princess Christina visited the community and was welcomed by about 200 people at Chisago Lake Lutheran Church. Traveling with her were Swedish Ambassador Hubert de Besche and his wife and Mr. and Mrs. Kurt Granstedt, a representative of the Swedish Foreign Ministry. Gifts were exchanged and Princess Christina was presented with a silver key chain and a key to

Princess Christina

the church from the congregation, indicating that she was always welcome. Violet Almquist hosted a tea in the parsonage to honor these dignitaries.

1972

Special Fund Appeals

In the fall of 1972, Mr. Lawrence Quanbeck was asked to come and assist the congregation in a building fund and current budget appeal. He used his expertise in organization to facilitate an every member visit. The result of this appeal indicated that more than $130,000 was pledged to the building fund over a three year period and there was an increase of $8,947 pledged for the general fund for the coming year. With this successful appeal, it was possible for the building committee to proceed with hiring an architect to design an education building addition for the church and also enabled the congregation to better meet its benevolence responsibilities. Thanks be to God! Subsequently the building committee contracted with the architectural firm of Bergstedt, Wahlberg, Bergquist, Rohkohl and Peeps of Stillwater, Minnesota.

Also in the fall of 1972, Lutheran Social Service conducted a capital funds appeal. The congregation accepted the goal of $7,616 as its contribution to this appeal. Each family was encouraged to give a minimum of $1.00 each month for 18 months to reach this goal.

Pastoral Concerns

Pastor Almquist viewed himself as a "hospitality pastor." He was very much interested in building relationships between his parishioners. He preached a "social gospel" emphasizing an individual's living out his faith in caring for others. This is the horizontal Christian relationship within the church family.

However, he was equally concerned for each individual's relationship and commitment to Jesus Christ—the vertical spiritual relationship. He was concerned for those members who neglected to attend worship services and to partake of the Eucharist. In his annual report given in October 1973, he said: "I plead with you, for the sake of your souls, re-dedicate yourselves anew to the program of Christ and His Kingdom!"

1973

He asked for help to get small group Bible studies started in the congregation. Gaylord Swenson volunteered his help.

For spiritual nourishment and enrichment Dr. David Tiede of Luther Seminary led a series of Bible studies on four consecutive Sunday evenings in April 1972. Pastor A. B. Walfrid conducted a Bible Teaching Mission February 17 to 19, 1974. Dr. Hagen Staack, professor and chairman of the department of religion at Muhlenberg College, Allentown, Pennsylvania presented a series of biblical lectures April 27 to 30, 1974, and again during Holy Week, March 24 to 26, 1975.

"Key '73"

This "Key '73" was an interdenominational, international effort to confront every person on the North American continent with the claims of Jesus Christ upon him. More than 100 religious groups and organi-

zations in the United States and Canada participated. National publicity was aired on television. Every Christian was called upon to witness
and to become involved in bringing the claims of Christ to the unwon.
Chisago Lake joined with other churches in the community in this
effort. A first step in preparation for sharing the gospel with others was
for all members of the congregation to spend time each day in reading
the Bible. To assist families in getting started, the American Bible
Society "Daily Bible Reading Plan" was given to all members.

On Sunday, March 11, a county-wide visit to every home took
place. The purpose of this event was to determine the religious affilia-
tion of every home in Chisago County and to leave with each family a
copy of the Gospel of Luke and the book of Acts. Chisago Lake
Lutheran Church was assigned the Shafer and Franconia area.
Information gathered was shared with a county committee, and names
referred to Chisago Lake were followed up on by the pastor and the
evangelism committee.

1973

Special Congregational Meetings

Two special meetings of the congregation were called in 1973.
On Sunday, March 25, a meeting was called to vote on the following
resolution:

> That we instruct the Decorating Committee to proceed with the
> installation of new pew seats." This resolution passed almost
> unanimously. The new pew seats were installed before the end of
> the year.

On August 22, a meeting was called at 8:00 P.M. to vote on two
resolutions concerning the building project. The resolutions were:

> BE IT RESOLVED that the preliminary plans for a parish edu-
> cation, administration and fellowship building, as submitted by
> the consultants Bergstedt, Wahlberg, Bergquist and Rohkohl,
> Architects, be approved in concept; and that the Building

Committee be allowed to make whatever minor changes are required to complete the project;

AND BE IT FURTHER RESOLVED that the Building Committee be authorized to permit the consultants to proceed with working drawings and receive bids."

There were 159 votes cast with 105 voting yes, 50 voting no, and 4 blank ballots.

The second resolution read:

WHEREAS it is deemed necessary and desirable to construct new facilities to provide for the parish education, fellowship and administrative needs of the congregation, and

WHEREAS the preliminary plans and design indicate an estimated cost of $445, 000.00 for new construction, remodeling, and site development, and $45,000.00 for consultants' fees and contingencies,

BE IT RESOLVED that the Church council in concert with the Building Committee be authorized to construct and equip a new parish education building.

1973

There were 158 votes cast with 105 voting yes, 50 voting no, and 3 abstaining.

It was announced that the building fund had $70,000 and that a capital funds appeal would begin immediately.

In retrospect, it would seem that 159 persons attending this important decision-making meeting for the congregation and only 105 of them voting affirmative was evidence of a great deal of apathy among the members. It certainly did not show an enthusiastic support for the building committee's many months of work and planning or for the Church Council. However, Pastor Almquist in his annual report looked forward to the 1973–74 year as a "year of excitement, hope and joy!"

Special Music Events

Three special concerts were held at Chisago Lake Church in 1973. On Palm Sunday evening, the choirs of the three local Lutheran Churches, Trinity, Zion, and Chisago Lake, presented *The Seven Last Words of Christ*, a sacred cantata by Theodore Dubois. Hollis Johnson directed the choirs and Kathleen DeBolt was the organist. Soloists were Dorothy Alshouse, soprano; David Hagar, tenor: and Steven Newton, baritone. The concert was well attended and was an inspirational beginning for Holy Week.

On May 15, the Chisago Lake Churchmen sponsored a concert by the Madrigal Singers from Golden Valley Lutheran College in Minneapolis.

On June 17, a concert was given by Mr. and Mrs. Allan Sjostrom and their seven children from Anasett, Vasterbotten, Sweden. The Sjostroms made their home on a small farm just 125 miles south of the Arctic Circle. Mr. Sjostrom was a public school music teacher. The family stayed in homes of members.

1973

There was also a change in the music staff when Mr. James Iverson resigned as music director effective August 31, 1973. Mr Iverson had served in this capacity for seven years. Miss Jeannine Dahl joined the staff as the new choir director. She was an elementary music teacher for the Chisago Lakes School District and a graduate of Augsburg College. Miss Dahl served in this position for two years. Mr. Iverson assumed the duties of Sunday school superintendent in the fall of 1974 when Myron Johnson resigned from that position.

Another special event was the December 13 Lucia Festival. This was the first year that this event was observed in our community and was under the direction of Mrs. Helen Fosdick. The festival was held in the evening and began with a potluck supper sponsored by the LCW. The climax of the evening was the crowning of the Lucia Queen. Since 1973, there has been a Lucia Day celebration for the community, not always held at the church. After several years, the

December 13 Lucia Festival

festivities were changed to the morning, which is the traditional time for Lucia to appear. Helen Fosdick continued to direct the festival each year until she moved away in 1999. At that time other members of the Swedish Club assumed this responsibility.

1974

"Celebration 120"

Several special events were planned for 1974, the 120th anniversary of the congregation. The first of these was a Bible study on the Gospel of Luke led by Pastor A. B. Walfrid of Scandia February 17 to 19. Sessions were held on Sunday morning and Sunday, Monday, and Tuesday evenings. This was an overview of the Gospel held early in the year to develop a better understanding of the Gospel texts for the year, most of which were taken from Luke.

On Sunday, March 10, Dr. Charles A. Puls was the pulpit guest. Dr. Puls represented the Lutheran Orient Mission and spoke about the work being carried on in Kurdistan. The mission began work there in 1910 and sponsored an evangelistic church in Arbil, Iraq, and a Christian hospital in Ghorveh, Iran. A congregational potluck was served after which Dr. Puls showed slides of the work among the Kurds.

A mother-daughter banquet was held on May 9 sponsored by the LCW. The theme was "120 Years with Ladies Aid and Lutheran Church Women."

May 12, the exact day of the anniversary, fell on a Sunday. Dr. Melvin Hammarberg, president of the Minnesota Synod of the LCA, was the guest preacher.

May 19 to 21, Dr. Hagen Staack conducted a series of Bible studies on understanding the Old Testament. Trinity Church in Lindstrom, and Zion Church in Chisago City also participated in these studies.

The Swedish National Chorus of Varmland, Sweden, presented a concert on

Dr. Hagen Staack

June 20. This group consisted of a men's chorus and a women's chorus, each singing separately. The groups, with about 100 voices, combined for the finale.

1974

Sunday, July 21, was "Pioneer Day." Pastors J. Walton Kempe, Gilbert Monson, and W. Burdette Benson and their families were special guests. Pastor Kempe was the pulpit guest for the day. A congregational potluck picnic was held followed by games and recreation for all.

On July 28, Chisago Lake Lutheran Church was honored by the presence of Archbishop Olaf Sundby of the Church of Sweden. The Archbishop brought a greeting at the 10:30 service. A reception was held in his honor after the service so that he could meet and visit with members of the congregation.

The annual Swedish communion service was held on Friday, October 4, with Dr. Bernhard Erling of Gustavus Adolphus College conducting the service.

The annual lutefisk supper was held on November 14.

Pastor Anders Hanson of Hong Kong was the guest preacher on Sunday, December 1. He had served as a missionary to China for four

Pr. Anders Hanson

years before the Communist take-over. He then moved to Taiwan for 10 years, and then to Hong Kong.

Pastor Hanson served as the director of a Lutheran publishing house involved in translation of literature into the Chinese language. He later served as an associate to the president of the Lutheran Seminary in Hong Kong. This was part of the synod's emphasis on world missions.

Building Program Delayed

As the congregation celebrated its past, things were not going as well in its plans for the future. Bids were received for the building addition in March 1974. The bids exceeded the budgetary requirement and were rejected by the building committee. The architect was asked to redesign the building so that it would come within budget guidelines.

1974

The new plan was ready in May and the congregation accepted the plan and approved the budget. The bids for the redesigned building were received in July and met the budget guidelines.

A special meeting of the congregation was called for 11:30 A.M. on Sunday, August 4, 1974, for the purpose of authorizing and empowering the Board of Trustees of the congregation to borrow not more than $400,000 from First Federal Savings and Loan Association of Minneapolis, payable over a period of not more than 25 years in equal monthly installments which shall include interest at a rate of $8\frac{1}{2}$ percent per annum. The results were 166 voting yes and 105 voting no. Although the majority voted in favor, the proposal failed because First Federal Savings & Loan Association had asked that the program be approved by a two-thirds vote. The building committee understood this to mean that an alternate plan of financing would need to be found.

A special congregational meeting was called for September 26 at 8:00 P.M. to vote on a resolution for an alternate method of financing the building program. The resolution was:

> To consider the issuance of bonds to provide funds for the construction of the educational, administrative, and fellowship addition to our church.

This proposal passed and the committee began to investigate the legal steps that needed to be taken in order to raise funds by selling bonds to members of the congregation.

The prospectus prepared for the sale of bonds to the congregation read in part:

> That Church bonds in an aggregate amount not exceed THREE HUNDRED SEVENTY FIVE THOUSAND DOLLARS ($375,000) be issued in denominations of $100, $250, $500, and $1,000 and larger if requested, with the aggregate of each denomination to be determined by bond subscriptions of record when such determination is made; bearing interest at the rate of EIGHT PERCENT (8%) per annum payable semi-annually.

1974

Bonds were dated April 1, 1975. A schedule of redemption was set up to begin October 1, 1976, with final payment to be made April 1, 1991. According to the financial report covering the fiscal year October 1, 1975, to September 30, 1976, a total of $170,400 was raised by selling these bonds.

Staff Changes

In August of 1973, Mike and Eldri Wittkamper completed their year of internship. A decision was made to not hire another intern, but to join with Zion Lutheran Church in Chisago City and Trinity Lutheran Church in Lindstrom to hire a full-time youth director for the three congregations. Mr. David Benson accepted a call to this position and began his work in the fall of 1974. Mr. Benson was a graduate of Gustavus Adolphus College. He moved to the community with his wife and two children.

In October of 1973, the church custodian, Harold Dombrock, suffered a fall at his home which resulted in multiple fractures to his body. Steve Grossmann was hired as interim custodian in hopes that Mr. Dombrock would be able to return to his position. However, as time went on it became evident that he would not be able to continue his work. In December of 1974, Mr. Robert Allen was hired as the custodian. He continued in this position for several years.

Robert Allen

In May of 1974, Barbara Wikelius was hired as an assistant secretary for Alma Hasselquist. When Alma retired at the end of 1974 after 20 years of faithful work, Barbara stepped into her position.

1974

New Fellowship Groups

In November of 1974 a couples club was started. This group was organized to offer opportunities for members to get to know each other better through social events. Their first event was attending the Lakeshore Players Theater in White Bear Lake. This was followed by a bowling event and then a progressive dinner.

On Wednesday, December 4, 1974, all retirees were invited to a noon dinner hosted by the Mary Circle. Purpose of this get together was to make plans for a senior citizen group. A second meeting was a potluck luncheon held on the first Wednesday of February 1975. This organization was named "O.K.'s" an acronym for "Older Kids" and has continued to exist with some changes.

Love Compels Action Hunger Appeal

In January of 1975, the Lutheran Church in America launched a World Hunger Appeal in response to the dire needs of countries in Africa and Asia where there was extensive famine due to drought and crop failure. Chisago Lake Lutheran Church participated in this appeal, which was included in an appeal called Love Compels Action (LCA). Members were urged to skip one meal each week and give the money that would have been spent on that meal to the Hunger Appeal. Each family was given an LCA Hunger Bank, which was to be placed on the table to remind us to give and to pray for those suffering from famine, malnutrition, and starvation. February 2 was designated as World Hunger Sunday. Ever since then, the first Sunday of each month has been World Hunger Sunday at Chisago Lake Lutheran Church when members are encouraged to give an extra offering to help feed the hungry in our world.

1975 — Building Construction Begins

Since the sale of bonds did not raise enough funds for the construction of proposed building, a special meeting of the congregation was called for Sunday, August 11, 1975, at 8:00 P.M. for the purpose of voting on

Groundbreaking September 21, 1975

a resolution to borrow the balance of funds needed. The resolution was to mortgage the church property and to obtain a loan from Lutheran Brotherhood Insurance Company of Minneapolis, Minnesota, not to exceed the sum of $175,000 for twenty (20) years at eight (8%) percent interest. This resolution passed making it possible to go forward with construction plans. The loan was not finalized until May 1978 at which time the amount needed was $110,000. Payments would be $921 per month beginning July 1, 1978.

Bids were opened on September 16, 1975. Bidders receiving construction contracts were: general contractor, George Olsen Construction, Stillwater; mechanical contractor, M. M. Peaslee, Stillwater; and electrical contractor, Maurie St. Martin, White Bear Lake.

1975

The groundbreaking service was held on Sunday, September 21, 1975, after the morning worship service. This was a special event with

Groundbreaking September 21, 1975

James Froberg bringing his team of Belgian horses and bucket scoop to move the first soil. He was assisted by Chester Carlson. Work began soon after the groundbreaking and by the end of October footings were ready to be poured.

Part-Time Pastoral Assistant Hired

The congregation had long recognized the need for an assistant for the pastor. Interns who served for one year each filled this need for a number of years. In 1975, the opportunity arose to hire a part-time assistant by the name of Melvin Schroeder. Mel had been a student at the

LCMS seminary in Saint Louis, Missouri, and was one of those affected by the division that occurred at the seminary at that time. He chose to continue his theological education at Luther Northwestern Seminary in Saint Paul. He worked part-time at the Hazelden Foundation and part-time at Chisago Lake Lutheran Church. Mel's primary responsibility at Chisago Lake was a ministry to young adults. An active group of young single adults was formed.

The Parish Enrichment Program (PEP) was started under the leadership of Pastor John Clawson to minister to the educational needs of the congregation, especially to young married couples. A Faith and Life Enrichment weekend program was developed for post-confirmation young Christians. Mel also assisted with confirmation and adult Bible classes, home visits, hospital visits, and Sunday worship services. He continued his ministry at Chisago Lake Lutheran Church until the end of November 1976, when he entered chaplaincy training at Hazelden.

1976

Bicentennial Celebration

The United States celebrated its Bicentennial in 1976. Everywhere in our country there were celebrations for this event. There were parades, flags flew, and school children put on Bicentennial programs.

His Majesty Carl XVI Gustav, King of Sweden, visited Minneapolis for the American Swedish Bicentennial Festival at the Minneapolis Auditorium on April 10. Rolf Bjorling, an internationally famed Swedish singer, participated in the program. Several from the Chisago Lake area attended the festival.

It was on June 1, 1976, that the Kichi-Saga Chapter of the American Swedish Institute was organized. Among the members of Chisago Lake who were charter members of this organization and served on the Board of Directors were Bertha Andersen, Myrtle Berglund, Helen Fosdick, Arnold H. Johnson, Carroll Westlund, and

Vincent Videen. Pastor Almquist took the presidency for one year to "get things started."

At Chisago Lake Lutheran Church, we had our own special celebrations. Most important of these was the laying of the cornerstone for the new education building on Sunday, July 4, 1976. A Festival Service of Celebration was held at 10:30 A.M. led by Pastor Almquist. The choir provided special music. The service was followed by a fellowship hour and refreshments.

During the year, the congregation also had a special bicentennial thank offering with a goal of $10,000. The offering totaled $10,400, and so exceeded its goal. This money was used to help meet the budget, provide for some non-budgeted items, and to help some families who were in need because of health difficulties.

During the month of July several events were scheduled to celebrate the Bicentennial and also to remember our Swedish heritage. Pioneers who settled at Chisago Lake began worship services, which led to the organization of the congregation. On Wednesday, July 14, a group of Swedish singers and folk dancers from Vastergotland presented a program. On Sunday, July 18, a Swedish service was held at 9:00 A.M. with Dr. Rudolph Burke of Willmar preaching. This service was a community event in connection with the Karl Oskar celebration. On Sunday, July 25, there was an organ and song concert by Ingegard Bjorklund, a music director from Växjö, Sweden. At the worship services on July 18 and July 25, the old Augustana liturgy was used.

1976

Picnic flyer

On Sunday, August 1, 1976, a bicentennial potluck picnic was held after the morning worship services on the east lawn of the parsonage. Members were encouraged to wear a costume depicting the

The Interstate Band directed by Duane Arnold

bicentennial theme. The Interstate Band, directed by Duane Arnold, furnished appropriate music and there were games and races for all ages. There was a fish pond for the children, and a cake walk for their parents.

The climax of the year was Reformation Sunday, October 31, 1976, when newly elected Synod Bishop, Dr. Herbert Chilstrom, came to preach at the 10:30 service and participate in the dedication of the new education building. Open house was held in the afternoon with Vespers at 4:00 P.M.

1976

Pr. H. Chilstrom, 1983

Not all activities of the year were involved with the bicentennial and the building construction. During the early part of the year, home Bible studies continued with four groups involved and an average attendance of about 40. The course studied was "Courage for Today—Hope for Tomorrow," a study of the book of Revelation.

During the Lenten season, the Wednesday noonday luncheons continued with meditations centering on the theme "Portraits of a Savior." Services were also held on Thursday evenings at 6:30 and included a light supper for commuters and families.

On April 4, 1976, John Hult, missionary to Liberia, was guest preacher. On Palm Sunday, April 11, the choir presented the cantata

Adoramus Te by James Clokey, under the direction of Kathleen DeBolt at the morning worship service. Soloists were Lois Barott, Barbara Wikelius, Marjorie Hawkinson, and James Iverson. In the evening, the Lutheran Brotherhood Singers presented a concert.

In June, Pastor and Mrs. David Lindell, missionaries to India, visited vacation Bible school. The children raised $150 to send to India through the World Hunger Appeal to be used to dig a well.

The merger of Luther and Northwestern Seminaries in Saint Paul also occurred in 1976. Preceding this merger, Northwestern Seminary held a funding appeal known as L.I.T.E., "Let's Invest in Theological Education," in which Chisago Lake took part.

Mrs. Marjorie Pohlmann had contracted with the congregation to make woven paraments for the altar. The designs for these paraments were approved and they would be ordered as money became available to pay for them. Many memorial gifts were given for this purpose.

Mrs. Pohlmann was also asked to help with the design and selection of furnishings for the new parish building. A generous donation was given to be used for a tapestry depicting the history of the congregation. This tapestry would hang in the room that came to be known as the Green Room. Mrs. Pohlmann agreed to design and weave this tapestry. She chose the highlights for the tapestry from reading the history of the congregation and ordered the yarn for the tapestry from Sweden. Thousands of people have come to view this tapestry over the years, many of them visiting from Sweden. The tapestry was completed and dedicated in 1979 with Mrs. Pohlmann and the donor participating in the dedication.

1976

Special Congregational Meeting

On Monday evening, August 9, 1976, a special congregational meeting was held to discuss and vote on a resolution to call an assistant pastor or a pastoral assistant. Only 56 persons attended this meeting. The resolution noted that 26 percent of the congregation was between the ages of 16 and 30 and that many of these people were not being reached by the ministry of the congregation. The discussion stressed that there would need to be a substantial increase in giving to cover the salary of another staff person. Several members present stated their belief that "if we proceed in faith, we will be able to meet the additional costs." It was also stated that "a dollar value cannot be placed on the spiritual blessings that will be received from this added ministry."

The resolution read:

> BE IT RESOLVED that Chisago Lake Ev. Lutheran Church call an Assistant Pastor or a Pastoral Assistant to assist in the following areas of responsibility: Junior and Senior High youth, Young Adult ministry, Confirmation instruction and in the pastoral ministry of the congregation.

The resolution passed with 46 voting yes and 9 voting no.

1976   Dr. Herbert Chilstrom, president of the synod, would be contacted and informed of the action taken at this meeting and the procedure for calling this person would begin.

Historical Park Proposed

When the Swenson-Peterson property was purchased in 1972, various uses were proposed for it. Since it was connected to the church property on two sides and bordered by Pioneer Lake on one side, it seemed logical for it to become a part of the church grounds. It would lend itself well to some low density senior housing. It could become a historical park with the house used as a museum. Or it might be used in the future as the site for a new parsonage.

The historical committee took the responsibility of brushing and cleaning the grounds around the house and painting the house on the outside. There was planning for making this area into a Historical Park. However, with funds needed for the new building and several maintenance projects in the church, including the windows, this was not an opportune time to be contributing to this park. At the annual meeting in 1975, the decision was made to create and ad hoc committee to look into the possibility of other groups in the area working with us to establish at this site a heritage Swedish Historical Park.

At the annual meeting in October 1976, the ad hoc committee reported back and offered the following resolution:

> That a separate Historical Park non-profit corporation be formed by interested members of the congregation and interested citizens of the Chisago Lakes community, and that the said corporation be instructed to procure funds so that this park can become a reality in the near future; and be it further resolved that the said corporation seek alternate means of financing by January 1, 1977, so that the monies now obligated for this property may be used by the congregation for their intended purposes.

This resolution was adopted. And, although this resolution was adopted, no corporation was formed. The property continued to be a financial burden for the congregation.

1977

At the next annual meeting, in October 1977, another resolution concerning this property was brought before the congregation. The resolution read as follows:

> Whereas: The Swenson-Peterson property is still held by the congregation and, whereas: it has been and continues to be a financial burden, we still owe $12,000.00, plus interest, we have had to sign notes at the bank and make additional interest payments, because of lack of funds to meet payments and, whereas: various attempts have been made to dispose of or change the use of this property, to historical park, etc.

> Therefore: be it resolved the matter of the Swenson-Peterson property be brought before the congregation for disposition.

The resolution was amended to read: "disposition at the current market value." The amended resolution was adopted.

A bid of $43,050 was received for the property, and on March 19, 1978, a special congregational meeting was held to vote on whether or not this property could be sold at this price. A total of 169 ballots were cast with 167 in favor of the sale.

On August 13, 1978, another special congregational meeting was held to vote on a resolution to sell the property to James D. Waddington for the sum of $43,050 as had been previously approved. The resolution to sell was unanimously adopted with 86 ballots cast.

After the closing costs had been paid on the sale of the property, the balance remaining from the sale was $42,367.48. These monies were disbursed in this way:

Benevolence:

Lutheran Social Services	$1,250.00
Northwestern Lutheran Seminary	1,250.00
A local community project to be determined later	1,000.00

1977

Building:

Repay loan to building fund	12,500.00
Window repair	7,623.00
Replenish funds which had been used for operating expenses	4,113.24
Elevator fund	14,631.24

Fun memories from the years that the Swenson-Peterson property belonged to the congregation include the Halloween parties that were held in the house. The parties were sponsored by the church youth and their advisors and were attended by children from throughout the community. A good time was had by all!

Building Improvements

With the building construction completed, there were still numerous improvements under way. The undercroft of the church needed to be remodeled to better accommodate Sunday school classes. Furnishings needed to be purchased for all the rooms in the new building. The church grounds needed landscaping and a parking lot prepared on the east side of the new building. Soffits were installed on the eaves of the church, and gutters and downspouts placed on the church to divert water away from the buildings. The elevator was not part of the construction cost, so a fund was started to pay for the elevator installation.

The church windows were to be repaired. These were examined and those in poorest condition were given top priority. The one that needed attention first was the large one on the south end of the church building. Since this large and beautiful window was not visible from the inside of the church, it was decided that it should be lighted from the inside so that it would be more visible from the outside. The congregation contracted with Continental Art Glass Company of Fridley for the repair work. Their bid was $10,688 and included re-leading, replacing of missing glass, repair of sills and frames, and new storm windows. The lighting of the window was not included and was done by members of the church. The top priority windows were repaired and all windows received new unbreakable storm windows. Since the stained-glass windows in the church were no longer available, it was necessary to protect them from storm damage or vandalism.

1977

At the annual meeting in October 1976, a great deal of discussion was held on the proposed budget. The result was that the budget was not approved. A special congregational meeting was called for January 26, 1977, to again vote on a budget. By this time the stewardship program had been completed and there was a firm commitment of income on which to build a budget. The budget was approved.

Opportunities for Growth in Faith and Fellowship

The work on the building did not diminish the opportunities for spiritual growth. The year of 1977 began with a series of Sunday night Bible studies on the books of Luke and Acts. These meetings were held in the church complex under the leadership of Pastor Almquist.

PASTOR JAMES ALMQUIST

+ A pre-Lenten Every Member Visit was planned with one-third of the members of the congregation making home visits to the other two-thirds. Visits were also made to the unchurched of the community.

+ The Lenten luncheons were continued on Wednesdays during Lent with the meditations based on the Lord's Prayer. Thursday evening supper meetings were held for commuters and families.

+ A Parish Enrichment Program (P.E.P.) for adults was begun during the Sunday school hour. Speakers were brought in from outside the congregation to conduct these sessions.

+ The LCW continued to provide a clothing bank for the needy and sewed blankets for Lutheran World Relief.

+ The Gustavus Adolphus College Choir presented a concert in the sanctuary in January.

1977

+ A mother daughter tea was held in the fellowship hall in May.

+ Bible school was held for 30 three- and four-year-old children May 9 to 13. The vacation Bible school for children from kindergarten to grade 6 was held June 6 to 10 with 84 in attendance.

+ Children from grades 5 through 12 were encouraged to attend Luther Point Bible Camp. A week of Bible camp cost $35 in 1977. A "Pennies for Camp" project was started with everyone in the congregation asked to save their pennies and bring them to church. Monies collected in this way were used to help with the cost of going to camp.

There had been several requests for a worship service during the Sunday school hour. Beginning on March 6, 1977, a third service was added at 9:15. This continued for several months but did not prove to be successful.

Staff Changes

Pastor Robert Knutson was hired as a part-time visitation pastor effective June 1, 1977. Pastor Knutson had been serving as the Protestant chaplain at the Veterans' Hospital in Fargo, North Dakota, but due to health problems he needed to change his work load. He purchased the photography studio near Forest Lake, formerly owned by George Johnson, and began work as a photographer. However, he did not want to demit from the ministry and was available to serve in a part-time position. This fit in well with the needs at Chisago Lake.

Pr. R. Knutson, 1987

Barbara Wikelius resigned from her work as church secretary effective May 31, 1977. Joyce Peterson filled in as interim secretary for two months until Mrs. Maxine Valley was hired for the secretary position effective August 1.

1977

Jim and Jane Iverson had served as Sunday school superintendents for three years. They resigned at the end of the school year. Their leadership duties were taken over by three people who divided the work. Judy Nelson assumed leadership for the primary department, Shirley Ganter led the intermediate department, and Carolyn Brottem, chairperson for the Christian education committee, was in charge of the confirmation department.

Eunice Anderson resigned from the treasurer's position after having served for 12 years. These duties were assumed by Richard Ruffcorn.

Jeannine Dahl, a music teacher at the Chisago Lakes Intermediate School, served as junior choir director from 1975 to 1977. Carol Johnson directed this choir next. When Carol and her family moved to Alaska, Gail Gaustad, who was hired by the school district to replace Jeannine Dahl, became junior choir director. She also started the Sunbeam choir for children from kindergarten to grade 2.

Mrs. Kathleen DeBolt served Chisago Lake Lutheran Church as organist well and faithfully for more than 10 years. When she resigned in March 1978, Rita Knutson, Pastor Knutson's wife, became the organist. The congregation was blessed in having such talented and faithful people on the music staff.

On October 15, 1977, a bazaar was held at the church sponsored by the LCW. Monies raised at this event were dispersed as follows: $1,987 for furnishings for the Green Room; $500 for the new library; and $600 for mission projects. Also in the fall of 1977 pictures were taken for a new pictorial directory of the congregation.

A lutefisk dinner was served on November 18, 1977. This was an "all you can eat" meal with tickets selling at $3.50 for adults and $2.00 for children 12 and under.

Records show that the total membership as of October 1, 1977, was 1,117, with 888 of these being confirmed members.

1977   Strength for Mission

Strength for Mission was an LCA outreach program to reach more people with the gospel of Jesus Christ. The LCA goal was to raise at least $25 million for this program. The outreach program was a three-prong approach: 1) Increased evangelism and stewardship within the local congregation; 2) Establishing new congregations throughout North America; 3) Joining with Christians around the world to spread the gospel.

To begin the program at Chisago Lake, Dr. Duaine Vierow, Minnesota Synod mission coordinator, was the guest preacher on March 12. The month of April was set aside as a time to study and learn about the program and to pray for its success. During the month of May there was an Every Member Visit to secure three-year pledges for the program. When all pledges were in, more than $40,000 had been pledged. This program ended on August 31, 1980.

During the year there was an emphasis on missions around the world. One interesting event was hosting the Youthsingers, a group of 45 young people from Guyana, South America. They represented the 230-year-old Lutheran Church in Guyana. This concert gave the community an opportunity to experience how the Lutheran tradition of good music has been carried on in a culture with dominant cultural patterns of Africa and India. To accompany their voices they brought congo drums, guitars, maracas, tambourines, and other instruments.

During the summer of 1978, a lay ministry program was begun. The purpose of this program was to bring together clusters of members to become a "church within a church." The lay ministers would visit the members in their cluster (zone) to become better acquainted and perhaps plan a social event such as a picnic. They would call on new members in their zone, and visit any that might be ill or have special needs. They would then notify the church office if someone was hospitalized or needed pastoral care.

To begin the program, seven couples were trained as lay ministers. Each was assigned 10 to 12 families in their zone. The program was a good one, but due to lack of volunteers to assume lay leadership roles, the entire congregation was never involved.

1978

Gordon Grimm

Pastor Gordon Grimm was a supervisor of clinical pastoral education at Hazelden for many years. He and his family were active members of the congregation. Before an assistant pastor was called, Gordy often helped Pastor Almquist with communion and filled in for him when he was gone. He was a "pastor's pastor" and helped many area clergy.

Parish Life and Ministry Development

In addition to the Strength for Mission program, the LCA provided congregations with materials for a Parish Life and Ministry

Development program (PLMD). This program was begun at Chisago Lake in December of 1977 with Synod consultant Jan Benson training a team of seven persons as leaders. Members of this team were Pastor Almquist, Susan Clawson, Richard Genung, Rita Knutson, Barbara Reichstadt, Marjorie Schrader, and Orval Starr. This committee prepared two questionnaires that were distributed to members of the congregation dealing with the hopes, concerns, and needs of the members. This survey was to assist the pastor and the committee in planning worship and spiritual growth opportunities to better meet the needs of the congregation.

One outcome of this survey was a Saturday evening outdoor worship service during the months of July and August. Services were held on the west lawn of the church at 7:00 P.M. These were informal services centered on the preaching of the Word and singing. The services were short and inspirational but few attended.

1978

September 17 to 20, 1978, a Bible teaching mission was conducted by Dr. A.B. Walfrid. The theme of this series of lessons was "Adventures in Building the Kingdom of God." Each evening of the mission a group gathered before the session to pray with Dr. Walfrid. This group found the time together for prayer such a meaningful spiritual experience that they continued to meet weekly for prayer for several years. The group became known as "Care, Share, and Prayer."

Later in the year, October 31 to November 21, Dr. Elof Nelson led a class on "Partners in Parenting" for parents who were interested in improving their parenting skills. Dr. Nelson was an associate professor of behavioral medicine at the University of Minnesota Medical School, Department of Family Practice and Community Health, and a member at Chisago Lake Lutheran Church. These four sessions were entitled: Understanding Ourselves First, How To Raise Healthy Children, Communication and the Family System, and You Can Make It Easier and Live Better.

Also in November, the Chisago Lake Good News Singers presented the Christian musical *He Lived a Good Life* by Richard Wilson. This was an inspiring presentation under the direction of Rita Knutson and the new choir director, Mark Johnson, who had joined the staff in the fall. He was on the music staff at Chisago Lakes Middle School and he and his family were members of Chisago Lake Lutheran Church.

New Hymnal

In preparation for the use of the new *Lutheran Book of Worship*, the 9:15 A.M. Parish Enrichment Program provided a series of four sessions during the month of November to become familiar with the new liturgy. Dr. Leland Sateren, a member of the Inter Lutheran Commission that developed the *LBW*, was the first guest speaker. He spoke about the background of the hymnal, emphasizing the music.

At the second session, a filmstrip, "With Heart and Hands and Voices," was shown giving an overview of the *LBW*. This was followed by a discussion of how this new resource could be used to bring about a renewal in worship.

1979

The Reverend Victor Gabeuer, professor of worship at Concordia College, Saint Paul, was the second guest speaker. He served on the liturgical text sub-committee for the *LBW*, and was well qualified to explain the various aspects of the new liturgy.

The fourth session was a practice session to become familiar with the musical settings of the liturgy.

With this preparation, *Lutheran Book of Worship* was dedicated and used for the first time on the first Sunday of Advent, December 3, 1978. This recalled the first time the people of Chisago Lake gathered indoors for worship, which was on the first Sunday of Advent in 1851.

125th Anniversary, 1979

The theme "A Jubilee of Thanksgiving" was chosen for the observation of the 125th anniversary of the congregation in 1979. A booklet was published with information about the congregation, its history, its people, and its faith. It was a time to rejoice over the completion of the new building and of rededication to the church and to Jesus Christ the head of the Church. The rededication statement follows:

> With the assistance of the Holy Spirit, we now also rededicate ourselves in love, loyalty and faithful service to God and His Church. We pray that our relation to Him may be an inspiration to others to come and share with us the joys and blessings of worshiping and working for Jesus, who died that we might live.

Irene Carlson, Melvin Dahlquist, Myron Johnson, Harold Tangren, and Barbara Wikelius served on an anniversary committee, which was chaired by Marie Cotch. They planned celebration events throughout the year.

A Kick-Off Banquet was held on February 13, 1979, with Pastor Laurel Lindberg from Mount Olivet Lutheran Church as guest speaker. Pastor Lindberg served as intern at Chisago Lake during 1946. The

1979 banquet was a fund-raiser for the elevator. It was a catered meal with tickets sold at $12.50 each. About $2,000 was raised at this event. A goal of $12,500 had been set as a special thank offering for the year to be used for the elevator, the blacktopping of the parking lot, organ repair, and other equipment including a new amplification system.

A mother daughter banquet was held on May 4, 1979. The program at this event was modeling of wedding dresses depicting the styles as far back as dresses were available and up to the present.

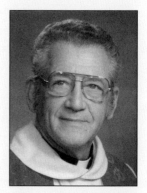

Pr. Laurel Lindberg

On Anniversary Sunday, May 13, 1979, Dr. Edward Lindell, president of Gustavus Adolphus College, was guest preacher. The celebration service was followed by a noon banquet and the dedication of the memorial tapestry in the reception room.

Memorial Tapestry

Section A · 1851–1865

First we see immigration from Sweden through the Midwest and up the Mississippi and St. Croix Rivers. Rural life is depicted—the forests, working the fields. Per Berg's haymow is the site of the congregation's organization in 1854. The first church building is completed in 1856.

Transition · 1860s

The Civil War in the United States of America. Chisago Lake Union Soldiers send gifts of communion ware. The hard times in Sweden encourage continued immigration.

Section B · 1865–1915

The church is the center of the community —an early morning Christmas Day service called *Julotta*, the Swedish summer school, the new brick church building. There is prosperity. In 1888 the church building is struck by lightning and burned. It is replaced the same year. New villages grow up in the area, new congregations in new towns. The railroad is introduced. The beginning of expansion is seen in 1891. The Augustana Synod meeting is held at Center City.

Transition

Now we see the introduction of the telephone, the automobile, and electricity. And then comes World War I.

Section C · 1915 and on

Shown here is increased mobility and expansion. People move to and from the larger cities. There is an expansion of the church facilities. People leave, but the church is still a focus in the community.

Marjorie Pohlman designed and wove this tapestry, which was dedicated at the congregation's 125th anniversary.

Portion of the Memorial Tapestry

Continuing the anniversary events, a confirmation reunion worship service was held on Sunday, June 24, 1979, at 10:30 A.M. At this service, Pastor Charles Anderson, from the Minnesota Synod office was the pulpit guest. He was assisted by Pastor Ralph Larson, a son of the congregation as liturgist, and by lay minister Phil Lindblom of Crystal Falls, Michigan, also a son of the congregation, as lector. Following the worship service, a potluck picnic was held on the parsonage lawn with games and a program and time for renewing friendships with those who returned for the confirmation reunion.

Pr. Charles Anderson

A very special day was Saturday, September 15, 1979, when the Lutheran Church Men of the Minnesota Synod held their annual convention at Chisago Lake. George Nielsen was the LCM president. At the 6:30 P.M. banquet, the Reverend W. Burdette Benson was the speaker and special music was presented by the men from Gibbon. During the afternoon, Mrs. Almquist hosted a tea at the parsonage

Pr. Ralph Larson

for visiting women, and there were bus tours provided for the entire group to Parmly Residence, Hazelden, and other points of interest.

Another son of the congregation, Dr. Emeroy Johnson, former archivist of the Minnesota Synod, honored Chisago Lake Lutheran Church by publishing a paper entitled, "First Swede at Chisago Lake." This paper was the first article to be published by the Archives of Gustavus Adolphus College and the Minnesota Synod of the LCA under the title of "Arkivfynd." The article documented Chisago Lake Church as one of the very first Swedish Lutheran churches in the state.

Dr. Emeroy Johnson

Other anniversary events included a Swedish communion service on October 11, with the Reverend William Hyllengren from Zion Lutheran Church in Anoka conducting the service; a Bible Teaching Mission by the Reverend A. B. Walfrid, October 14 to 17, centered on the theme "The Word of the Lord Came with Power"; a bazaar on October 20; and the annual lutefisk dinner on November 15, 1979.

1979

Staff Changes

In the spring of 1979, the custodian, Bob Allen, resigned to accept a position on the maintenance staff at Hazelden. To replace him, Doug Jurek was hired.

There was also a change in the secretarial position. Gladys Moe was hired to be the Christian education director as well as to care for secretarial duties. This brought Maxine Valley's position to a close after she served for two years. Mrs. Moe had many years of experience in Christian education. Alma Hasselquist assisted in the office part-time with secretarial duties.

Gail Gausted married and resigned her position as children's choir director. Jane Iverson filled this position, but returned to the practice of one choir rather than two. Rita Knutson started a youth choir for the youth in grades 7 through 12.

Pastor Robert Knutson had been hired to be the visitation pastor for the congregation. During the summer of 1979, seeing the need for more work with the youth, Pastor Bob (as he was affectionately known) asked the Church Council if he could have a change in his job description to become the youth pastor. This was granted and he immediately began some new programs for the youth. One of these was "The Order of St. Andrew" group for grades 7 through 12. This group received training in the liturgical traditions of the Lutheran Church including acolyte training.

Other Church Activities

1979

As the congregation added worship services to its schedule, there was considerable discussion as to how often the Sacrament of the Altar should be offered. One schedule tried offering it at one 8:00 A.M. service each month and one 10:30 A.M. service. This proved to be unsatisfactory for those who were not always able to attend one of these two services. On March 4, 1979, a schedule was begun that offered the sacrament at both services on the first and third Sundays of each month. This schedule satisfied most members and has been continued.

It was also decided to try a Saturday evening worship service to be held in the reception room. These services began on May 26 at 5:30 P.M. and continued through the summer.

On Sunday May 20, after the 10:30 A.M. worship service, a special meeting of the congregation was held to accept a bid on the elevator. The bid proposed was from Lagerquist Elevator Co. of Minneapolis for $26,414. This bid was accepted. However, the elevator was not installed until January of 1980. Final cost of the elevator was $27,430.85. It was dedicated on May 18, 1980.

Troop 135 Boy Scouts at Chisago Lake receiving their Pro Deo Et Patri church awards: Mr. & Mrs. Elmer Althaus and Joe; Mr. and Mrs. Gordon Grimm and John; Mr. & Mrs. Gerald Faanes and Brian; Mr. & Mrs. Vernon Lundberg and Scott; Louis Anderson, Scoutmaster; Pr. James Almquist.

The Parish Life and Ministry Development Committee continued to meet and work throughout the year. They did an in-depth study of five areas of parish life, 1) witness, 2) learning, 3) worship, 4) service, and 5) support. When this study was completed, they developed objectives for the program and set priorities. The committee then prepared a report, which was sent to the Division for Parish Services in Philadelphia. They in turn sent to the congregation a custom-designed proposal with a wide range of information and resources to fit our particular needs. This proposal was to assist the congregation in reaching the objectives that had been set as the program was implemented.

1979

A gift of $600 was received for the library from the estate of Emma Johnson. This money was designated for reference books and was used to purchase the fine selection of reference books that have been available for use by the congregation.

The year 1979 was also when members of Chisago Lake became active in the Meals on Wheels program. Marjorie Hawkinson has been the coordinator for this worthwhile program for our congregation.

In 1970, the congregation had changed to a fiscal year from October 1 to September 30, with the annual meeting being held in

October each year. The reason for this change was primarily the weather. Often the annual meeting was held on an evening in January that was extremely cold or snowy. By moving the annual meeting to October, it was anticipated that more people would be able to attend. Attendance did not increase significantly and making financial reports to the Synod at the end of their fiscal year was more difficult. At the annual meeting in October 1979, a resolution was passed to return to a fiscal year that ended on December 31. This resulted in a 15-month fiscal year, which ended on December 31, 1980. Changes were made in stewardship pledges and the yearly budget to reflect this calendar adjustment.

There was also a change in staff when Richard Ruffcorn resigned as treasurer during the summer of 1980, and Carrie Ann Holmquist assumed his duties.

In the early part of 1980, it became evident that 10 hours a week was not sufficient for the work Pastor Knutson was doing for the

1980

Pr. Orville Martin

congregation. After discussing this for several months, a special congregational meeting was called for Sunday, June 1, 1980, to vote on issuing him a call to serve as an assistant pastor half-time. The call was extended, and he was installed on Sunday, September 7, 1980.

At the end of July, however, Pastor Almquist accepted a call to Beaver Lake Lutheran Church in Saint Paul and resigned from his duties at Chisago Lake effective October 1, 1980. This included a month of vacation, so his last day of active ministry was August 31. Therefore, Pastor Knutson assumed most of the pastoral duties after his installation. Pastor Orville Martin was assigned to serve as vice pastor of the congregation during this vacancy.

During his years at Chisago Lake, Pastor James Almquist had also served the wider ministry of the church in several positions. He served on the Board of Social Ministry of the Minnesota Synod from 1972 to 1981 and was also on the executive committee of the board. He also served as an interviewer on the committee on professional leadership for the synod. He was on the board of Margaret S. Parmly Residence in Chisago City from 1972 to 1982 and chairman from 1975 to 1981. He was a member of the Luther Point Bible Camp board for several years. Pastor Almquist was a clergy

Vi & Pr. James Almquist

consultant for the Hazelden Foundation from 1970 to 1980. During that time he also took training in alcoholism counseling.

Pastor Robert Knutson, 1977–1987

1980

Robert Knutson grew up in Pelican Rapids, Minnesota and graduated from high school there. He earned his college degree at Concordia College in Moorhead, Minnesota, and then went on to seminary. He graduated from the Lutheran School of Theology in Rock Island, Illinois, in 1967. He was ordained in his home church, Central Lutheran in Pelican Rapids, in June 1967 having accepted a call to Big Spring, Texas. He served that congregation for three years and then moved to Fargo, North Dakota, where he served as full time chaplain at the Veterans' Hospital.

Rita Avoles Knutson grew up in Saint Paul and graduated from Minnehaha Academy. She attended Concordia College in Moorhead where she studied music. She met Bob there and they were married in 1963. While they were in Big Spring, Texas, she served as organist and choir director for their church. In Fargo, she served as organist at Saint Mark's Lutheran Church.

The Knutsons have three children: Rebecca, born in 1966; Robyn, born in 1969; and Randy, born in 1971.

Bethel Bible Studies

At the annual meeting in October 1978, the Bethel Bible Studies had been approved for use in our congregation. The first step of the program was training for the pastor. Pastor Almquist and his wife, Vi, attended this training session in August 1979. The second step was training teachers for the classes. Pastor Almquist started a class for teachers soon after he completed his training. This class had not completed its training when Pastor Almquist resigned. In order not to disrupt the training, Mrs. Valaria Fredell, a member of Trinity Lutheran Church in Lindstrom, was asked to complete the course. Mrs. Fredell was a public school teacher and had been trained in Bethel Bible Studies and had also taught the course at Trinity. Under her leadership the training class was completed.

1980

Music Enrichment

The music department also provided some excellent opportunities for the congregation during the year. On Sunday, February 10, 1980, Paul Manz came to Chisago Lake to lead a family night hymn festival. Paul Manz is known nationwide for his compositions for both piano and organ, and is an outstanding organist. In addition, there was a mass choir from the area churches to sing and to lead the congregational singing. It was a great evening of music.

On Palm Sunday, March 30, 1980, the choir presented their spring concert.

On Friday evening, April 18, the chamber orchestra and stage band from Bethany College, Lindsborg, Kansas, presented a concert in the sanctuary. Sixty-five students participated in this event.

In the fall a new Mason and Hamlin seven-foot grand piano was purchased for the sanctuary for $9,995. The Chouinard family, who were residents of the Chisago Lakes area, gave a benefit piano and organ recital in September to help raise money for the piano. This talented family presented a recital that was enjoyed greatly by those who attended.

In November, the Chisago Lakes Good News Edition, a group of people from the area churches, presented Festival of Praise by Thurlow Spurr, under the direction of our music director, Rita Knutson.

Calling a New Pastor

By the first of September 1980, a call committee had been formed to aid in the selection of a new pastor. Those appointed to this committee were Donald Hackman, David Kaasa, Nancy Grossmann, Marjorie Hawkinson, Larry Wikelius, Gaylord Swenson, and Myron Johnson, with Susan Clawson and John James as alternates. This committee visited prospective pastors at six churches. After 13 interviews and meetings they came up with a unanimous selection of Pastor Russell Peterson.

1980

The Petersons came to visit the congregation on Sunday evening, November 23, and the congregation met in special meeting after the Thanksgiving Eve service on November 26 to vote on extending a call to Pastor Peterson. The vote was unanimous and Pastor Peterson accepted the call to begin his work at Chisago Lake in February 1981.

The Petersons would have preferred to purchase a home of their own, but after looking at available homes for sale, they decided that they would live in the parsonage. The congregation at its annual meeting on January 18, 1981, passed a resolution to allow the Church Council to enter into an indebtedness up to $20,000 for remodeling and repairs to the parsonage in preparation for their coming.

The annual report shows a membership as of December 31, 1980, of 1,209. Of these 253 were unconfirmed children.

1980

Pastor Russell Peterson
1981–1988

PASTOR RUSSELL PETERSON grew up on a farm near Hector, Minnesota. He graduated from Gustavus Adolphus College in Saint Peter, Minnesota, and Augustana Seminary in Rock Island, Illinois. Prior to his call to Chisago Lake Lutheran Church, he served congregations in East Chain and Pilot Grove, and Cokato, all in Minnesota.

Pastor Peterson and his family arrived to assume the Chisago Lake pastorate February 6, 1981. At that time, their son, Wayne, was in his last year at Luther Northwestern Seminary; their daughter-in-law, Jackie, was working at Pillsbury; and their daughter, Joy, was teaching second grade at Hector, Minn. Pastor Peterson had just celebrated his 25th year of ordination.

Most of the remodeling and repairs to the parsonage had been completed. Walls and ceilings on the main floor were redone with drywall and texturing and spraying of the ceiling. New carpeting was installed and new draperies purchased. The heating system was renovated. Upstairs bedrooms were painted after their arrival. New roof and insulation had to wait for warmer weather.

Pastor Peterson's first Sunday was February 15, 1981. One week later, on February 22, Pastor Peterson was installed at a special installation service at 7:30 in the evening. The Reverend George Lundquist, vice president of the Minnesota Synod, was guest preacher and conducted the installation rite.

The Lenten season began at the beginning of March. Plans were already in place for the Lenten noon luncheons; special services were also held on Wednesday evenings at 7:30 P.M. During Holy Week, short devotional services were held at 7:00 A.M. Monday through Thursday.

The Petersons had used the Bethel Bible studies in their previous congregation and were able to conclude the teacher training for the series that had begun under Pastor Almquist and continued under the tutorage of Valeria Fredell. Preparation was made to begin classes for the congregation in October.

1981

Special Congregational Meeting

In addition to the renovation at the parsonage, it was necessary to do some repair work on the church building. A special congregational meeting was called for Sunday, March 1, 1981, after the 10:30 service, to discuss and vote on insulating the church attic. The proposal was to add eight-inch batts of class one cellulose with an R-30 rating to the four to six inches of blown fiberglass already in the attic. This would give an insulation rating of R-38-43, which would result in a 30 to 35 percent savings in heating costs. Plans were to have the wiring for the new sound system and ceiling fans completed before the insulation was installed. Completion of this work and authority for the council to borrow the necessary funds was approved at this meeting. (It is interesting to note that interest at this time was 17 percent—an incentive to borrow as little as possible.)

In addition to these projects that were carried out during the year, the church basement was waterproofed, the chimney on the church was repaired, and the new sound system was installed.

Change of Custodian

Doug Jurek served as church custodian for two years. In January of 1981, he resigned this position. During February applicants were interviewed for the position; Gary Johnson was hired as senior custodian, effective March 1. His duties were listed as responsibility for the maintenance of the church, the education wing, and the grounds; routine repairs; and preparing the rooms for whatever function is occurring. Gary was a member of the congre-

Gary Johnson family

gation along with his wife, Diane, and two children, Dan and Becky. They resided in Center City.

1981

A separate position was open for care of the cemeteries and the parsonage grounds.

Gladys's Bible Studies

When Pastor Russell and Gladys Peterson came to Chisago Lake, they indicated that they came as a team. Gladys was well known for conducting Bible studies and retreats. In their previous congregation she had been instrumental in starting many small group Bible studies. In May of 1981, she started her first Bible studies in our congregation. The studies were held on Wednesdays with classes at 9:30 A.M., 1:30 P.M., and 7:00 P.M. This

Gladys Peterson

allowed for participation at whatever time of the day was convenient. There were 169 present weekly for these studies. This was the beginning of many years of Bible study with Gladys, which contributed to the spiritual growth of a large number of people in the Chisago Lake community.

Born Anew to Share

At the Minnesota Synod Convention in 1980, the delegates voted to have a synod-wide emphasis in 1981 in preparation for 1982. The theme of this program was "Born Anew to Share." During 1981, informational meetings were held and literature distributed to help people become more aware of the needs of the church in the world. This was a stewardship program that encouraged members to increase their giving by one percent for 1982. The plan specified that any increase in giving be divided 65 percent for the local congregation and 35 percent for the synod outreach.

1981
The theme for 1981 was "Born Anew to be Good Stewards," and the theme for 1982 was "Born Anew to Serve." This emphasis was much more than stewardship. It involved evangelism—reaching the world with the gospel, and social ministry—reaching out to the disadvantaged in our community.

Pastor Peterson stated in his newsletter column for April 1, 1981:

But being born anew we have a responsibility to share—ourselves, our prayers, our lives, our possessions. Life has purpose. We are born anew to share as a congregation and as individuals. We are not an island. We touch and live in relationships with others.

Again a quote:

We are blessed to be a blessing—we are Born Anew to Share! May we learn to express our faith more and more.

Special Congregational Meeting

A special congregational meeting was called for Sunday, June 28, 1981, at 9:15 A.M. Three items were considered at that meeting: 1) adoption by substitution of a new constitution for the congregation; 2) extending a call to Pastor Robert Knutson to be associate pastor of the congregation (his previous call was for one year and was expiring); and 3) to act upon the recommendation of the social ministry committee to construct low-rent housing for the elderly.

1. This was a first reading of the approved constitution for congregations of the LCA—1980 edition. The second reading occurred at the annual meeting in January 1982. Resolution for adoption passed.

2. Pastor Knutson's call was for four years, the maximum for part-time clergy. He accepted the call and job descriptions were drawn up for the pastors.

3. In the brochure "To Burn Again," developed in 1972, provision was made for senior housing to be located on the church property. Although this idea had received low priority during the construction of the education wing, it had never been forgotten. In 1981, the social ministry committee had been enlarged to 22 members to plan for a building project for the elderly and handicapped. This committee completed a market survey that defined a significant need for this type of housing. The recommendation to construct low-rent housing was approved and application for financing was submitted to FmHA by the committee in August of 1981. The committee was notified in November of that year that the application had been denied. The committee decided not to reapply for a government loan, but to look at and identify alternate forms of financing.

1981

This resulted in an organization called Center City Housing Partnership Ltd. being formed in 1982. The congregation met and voted to sell a piece of land southeast of the church to this organization

for construction of housing for the elderly. This did not work out, however, and the plan was eventually abandoned.

Church Basement Renovated

When the education building was constructed, the plan was to reno-
vate the church undercroft so that it would provide classrooms for the
church school. This
project had been
delayed while the new
building was fur-
nished and the par-
sonage was redecorat-
ed and repaired. On
Sunday, June 27,
1982, a special con-
gregational meeting

Renovated church basement

1982

was held in the fellowship hall at 9:15 A.M. to discuss and vote on this
renovation. The plan accepted was from Erlandson and Nelson for
three classrooms on each side with an open space in the center for an
assembly area. Cost of this plan was $3,250. An additional $500 would
provide storage cabinets in each room. The rooms would be open on
one side with sliding curtains installed to provide for privacy and prevent distraction. The tower clock was also repaired in 1982.

Memorial Lectern

A suggestion had been made that we have a lectern at the front of the
sanctuary that would be constructed similarly to the pulpit and add balance and beauty to the worship area. Rodney Larson from Lindstrom
was asked to do this work. Rodney was a skilled woodworker and
agreed to build the lectern for $1,600, which included materials and
labor. Cost of the lectern was covered by gifts to the memorial fund.

Spiritual Growth Opportunities

The Bethel Bible studies, which had begun in the fall of 1981, were continued into the next year. Four classes were held with Eunice Anderson, Gertrude Lindo, Duane and Lou Arnold, Bonnie Anderson, and Pastor Peterson as instructors. Classes were held on Tuesday afternoons and Wednesday evenings.

The Prayer, Care, and Share Fellowship moved to Thursday evening so as not to conflict with the Bethel studies. This was a small group that met to pray for the church, the staff, and any special needs of members.

In January, Gladys Peterson started a prayer chain for the purpose of praying for those who requested prayer support while going through some difficulty in their life. About 30 people volunteered to be a part of this ministry.

The Lenten luncheons were discontinued and Lenten services were held on Wednesdays at 2:00 P.M. and 7:30 P.M., with the theme "Love Road to Calvary." During Holy Week, morning devotions were held at 7:00 A.M., Monday through Thursday in the sanctuary.

1982

On Friday, April 23, Dr. Vernon J. Bittner conducted a one-day retreat on "Wholeness and Self-Esteem." This retreat was sponsored by the LCW.

In June, Sunday services were taped and a new ministry was begun of bringing the tapes to homebound members who were unable to attend church. The tape was reproduced by Cleab Bowles. Several tape players were purchased for this purpose, and members of the social ministry committee volunteered to bring them to those who requested their use.

Lutheran Church Women Activities

In addition to the retreat, the LCW sponsored a number of activities under the leadership of Ruth Grandstrand, chair.

During Lent, Marlene Hackman led a celebration of the Seder, the Jewish Passover feast. The meal, together with the accompanying explanations, enlarged and clarified the meaning of the Passover feast that Jesus celebrated with his disciples before his crucifixion and how Christ became the Passover Lamb for all believers.

On July 8, there was a 6:30 A.M. sunrise service at the Hackman home on the west side of South Center Lake. Since this congregation is named "Chisago Lake" and many members live by a lake, for several years the LCW had sunrise services and sunset services on alternating years. This was a reminder of how Jesus and his disciples often worshiped by a lake.

The LCW had 12 circles with 167 members. During the year they planned and served a father-son banquet in February, a mother-daughter banquet in May, the Hazelden alumni banquet in June, the 4-H banquet in October, and the lutefisk dinner in November.

1982

Synod Highlights

The synod report showed the promise of a 14 percent increase in benevolence giving as a result of the "Born Anew To Share" program. This was an indication that the synod program had been successful in promoting greater giving for outreach.

The merger of Luther Theological Seminary and Northwestern Seminary located next door to each other in Saint Paul became effective on July 1, 1982. For several years the seminary went by the name Luther Northwestern before it became simply Luther Seminary.

In 1982, The Lutheran Church in America, The American Lutheran Church, and the Association of Evangelical Lutheran Churches, separately voted to join together and form a new Lutheran church. A 70-member commission was formed to work out the details for this merger. A time line was established with a goal for the new church beginning to function on January 1, 1988. Thirty-one members of the commission were from the LCA including four from the

Minnesota Synod: Bishop Herbert Chilstrom, Carl M. Johnson of Saint Peter, Dr James Raun of Minneapolis, and Paul N. Schultz of International Falls.

Parsonage Wedding

In July, the congregation was invited to join Pastor Peterson's family as

they gathered to celebrate the marriage of their daughter, Joy, to Rodney Sietsema. The wedding took place at the church on Saturday, July 31, at 2:30 P.M. The marriage rite was followed by a reception on the parsonage lawn. This was a gala event

Joy, Rod, Glad, Pr. Russ, Wayne, and Jackie

1982

enjoyed by all those who participated. This was the fourth consecutive pastor to have a daughter married in the sanctuary.

Wedding reception on parsonage lawn

PASTOR RUSSELL PETERSON

Financial Secretary Retires

Lois Johnson served the congregation as financial secretary for nine years. She retired, effective August 1, 1982, to enjoy retirement years with her husband Lester. By decision of the council, this position was given to Carrie Ann Holmquist in addition to her work as congregational treasurer.

Organ Rebuilding Planned

For several years the congregation had been aware of the need to have the pipe organ rebuilt again. When it was rebuilt in 1953, it was considered to be in good condition for 20 years.

It was now almost 30 years since that work had been done. During the summer of 1982, the worship and music committee contacted companies that could do the organ work and also visited a number of churches to listen to organs that had been rebuilt by these companies. The committee wanted to retain the sound of the organ if possible.

1982

In October three meetings were scheduled to show slides and discuss the work that needed to be done. The committee recommended that the congregation contract with the Johnson Organ Company of Fargo, North Dakota. Mr. Johnson was present to explain his proposal and to answer questions. His estimate for the work was $109,000. He set a completion time at 10 months.

A special congregational meeting was called for the last Sunday in November after the 10:30 A.M. worship service. The resolution to enter into a contract with Johnson Organ Company for the rebuilding of the organ was passed. The work would be done in 1983.

There are a number of interesting statistics from 1982. The total membership at the end of the year was 1188 with 925 of those confirmed members. The attendance on Easter Sunday was 829 and on Christmas Eve 777. Average Sunday attendance in 1982 was 392.

The pastor's article in the January 1983 newsletter indicates that we met all financial obligations in 1982 including repaying $7500 to the building fund, which had been borrowed for parsonage repair. The benevolence to synod and church was paid in full and $3,696.14 was given to the LCA World Hunger appeal.

Pipe Organ Rebuilt

With the need for more than $100,000 to pay for the rebuilding of the organ during the first half of 1983, the issue of raising money with fund-raisers was discussed. In the January 1983 issue of the *Kichi-Saga*, Pastor Peterson quotes from the LCA Statement on Commercialism adopted in 1964.

> Commercialism, the selling of goods and services in the name of the church, with the purpose of securing funds for the operation and mission of the church, its auxiliaries and church related institutions, vitiates the clear relationship between the giving of the Christian and the mission of the church. It fails to bear testimony to the mission of the church and creates a false image of the church. "Commercialism" further weakens the life of the church and a true sense of stewardship for the following reasons:
>
> a. It involves the church in other than its true business of giving—giving the gospel.
>
> b. It is used instead of giving. The church languishes and suffers from a lack of support, due to the improper understanding of and commitment to giving by its members.
>
> c. Buying from the church often suggests supporting the church. This leads to a false sense of security which satisfies the consciences of people not vitally related to the church."

1983

Pastor Peterson supported this statement. And so instead of trying to raise money for the organ, the congregation decided to have a prayer goal. It was exciting as each goal was reached. The Lord is faithful.

The contract signed with the Johnson Organ Company for the rebuilding of the organ was for $101,000. At the time the contract was signed, $25,250 was to be paid; about Easter time, $50,500 was due; and at the completion of the project, about June 1, the final $25,250 was due.

There was about $15,000 in the memorial organ fund when the contract was signed. One day a check arrived in the mail for $10,000, a bequest from the estate of a deceased member. Of this bequest, $1,500 was designated for new choir robes for the junior choir and the remainder was given to the organ fund. With other gifts that had come in it was possible to make the down payment.

Sunday, February 13, was designated for an organ fund appeal. Pledge cards were mailed to members of the congregation to be returned on that day. Gifts continued to come in for the organ and the $50,500 was paid in full within a week after Easter, April 3, 1983.

In addition to the rebuilding of the organ, it was enlarged to 39 ranks. Considerable work needed to be done in the organ chamber—

1983

rebuilding walls, insulating the window, and doing electrical wiring. A small chamber was constructed in the attic by the choir for two ranks of pipes, which would enable the choir to hear the organ better when it was played more softly as for choir accompaniment. This

Rita Knutson at the rebuilt organ

brought the entire cost of the organ project to $109,518.41. As of June 22, $95,095.20 in cash had been received, plus $1,150 of donated labor. The organ was ready for use on Pentecost Sunday, May 22, and dedication was set for October 9. In Pastor Knutson's annual report he states,"Mr. Johnson, the builder, still shakes his head when he thinks of how our congregation responded to this need."

In August, the congregation decided to sell the old organ pipes at an auction. Many people had expressed an interest in owning one and this was a fair way to disburse them. The church closets were cleaned and any articles not in use were also put on the auction. Money from the auction went to the organ fund. The annual report shows that the balance left to be paid on the organ project at the end of 1983 was $1,465.61. Some of the smallest pipes were used by Raymond Wikelius to build a replica of the first organ, which was in the balcony. This replica can be seen in the church archives.

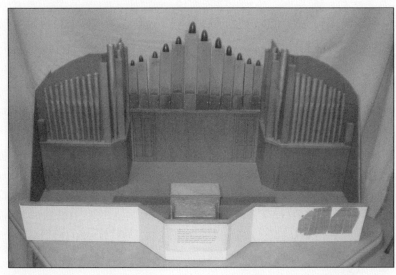

1983

Replica of first church organ built by Raymond Wikelius

Hazelden Ministry

At the time the decision was made to have services at 8:00 and 10:30 A.M., one of the reasons for choosing these times was to accommodate the Hazelden community. Many of the patients at that facility desired an opportunity to attend a local church for worship on Sunday morning. Due to the scheduling at Hazelden, the only time they could attend worship was between 10:30 and 11:30. The congregation was willing to schedule a service at a time they could attend. Many times Chisago Lake Church has been thanked by those who have been blessed by attending worship with this congregation.

PASTOR RUSSELL PETERSON

One story deserves to be related here. A young man from Iceland, Hrein Lindahl, was an opera singer who had sung all over Europe. Through some mishap in his life, he vowed he would never sing again and had not done so for one and a half years. He came to Hazelden to be treated for some addiction in his life, and first attended services at Chisago Lake in April 1982. He attended services several times after that and in June he spoke to Rita Knutson, the organist and music director. He said that he would like to sing for the congregation some Sunday as a thank you for the opportunity to worship with them. This he did in July. It was a joyous experience to hear this young man sing. It was even a greater joy to know that because of Hazelden and Chisago Lake Church this man of great talent would once again use his voice to sing for the Lord. In February 1983, Hrein Lindahl gave a concert at Chisago Lake for the community. His concert included songs by Italian, German, Swedish, and Icelandic composers and was a concert equal to what you might hear at Orchestra Hall.

1983

This is only one story of the many lives that have been touched by worshiping with this congregation and hearing the gospel preached and the beautiful music of the organ.

Second Custodian Hired

Gary Johnson, who had been serving as custodian since March 1, 1981, desired to work on a part-time basis. To assist him, Irene Potter was hired in January as a part-time custodian. Each was to work four hours a day during the week and every other weekend. Irene worked mornings and Gary worked evenings. This made it possible for Gary to hold another position during the day.

Irene Potter

Lenten Visitation

Prior to the 1983 Lenten season, the congregation was divided into areas with a "shepherd" appointed for each area. The shepherds were given Lenten materials and a questionnaire to distribute to each home in their area. The questionnaire was designed to give helpful information about the strengths and weaknesses of the congregation, which would enable the congregation to better serve its members. The questionnaires were to be filled out and returned to the church during the Lenten season. This process was not entirely successful because not everyone received a questionnaire and not all that were distributed were returned, but it did help the Church Council to set some goals for the future.

Storm Damage

On July 3, 1983, a severe wind storm swept through Chisago County. Many trees were downed at the parsonage and there was some proper-

ty damage. This photo shows willow branches that blew up against the parsonage windows. The windows did not break. Most of the damage was minor, but one of the clock faces in the bell tower of the church was damaged. Insurance received for this damage

1983

Storm damage at the parsonage

was $2,255. The clock movement had not worked properly for some time, however, and there was a need for a new electric bell ringer. To do all of the work would require an additional $5,000, which was not in the budget. The Church Council approved a recommendation from the property committee to go ahead with the needed repairs. The goal was to have this work completed before the sanctuary centennial celebration October 9.

Another project completed during the summer was the installation of a second set of doors for the lower entrance. These doors would provide an air space and prevent some heat loss. Cost of this project was about $4,000. There was also a new well that was dug at the parsonage.

Youth Activities

After Pastor Peterson was installed as the senior pastor, Pastor Knutson (Pastor Bob) was able to concentrate on the youth work he was called to do. He worked with the Christian education committee and the Christian education director, Gladie Moe, to see that the Christian education program ran smoothly. He planned the adult education program (Parish Enrichment Program) for Sunday mornings. He also helped with the summer vacation Bible school.

The youth were involved in several athletic leagues with other churches. They played volleyball in the winter and softball in the summer. They participated in ski outings in the winter and went to Luther Point Bible Camp in the summer. They went to Valley Fair and to youth conventions.

1983

One of the conventions some of the youth attended during the summer of 1983 was in Marquette, Michigan. After the convention, they went to visit an inner-city black church in Chicago. The pastor there was a friend of Pastor Bob's and

Youth leaving for Chicago, Illinois

he invited our youth to come back in 1984 and conduct a vacation Bible school for them. The invitation was accepted, and the youth at Chisago Lake spent the next year planning for this week.

Lutheran Church Women Activities

One of the projects of the LCW was the partial support of a missionary family. The family to which they contributed at this time was the Rick and Helen Meier family who served as missionaries in Argentina. In February, the Meiers visited Chisago Lake with their four children, six-year-old-triplets and a baby. The congregation was invited to a 6:30 pot-luck supper and social hour, followed by a program.

There was a mother-daughter banquet in May as well as a cradle roll party for all preschool children and their mothers. The women also served the Hazelden Alumni Banquet in June.

A sunset service was held in July at the Watersedge Apartments .

1983

Sanctuary Centennial

The first phase of the sanctuary construction began in 1882 and the building was ready for use in the fall of 1883. October 1983 was set aside as a time to celebrate 100 years of worship in this sanctuary.

On Friday, October 7, at 11:00 A.M., a Swedish communion service was held. Pastor Stig Demker from Sweden, the interim pastor at Long Lake Lutheran Church in Isanti, was the guest preacher for this event. The service was followed by a noon lunch in the fellowship hall.

On Sunday, October 9, at the 10:30 A.M. service, Dr. Herbert Chilstrom, bishop of the Minnesota Synod was the guest preacher; he also officiated at the dedication of the rebuilt organ and the rededication of the 100-year-old sanctuary. Also invited to be present were Dr. Emeroy Johnson, the Almquists, and Pastor and Mrs. Burdette Benson. Following the worship service there was a pot-luck dinner and at 2:00 P.M. an organ concert was presented. Organist Rita Knutson and previous organists Faylon Geist and Kathleen DeBolt participated in the concert.

On Reformation Sunday, the Saint Croix District held their meeting and service at Chisago Lake. For this event a mass choir of 85 voices from the various churches in the district sang. Mark Johnson directed this choir.

Choirs

In the fall of 1983, there were four choirs. The Sunbeam choir, age 3 through grade 2, was under the direction of Jane Iverson. The junior choir, grades 3 through 7, was under the direc-tion of Joy Sietsema. The youth ensemble, grades 8 through 12, was under the direc-tion of Rita Knutson. The senior choir was

1983

The Sunbeam choir

under the direction of Mark Johnson. All choirs were scheduled to par-ticipate in worship services.

On the first Sunday in Advent, a community choir of 75 voices presented portions of Handel's *Messiah*. Mark Johnson directed this choir and Rita Knutson was the organist. Pastor Knutson read each scripture verse before it was sung. The sanctuary was well filled for this event. The *Messiah* concert was held annually on the first Sunday in Advent for several years.

Mark Johnson and Rita Knutson

Seminary Scholarships

Jeff Sandgren, a son of the congregation, was now a student at Luther Northwestern Seminary. The congregation wanted to do something to

assist Jeff with his education, so the seminary scholarship fund was reactivated. The decision was made to pay his full tuition, which was $1,500 a year. Janet Tengbom, another semi-nary student also joined our church. Janet Tengbom was a daughter of Pastor Luverne and Mildred Hasselquist

Jeff Sandgren

Tengbom. Mildred Hasselquist grew up at Chisago Lake, which helped Janet to feel at home in this congregation. Janet also received some tuition assistance.

Janet Tengbom

1983

Spiritual Enrichment Opportunities

Bible studies were a top priority for Pastor Russ and Glad Peterson. Teaching the Bible was one of Glad's greatest gifts. The first three class-es of Bethel students had completed their course and Pastor Russ was teaching the final parts for the fourth class. Glad conducted a five-week course on the book of James during Lent, and plans were made to start the Search Bible studies in the fall. The Bethel course was an overview of the Bible; Search was a five-year, in-depth course. Classes were to be held on Wednesday mornings and Thursday evenings, beginning the first week in September. By May 30, 75 people had already enrolled.

In addition to these studies, there was a senior high Bible study on Wednesday evenings led by Pastor Bob, and many of the P.E.P. (adult Sunday school) sessions were Bible-based. The circles continued with their monthly Bible studies and the vacation Bible school for children was well attended in the summer.

In March, there was a one-day retreat featuring Mildred Tengbom as leader. Her topic was "Friends Can Be Good Medicine" and the retreat was open to both men and women.

To promote friendships within the congregation, three organizations were active for different age groups. The OKs (Older Kids) was an organization for retired members. This group met monthly for lunch and a program. In the summer they often took a one-day bus trip to some point of interest. The 3Ms (Make the Most of the Middle years) was for members between 40 and retirement. This was a less struc-

The OKs on a boat trip

tured group that would get together occasionally to attend a concert, see a play, enjoy a corn roast, or have a progressive dinner. The Odds and Ends were the young members under 40. These were young married couples or singles that would gather to play games or go bowling, etc.

Youth Conduct Bible School in Chicago

The big event for the youth during 1984 was making the trip to Chicago to conduct a vacation Bible school. The early part of the year was spent in preparation. Materials were secured through Augsburg Publishing House, and time was spent becoming familiar with the material in preparation for teaching. Fund-raising events were held to cover the expenses for the trip, which was anticipated to cost about $5,000 including materials to create a playground for the children. A car wash and Easter breakfast brought in $926.18 for the ministry, which was partly matched with funds from Lutheran Brotherhood.

Eighteen young people and five adults made the trip to *Messiah* Lutheran Church in Chicago. They were able to rent a bus from the school district for the journey. This mission venture was very successful. *Messiah* had never been able to find enough teachers to staff a Bible school, so this was a new experience for these children. In the evenings the youth from *Messiah* and Chisago Lake had an opportunity for fellowship and building bridges between a Minnesota white rural congregation and an inner-city black church in Chicago. It changed lives for members of both congregations.

After they returned home, there were several opportunities for Chisago Lake youth to share their experience with others. They first gave a presentation in their home church and then went to Parmly, Trinity Lutheran Church in Lindstrom, and St. Paul Lutheran Church in Wyoming. They were also invited to Central Lutheran Church in Pelican Rapids, Pastor Bob's home church, to share their story.

1984

Special Meeting to Discuss Sprinkler System

At the annual meeting in January 1984, the Church Council was authorized to look into the possibility of installing a sprinkler system in the church and to find out the approximate cost of such a system.

A special meeting of the congregation was called for September 9, 1984, at 11:30 A.M. to consider the following resolutions:

RESOLVED:

1) That the Church Council be authorized to secure bids and to install a dry pipe fire protection system in the church building at a cost of approximately $42,000.

2) That the Church Council be authorized to arrange for funding of the project by borrowing and/or by conducting a financial appeal.

PASTOR RUSSELL PETERSON

Plans had been made to blacktop the parking lot on the south side of the church, but if a sprinkler system was to be installed, these pipes needed to be in the ground before the blacktop was laid.

The resolution was not passed.

Pony Express Stewardship

In the fall of 1984, the Pony Express stewardship program was introduced. Wally Carlson was the campaign general manager. Under his leadership, the stewardship committee served as station agents. Each of these supervised five or six trail bosses. Each trail boss would oversee a pony express route composed of 10 families.

The pony express theme was chosen because of the example set by the highly dedicated riders of the original pony express. The secret of their success lay in their ability to work as a team—each rider was

1984

Stewardship committee: David Oftelie, George Mickelsen, Wally Carlson, Melvin Dahlquist, Tom Miller, Eleanor Shogren, Glad Peterson, and Jeannette Dahlquist

dependent on the other to make the relay system work. Likewise the success of the pony express stewardship program depended on the dedication, commitment, and teamwork of each member of the congregation.

Each saddlebag contained a stewardship booklet and "Estimate of Giving" cards for each family. A family would fill out their card, place it in a sealed envelope in the saddlebag, and then pass it on to the next family. One family even passed their saddlebag on horseback.

This program was very successful. The annual report covering 1984 indicates an increase of 23½ percent in dollars pledged for 1985 and an increase of 49 percent in "Estimate of Giving" cards returned. Because of this success, the same program was used again the following year.

Pastors Visit Israel

From November 27 to December 8, 1984, Pastor Peterson had the opportunity to travel with a group to Israel. The group also made a stop in Rome. After he returned, he shared his impressions of Israel with groups within the congregation.

Before this opportunity came to Pastor Peterson, Pastor Knutson and Rita had already been planning to lead a group on an 11-day trip to Israel in April of 1985. There were 41 people who took advantage of this opportunity, but only seven of them were from Chisago Lake Lutheran Church. Several were area people who were members of other churches, and some were friends of members. An anonymous donor gave a sum of money to enable two young men of the congregation, Kurt Schrader and Todd Elkerton, to go on this trip. In addition to visiting Israel, the group went to Amman, Jordan, and Cairo, Egypt. Some of the group also took advantage of an add-on trip of five days in Athens, Greece.

1984

Hospice: Chisago County, Inc.

Hospice, a program dedicated to care for and to serve those individuals and their families who are terminally ill, was introduced into Chisago County in 1984. Cheryl Fish, a part-time director of the program, was a member of Chisago Lake Lutheran Church. Dr. Elof Nelson, who was also a member of the congregation, served on the board of directors. In order to get the program functioning, a county fund drive was under way to raise

Cheryl Fish

$100,000. The congregation was challenged to give its support and encouragement for this worthy volunteer service. There was a plea for qualified personnel to volunteer for this program.

Pictorial Directory

During 1984, plans were made to have United Church Directories produce a new pictorial directory for the congregation. Glad Peterson chaired the directory committee and pictures were taken in September. Due to some delays in printing, the directories were not ready for distribution until the middle of 1985.

Other interesting information from 1984:

1984

+ The ladies completed 79 quilts for Lutheran World Relief.
+ A father-daughter banquet was held in February.

Ida Johnson, Helen Leander, Hazel Swenson, Myrtle Medin

+ Reid Peterson, a young man from Lindstrom, presented an organ concert in March.
+ The junior choir presented "Vinegar Boy" for Mother's Day.
+ Liv Iverson, a college student from Chisago Lake, went with a Campus Crusade for Christ team to witness in Africa.
+ Sunday school enrollment was 239 with a staff of 46.
+ A second *Messiah* concert was given on the First Sunday in Advent with a community choir of 75 voices under the direction of Mark Johnson with Rita Knutson, organist.
+ The Lutheran Church in America World Hunger Appeal brought in $8,489,559 during 1984. This was $1,489,559 above what was expected. $1,100,000 of this money was given to help the people of Ethiopia who were experiencing a famine. Chisago Lake gave $7,638.89 to this fund.

Gladys Moe Resigns

Gladie Moe, parish education director and
church secretary, resigned effective May 31,
1985. She had served faithfully for six years. A
retirement reception was held in her honor on
Sunday, June 6, between services. She went on
to work at Gustaf's, a gift shop in Lindstrom.

Gladys Moe

In replacing her, new job descriptions
were developed separating the church secretary duties from the Christian education
duties. Eunice Anderson was hired to be the
church secretary beginning June 17; in September, Sue Wehrenberg
was hired as a part-time Christian education director.

Two more staff changes were made in the fall. Irene Potter
resigned her position as part-time janitor for health reasons; Jane
Loehlein was hired to replace her. Joy Sietsema resigned as junior choir
director; her replacement was Ann Towler, an elementary music
teacher in the Chisago Lake School District.

1984

Special Congregational Meeting to
Renew Pastor Knutson's Call

A special meeting of the congregation was called for Sunday, June 16,
at 9:30 A.M. to renew Pastor Knutson's call as half-time associate pastor. The call was issued for two years. Two reasons given for this were:

1. the custom of issuing special service calls for two years, and
2. the possibility of needing a full time associate in two years.

Come Celebrate! Go Proclaim!

Beginning in 1985 and for two-and-a-half years, Bishop Chilstrom
asked congregations to place a strong emphasis on Bible study and

evangelism. The theme for this emphasis throughout the synod was "Come Celebrate! Go Proclaim!" At Chisago Lake we were already involved with the Search Bible studies and other learning opportunities. At this time, Glad Peterson served on the synod council and was one of the synod evangelists. She had many opportunities as she preached in many churches.

Glad Peterson teaching Search

The evangelism committee established as a long-range goal for our congregation:

1985

> To effectively train the members of the congregation in Outreach and Evangelism so that they will begin to develop a lifestyle that radiates the love of Jesus Christ in all areas of their lives.

Pew registration pads were used at Sunday morning worship services to enable those worshiping together to get to know each other better and to be able to recognize visitors. In addition to this, a program of sponsorship for new members was started. Members were paired up with those joining the church to assist them in becoming involved in all aspects of the congregational life.

In November a "Preaching, Teaching, Reaching Mission" was held with Pastor Marvin Palmquist as presenter. He used the synod theme "Come Celebrate! Go Proclaim!" with an emphasis on putting faith into action.

Musical Events

Chisago Lake has always showed a strong interest in music. Several opportunities for musical enjoyment were made available in 1985.

+ Sunday, February 10, the Gustavus Adolphus College Concert Choir sang at the 10:30 service. After the service, the choir was served a pot-luck dinner by the congregation.

+ Monday, March 18, the Bethany College Concert Choir from Lindsborg, Kansas, gave an evening concert in the sanctuary. This concert was sponsored by the area churches including, Trinity, Lindstrom; Zion, Chisago City; and Immanuel, Almelund.

+ On Sunday, May 5, there was a polka service led by the Polkateers of Prince of Peace Lutheran Church in Brooklyn Center. Although polka services have been used in many congregations, this service was not well received at Chisago Lake.

+ On a Sunday in June, the St. Thomas College Liturgical Choir was present to help lead the worship and sing.

+ On Friday, August 9, a Lutheran Youth Encounter team presented a concert. The "Spoke Folk" were on a bicycle tour in Wisconsin and Minnesota from July 26 to August 11. This group traveled about 60 miles each day and gave a concert each evening. They were housed in community homes where they could refresh themselves at the end of a long day on the road.

1985

+ On November 8-10, several of the youth from Chisago Lake congregation attended a youth choir seminar at Prince of Peace Lutheran Church in Burnsville. This was the "Sounds Like Love" seminar that our youth participated in for several years.

+ On December 1, the third annual *Messiah* concert was presented with about 90 community members participating.

+ The "Folk Service" which had been introduced at the Thanksgiving Eve Service in 1984, was used about every fifth week during the year. Comments from the congregation indicated that the service did provide a meaningful worship atmosphere, and it continued to be used as long as the Knutsons were at Chisago Lake.

National Youth Convention

July 1 to 5, 1985, were the dates of the National Youth Convention, which took place at Purdue University in Indiana. With the Lutheran church merger on the horizon, this would be the last LCA youth convention. Youth were encouraged to plan to attend this convention but only four were able to go along with Pastor Bob. The Chisago Lake group stopped at *Messiah* Lutheran in Chicago and four youth and two adults joined them and were "adopted" as part of the Minnesota delegation.

New Chapter of Lutheran Church Library Association

The LCLA is a national organization of church libraries, with chapters all over the United States. For many years members of the Chisago Lake Church library committee had attended meetings of the Metro chapter. In 1985, the Metro chapter was invited to hold their meeting at Chisago Lake, but the invitation was not accepted. Instead, it was suggested that we form a chapter in our area.

1985

Eunice Anderson, church librarian for Chisago Lake, contacted area churches to determine if there was enough support for a new chapter. This resulted in Chisago Lake hosting a meeting on Saturday, September 21, to which all churches from Marine to Rush City, Minnesota, and from Cambridge to Amery, Wisconsin, were invited.

Several of the staff from the LCLA office in Minneapolis were present at this meeting to conduct workshops and to determine if our group would be viable as a new organiza-

Eunice Anderson

tion. This was the beginning of the St. Croix Valley Chapter of the Lutheran Church Library Association. Elected to the executive committee of the new chapter were Eunice Anderson, Chisago Lake, Center City, president; Sue Berry, St. Paul, Wyoming, vice-chairman; and Fran McLeod, Fristad Lutheran Church, Centuria, Wisconsin, secretary-treasurer. This chapter was still very active 10 years later but has since disbanded.

In our own local library, hundreds of books were added to our selection after the education building was constructed with a large room designated for a library. The library was funded first by the LCW and later by the church budget under Christian education. Many books were purchased with memorial monies designated for the purchase of books. For several years, books were brought to Chisago Lake Lutheran Church on consignment from a Christian book store in Saint Paul to be sold at church for about three weeks in late November and early December. Money earned at these book sales was used to purchase more books. There were also other private donations of books, both new and used.

1985

Property Upkeep

Several repair needs for the building became obvious during the summer of 1985. There were leaks in the flat roof on the education building, and there was also a leak on the southwest entry of the church building. And work needed to be done on the steeple. The louvers were in very poor condition and the entire steeple needed painting or some other covering.

Sealing of the roof on the education building and also on the west

Working on the steeple

PASTOR RUSSELL PETERSON

entry to the undercroft was estimated to cost $4,485. The estimate to cover the steeple with vinyl or aluminum was $7,640. Annual meeting reports show that these repairs and some others were completed in 1985. There was also a considerable amount of landscaping done around the church during the summer.

Pew cushions were installed as a gift from two brothers, Oscar R. Johnson and Paul F. Johnson, who were life-long members of Chisago Lake.

Plans were being made to blacktop the upper parking lot; however, of the $12,000 needed for this project, only $3,100 was available.

Lutheran Church Women Continue Active

The LCW continued to hold monthly meetings in 1985. They sponsored events such as a talent show/family night in March, a mother-son banquet in May, an all-day mystery tour in October, and a festival of carols family night in December.

1985

In the early part of the year, ladies made quilts and soap—360 pounds of quilts, soap, and clothing were delivered to Lutheran World Relief. A group of ladies also visited the Marie Sandvik Mission in

LCW tour to the State Capitol

Minneapolis in August. This included presenting a program, serving a light meal, and helping to distribute clothing and bedding to the needy who had come there for help. This was a yearly service to the mission for many years.

The lutefisk dinner was revived this year with more than 140 people volunteering their help. A delicious dinner served to more than 450 people. Co-chairs for the kitchen work were Kathy Lindo and Barb Wikelius; co-chairs for the dining room were Vicki Mickelsen and Sue (Mrs. Lorens) Johnson. Some of the proceeds of this dinner were given to the food shelf.

Healing and Wholeness

Several people in the congregation had approached Pastor Peterson about the possibility of having a regular service of healing. There is a Service of Healing and Wholeness in the pastor's book of *Occasional Services*. It was decided that these services would be made available on the fourth Sunday of each month at 7:30 P.M. The services were a time of singing, fellowship, and prayer. Prayer requests were received from those who were ill or needed encouragement in times of stress or personal crisis. Attendance was not great at these services, but they were important and beneficial for all who came.

1985

On Saturday, September 14, the Christian education committee sponsored a seminar on "Dealing with Loss and Grief in the Christian Community." Presenter for this seminar was Janice Nadeau. This was an opportunity to learn how to minister to those persons dealing with grief. This was also a way to bring healing and wholeness to others.

Confirmation Task Force

In February of 1985, the Christian education committee appointed a task force of eleven people to study the confirmation program and to make recommendations as to how it could be improved. Following are excerpts from the report, which was adopted by the Church Council and implemented in September of 1985.

- ✦ Confirmation classes to be held on Wednesday evenings from 5:30 to 6:45 P.M. for students in 8th and 9th grade.
- ✦ Materials will be the same, but the format of instruction will change.
- ✦ Students will be divided into small groups with a parent volunteer to assist them when needed.
- ✦ Pastors will present a 15-minute introduction to the day's topic and the remainder of the time will be spent in small groups.
- ✦ Students are also required to attend Sunday school.
- ✦ Memory work is the student's responsibility and parents will be asked to help.
- ✦ Each class will have a retreat — 9th grade in October and 8th grade in February.
- ✦ Pastors should visit each home to explain the program, to recruit parent volunteers, and to get to know the families.
- ✦ Parent volunteers will receive training.

1985

The Computer Comes to Chisago Lake

Pastor Bob was an Osborne computer fan. He was becoming adept at using it himself and sometime during the year began to do his page for the newsletter on the computer. He started some database programs for use in keeping attendance, and for the organist the hymns used each Sunday were recorded.

He installed a financial records program for the treasurer,

C.arrie Holmquist

Carrie Holmquist, and taught her how to use it. As the computers were upgraded to IBM-compatible she attended classes at Cambridge Junior College.

He installed a WordStar word processing program for which he found many uses. The church secretary took an evening class at the high school to learn how to use the program. Before long Pastor Knutson purchased a second Osborne.

This was the office's early introduction to the computer age.

Benevolence Priorities

Pastor Peterson had two high priorities for the churches he served. The first was to always have opportunities for Bible study, and the second was to be generous in benevolence giving. Education, stewardship, and evangelism were high on his agenda.

Evidence of this can be found in the proposed budget for 1986, where the line item for the Minnesota Synod is $36,000. One of the resolutions passed at the annual

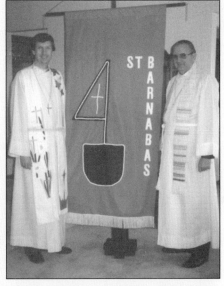

1986

Pastors Wayne and Russ Peterson

meeting in January 1986 stated that Thanksgiving and Christmas offerings were to be designated for unbudgeted benevolence causes. The Christmas offering was $2,675 and was divided equally between three new mission congregations: Christ Lutheran in Faribault, St. Barnabas in Plymouth, and Christ Lutheran in Elk River. Chisago Lake had a special interest in St. Barnabas because the mission developer/pastor was Wayne Peterson, son of Pastor Russ and Glad Peterson. St. Barnabas held their first worship service on the last Sunday of November 1985. In 1985 Pastor Russ was pastor of the oldest Minnesota congregation and Pastor Wayne was pastor of the youngest congregation.

In the pastor's annual report covering 1985, it states that "our financial stewardship reveals that all responsibilities were met. 97% of the pledged income was received." This indicates a growth in steward-ship over the years. Offerings for World Hunger in 1985 totaled $6,550. There was also a balance in the treasury at the end of the year of more than $4,000.

Membership statistics at the end of 1985 show:

✦ 1,245 baptized members

✦ 925 of these were confirmed members

✦ 800 of these were active members

✦ 125 were inactive

✦ Average attendance at Sunday worship was 407

1986   Leadership for Tomorrow/ One in Mission

The Lutheran Church in America had two areas of emphasis for 1986. The first was to continue with the "Come Celebrate! Go Proclaim!" program, which had already begun. This was done at Chisago Lake by continuing the Search Bible studies and other Bible study opportuni-ties and with a strong emphasis on evangelism.

The second emphasis, new in 1986, was the Leadership for Tomorrow/One In Mission Appeal. The purpose of this appeal was to begin new mission congregations in the United States and to have money available for start-up costs for the new Lutheran church. The LCA goal was $36,000,000. Of this money, $30,000,000 was for new congregations and the other $6,000,000 for the new Lutheran church. The Minnesota Synod share was $6,000,000, with $3,000,000 for the synod and $3,000,000 to be given to Gustavus Adolphus College,

Luther Northwestern Seminary, the Lutheran Camp Board, and Campus Ministries.

The goal of this appeal for Chisago Lake Lutheran Church was $41,598 over a three-year period of time. The resolution to accept this goal was passed at the annual meeting. Marie Cotch was chairman for the committee to conduct this appeal. When all pledges for LFT/OIM had been received, the total amount pledged was $64,346. Chisago Lake exceeded its goal by pledging 155 percent! This was the first congregation in the synod to exceed its goal.

Parsonage Committee Appointed

A resolution, which passed at the January 1986 annual meeting, was to appoint a parsonage review committee. The responsibilities of this committee were as follows:

1. Inventory the condition of the parsonage
2. Develop a proposal, time plan, and cost estimate
3. Make recommendations as to the future disposition of the parsonage

1986

Those appointed to this committee were Elliott and Marjorie Hawkinson, Richard Hofmann, Rodney Sietsema, Avis Nelson, LeeVerne Peterson, and George Mickelsen. The recommendations of this committee were:

1. That the parsonage building be kept and maintained for its aesthetic, character, and historical value.
2. That the senior pastor of Chisago Lake Lutheran Church be required to occupy the parsonage as a residence.
3. That there be a committee comprising 3-5 members of CLLC to act as intermediary between the church and the contractor in regard to recommended repairs.
4. It is desirable that the repairs be completed over a three-year time period beginning in 1987.

5. That the above list (of recommended repairs) be looked upon as recommended repairs in order of priority. The recommended repairs and renovations totaled $50,000.

Not all members of the congregation thought that it was prudent to spend $50,000 on the parsonage. A request was made that a committee of Church Council members be formed to look into other options. This committee worked throughout 1987 and by September had some options ready for presentation. These were:

1. Construct a new parsonage on a different lot
2. Rent out the parsonage and give the pastor a housing allowance
3. Tear down the parsonage and build on the same lot
4. Have the parsonage moved and sell it

There were some variations of these options, and pros and cons and costs of each option were made available to the congregation. A meeting to discuss all the options was held on Sunday evening, October 4, 1987, at 7:00 P.M.

1986

At the annual meeting in January 1988, the congregation still was not ready to make a decision on the parsonage issue. A resolution to hold a meeting later in the year was passed. This meeting was held on Sunday, June 12, 1988, at 9:15 A.M. The meeting was called to make a decision on whether to offer a parsonage or a

The parsonage from the west

housing allowance to a future pastor and if the decision was a parsonage, then there would be a further decision on whether to repair the present parsonage or build a new one.

The decision was to continue offering a parsonage and to spend the monies needed to repair and update it. A new committee was formed to handle the taking of bids on the projects to be completed. The first of these were for new exterior siding and replacement of all windows.

Minnesota Foodshare Month

The State of Minnesota designated March as the month in which to gather food for the state's many food shelves to help the hungry. During that month, donations would be matched by Minnesota corporations. The goal set for Chisago Lake Lutheran Church was one pound of food and $1.00 from each member. The drive resulted in 579 items donated and more than $1,000 in cash. To this amount, the LCW added $500 from the proceeds of the lutefisk dinner held in November.

March has continued to be Foodshare month in Minnesota, and Chisago Lake has an ongoing program of giving to both World Hunger and the local food shelf.

1986

Worship and Music Survey

The worship and music committee continued to explore alternate worship services. In May, John Ylvisaker was a guest at a morning worship and led the congregation in a folk service that he had written. In September, a survey was included in the newsletter and the results were printed in the October newsletter.

There were 247 responses to the survey and 56.7 percent of these came from members who were 46 years of age and older.

A summary of the report showed that the majority supported a variety of worship services and wanted to keep the hours of worship at 8:00 and 10:30 A.M.

Other 1986 News Items

+ A one-day retreat was held on April 12, with Ruth Lofgren of Arlington Hills Lutheran Church in St. Paul as presenter. Theme for the retreat was "Celebrate Life."

+ A "Spring-Fling" banquet was held for all women on May 10.

+ At the Minnesota Synod convention, a special offering was received for ministry to the Asian community. More than 12,000 Asians had immigrated to the Twin Cities area.

+ The social ministry committee divided the members of the congregation into twelve service groups. These groups were to serve at funerals and other church functions.

+ The Spoke Folk team, sponsored by Lutheran Youth Encounter, used Chisago Lake Lutheran Church for their training session from July 11 to 15. The group was comprised of 23 young people and counselors. These were bikers who would travel about 600 miles in 10 days and give an inspirational concert in a church each evening. They stayed at the church.

+ Fourteen youth accompanied Pastor Bob to Pine Ridge Indian Reservation in South Dakota from August 13 to 19. While there, the group painted one of the churches on the reservation. They also attended an Indian pow-wow. Before returning home they attended the Passion Play in Spearfish, South Dakota, and did some sight-seeing in the Black Hills.

+ The annual Swedish communion service was held on October 10 at 11:00 A.M. with Dr. Rudolph Burke as guest preacher.

+ The fall "Preaching, Teaching, Reaching" mission was held November 9 to 11 with Dr. William E. Berg speaking. His theme was "Journey Into New Life and Hope." Dr. Berg had served more than 100 congregations with his PTR missions, and was a well-known evangelist in the Augustana Lutheran

1986

Church prior to its merger into the Lutheran Church in America.

+ The annual *Messiah* concert was held on November 30.

+ In December, the Parmly van was made available to bring members to church who were residents of the Parmly complex. Donald Johnson volunteered to be the driver, with Wally Carlson as his back-up. Drivers needed to have a Class B license.

+ The new carillon, which was purchased with memorial gifts, was used for the first time on Christmas Eve.

Parking Lot Blacktopped

For several years the congregation worked toward getting the upper parking lot blacktopped. There were delays in getting this accomplished when other projects received a higher priority. There was discussion of running a large water pipe into the church, and if this was to be done, it should be done first. The estimated cost of the parking lot project was $12,000. There was a fund for this project, which had **1986** grown to $6,000. In July bids were received from three companies, and all exceeded the estimated amount. The bid accepted was from E. F. Hals Company for $17,217. This included drainage work on the hillside. The work was completed in the fall. Monies continued to come in for this project during the year and the balance of $4,300 was paid from undesignated memorial funds.

Another property project during 1986 was replacing the septic system at the parsonage at a cost of $3,950.

Replacing septic system

Mutual Ministry Committee

In 1985, a mutual ministry committee was established. The purpose of this committee was: 1) to identify the professional leadership and support staffing needs of the congregation and to seek persons to meet those needs; 2) to provide for the evaluation of the ministry and mission of the congregation; and 3) to serve as a personal and confidential support group to the pastors and to serve as a communication channel regarding conditions and attitudes within the congregation.

Within these general areas, responsibilities of the committee were to provide for:

1. Open communication concerning the attitudes and conditions within the congregation.
2. Early warnings of misunderstanding within the congregation
3. A "listening post" for the pastor, the lay professional, and the congregation.
4. Conflict resolution.
5. Appraisal of the ministry of the pastor, the lay professional, and the congregation.
6. A sounding board for the pastor and lay professional in time of personal or professional stress or anxiety.
7. Identifying continuing education that would assist the ministry of the pastor and lay professional and the goals of the congregation.
8. Concerns for the spiritual, emotional, and physical needs of the pastor and lay professional.

The intent of this committee was to resolve any conflicts between members or between members and staff before they caused a division in the congregation.

On December 21, 1986, the committee conducted a survey at the church services. A questionnaire was distributed in an effort to gain a better understanding of the congregation's view of the church's ministry. The questionnaire addressed five areas of ministry: service, wor-

1986

ship, support, learning, witness. In all areas, an overwhelming majority of the 186 people who returned the questionnaire felt that the congregation was doing a satisfactory job. In the area of witness, 32.3 percent felt that the congregation should improve or expand its ministry.

Constituting Conventions for the ELCA

During 1987, the conventions were held that would prepare for the beginning of the new Evangelical Lutheran Church in America in January 1988. The constituting convention of the ELCA was held in Columbus, Ohio, from April 28 to May 3. Two members of Chisago Lake Lutheran Church were delegates to this convention. They were Gladys Peterson and Wallace Carlson. At this convention, Dr. Herbert Chilstrom, bishop of the Minnesota Synod, was elected presiding bishop of the new ELCA.

The organizational meeting for the East Metropolitan Minnesota Synod was held at the Saint Paul Radisson Hotel from June 12 to 13. Delegates to this constituting convention from Chisago Lake Lutheran Church were Wallace Carlson, Gertrude Lindo, George Mickelsen, Pastor Knutson, and Pastor Peterson. Elected bishop for this synod was Pastor Lowell Erdahl. From Chisago Lake Lutheran Church, Wallace Carlson was elected to the Synod Council, Pastor Peterson was elected to the Board of Finance, and Eunice Anderson was elected to the Board of Church and Society. The Reverend Gordon Grimm was also elected to the Board of Church and Society as a representative of Redeemer Lutheran Church in White Bear Lake where he was still a member.

1987

The constituting convention of the Women of the ELCA was held in Milwaukee, Wisconsin, from June 11 to 14. Theme of the convention was "Embrace God's World." There was no delegate at that convention from Chisago Lake. The East Metro synodical women's organization constituting convention was held at Bethel College in Arden Hills from August 3 to 5. Jane Iverson was a delegate to that convention. Irene Carlson and Barbara Wikelius, from Chisago Lake, were synodical women's organization task force trainers to help local congregations with the transition.

Stained-Glass Windows

At the same time as the congregation was struggling with the disposition of the parsonage, the stained-glass windows in the sanctuary became an issue. They were nearly 100 years old, and it was expected that they should be re-leaded at least every 75 to 80 years. A few windows had been repaired in 1977, but the others were in need of restoration. During the summer of 1987, a consultant from the Swedish Institute examined the windows and recommended that the windows all be re-leaded. The approximate cost would be $85,000.

The property committee proceeded to secure bids for the work, and by the annual meeting in January 1988 they presented a resolution to the congregation and the resolution passed:

1987

> That the bid of Warren Keith Studio be accepted for the repair and restoration of the stained-glass windows in the church at a cost of $82,739.00, and that the price not exceed $90,000.00 if the project is to be completed over a period of years, with the understanding that if the project is to be completed over a period of years we would have to absorb "cost of living" increases and that the Church Council be authorized to arrange the repair schedule and the financing.

Pastor Knutson Resigns

A special congregational meeting was called for Sunday, May 31, 1987, at 9:15 A.M. to extend a call to Pastor Bob as part-time associate pastor for three years. Also on the agenda for that meeting was an item dealing with increasing the call to Pastor Bob to a full-time position. It was pointed out that the majority of congregations comparable in size with

Robyn, Randy, Rita, Pr. Bob, and Becky Knutson, 1986

Chisago Lake Lutheran do have two full-time pastors. The resolution to issue the call for part-time was passed.

At the October meeting of the Church Council, Pastor Bob submitted his resignation stating that he had accepted a call to be senior pastor at First Evangelical Lutheran Church in Worthington, Minnesota, effective December 1. Since his wife was the director of music and the organist, she also submitted her resignation. These resignations were accepted with regret.

A farewell reception was held in their honor on Sunday, November 22, at 2:00 P.M.

1987

Staff Changes

Pastor Bob's areas of responsibility had been youth, Christian education, and together with his wife Rita, worship and music. As the Knutsons prepared to leave, they left these areas with strong lay leadership. Sue Wehrenberg was already serving as part-time Christian education director, and Cheryl Fish was chairperson for the Christian education committee. Vicki

Jim and Jane Iverson

Mickelsen was chairperson for the worship and music committee. James Iverson was senior choir director and his wife, Jane, was directing both the Sunbeam choir and the junior choir. Together they assumed the position of director of music.

David and Virginia Johnson took over the leadership of the senior high youth program. Barbara Reichstadt assumed responsibility for the 7th- and 8th-grade confirmation program. Julie Lauritzen offered to direct the youth ensemble and to be the organist on Sundays when she was not working at Hazelden.

There had also been a change in the janitor position. Jim Atkinson had been hired to replace Gary Johnson, but he stayed only a short time and was replaced by Richard Fisk. Jane Loehlein had worked as day janitor, while Gary Johnson worked as evening janitor. She moved to the evening janitor position when he resigned.

Advertisements were placed in several publications for an organist. The person chosen for this position was Ron Crowl, who assumed

1987 the position of organist and music director effective February 1. Mr. Crowl had a master's degree in organ and many years of experience as church organist in the Catholic church. He had previously served a church in Louisville, Kentucky, and was working with Schmitt Music Company. He was hired for a three-month trial period and at the end of that time was hired for the position on a more permanent basis.

Pastor Peterson knew that he was reaching retirement age and preferred to work with lay staff for the remainder of his time at Chisago Lake. His rationale for that was that it would be better for the next senior pastor to help select the assistant. The decision was then made to look for someone to assume the responsibilities of youth director.

The mutual ministry committee worked with synod personnel and decided to offer a contract to Deborah Nolby through the

Deborah Nolby

Tentmakers program. Miss Nolby was a graduate of Golden Valley Lutheran College with an A.A. degree and she had a B.A. degree in music therapy from the University of Minnesota. The contract was for a full-time position. She accepted the two-year contract and began her work on April 11, 1988.

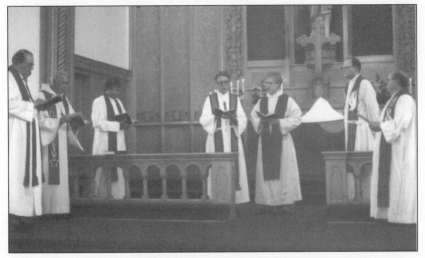

Ordination of Jeff Sandgren

1987

Jeff Sandgren Ordained

Jeff Sandgren completed his seminary studies in the spring of 1987. He received a call to be associate pastor at First Lutheran Church in Harvey, North Dakota. Jeff's roots were deep at Chisago Lake Lutheran Church; his parents, grandparents, and great-grandparents had all been members. Jeff grew up in Center City and spent his childhood and youth in activities at Chisago Lake. He chose to have his ordination service in his home congregation.

Sunday, June 28, 1987, at 3:00 P.M. was the time chosen for this service. The service was beautiful and inspirational and well

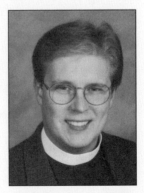

Jeff Sandgren, 1997

attended by family, friends, and members of Chisago Lake.

The presiding pastor for the service was the Reverend Russell Peterson, senior pastor at Chisago Lake and the ordainer was the Reverend David Hernes, pastor of First Lutheran Church in Glenville, Minnesota, where Jeff had served his internship. The Reverend Nils C. Hellevik of Bethel Evangelical Lutheran Church in Minneapolis was the preacher.

Other pastors who participated in the service were the Reverends Robert Knutson, James Almquist, John Twiton, and Marvin Holje, senior pastor at First Lutheran in Harvey.

News Tidbits from 1987

1987

- Point Pleasant Heights, a new part of the Parmly complex, had a grand opening from January 31 to February 1, 1987.
- Chisago Lake Lutheran Church received a letter of thanks from Bishop Chilstrom of the Minnesota Synod for going beyond their synod commitment of $36,000.
- Glad Peterson started a Bible study on Galatians for those wanting to continue their study of the Bible to supplement the Search series. This series was followed by a study of Psalms in the fall.
- Pastor Bob started a senior high Bible study on Sundays at 6:00 P.M.
- Programs that continued to be a part of the congregation's life were the Sunday morning adult class known as P.E.P. (Parish Enrichment Program), the senior citizen organization known as OKs, the adult fellowship group known as Odds 'n Ends, and the summer vacation Bible school. The LCW continued to hold monthly meetings and/or special events.
- The service of taping the Sunday worship service and distributing it to homebound members also continued.

- A clown service was held on March 8, led by a group from Gustavus Adolphus College called Disciple Ship.
- On Saturday evening, April 25, the Gustavus Adolphus College Chapel Choir and Bell Choir gave a concert in the sanctuary. Dr. David Johnson, dean of the college, was guest preacher for the services on Sunday morning.
- Gladie Moe continued to teach the 5th grade first communion class during Lent with the class having their first communion on Maundy Thursday.
- There was a May 9 medley banquet for all women and girls.
- In the summer, 41 children attended Luther Point Bible Camp.
- Thirty-eight people with Spoke Folk held their training at Chisago Lake for the second year. They presented their homecoming concert at the church on August 9.

1987

- Dawn Reichstadt, a member of Chisago Lake attending college, spent the summer working in Christian ministry in Yellowstone Park.
- William Johnson, Hinckley, Minnesota, translated into English the book that was published after the

William Johnson

fiftieth anniversary celebration of the congregation in 1904. Two copies were put on acid-free paper, one for the archives and the other to be kept in the safe.
- Melvin Dahlquist, a member of the evangelism committee, erected a sign pointing the way to Chisago Lake Lutheran Church on property owned by Richard Gustafson along Highway 8 east of Center City.
- A fence was erected around the roof of the education building to deter children from playing there, both to protect them from danger and to prevent roof damage.

+ A double bulb light on a pole was erected in the lower parking lot at a cost of $1,312.

+ The *Spirit Touching Spirit* hymnal was introduced and used for the contemporary worship services.

+ A synthesizer was purchased and a stand was made for it out of old parts from the organ by Raymond Wikelius.

+ There was a congregational picnic at the parsonage on Rally Day, September 13.

+ The annual Swedish communion service was held on October 9, at 11:00 A.M. with Dr. William Hyllengren. A noon luncheon was served after the service. The decision was made that this would be the last annual Swedish service.

+ Dr. Rudolph Burke conducted a Spiritual Renewal Days series of meetings November 8-10.

+ The last Sunday of Advent the senior choir presented the cantata *The Song of Christmas* by Roy Ringwald at both services.

1988

+ The Thanksgiving offering of $1,407.25 went to World Hunger.

+ The Christmas offering of $3,269.87 was divided between Our Savior's Shelter in Minneapolis and the local food shelf.

+ End of the year financial reports showed that all financial obligations for 1987 were met and all building bonds were paid. The only debt was the Lutheran Brotherhood loan for the education building amounting to $77,305.91, which was scheduled to be paid in full by 1998.

Beginning of the ELCA

January 1, 1988, was the official beginning of the new Evangelical Lutheran Church in America. This merger brought into one united Lutheran church body 63 percent of the Lutherans in the United States. Membership was approximately 5,316,500 in 11,035 congregations. The ELCA was divided into 65 Synods. Chisago Lake was one of 17 congregations in the North Conference of the East Metropolitan

Minnesota Synod. This synod was the smallest one geographically and was comprised of 113 congregations in four counties: Chisago, Washington, Ramsey, and Dakota. Membership of these congregations totaled about 135,000, making it one of the largest synods numerically.

The installation service for Bishop Erdahl and all members of the new synod boards and council was held at Gustavus Adolphus Lutheran Church in Saint Paul on Sunday, January 10, at 3:00 P.M.

The theme for the ELCA was "Come Share the Spirit." Come — have an open door to all people. Share — witness and share your faith with others. Spirit — there is excitement as the fruit of the Holy Spirit is shared.

With the beginning of the new church came the necessity of updating the congregation's constitution to coincide with the constitution of the ELCA. Jane Iverson volunteered to chair a committee for this purpose. Serving with her on that committee were Eleanor Shogren, Elaine Lundberg, Gaylord Swenson, and Howard Johnson.

1988

A special congregational meeting was held on Sunday, October 16, 1988, for the first reading of the proposed constitution changes. The second reading was scheduled for the annual meeting to be held in January 1989.

Financing for Window Project

The contract with Warren Keith Studios for the window restoration was signed in April 1988. In May the first six windows on the west side of the sanctuary had been removed. A committee was needed to plan for financing the window project. David C. Johnson and Gertrude Lindo volunteered to serve on the committee along with George Mickelsen, council president.

Some people had indicated a desire to pay for a window in memory of a loved one. The cost of one window was $3,300. Several windows were paid for in this way. Also during these months several bequests were received from estates of deceased members. In some cases, a window was paid for with money from a bequest. As the project was under way, donations came in from many sources.

Organist Ron Crowl offered to present a benefit organ concert for the window fund. This concert was presented on Sunday, October 2, 1988, at 3:00 P.M. A free-will offering was received, which amounted to $3,011. An additional $1,200 was received for the fund the following Sunday, bringing the total of the fund to $36,000, or 42 percent of the total amount needed.

The six windows were completed and paid for; however, in the middle of 1989 some internal problems occurred at the Keith Studios and the project was put on hold. It took more than a year for these problems to be resolved and the project was not continued until August 1990.

Pastor Peterson Resigns

1988

At the council meeting in March 1988, Pastor Peterson presented his letter of resignation, effective in August. He had originally planned to retire in August 1989, but after much consideration and prayerful deliberation felt that this would be the right time to step down.

The workload for only one pastor at Chisago Lake was very heavy. The double services on Sunday, the many committees to oversee, and the many baptisms, weddings, and funerals—all this made for a very demanding schedule, even with many lay people on the staff.

The Reverend Marilyn Breckenridge, assistant to Bishop Erdahl, was assigned to be the council advisor and to guide them through the call procedure. She made several visits to Chisago Lake and on Sunday, May 15, was the guest preacher. She had led the council retreat in March, and on June 20 she met with the council to discuss the interim pastor position.

By July, the decision had been unanimously made to call Pastor

Paul H. Knuston to be the interim pastor. His duties would begin on August 16, 1988, and his first Sunday would be August 21.

A farewell party in honor of Pastor Russ and Glad Peterson was planned for Sunday August 7, at 2:00 P.M. In spite of the sorrow at seeing the Petersons leave, the party was light-hearted. Many people came to share this parting time with the Petersons. The choir sang and many tributes were given and memories shared. Since the Petersons were retiring, they weren't really moving away; they only went to Chisago City where they had purchased a home.

Glad and Pr. Russ Peterson

Contemporary Service Survey
1988

Rita Knutson had spent a great deal of time looking at various options for a contemporary service. She wanted one that was doctrinally correct and simple to use—one with hymns that were easy to learn. The *Spirit Touching Spirit* book met her expectations. The congregation was using this service every month and was becoming familiar with it. Ron Crowl, the new organist was not familiar with this service and was uncomfortable using it.

The worship and music committee conducted a survey to determine how to proceed with this service. Nearly 300 people responded to this survey. Although 247 people responded that they liked the contemporary service and 174 of these liked the *Spirit Touching Spirit* book, only 11 said they were willing to help lead the music and only 8 were willing to serve on the worship and music committee. In response to the question "Do you make it a point to attend the contemporary service regularly?" there were 104 who responded yes and 176 who responded no.

Without people to help lead the music with voice and instruments, the contemporary service as it had been used was dropped.

Plans for Billy Graham Crusade

Most of the churches in the extended area, including Chisago Lake Lutheran, were making plans for a Billy Graham Crusade to be held at the Forest Lake High School Stadium in 1989. A crusade requires planning and preparation for a year or more in advance. The evangelism committee began attending meetings and working on publicity for this event.

New Cemetery Guidelines

Care and mowing of the cemeteries is a difficult and time consuming task. To increase the efficiency of the work, the following guidelines were proposed:

1988

+ Small flowers may be planted within 18 inches of the monument or marker in the Glader and Chisago Lake Cemeteries.
+ In the Hillside Cemetery, flowers may be placed (not planted) prior to Memorial Day but must be removed by June 15. Flowers not removed by June 15 will be removed by the cemetery caretaker.
+ Small flowers planted in the other two cemeteries may remain throughout the season if properly maintained.
+ Potted plants or urns are permitted in Hillside.

Change of Missionary Support

Chisago Lake Lutheran Church, through the women's organization, had been contributing $1,000 each year to the support of the Richard Meier family, serving as missionaries in Argentina. They completed

their work there and returned to the
United States. Since they did not need
support any longer, our support was
transferred to the Reverend Allen and
Jean Swanson, missionaries in Taiwan.
So that they might get to know us and
we them, they visited Chisago Lake on
June 16, and participated in the
Women of the ELCA meeting.

Pr. Al and Jean Swanson

During the summer, the vacation Bible school gathered an offering of $210, which was given to Pastor Al and Jean Swanson.

News Tidbits from 1988

+ Pastor Russ and Gladys Peterson attended Cursillo weekends.
  This was the beginning of Chisago Lake's involvement with
  Cursillo. From this beginning many members have become
  involved, and Chisago Lake Lutheran church has become a
  host congregation for Cursillo weekends.
+ Dr. Wilton Bergstrand conducted the Lenten midweek services.
+ Chisago Lake congregation collected $935 and 726 pounds of
  food for Minnesota Foodshare in March.
+ The year 1988 was the 350th anniversary of the arrival of the
  first Swedish immigrants in the United States. Many tour
  groups came from Sweden during the year to visit the places
  where their people had settled. Although this area was not settled until 1851, many tours came to the Chisago Lakes area
  and this church was one of the places on their itinerary.
+ The South East Asian Ministry was part of our synod's
  responsibility. Thousands of South East Asian immigrants
  were already living in the Twin Cities area and another two
  thousand Hmong were expected in 1988. All churches were
  asked to help meet the needs of these new neighbors.

1988

+ On July 30, 1988, Rebecca Knutson, daughter of Pastor Bob and Rita Knutson, and Wayne Herrmann were married at Chisago Lake. The congregation was invited to attend the wedding and to participate in the reception.

+ Robyn Knutson, the Knutsons' other daughter, was also married at Chisago Lake on September 20, 1997. Robyn was the bride of David Schrader. The congregation was invited to attend the wedding.

Pr. Bob, Rita, Wayne, Rebecca, Robyn, and Randy

1988

+ The new Women of the ELCA organization continued to function much as in the past. Quilts were made in the winter, a Ladies Night Out was held on May 6, and the annual visit to the Marie Sandvik Mission was made. Some activity was planned for each month and circles met monthly.

+ Glad's Bible study in the winter and spring was on the Gospel of John. P.E.P. continued on Sundays with the Christian education director as coordinator.

+ Odds 'n Ends and OKs continued their monthly activities.

+ Average attendance at worship in 1988 was 357.

Call Committee Appointed

Beginning in May 1988, the Reverend Marilyn Breckenridge, assistant to Bishop Erdahl, met with the Church Council on a regular basis to help with the call process. The synod had guidelines to make the process work, but the procedure had flexibility to adapt to each congregation's needs. She also assisted the council in selecting an interim pastor.

Pr. P. H. Knutson

By August, the Reverend Paul H. Knutson was called to be the interim pastor. He had served as campus pastor at Luther Northwestern Seminary since 1976. Prior to that time, he had served two churches and been chaplain at Mercy Medical Center. This was his first interim call, which he felt would enable him to reach his goal of returning to congregational ministry. He began his work at Chisago Lake on August 16. Pastor Knutson had also been a docent at the Como Park Zoo, and he adorned his office with pictures of some of his favorite zoo animals.

1988

The call committee was finalized by August. Members were Kermit Christensen, James Iverson, Marie Cotch, Bonnie Anderson, Linda Lindgren, Deborah Nolby, and Clarence Johnson. Kermit Christensen was elected chairman.

Members of the congregation were given the opportunity to fill out a congregational profile to determine what kind of leadership they were looking for. Results of this profile showed the following as highest in priority: preacher, worship leader, evangelism, minister in crisis, administrator, counselor, share leadership, interpreter of theology, teach adults, and youth leader. These needs were summarized as follows:

1. Conduct a meaningful worship service. Preach and proclaim the inerrant and infallible Word of God.

2. Visiting those in need; homebound, ill, bereaved, crisis.

3. Evangelism; visit inactive and unchurched people.

4. Work well with the staff and council effectively.

5. Skills in making the church real and meaningful and alive to all ages.

6. A pastor whose life is a true witness to Christ.

The call committee received profiles of 12 pastors. Eight of these were given further consideration.

A special congregational meeting was called for March 12, 1989, after the 10:30 worship service for the purpose of voting to call a pastor. The call committee submitted its recommendation to extend a call to Dr. Dale L. Peterson. Dr. Peterson was currently serving St. Paul Lutheran Church in Farmers Branch, Texas.

The meeting was held and the resolution to call Dr. Dale Peterson to serve as senior pastor of the Chisago Lake Evangelical Lutheran Church passed with 171 voting yes and 15 voting no.

1988

Dr. Peterson accepted the call to Chisago Lake with plans to arrive in Center City the first week in May. His first Sunday in the pulpit was May 7, 1989.

Parsonage Repaired

After Pastor Russ and Glad Peterson moved out of the parsonage, it was offered to the organist, Ron Crowl, since the interim pastor was commuting from his home in Roseville and not using the house. Ron lived there for several months. In March 1989, the Church Council received a letter of resignation from Ron, effective June 1, which was read and accepted. He was asked to move out of the parsonage so that it could be repaired and readied for the new pastor and his family.

A bid was received for new seamless steel siding for the parsonage and replacement of all doors and windows. This bid, together with a bid to upgrade the electrical system came to approximately $32,000.

The memorial committee transferred $15,000 from undesignated funds to the parsonage restoration fund to enable the project to be started.

An appeal was made to the congregation to contribute to this fund so the work could be completed. Other work to be done included new kitchen cupboards, repair of the front porch including combination windows to make it a three-season porch, and some interior redecorating. More than 40 people volunteered their time on this project.

Staff Transition

The last Sunday for Pastor Paul Knutson, the interim pastor, was April 9. Confirmation had originally been scheduled for May, but since Pastor Knutson had taught the class for eight months, parents requested that confirmation be on his last Sunday. The other Sundays in April were provided for with guest preachers. April 16 was designated as Chemical Awareness Sunday, and Per Nilson, a student at Luther Northwestern Seminary and an intern at Hazelden conducted the worship services.

1988

With Ron Crowl's departure June 1, James Iverson assumed the tasks of music director and Kathleen DeBolt was hired as interim organist for the summer. By fall, Janelle Schauer/Anderson was hired as organist.

Carrie Ann Holmquist, who had served the congregation as treasurer for nine years, presented her letter of resignation to the Church Council in March, effective June 1. Duane Arnold was hired to take care of the treasurer's duties, and Norma Sellman, who had assisted Carrie Ann with the financial secretary's duties, assumed those duties. Deborah Nolby, youth director, was married to Sidney Wolterstorff at her home church, Christ the King Lutheran in New Brighton on June 17.

Youth Work

Under Debbie Nolby Wolterstorff's direction, the youth work continued to grow and flourish. She enjoyed sports (especially softball) and
helped organize the inter-church softball league in the summer and the
volleyball league in the winter. Youth activity pages in the newsletters
listed bowling tournaments, ski trips, and camping excursions.

Together with other youth directors in the community, a group
called YOWSA (Youthworkers Organizing Wonderful Situations and
Activities) was formed. Many of the youth activities were with the
other community church youth groups. There were day trips to Valley
Fair or inner-tubing on the river at Somerset, Wisconsin. There were
family trips to Twins' Games, all-night parties on prom night, and lock-
ins for different grades. There were progressive dinners, hayrides, and
swimming parties—all the things that youth enjoy.

She also was concerned about their spiritual growth and had a
youth forum for grades 7 through 12 during the Sunday school hour
and Bible study for grades 6 through 12 on Wednesday evenings at
7:00 P.M. Debbie also participated in the confirmation retreats at
Luther Point. She had a youth choir, and with other churches the
youth presented the musical *Live it to the Max*.

The youth continued to participate in "Sounds Like Love" at
Prince of Peace Lutheran Church in Burnsville, and to attend the
Lutheran Youth conventions. During the summer of 1989 four youth
made a trip to Appalachia for a week with the Appalachia Service
Project, traveling with the young people from Christ the King
Lutheran Church in New Brighton.

While Deb was working with the youth, Sue Wehrenberg, the part-time Christian education director, was busy providing educational opportunities for all ages. Records show that during the 1988–89 Sunday school year, 147 children were enrolled from age 3 to grade 6, with 20 teachers.

Sue Wehrenberg

- ✦ Vacation Bible school for a week in June had 90 children.
- ✦ A special Advent program by the Sunday school children was presented at a 10:30 A.M. Sunday service.
- ✦ In the summer of 1988, 38 children attended Luther Point Bible Camp; the next summer 32 children attended.
- ✦ The P.E.P. (Parish Enrichment Program) for adults continued with about 20 to 25 attending each Sunday.

One of the interesting projects the children were involved in at this time was raising money to bring a child from the inner city of New York City to Camp Connection near Moose Lake, Minnesota. The camp was owned and operated by Dan Celantano who had grown up in New York City himself. It was his goal to bring children to Minnesota to experience life in a completely different environment and to help them become aware of opportunities outside the New York slums. It cost about $500 for a child to come for a week, and our children sponsored one child in 1988 and one in 1989. It was also possible for a few people to go to the camp and meet the sponsored child.

1988

Dr. Dale Peterson
1989–1998

PASTOR DALE LORLIN PETERSON was born in 1949 in Fort Worth, Texas. He graduated from the University of Texas at Arlington in 1971 and received his master of divinity degree from Northwestern Theological Seminary in Saint Paul, Minnesota, in 1975. He was ordained on June 15, 1975, and began his ministry at Peace Lutheran Church in Vernon, Texas. In 1979, he accepted a call to House of Prayer Lutheran Church in San Antonio, Texas, where he served a short time before being called to Saint Paul Lutheran Church in Farmers Branch, Texas, in 1980. It is from Saint Paul Lutheran that he was called to be the senior pastor at Chisago Lake Lutheran Church. In 1983, Pastor Dale Peterson received a doctor of ministry degree from McCormick Theological Seminary in Chicago, Illinois.

Dale Peterson married Tamra An Womack on June 26, 1971, shortly before he entered the seminary in Saint Paul. They have three

Pastor Dale Peterson and family

children, Angela born in 1975, Kelli born in 1977, and David born in 1979.

Dr. Peterson was installed as senior pastor at Chisago Lake on Sunday, June 11, 1989, at the 10:30 A.M. service. Pastor Ron Peterson, assistant to Bishop Lowell Erdahl, participated in the service.

Pastor Peterson's introductory article in the May newsletter revealed some of his aspirations as he began his ministry at Chisago Lake.

> I wish I could begin this pastorate with an immediate, healthy relationship with you and every member of Chisago Lake Lutheran Church. Wouldn't it be great if somehow we already knew each other's faith stories? I'm interested in knowing the people events, and dreams that form your spiritual side of life. But healthy relationships take time. Trust is built best for healthy relationships by sharing some of life's experiences together.... From the beginning let's work on becoming "One in Christ" as St. Paul encourages believers (Ephesians 4:3-12).

Education Rooms Used for Court

During 1989, a new courthouse was under construction in Center City. While this construction was taking place, it was necessary to find a place where some of the court business could be conducted. The county officials approached the Church Council about using space on the lower level of the education building for some court proceedings. After due consideration, a contract was drawn up with Chisago County wherein they agreed to give the church a donation of $500 per month to cover extra expenses for utilities and janitor services. The county moved some necessary furnishings into the large room on the lower level early in the summer and their use of these facilities continued well into 1990.

John Wesley White Crusade

After many months of planning and work by volunteers from more than 20 congregations including many denominations, a John Wesley White Crusade was held in Forest Lake July 23 to 30, 1989. John Wesley White was a Billy Graham associate evangelist whose crusade ministry was built on exactly the same model and principles of a Billy Graham crusade. He had been in this ministry for more than 20 years and had preached the gospel of Jesus Christ in more than 100 countries around the globe.

1989

Chisago Lake Lutheran Church was a participant in this ecumenical evangelism program, which covered the Chisago–Washington County area. Sessions were held at the Forest Lake High School athletic field, and buses transported people from around the area who chose not to drive their own cars. This was an opportunity to strengthen the spiritual life of individuals and congregations throughout the community. The stadium was well filled each evening and even when the rains came, people did not leave.

Synod Campaign for Namibia

When the ELCA was formed, the goal was to continue any programs that were already in progress in the merging synods. One of the programs that came from the ALC was a concern for the Lutheran Church in Namibia. Namibia is the most Lutheran country in the world, and these, our brothers and sisters in Christ, were struggling under the apartheid system imposed on them by the government of South Africa.

July 4, 1989, our Independence Day, was chosen as the kick-off date for a Saint Paul Area Synod fund-raising campaign to assist the Christians in Namibia in resettling more than 70,000 exiles who were returning to their homeland to participate in their first free elections in November 1989. Goals for this synod were prayers for the people of Namibia and a donation of one dollar per baptized member. The children contributed with their "Quarters for Namibia" Sunday school mission project. The campaign would end at our Thanksgiving time, which would coincide with their election time. Financial records show that Chisago Lake Lutheran Church contributed $1,265 to this fund. The Republic of Namibia became independent on March 21, 1990.

1989 New Christian Education Programs

Pastor Dale Peterson brought with him several innovative ideas for improving our Christian education program. New confirmation materials had already been discussed and he brought to Chisago Lake an intergenerational approach, which he had used in his former congregation. Confirmation would now take place on Sunday mornings during the Sunday school hour and each child was required to bring a parent or other adult to the class. At first adults found this somewhat distressing, but before long parents were enthused over this new approach. This was a two-year program with one year being an overview of the Bible and one year a study of Lutheran liturgy from the *Lutheran Book of Worship*, which included study of the Apostles' Creed and the Lord's Prayer.

In 1986, an addition was built to the local high school and the 9th grade students were moved from the junior high school to the senior high school. The 9th graders were given the opportunity to participate in extra-curricular activities after school, which made it very difficult to schedule confirmation classes for these students. Parents and confirmation teachers soon realized that a change would be needed and the decision was to have confirmation classes for children in 7th and 8th grades with students confirmed in the spring of their 8th grade.

To prepare children for confirmation in 7th and 8th grades, a Y.S.L. (Young Searcher's League) was started for children in grades 3 through 6. These classes were held on two Sunday afternoons each month from 2:00 to 3:30 P.M. The first hour was spent in Bible study, using workbooks prepared for each student, and the last half hour included a time of recreation and refreshments. Peg McCubbin volunteered to lead these sessions with help from several parents.

Small Group Stewardship Meetings

Pastor Peterson and Tamra decided they would like to host a series of stewardship meetings at the parsonage to give the members of the congregation an opportunity to see what work had been done on the parsonage. Seventeen meetings were scheduled, five of which were held in

1989

the Green Room at church, and the other 12 were held at the parsonage. There were five morning meetings, five afternoon meetings, and seven evening meetings. Parishioners were asked to sign up for the meeting that best fit their schedule. After the meet-

Parsonage

ings had been held, council members were available on Sunday afternoon, October 22, to meet with members who may not have had an opportunity to attend a small group meeting.

Stewardship month ended with a loyalty supper on Sunday, October 29, at which time Cathy Leestma was the guest speaker. Cathy was a motivational speaker from Garden Grove, California, who was in the Twin Cities area of Minnesota for several days. She came to Chisago Lake to conduct a seminar for all women of the church on Saturday, October 28. She was also an author and wrote the book *Supermom/Superpooped*.

Along with financial pledges received during the stewardship meetings were pledges of time and talent. In order to organize the volunteer commitments received, three volunteer coordinators were trained to serve the congregation by connecting the volunteers to the places within the church program where their talents could be best used. These coordinators were Judy Nelson, Dorothy Starr, and Barbara Wikelius. The ladies worked hard to make the volunteer program a success, but after a period of a few months their committee disbanded.

Space Assessed

As the number of people on the church staff increased, office space became more and more congested. A space committee had been looking at these needs during the time of the interim pastor. However, it was decided not to make any major changes until the new pastor was involved in the decision making. When the education building was constructed, the room between the Green Room and the offices was designated as the library. When office space became crowded, the library was moved to the first office space and served as a reception room.

1990

The secretary and finance staff then shared the room that had been the library. This proved to be unsatisfactory, especially after computers made their appearance.

After Pastor Peterson arrived, a space task force was organized to study the space needs and to make recommendations. Once again the library was relocated, this time to the hallway leading into the undercroft. The sacristy behind the organ had been used as a music office, and the music supplies were moved to an area next to the choir room. This area had been used as a youth room and the youth moved to a room on the lower level.

The Christian education director's position had been increased from 10 hours to 25 hours each week and Sue Wehrenberg was given her own office. However, Sue Wehrenberg also had other part-time work and felt that this would be too many hours for her. She resigned from this position effective January 1, 1990. Larry and Midge Nelson accepted the responsibilities for Sunday school for the remainder of the year, and the Christian education committee with the help of parent volunteers and other staff persons kept the education program going.

Befriender's Ministry

Pastor Peterson had been trained in the Stephen Ministry program and had used this program in his previous congregation. Some other congregations in this area were using a program known as "Befriender's Ministry," which was a program of the Wilder Foundation. After studying the two programs, Befriender's Ministry was chosen as the one to be used in this congregation. Marie Cotch, Esther Grimm, and Eleanor Trippler were trained as leaders and the program was put into place in the fall of 1990. Befriender's is a program designed to provide a friend to someone who is dealing with grief, illness, divorce, depression, job loss, or some other trauma in their life.

1990

Mission Statement

In 1990 a new mission statement was adopted for Chisago Lake Lutheran Church. It read as follows:

Led by the Spirit...

We, the people of Chisago Lake Lutheran Church, being led by the Holy Spirit, are gathered to share in God's love; to strengthen our purpose of worship, witness, learning, support and service by:

Proclaiming the Word of God and rightly administering the Sacraments, providing worship experiences in a variety of ways through music, prayer, praise, and thanksgiving;

Showing concern for the needs of others, both young and old, ministering to those needs, and caring for one another;

Preparing God's people to understand and deal with their role as Christians in everyday life by education and training both youth and adults in the Word of God;

Sharing our faith with one another, reaching out to bring Christ to others by our personal witness, telling all people of God's love, and encouraging them to believe in His Son, Jesus Christ, as Lord and Savior;

Encouraging each other to use our time, talents, and financial resources to carry out the ministries of our congregation.

Having a sense of unity in the Spirit, we can do all these things through Jesus Christ who gives us our strength!

Annual Meeting 1990

1990

The pastor's report covering the year 1989, shows that Chisago Lake members generously supported the work of the church:

> $40,000.00 was paid in full to synod benevolence.
> $4,745.87 was given for World Hunger.
> $1,265.00 was given to the Namibia Support Fund.

Although the congregation had begun the year with a $5,000 deficit, the year ended with all bills paid and about $5,000 in the bank.

A resolution to accept the recommendation of the Church Council to establish a youth committee separate from the Christian education committee was passed. This is to be a permanently established committee made up of adults, but also open to youth. The committee will have a council representative.

A bequest from the Arnold and Edith Johnson estate was acknowledged. This bequest was specified to be invested and the interest used to provide scholarships for Christian education such as college, seminary, Bible camp, etc.

Distributions from the fund are to be in accordance with the following conditions and procedures:

1. Only members of the congregation may apply.

2. Each spring the committee shall announce the amount available via the church bulletin and Kichi-Saga, and request applications consistent with the bequest.

3. Distributions may be made to one or more individuals.

4. A committee comprised of the Senior Pastor, the Youth Director (ex officio), and Chairpersons of the Youth, Social Ministry and Christian Education Committees shall determine the distribution.

This fund continues to grow and to provide scholarships for members of Chisago Lake Lutheran Church who wish to attend a Christian college or seminary and to help children attend Bible camp.

———

1990

Organ Console Rebuilt

A special congregational meeting was held on April 8, 1990, at 11:30 A.M. to consider a motion presented by the Church Council to have the organ console replaced with new solid state controls, using the existing cabinet. The congregation voted unanimously to approve a contract with Gerald A. Orvold for this work in the amount of $18,300. Special envelopes were made available for donations for this project. The project was completed in September and the account was paid in full. Mr. Orvold's opinion was that this console should last at least 25 years. The organ had 39 ranks, 21 stops, and 2,025 pipes. The organ dedication service took place on Sunday, October 21, with organist Janelle Anderson playing a concert of selections that illustrated the flexibility of the instrument.

New Personnel Added to Staff

In January 1990, the Church Council received a letter from Jim and Jane Iverson requesting a leave of absence. Their positions as choir directors were filled temporarily by Rodney Sietsema, Roxy Bahn, and Jane Miller.

With the positions of music and choir director and Christian education director open, the Church Council began a study of how the staff should be structured to provide the most effective leadership for the congregation.

The Iversons did not return, and by September a decision had been made to hire two part-time staff who were students at Luther Northwestern Seminary. Evey Phillips had previously worked in a congregation of 4000 families in San Diego, California. She was a talented musician and became the music and choir director at Chisago Lake. LaDonna Lee's expertise was in Christian education and she became the Christian education director. Both were introduced to the congregation on Rally Day, September 9, 1990.

1990

In January 1991, they both began their contextual education program at Chisago Lake. This program would fulfill their seminary practical studies requirements with Pastor Dale as their supervisor over a two-year period. The studies included projects including teaching, preaching, social ministry, and cross-cultural studies. Each student had a committee of seven lay members to serve as supportive supervisors.

Both of these women became active members of Chisago Lake Lutheran Church, and LaDonna Lee asked that this congregation sponsor her seminary candidacy.

Jane Loehlein resigned from her position as evening janitor and Gordon MacDonald was hired to replace her. Donna Anderson continued as morning janitor. For many years Len Kobeska took care of the church boiler and heating system. When he was no longer able to do this, DeWayne Weise replaced him.

With changes being made in the organization of the nursery, Kelly Ford was put on the staff as a nursery professional. When Kelly was no longer able to continue, Ruth Selden and Dawn Meredith, were hired to serve as nursery attendants. Each would serve on alternate Sundays and other times as they were called for special events.

Pastor Russ Peterson Returns Part-time

At the March 20, 1990, Church Council meeting, Pastor Russell Peterson was approved as visitation pastor for Chisago Lake. He would spend one day each week visiting the elderly, sick, and shut-in. He

Pr. Russ Peterson

would make routine visits and offer communion to those not able to attend church. He visited members in nursing homes and occasionally made hospital calls. At a special worship service on October 21, 1990, Pastor Russ Peterson was commissioned "Pastor Emeritus" of our congregation. This honorary title emphasized the blessings our faithful, retired pastors are to our community. Gladys Peterson also continued her connections with Chisago Lake by teaching a Bible study class each Thursday morning and evening.

1991

Iringa Diocese—Companion Synod

The ELCA developed a program in which each of its 65 Synods became a companion synod to a synod of the Lutheran church in another country. The companion synod for the Saint Paul Area Synod is the Iringa Diocese in Tanzania. At the synod conference in 1990, it was decided to help the Iringa Diocese build a Bible college/seminary. Chisago Lake Lutheran Church became one of 20 churches in the

Saint Paul Area Synod to pledge $20,000 to the building of this school. This outreach became part of the yearly budget at $4,000 for five years. The Iringa Diocese had a total of almost 53,000 members in 155 congregations in 1989. These congregations were served by 47 pastors.

Mission90

Mission90 was a church-wide emphasis on believers returning to regular Bible study, witness, and service. All ELCA members were encouraged to read the entire Bible during 1991. We were asked to support a young congregation in the United States and one overseas. At Chisago Lake we participated in Mission90 in a variety of ways. Gladys Peterson was willing to become a Bible study leader. The prayer partners program was begun—a program where the youth were paired with an adult in a prayer fellowship. The budget item for the school in Tanzania was our world outreach. We participated in the homeless ministry at Our Savior's Lutheran Church in Minneapolis. And helps were provided for the Bible reading in 1991.

1991

As a reminder of Mission90, the following statement was printed in the bulletin each Sunday:

> Members of Chisago Lake Lutheran Church believe that we have been sent by God, called by Jesus, and empowered by the Holy Spirit to:
>
> CELEBRATE our life together in Christ;
> CULTIVATE personal growth in Christ Jesus;
> COMMUNICATE the Good News of Christ with others, and
> CARE about one another in the spirit of Jesus!

Summer Events

During the summer of 1990, Julie Oftelie, a college student from Chisago Lake, participated in a Campus Crusade for Christ international summer project in Europe. The congregation helped to support her with an offering of $800, which was matched with $600 from Lutheran Brotherhood.

The first Triennial Convention of the church-wide Women of the Evangelical Lutheran Church in America (W/ELCA) organization was held in Anaheim, California, in July. Barbara Wikelius, vice president of the synodical women's organization, was a Saint Paul Area Synod delegate to this convention.

Eleven youth with youth director, Deb Wolterstorff, and adult leader, Bea Nelson, went to Hancock County, Tennessee, from June 8 to 17 on an Appalachia Service Project mission trip. They went with a group from Deb's church, Christ the King in New Brighton.

The Pilot Outreach Jail Ministry began in July. Members of this congregation took turns with other churches in the area to meet with the jail inmates on Sunday mornings for Bible study and fellowship. Several members have participated in this ongoing program.

Fall Programs

1990

Rally Day was celebrated for the purpose of gathering the congregation at the beginning of the fall season for worship and fellowship, to introduce Sunday school teachers, and for classes to meet each other. In 1990 the worship service was followed by a booya soup picnic on the parsonage lawn. The booya was cooked by Dick and Jackie Genung and Steve Grossmann. Members were asked to bring breads and desserts. The picnic ended with a tug-o-war—Swedes against non-Swedes! Guess who won—the non-Swedes!! Evidence that this is a changing community!

In the afternoon at 3:30 P.M., the Linjeflyg Chorus, sponsored by the Swedish Airline, presented a concert at Chisago Lake Church. Carl Werner Peterson, a pilot with Swedish Airline who had relatives who were members of Chisago Lake Church, arranged for this group to come.

Also beginning the first week in September 1990 was the men's brotherhood breakfast. Men would meet for breakfast and Christian fellowship at 6:30 A.M. each Wednesday morning. This early hour would allow for men to join in before going to their daily work. The purpose of this gathering was to bond and support one another and to begin the day with scripture and prayer.

The "Joint Committee Night" was also begun in September. Having all committees meet at the same time was an attempt to avoid wasting time and effort, to better coordinate the ministry of the church, and to enable the committees to meet together when needed.

The "Adopt A Highway" program also came to Chisago Lake in the fall of 1990. The congregation has continued to participate in this effort to keep our Minnesota highway ditches clean by being responsible for a two-mile stretch of Highway 8. Members collect trash three times each year.

In November the first "Saturday Night Alive" was held. The purpose of these events was to provide a fun family night out. This first event featured Janet Kay (Grossmann), daughter-in-law of Herb and Joan Grossmann. Janet became involved with Teen Missions International in 1977 as a part of an evangelistic team. She and six others sang together and traveled for one year giving concerts and church services in the New England states. They also toured in Scotland for two months. From 1978 to 1980 Janet was on staff at Teen Missions as a worship leader. In 1990 she completed her second album and had a summer tour through Eastern Europe.

Children's church was begun on alternate Sundays with volunteers as leaders. Before the sermon, children age three through grade two left the sanctuary to go to the Green Room. There, Bible stories were told, songs were learned, and activities were provided to enhance the learning experience.

1990

Gleanings from the 1991 Annual Report

+ At the end of 1990, there were 1,230 baptized members; 941 were confirmed members.

+ At the request of Lutheran Social Service, the Church Council approved an every member appeal for contributions. The goal for our congregation was $16,500 over a three-year period.

+ A bequest of $39,258 was received from the estate of Viola E. Peterson to be used for current needs. The bequest was partially used as follows:

> $4,000 designated as benevolence
>
> $4,000 for a new lawn mower for the cemetery
>
> $11,000 for new carpeting on the building's second level
>
> $2,500 for gutters on the parsonage
>
> $5,000 for a computer system for the office

+ Between $20,000 and $25,000 was needed to complete the window project in 1991.

1991

New Summer Programs

At a goal-setting meeting of the Christian education committee on March 9, 1991, a decision was made to have a Sunday education program during the summer. This was an intergenerational program held between services, June through August. Families gathered on the lawn or in the fellowship hall for storytelling, singing, games, videos, and the like. Programs were planned to emphasize special events. One example would be "Proud to be an American," which was held on the Sunday before the 4th of July reminding us of the blessings we enjoy as Americans.

A summer activities program was planned for children ages 3 to 8 from 9:30 to 11:30 A.M. eight times during June and July. Kathy

Lindo and Betty Ness coordinated the program, which involved sports, games, storytelling, baking, and crafts. The purpose of these activities was to provide safe play in a Christian setting for children who may otherwise have been home alone or playing on the street. About 40 children participated in these activities. Youth from the church, as well as other adults, formed the staff.

Service Saturday was also begun. This was a program for the youth and their adult leaders to perform work projects for members who were not able to do them alone. This included washing windows, cleaning up lawns, painting, or any other chores that might require climbing a ladder or something difficult. The first Saturday of each month was set aside for this purpose.

Vacation Bible school was moved from June to August. Daily attendance reported during the week was as high as 94. The special VBS offering amounted to about $250, which was sent to People's Primary School in Namibia to be used for books for their library.

1991   Another project started in 1991 was a sister relationship with First Lutheran Church in Saint Paul. Their church is located in a part of Saint Paul where there are many recent immigrants and people living in poverty. Their food shelf was in need of additional items for stocking their shelves. Food would be collected by the circles and brought to the church kitchen. Dormon Trippler offered to drive to Saint Paul once each month to deliver these supplies. This project spread to include the entire congregation and has continued.

Staff Changes

As summer approached, LaDonna Lee was offered an opportunity to serve in a tourist camp in Pennsylvania. This position included preaching weekly and visiting with and helping tourists with their spiritual needs. She decided to accept the position, which meant a lack of staff in the Chisago Lake Lutheran Church office. Bonnie Anderson continued as chairperson for the Christian education committee

Deb Wolterstorff was offered the position of youth director in her home church, Christ the King in New Brighton. This was nearer her husband's work and gave them the opportunity to buy their first home, so she accepted that position. Deb's last official day was July 14, and one of her last official duties was accompanying 10 youth and adults to the ELCA National Youth Gathering in Dallas, Texas, July 2 to 8. She had served Chisago Lake well for three years. Ginny Johnson continued as chairperson of the youth committee.

With two vacancies, the Church Council and the pastor began to consider the possibility of calling a second pastor.

On June 23, 1991, a congregational meeting was held to discuss and vote on calling a second pastor. The first concern raised was that a person was needed who could continue the youth program.

The second concern was financing the second pastor position. The combined salary of the two vacant positions was about $34,000, and the synod would be asked if there would be someone available in that price range. The vote to call a second pastor was 81 voting yes and 22 voting no.

1991

The Reverend Marilyn Breckenridge of the synod office was contacted to assist the congregation in issuing a pastoral call. She was asked to help find a person who could do "general" ministry well and who would have a special interest in youth work. Of special concern was finding a person who would be a "team player" and would work well with the present staff.

A call committee, appointed by the Church Council, included Joe Johnson, chairman, Jackie Genung, Bernette Wikelius, Rodney Amundson, and Darin Bourasa. On December 1, a special congregational meeting was held at which there was a unanimous decision to extend a call to Marilyn Witte.

Marilyn Witte earned bachelor's degree and master of arts degree from Notre Dame University, and a master of divinity from Luther

Northwestern Theological Seminary. While attending the seminary, she was an associate professor for music and liturgy. Pastor Witte's call was to serve as associate pastor.

Pr. Marilyn Witte

Miss Witte accepted the call and was ordained at the seminary on January 18, 1992. Her installation service was on Sunday, February 23, with the Reverend Marilyn Breckenridge, assistant to Bishop Lowell Erdahl, as guest preacher.

After a few brief weeks, Pastor Witte resigned. At a special meeting of the Church Council on March 19, 1992, Pastor Witte's resignation was accepted. She was given a severance package to enable her to meet her living expenses while she looked for another position.

Pastor Mwaluvinga
Resident Pastor from Tanzania

1991

In 1991, the Saint Paul Area Synod arranged for Pastor Ernest Mwaluvinga to come as an exchange pastor to Minnesota for nine months. He spent three months in each of three churches, staying with three families in each parish. Chisago Lake Lutheran Church was privileged to host him during January, February, and March of 1992. He also spent time at Shepherd of the Hills Lutheran Church in Shoreview and North Heights Lutheran Church in Roseville.

Ernest Mwaluvinga was born in Kitowo village in the Pommern District of south-central Tanzania, about 350 miles west of Dar Es Salaam. He studied at Ihimbo Primary School and Kidugali Bible School. In 1978 he was chosen to attend Makumira Theological College in Northern Tanzania, near the slopes of Mount Kilimanjaro. He was ordained in 1982 and served the Idete congregation from 1982 to 1986. Since then he had served as Pommern District Pastor in the Iringa Diocese of the Evangelical Lutheran Church in Tanzania. This district was made up of seven congregations with each congregation consisting of several parishes.

During his time at Chisago Lake, he participated in the regular life of the congregation. He also spent some time at Hazelden where he studied treatment for those suffering from an addiction. He hoped to start a rehabilitation program when he returned home.

Pr. Mwaluvinga with Tamra and Pr. Dale

Families who provided a home for Pastor Mwaluvinga during his stay at Chisago Lake were Wally and Irene Carlson, Gary and Julie Lauritzen, and Stan and Mary Smidt.

The Slanted Cross

1991

The ELCA "Mission90" emphasis was the inspiration for the "year of the cross" for Lutherans across the country. Biblically, grace means unmerited favor from God to God's people. As a symbol of our grace-oriented theology, a slanted cross was placed in the churchyard. The cross was constructed by Kermit Christensen and was placed where it

PASTOR DALE PETERSON

would be seen by all people passing by. Pastor Dale stated the following in the October 1991 newsletter:

> Our hope is that the slanted cross that touches the ground in two places will confront travelers with the question, "Why doesn't that church plant their cross upright?" The answer, "Because we are picking it up daily to follow Christ!" (Matthew 16)

Other 1991 Highlights

+ January 1991 was the time of the Gulf War. Michael Germain, a member of Chisago Lake, was called to active duty with the Medical Corp. His wife, Cindy, and three sons waited at home for six months. Thankfully he arrived home safely when his tour of duty was completed.

+ Saturday Night Alive continued with three programs during the year: Sweet Adelines in February; Else Maria, a soloist, in June; and the Barbary Coast, a Christian jazz group, in October.

1991

+ Early in the year a synthesizer was added to the music for the folk service. Guitars and flute were also used, along with a few singers to lead the service. The "Victory Feast" service was introduced to the congregation as well.

+ In April, the "Lunch Bunch" began. On the first Sunday of each month, anyone who was alone and wanted to eat out after the second service was asked to meet in the narthex to plan the outing for the day. Many people have enjoyed this over the years.

+ Healing services were begun on the third Sunday of October at 2:00 P.M. These continued on the third Sunday of each month for several months. There were many conflicts with the Sunday afternoon time, and as the attendance decreased, these were discontinued.

+ The music department presented the musical *Tales of Wonder* by Haugen, on Saturday, November 16, at 7:00 P.M. Between 75 and 100 persons participated.

The congregational unit of Women of the Evangelical Lutheran Church in America (W/ELCA) continued to meet each month and there were 10 circles. The quilters made 61 quilts and 7 baby quilts.

Change in Missionary Support

The church, through the W/ELCA organization, had been sending monies toward the support of the Reverend and Mrs. Allen Swanson in Taiwan. When they returned home, this support was channeled to Pastor Phil and René Johnson. The Johnsons, who were members of Our Savior's Lutheran Church in Circle Pines, were serving in Kenya, Africa.

Pr. Phil and René Johnson

Pastor Phil was asked to fill the supervisory position for the Nairobi Parish, which was composed of four congregations. The Johnsons had two little boys, Simon and Neil.

1991

Other Staff Changes

Eunice Anderson, who had served as secretary for seven years, reached retirement age and resigned effective July 1, 1992. Elizabeth (Liz) Sterbentz was hired to replace her. Evey Phillips had completed her two years of seminary education and left to begin her intern year. Julie Lund was hired to replace her as the music minister.

Summer Project

The youth of Chisago Lake Lutheran Church participated in the Appalachia Service Project again in 1992. The group left on Sunday, June 28, and returned on Sunday, July 5. Ten youth and four adults made the trip to Hurley, Virginia, where they worked on home repair. The summer program for children age three to grade five was conducted again in June and July. The program was held on two mornings each week for four weeks. Goals for this program were: to provide constructive activities for church and community youth; to teach leadership skills to church youth; to witness to our community that our church is open and welcoming to everyone; and to introduce devotions appropriate to age level

Each day the program was held, 20 to 32 children participated. Daily leadership involved two to four adults and nine to 15 youth. Funds for the program came from a bequest.

Vacation Bible school was held in August and many young people attended Luther Point Bible Camp during the summer months.

Ribbon Around the Earth

1992

October 24, 1992, was officially declared "Ribbon Around the Earth Day" in Minnesota. As daylight dawned in New Zealand, Australia, Japan, Indonesia, Israel, Italy, Ireland, and the Americas, the ribbon was unwinding around the earth in local events. As people of all nationalities and all faiths came together to connect pieces of the ribbon, the entire earth was embraced in love and hope of reconciliation. The Saint Paul Area Synod Women of the ELCA participated in this event by

Ribbon around Minnesota's State Capitol

CHISAGO LAKE EVANGELICAL LUTHERAN CHURCH

gathering at the State Capitol in Saint Paul to tie their ribbon together around the building. This was the only event of its kind in Minnesota. Members of the Chisago Lake W/ELCA participated in this international event and contributed a piece for the ribbon.

Pastor Voelker Called as Associate Pastor

In September 1992, a call committee was appointed to search for a second pastor. This person would have major responsibilities for youth ministry, education ministry, and evangelism. Those appointed to this committee were Jim Jordal, chairman, Sally Barott, Joe Johnson, Craig Johnsen, Britta Westman, Gordon Grimm, and Dorothy Person.

At the annual meeting on January 31, 1993, this committee presented the name of Pastor John Voelker to be called as the associate pastor. There were 86 voting yes and 7 voting no.

Pastor Voelker had been serving a church in North Pole, Alaska for four years. While there he had married his wife, Julia, and they were

1992

expecting their first child. Pastor Voelker accepted the call and plans were made for them to move to the Chisago Lakes community as soon as possible after the birth of their baby.

Madeline arrived safely on March 20, and two weeks later the family drove down the AlCan Highway in order to be at Center City by Easter Sunday. On Sunday, May 2, a shower was held for Madeline at the church, with the congregation invited to come to meet her and her mother, Julia.

Clockwise: Julia, Pr. John, Madeline, Janie in Jan. 2000

The installation service for Pastor Voelker was held on Sunday, May 30, at both worship services. Assistant to the bishop, Pastor Ron Peterson, was the presiding official at the service. After the services there

was a reception to give the congregation an opportunity to meet the
Voelker family and present them with monetary gifts for their newly
purchased home.

Memorial, Mission & Ministry
Fund Established

At the annual meeting on January 31, 1993, a resolution was presented
to implement the Chisago Lake Lutheran Church Memorial, Mission
& Ministry Fund. The purpose of this fund was to enhance the mission outreach of CLLC apart from the general operation of the congregation. This committee would have five members elected by the congregation. One of the by-laws reads:

> The committee shall report on a quarterly basis to the church
> council and, at each annual or duly called special meeting of the
> congregation, shall render a full and complete audited account of
> the administration of the fund during the preceding year.

1993

A perpetual fund would be established from which only the income
could be used. (A complete copy of the resolution and by-laws covering
this committee can be found in the January 31, 1993, Annual Report.)

Goals of the committee were to encourage the use of named
endowment funds, increase the perpetual fund, hold meetings relating
to planned giving, recommend that all memorial gifts be handled
through this committee so a full record could be maintained, expand
charitable giving, improve coordination with the council and financial
officers, and improve the earnings on these funds.

The resolution was adopted and the following people were elected to the committee: Don Bungum, Eleanor Trippler, Harriet Ryberg,
Brad Mattson, and Stan Smidt.

Singles Ministry

One of the active fellowship groups at Chisago Lake Lutheran Church was F.O.C.U.S. (Fellowship of Christian United Singles). This group had planned monthly meetings and events to accommodate singles. There was also a "Single Again" group from the community meeting at Trinity Lutheran Church in Lindstrom. These two groups offered opportunities for recreational activities and culture nights.

Worship and Music Task Force

In April 1993, a task force was appointed by the worship and music committee to study the pros and cons of providing a third worship service. Why have a service at 9:15 A.M.? An answer to that is quoted from a book by Don Brandt where he writes:

> A service concurrent with Sunday School is the single most effective strategy for insuring the creation of a younger worshiping constituency.

1993

This service would be a shorter one with emphasis on Bible study and singing. It was designed to reach out to the unchurched, folks who might feel uncomfortable in the sanctuary, or left out because they have limited biblical knowledge.

Beginning on September 19, 1993, a worship opportunity was offered in the youth room at 9:15 A.M. This service was meant to fill a need for those who wanted to attend church while their children were in Sunday school, those who enjoyed more contemporary music, and others who might find a small group worship more fitting for their needs. Average attendance at this service was 12, and after several months with little or no growth, the service was abandoned.

Staff Changes

After serving as the church treasurer for three years, Duane Arnold resigned effective July 1, 1993. Jim Berling was hired to replace him. Jim and his wife lived in Center City with their family of young children. He was employed part-time at the Chisago County Court House. His job description indicated that he would work about eight hours per week for the church.

Pastor and Mrs. Richard Johnston moved to the Chisago Lakes area to retire. Pastor Johnston was hired for eight hours per week to call on prospective members and to conduct classes for those wishing to join the Chisago Lake Lutheran Church. Margaret Johnston became the congregation's wedding coordinator. She was paid by the hour, by the wedding party.

During the summer, Janelle Anderson resigned as church organist.

1993

Elwood (Woody) Bernas was hired to replace her effective August 1, 1993. Woody Bernas was from Wheeling, West Virginia. He earned a bachelor of arts degree in English literature and a master of divinity in theology and liturgy at Pontifical College Josephinum in Columbus, Ohio. He was associate direc-

Woody Bernas

tor and music coordinator for the office of worship for the Diocese of Steubenville, Ohio, from 1987 to 1989 where he became interested in pursuing counseling as his primary field. He completed the counselor training program at Hazelden in 1989 and was a certified chemical dependency counselor there.

There were also changes in the janitor position when Rick Moren was hired to replace Roger Lee, and then again when Dick and Hazel Underhill replaced Rick Moren. Dawn Meredith resigned from her nursery duties and Toni Sower-Christensen was hired to replace her.

Other Highlights of 1993

✦ In January 1993, Pastor Dale traveled to the Holy Land with a tour group. This was a wonderful experience for him and he shared many of his experiences and impressions with the congregation.

✦ Hollywood came to Chisago Lake Lutheran Church. The wedding scene at the end of the movie *Grumpy Old Men* was filmed at the church. Hollywood celebrities in the movie were Ann

Pr. Dale, Jack Lemmon, Walter Mathau

Margaret, Jack Lemmon, and Walter Mathau. It was quite an event for the community to be a "set" for a movie scene. Many local residents were extras in the wedding scenes. It was an

1993

Many local residents were extras in the wedding scenes

interesting experience, but when the congregation was asked to allow the facilities to be used a second time, they said no. The language used in the movie was not acceptable and although it brought fame to Center City, it was the kind of fame some members felt they could do without.

✦ Dale and Pam Snyder introduced the congregation to the "Haiti Project," with which they were involved. They had both visited Haiti. This project concentrated on education, medical care, and agriculture. It raised funds to provide a school for children in Haiti. They also were involved with food for the hungry of Haiti. The Sunday school and vacation Bible school raised money for the "Heifer Project." The goal of this project was to give a cow to a needy community to provide milk for the children. The children in VBS provided more than $300 to supplement the Sunday school mission offerings.

✦ A new schedule was worked out for Wednesday evening youth activities, which included a light supper. The Sunbeam choir and children involved with Young Searcher's League had their supper at 5:30 P.M., followed by their Bible studies. They ended the evening with choir and tone chime rehearsal. Tone chimes were purchased with a memorial gift. A tone chime choir was begun by adults called "Joyful Ringers," but children also used them. The middle school and senior high youth had their choir and tone chime rehearsal at 5:30 followed by supper and ending with their Bible studies. The program ended at 7:10. Parents took turns providing the supper.

✦ For several years the congregation had a tape ministry, which brought tapes of the Sunday morning worship service to shut-ins. In 1993, a video camera was purchased making it possible for people to see the service as well as hear it. Gordon Meland taped the services, and videotapes were brought to Parmly, Green Acres, and the extended care wing at the hospital.

1993

Bernette Wikelius, Gertrude Lindo, and Leona Warndahl brought the tapes to these locations each week.

+ A new sound system was installed in the sanctuary including cordless microphones for the two pastors. This system included a control unit located in the sanctuary. There were repeated problems with this system and the cause was traced to tampering with the control unit. A new lock was secured with only one key to be controlled by the senior pastor.

+ The historical committee hosted 32 tours with more than 1,000 persons involved.

+ This was the summer of unusually heavy rains and extreme flood conditions on the Mississippi River in July. Members were urged to contribute to the ELCA Disaster Fund.

+ The Green Room was redecorated with new furniture and other furnishings, both utilitarian and decorative, and a new sidewalk was put in from the parking lot to the narthex, including a railing on both sides of the sidewalk.

1993

+ Pastor John Voelker took seven senior high youth on an a week-long outing to the Boundary Waters during the summer. Pastor John and Julia brought 15 youth to the "Sounds Like Love" weekend at Prince of Peace Lutheran Church in Burnsville in November.

+ The youth sold Chisago Lake Lutheran Church T-shirts and sweatshirts as a fund-raiser. These proved to be an evangelism tool as more than 200 members began wearing these around the community. When the youth went to "Sounds Like Love" in November they wore their CLLC shirts.

+ There were 21 children who received camperships to attend Luther Point Bible Camp. Pastor John accompanied a group of 12 students on a four-day stay at Luther Point Bible Camp. He was invited by the camp director to serve on a committee to improve the Bible study offerings at the camp. This he did.

"Stir Us, Lord"

The theme for the 1993 stewardship program was "Stir Us Lord." This theme was inviting the Holy Spirit to come into our congregation and "stir us" to greater commitment, greater giving, and greater service. Homes were visited and members were given a "prayer tent" to place on their table as a reminder to pray for the church for 30 days.

The program also "stirred" the congregation by asking half the members to make an 18-month pledge while the other half would make the usual 12-month pledge. The purpose of this was to divide the stewardship responsibilities into spring and fall programs instead of having all pledges made in the fall. This sounded reasonable but it became so confusing that it was used only once.

The congregation was also stirred by the arrival of the first draft of the proposed statement on "The Church and Human Sexuality." The news media picked up some very controversial statements in this draft, which caused "stirring" throughout the ELCA. This controversy continues and the statement was never adopted.

1994

In an effort to improve committee work, new objectives were drawn up for each committee. Each committee reviewed and amended their objectives and these were then adopted.

The purpose of this was to coordinate committee work without having "overlapping."

Stephen Ministry

The Befrienders/Caregivers program was dropped in favor of the Stephen Ministry program. Four members of Chisago Lake, Martha Westman, Marian Johnsen, Esther Grimm, and Sanna Raedeke, went to Florida in January 1994 for the teacher training.

In September of that year they began teaching a class of 11 persons who became trained in this caring ministry. Since that time several other members have taken the teacher training.

140th Anniversary

In May 1994 Chisago Lake Lutheran Church celebrated the 140th anniversary of the organization of the congregation. Sunday, May 15, was the Sunday nearest May 12, the actual anniversary date. The theme for this celebration was "Recall Our Past, Celebrate Our Future." Former

pastors were invited to return to help commemorate the day. There was a single service at 10:30 a.m. attended by nearly 600 people.

Pastor Jeff Sandgren, a son of the congregation, was the guest preacher. The service was followed by a catered lunch and an afternoon filled with special music, recognition of visiting pastors, and renewing of acquaintances. During the afternoon, families were given the opportunity to tell their memories on video-

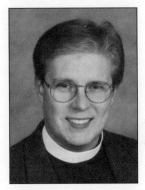

Jeff Sandgren, 1997

tape. These tapes will be shared at the 150th anniversary celebration.

1994

New Cemetery Guidelines

The cemetery committee had decided that to decrease the amount of time and money spent in keeping up the cemetery, a new guideline for placing flowers on the graves would go into effect on June 15, 1994. The guideline read as follows:

> Beginning in 1994, flowers may be placed on graves in both cemeteries prior to Memorial Day, but must be removed by June 15. Flowers not removed by June 15, will be removed by the cemetery caretaker. If you need to make arrangement regarding urn removal, please call Lester Johnson or John Nelson.

This new guideline had been publicized for about three years; during that time there was considerable confusion and disappointment about the policy. A task force was formed to study the matter, but they came to agree with the committee.

Plans were made to build permanent flower planters at the cemeteries and these were built during the summer. Families and friends were encouraged to donate funds in memory of loved ones for the planters and the plants. Cost of the planters was $3,300. These have been a beautiful addition to the cemetery.

The Nehemiah Project

The Nehemiah Project was a long-range project to repair our buildings before the 150th anniversary in 2004. The name was chosen from the book of Nehemiah in which he took up the task of rebuilding the walls of Jerusalem. The Bible verse used as a theme for this project was Nehemiah 2:20, "The God of heaven will give us success; Therefore, we, his servants, will arise and build." A task force was appointed to head up the project. Members of the task force were Gordon Grimm, chairman, Leona Warndahl, Valarie Mattson, Lynnell Rice, Orris Erlandson, and Gerald Vitalis. During 1994, this task force, together with the property committee, studied the needs of the building and made a tentative long-range plan for the project. By the end of 1995, this study was completed and the task force was ready to make a recommendation at the annual meeting in January 1996.

1994

The entire project included repair of the chimneys on the church, tuckpointing of the church exterior, new roofs for the building, steeple and clock repair, water control and landscaping, technology update for the offices, parsonage repairs, organ repair, and some expenditures for the archives. The entire proposed capital expenditures were estimated at $245,500. The congregation approved this project and authorized the Church Council to borrow money as needed for this project. The goal was to have the project completed by the end of 1998.

The Nehemiah project annual report for the year 1998, given at the annual meeting on February 7, 1999, stated:

> This congregation can look back on these last three years with great gratitude to God and its members for the work that has

been accomplished and give thanks to those who supported this project. For the most part, most of the work is complete... As most of this task force's work is complete for the short term, we are disbanding.

The financial accounting for this work shows receipts of $204,771 and a transfer from the memorial fund of $30,000, a total of $234,771. Expenses paid were $235,836, which left a balance of only $1,065 to be paid at the end of 1998.

Worship and Music

Chisago Lake Lutheran Church had begun the imposition of ashes on Ash Wednesday, and now the worship and music committee discussed having foot washing on Maundy Thursday. After a great deal of discussion, there was foot washing offered for at least two years. Several people participated. There was also a task force to look into the possibility of using home-baked bread for the communion services. There was a recipe available and it was hoped that different families would volunteer to do the baking. Home-baked bread was used on Maundy Thursday in 1994 and for the communion services on the first Sunday of each month for some time. Wafers were used for the intinction method of communion.

1994

The committee was still searching for an alternate worship service that would be acceptable to the congregation. A decision was made to use memorial monies for the *Hymnal Supplement* that had been published in 1991. This supplement continues to be used as an addition to the *Lutheran Book of Worship*. Altar candles that burn mineral oil were purchased with a memorial gift.

Youth Outings

On Saturday, April 9, 1994, sixteen youth and five adults visited the Union Gospel Mission in Saint Paul. This was a Service Saturday

Project and the purpose in going was to help work in their warehouse. The day also included a tour of the facility.

Also in April, five youth attended a TEC (Teens Encounter Christ) weekend at Shepherd of the Hills Lutheran Church in Shoreview. This was the first group of teens from Chisago Lake to participate in TEC. Pastor John was one of the leaders. Since then many youth have participated in TEC.

Fourteen youth and Pastor John joined youth from two other congregations in attending Faith Quest July 16 to 24. This was a week at a YMCA Camp, "Snow Mountain Ranch," in Colorado. It was a time of inspiration and Christian fellowship for those who attended. One problem—the bus broke down on the way home and they were delayed for several hours.

Stewardship

1994

In the fall of 1994, Pastor Dale decided to visit families personally. He wanted to visit people in their homes, to get to know them better and to concentrate on stewardship of time and talents. His main thrust was to ask these questions: 1) What should or can the church do for you? and 2) What should or can you do for the welfare of the church? It was hoped that more members would offer their time to volunteer for committee work and youth leadership, and that the talents of more members could be used to serve the Lord and produce a more vital and progressive community of believers. He was not able to visit every home.

Other 1994 Activities

+ Pastor Dale Peterson attended a "Head of Staff" seminar in Delray, Florida, which was conducted by the ELCA. He also attended a second session of this seminar in 1995.
+ Pastor Voelker attended the National Youth Work Convention in San Diego, California, sponsored by a ministry called Youth Specialties.

- Four pastors from Chisago Lake served on synod boards: Pastor Voelker, congregational life; Pastor Peterson, global mission; Pastor Johnston, church in society; (former) Pastor John Clawson, health, education, social service, institutions.

- Carrie Johnson, daughter of David and Virginia (Ginny) Johnson graduated from Luther Seminary with a master of arts degree in youth ministry.

Carrie Johnson

- Leona Warndahl made several "Rainbow Bags" for small children to use during the worship services. These were filled and kept in order by the members of the worship and music committee.

- Judy Nelson had taken care of the cradle roll for about 15 years and asked to be relieved of this task. It involved sending materials to all children for about three years after their baptism. These materials were to help parents and to acknowledge that these children were not forgotten. Muriel Bloom volunteered to continue this program.

1994

- A pictorial directory was published.

- In November an ecumenical choir concert was given at Saint Bridget of Sweden Catholic Church in Lindstrom. Choirs participating were from Chisago Lake, Trinity, and Zion Lutheran Churches, United Methodist Church, and Saint Bridget's. It was an uplifting evening for all who participated in the singing and for those who listened.

Pastor Voelker Resigns

Pastor Voelker wanted to continue his education, working for a doctorate. In 1995 the opportunity came for him to enroll at Marquette University's department of graduate studies for the fall term. In June he gave formal notice of his resignation, effective July 30. Based on his final report to the congregation, a decision was made that before calling

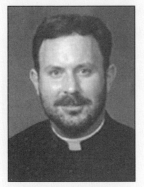

Pr. John Voelker

another associate pastor or youth worker, staff and congregation have a professional analysis.

At a Church Council meeting on August 8, 1995, a motion was made to ask the Saint Paul Area Synod for someone to come and work with us on this. In response to this request, Bishop Charles Anderson was appointed and he met with the council on August 15. Bishop Anderson recommended Dr. John Davis to work with the congregation and he met with the council on August 29.

A task force of four persons worked with Dr. Davis in facilitating his work.

The method chosen by the council to work with was the "listening post." Sunday, October 15, was the day chosen to have the synod mediation team come to Chisago Lake Church. All members of the congregation were invited to participate and were randomly placed in small groups as they came. Each group had a facilitator from the synod mediation team and someone from the congregation to record what was said. There were 134 persons who attended the "listening post" discussions. After the small group meetings, a member of each group met with the council subcommittee, the consultant, and the mediation team. They processed the results and then reported their findings to the council. There was also an opportunity for individuals to meet with Dr. Davis on the evenings of October 25 and 26, and on Saturday, October 28. There were 65 persons who participated in these interviews.

A questionnaire was mailed to each family in the congregation asking them to fill it out and return it to the church before November 10. Two members of the congregation tabulated the information in the 101 questionnaires that were returned.

1994

On November 21, 1995, Dr. Davis made his final report to the Church Council and the congregation. This report reviewed the process that had been followed in compiling his information and made recommendations to the congregation based on his findings. Some of the recommendations he made were:

1. Appoint a task force to contact other congregations who have or are experiencing transition from being primarily a Scandinavian-American parish to a more divergent one to learn how to retain cherished traditions as new ones are being created.

2. In lieu of no common vision, enter into a process where the congregation can focus each year on one or two goals whether the targeted area be intergenerational unity, worship, spiritual life, evangelism, education, stewardship, property renovation, community service, regional, national, or global mission. These goals, which need to be measurable and attainable, can be adopted during the annual meeting.

3. Establish a grievance process for congregational members based upon biblical guidelines for dealing with personal complaints. See Matthew 18:15-20.

1994

4. Form a personnel committee separate from the executive committee.

5. Design and implement a program to equip present and future lay leaders for their callings to leadership in the congregation.

6. Institute annual recognition for church staff, with appropriate messages and acts of appreciation being expressed.

7. Review provisions for staff development in light of increased stress being placed upon parish staffs. Informed observers report that one of the most significant changes that has taken place during the past twenty-five years in congregational life is the shifting from a volunteer based parish to a staff based one.

8. Grant Pastor (Dale) Peterson a sabbatical leave of three months for the purposes of rest, discernment, and renewal.

9. Declare a moratorium from criticizing others during Advent
   and Christmastide, given the fatigue and pain being experienced by parishioners and staff. Rather than turning outward
   to negate, the emphasis would be placed on turning inward to
   search. In this way Advent–Christmastide can become peni-
   tential seasons in addition to Lent and thereby release parishioners to welcome the Christ child.

Congregational Activities of 1995

While the congregation was going through this analysis, many good
things were happening.

- ✦ Early in the year plans were underway to host two Cursillo
  weekends at Chisago Lake in March. The men's group met from
  March 9 to 12, and the women's group from March 16 to 19. For
  these weekend activities, every part of the building was used to
  its maximum. Participants were very pleased with the facilities
  and the welcome they received. It was good for the congregation
  to share their space with the Cursillo program. Cursillo participants provided choral music for Sunday worship when they
  were there, which was an inspiration to worshipers.

- ✦ Ecumenical prayer breakfasts during the Lenten season were
  started in 1995. These prayer times were held Friday mornings
  at 7:30 A.M. Churches participating were Chisago Lake Ev.
  Free Church, Saint Bridget of Sweden Catholic Church,
  United Methodist Church, Chisago Lake, Trinity, and Zion
  Lutheran Churches, and also the Parmly campus. Each hosted
  a prayer breakfast, which included scripture reading and meditation, singing, prayer time, and a light breakfast. Gathering as
  people of God in our community during the Lenten season
  became a yearly event greatly appreciated by all who attended.

- ✦ The Christian education program was going well. There were
  23 children enrolled in the YSL (Young Searchers League)

program during the 1994–95 year. There were 79 children who attended vacation Bible school in August. Their special offerings amounted to $280 for the Haiti Project. This was enough to send nine children to school for a year. There were 168 children enrolled in Sunday school in the fall of 1995. Carol Hawkinson completed five years of serving as Sunday school superintendent.

✦ Chester Kukuk introduced the "Fireflies" program to our church. This was a program of home Bible study and home Bible verse memory. The program provided badges as incentives for children of all ages to memorize Bible verses. Chester and Bonnie Kukuk offered the initial funding for the materials as a gift to the children and families of Chisago Lake Lutheran Church.

✦ The Wednesday evening youth study and music events continued, but the meal was eliminated. The YSL program continued for the children, and Gladys Peterson continued her Thursday morning Bible study for adults.

1995

✦ The youth program continued with a large committee committed to both spiritual growth and fun times. Many activities were carried out in cooperation with the other church groups with an organization known as YOWSA.

✦ "The Refreshment Committee," a highly-acclaimed Christian drama troupe, came to Trinity Lutheran Church in Lindstrom on February 8. This was a YOWSA event that included our youth.

✦ There was a ski trip to Bridger Bowl near Bozeman, Montana.

✦ Some attended a youth rally at Central Lutheran Church in Minneapolis with Bernice King, daughter of Martin Luther King, and the Jay Beech Band.

✦ Tiger McLuen, director of Youth Leadership in the Twin Cities, came to speak on May 17, and 57 people attended.

+ Duke and Kathy Millington took five youth on an ASP mission to Sneedsville, Tennessee.

+ Some of the youth participated in the annual "See you at the Pole" event, which was a prayer gathering at the flagpole at the high school.

+ Bible studies, fund-raising events, lock-ins, athletic events, and the confirmation retreat went on as usual, although the attendance was small at most events.

+ The Church Council and committees also took care of some "housekeeping" concerns. On March 28, a special meeting was held to discuss committee structure and how it could be improved. Items discussed were recruitment of and term limits for committee members. There was also concern that the mutual ministry committee had not been functioning and was not being used as intended.

1995

+ Also at this meeting the *Model Constitution for Congregations and the By-laws*, which had been adopted in 1989, were distributed to council members for study. This resulted in a by-laws and policy committee being established in May to review these documents to see that they were all in proper order and up-to-date.

+ The worship and music committee created a new policy for special worship services asking that they be asked three months in advance for a special worship so that the staff could work out any changes in their responsibilities for that service. They also made a decision to use the *LBW* Setting One for the liturgy in the Advent, Christmas, Epiphany, and Lenten seasons; Setting Two for the Easter and Pentecost seasons; and to use the *Hymnal Supplement* liturgy on the third Sunday of each month.

+ Another committee worked on a rental agreement and facility use fee schedule.

+ The historical committee sponsored a Swedish communion service on Wednesday, October 4, 1995. Pastor William J. Hyllengren conducted the service at 11:00 A.M. The service was followed by a noon luncheon. There were 75 people who attended.

- On Sunday, October 22, 1995, The Gospel Stompers from Sweden provided the music for both services. This was a jazz team that found their mission in expressing their Christian faith in music that brings joy to many people. The group were pioneers in making a break-through for happy jazz and gospel music in the church in the early 1960s.
- Lutheran World Relief celebrated its 50th anniversary in 1995. LWR reported that in those 50 years 115,378 tons of quilts, clothing, and blankets were sent to more than 40 countries of the world. The women of Chisago Lake had made their contribution to this project. Also during that time, 1,183,669 tons of food were sent to hungry people around the world through LWR.

New Bishop Elected

1995

At the synod convention in April 1995, Pastor Mark Hanson was elected to succeed Bishop Lowell Erdahl as bishop of the Saint Paul Area Synod. He officially began his duties in September.

At the ELCA convention, H. George Anderson was elected to succeed Herbert Chilstrom as bishop of the Evangelical Lutheran Church in America. Bishop Anderson left his position as president of Luther College in Decorah, Iowa, to accept this position as leader of the ELCA.

Music Minister Resigns

Julie Lund had resigned her position as music director in July of 1994 and Kim Simon had been hired to replace her in September. In a letter to the Church Council dated December 11, 1995, Kim Simon, the CLLC music minister resigned, effective December 31, 1995.

The organist, Woody Bernas, agreed to direct the choir on an

interim basis and other duties of the music minister were handled by
the staff and worship and music committee.

Implementing the
Recommendations of Dr. Davis

When Dr. Davis's final report had been made to the Church Council,
the council began to make plans for implementing the recommendations he had made. One of the first items to be considered was Pastor
Peterson's sabbatical leave. The Saint Paul Area Synod Sabbatical
Leave Policy states:

> An Extended study leave (sabbatical) is understood to be a time
> of release from normal duties in order that a person may devote
> time to study, to renew and to increase and extend knowledge and
> competency in his/her fields of specialization. This may be
> accomplished through a sabbatical leave, normally a period of one
> to three months, during which time full salary and benefits will
> be continued.... Requests for sabbatical leaves including the pro-
> gram of study are to be submitted in writing to the church coun-
> cil.... A full report on the work completed shall be made by the
> pastor to the church council within two months after completion
> of the leave.

In keeping with Dr. Davis's recommendation, a three-month sabbatical leave was approved for Pastor Peterson.

A five-member steering committee appointed by the council was
to oversee the implementation of the Davis report. This committee
worked out the congregation's responsibilities for the sabbatical according to the synod leave policy and Pastor Peterson sent a report of his
goals and objectives to the Church Council.

1996

Securing an Interim Pastor

As Pastor Peterson carried out his plans for his sabbatical, the Church Council turned their attention to securing an interim pastor.

Pastor John E. Fahning was the pastor chosen for this position. Pastor Fahning had experience as an interim in several parishes and came to Chisago Lake highly recommended. A special congregational meeting was held on February 4, 1996, to approve Pastor Fahning as the interim. He arrived to take over his duties in the middle of February, and on Sunday, March 3, there was a dinner reception for him and his wife, Vendla (Vennie).

Pr. John Fahning

At the same time, the youth committee and the Church Council began to work with the Tentmakers Youth Ministry Network on options for a youth director. This was a need recognized by most of the members of the congregation who responded to the Davis survey. Another staff change was the resignation of Norma Sellman as financial secretary due to ill health. Her position was assumed by Harriet Ryberg and Vida Meland who worked as a team.

1996

Dr. Peterson's sabbatical was supervised by the Church Council and Bishop Mark Hansen. Other recommendations in the Davis report were supervised by the implementation committee.

At the annual meeting on January 21, 1996, all council incumbents on the ballot were defeated and five new council members were elected.

The implementation committee began work toward establishing a personnel committee and a conflict resolution committee as Dr. Davis had recommended. This necessitated making some amendments to the constitution of the congregation. A special congregational meeting was called for Sunday, May 12, 1996, to discuss and vote on these matters. As a result, proposed changes in the constitution were approved to be ratified at the annual meeting in January of 1997. Provisions were made for the two new committees and persons were elected to serve on them. The committees were a conflict resolution committee and a personnel committee.

Another recommendation made in Dr. Davis's report was the need for all members of the congregation to work for reconciliation and/or healing. This process should include contrition, confession, repentance, pardon, and words and acts of restitution. The members of the conflict resolution committee participated in training sessions to help in the reconciliation process. After the members of this committee had completed their training, they planned for cottage meetings to be held in the fall. These meetings would offer the opportunity for concerned persons to discuss their thoughts and feelings about the issues related to the growth and work of our church.

1995

Pastor Peterson Returns from Sabbatical

Three months passed quickly, and by mid-May Pastor Peterson returned from his sabbatical.

During Pastor John Fahning's time at Chisago Lake, he often mentioned his love for a piece of pie, his favorite being lemon meringue. On his last Sunday, May 19, the congregation honored him by having a "pie-fest" between services. The pie was delicious and a good time was had by all.

As Pastor Dale Peterson returned, the Church Council members received a report from Bishop Mark Hanson that dealt with the goals and objectives the pastor had set for his sabbatical and what had been done to carry out these goals. Pastor Peterson also submitted his report to the council.

Welcome John Wind

The youth committee, working with Tentmakers, announced to the congregation in July 1996, that they had found and hired John Wind to serve as youth director. John graduated from Fergus Falls High School and Northwestern College in Saint Paul. After finishing his college education, he connected with Tentmakers Ministry and the search committee met him there. John began the Tentmakers six-week intensive course of study on June 23,

John Wind

which brought him to Chisago Lake to begin his work on August 15, 1996—just in time to get ready for the fall season.

The youth committee chose to use the Youth Ministry Management Plan for this congregation. Its mission statement is:

> To inspire youth to be disciples of Jesus Christ and to make a difference in their church, community, and world.

1995

The plan states:

> The primary focus of our Youth Ministry is to have our youth learn about the life and teachings of Jesus Christ, to practice Christian values, and to be closer to Christ and to God... All that we do in Youth Ministry at Chisago Lake Lutheran Church will be done for this purpose.

The first goal of the plan was:

> to hire a youth director by 7/1/96." John Wind was the answer to that goal. The personnel committee worked with the youth committee and Pastor Peterson in accomplishing this goal.

With John working full time, and with the Youth Ministry Management Plan to assist them, the youth committee began rebuilding the Chisago Lake youth ministry. In his first annual report John wrote, "With Christ as the foundation already laid, we are his house-builders. We have gathered to build [the youth ministry] on his foundation together." John came as a young man "on fire" for the Lord. His goal—that every youth should come to a deep relationship with Jesus Christ. John is a man of prayer. His ministry is built on prayer—he prays, the youth pray, and he asks for prayer for himself and the youth with whom he comes in contact.

John and Rachel Wind

On December 28, 1996, John Wind married Rachel Roelofs. Rachel was a student at Northwestern College majoring in vocal music. She graduated in December 1998. She used her talents at Chisago Lake by singing in the choir and serving as liturgist and cantor.

1996

Should Lutherans Support Billy Graham?

A Billy Graham Crusade was held at the Metrodome in Minneapolis June 19 to 23, 1996. Chisago Lake Church had participated in planning and supporting the John White (Billy Graham Ministries) Crusade, which was held in Forest Lake in 1989. As the evangelism committee made plans to be involved in the 1996 crusade, the question came up, "Should the Lutheran Church support a Billy Graham Crusade or any other para-congregational emphasis that is not theologically Lutheran?"

Pastor Peterson answered that question in the June 1996 issue of the *Kichi-Saga* with these words:

> Yes and No. Most of us agree that we are not the only denomination of true Christians, nor do we claim to hold exclusive truths that must be followed to the letter in order to be saved by Christ. We do feel strongly that salvation by faith through Grace is the Gospel truth that frees us in Christ Jesus to enjoy our relation-

ship with God and one another. At the same time, however, Lutherans do not judge nor condemn those who do not find our theology meaningful for their particular spiritual journeys. Lutherans are "both/and" people rather than "either/or" types. Theologically Luther taught us to leave judgement to God. In the meanwhile, we die daily to our own sins as we arise from bed, say our prayers, and engage in living the faith on a daily basis!

...I advise moving with caution, individually staying tuned to God for guidance through personal Bible reading and prayer, and congregationally staying focused on MISSION. Then these extras can be helpful, excellent, and inspirational.

The congregation did participate in this event. The committee from Chisago Lake that worked with the planning stated in their report to the Church Council:

> The Lord richly blessed us as a committee, in our attendance at the numerous meetings, Bible studies, Word and Witness classes, preparation for follow-up classes, and in the opportunity to serve as counselors and as members of the co-labor team which took care of all the response cards.... Numerous response cards were returned to our church and to our community for which we will organize neighborhood Bible studies.... The Lord more than adequately provided the funds for covering all of the expenses and even more.

1996

The Metrodome was filled to capacity, and sometimes spilled over to the courtyard.

Other 1996 News Items

- ✦ A men's and boy's banquet was held on April 19 with a speaker from the Fellowship of Christian Athletes.
- ✦ About $900 was spent to replace leaking gaskets in the organ. Gould and Schultz Co. was hired to do the work.
- ✦ A contract was signed to have the church re-roofed for approximately $70,000.

+ The SAAD Restoration
Co. of Hugo, Minnesota,
tuckpointed the exterior of
the church for $36,750.
These items were part of
the Nehemiah Project.

+ A Habitat for Humanity
home was built in Center
City. Several members participated in this project with
financial   contributions,

Roof repair in 1996

working on the home, or bringing lunch to the crew.

+ An Appalachia Service Project group of four young people went
to the State of Virginia with Rich and Trina Berg as advisors.

+ On the night of July 29, 1996, more than 100 monuments in
the Chisago Lake Cemetery were tipped over. Some were so
badly damaged that they could not be repaired. This kind of
vandalism was not covered by insurance. The vandals were 10

1996

or 11 years old and
apparently did not
realize the magni-
tude   of   this
escapade. The boys
confessed and were
required to pay a
fine and to do 40
hours of community

Monuments tipped at the cemetery

service. Much of this service was done for the church.

+ The Church Council received a request from two residents of
Center City to use part of the education building for a Charter

School. A committee worked on this for several months. At the annual meeting on January 26, 1997, the congregation voted on a resolution to enter into an agreement with the Charter School for the rental of space for the period of one year. The resolution was defeated with 38 voting yes and 91 voting no.

+ Gladys Peterson declined the invitation to continue with Thursday morning Bible studies. Pastor Dale added this class to his schedule.

+ The historical committee sponsored the Swedish communion service on Friday, October 11, at 11:00 A.M. Pastor William Hyllengren conducted the service. A lunch was served in the fellowship hall following the service.

+ Bibles for the church were purchased in memory of LaVerne Mattson by her family. The family also provided racks under the pews to hold the Bibles.

+ Youth were given the opportunity to attend the annual "Sounds Like Love" weekend at Prince of Peace Lutheran Church in Burnsville in November. Only three girls attended.

1996

+ The stewardship committee used the "Consecration Sunday" approach to their fall program. Bishop Charles Anderson, Redwood Falls, Minnesota, was the guest leader. (His parents and all of his grandparents were baptized at Chisago Lake.) More than 400 members attended the Consecration Sunday brunch on November 10. This program focused on the "need of the giver to give" as part of his/her own spiritual development and Christian commitment. The estimate of giving increased by 23 percent over the previous year.

+ The annual report shows 1,322 baptized members at the end of 1996. Of these, 1,005 were confirmed members.

Stephen Ministry

When the Stephen Ministry program began in 1994, four women went to Florida to be trained to train others. These women then conducted a training session for several others from the congregation. Stephen Ministry is "Christ Caring for People through People." It is a way for lay people to become actively, meaningfully involved in ministry. It is also a way for pastors to lighten their workload while at the same time they multiply their ministry. People who need help get help because a trained staff of lay caregivers is at work. People who may need a Stephen Minister are those who are experiencing divorce, grief, terminal illness, job crisis, hospitalization, loneliness, and other maladies of contemporary life.

Trainers are expected to give two years to training others and then may retire. In 1996, Wendy Hickman went to Seattle, Washington, to receive training so that she could replace a retiree.

1997 The Stephen Ministry report to the Church Council on December 9, 1997, listed 11 active Stephen ministers, five inactive, two leaders (Pastor Dale and Wendy), and three former leaders still working as mentors for Wendy. In February 1998, John Wind, Kristi Mitchell, and Kathy Lindo traveled to San Antonio, Texas, for their training. Plans were to have three more leaders train in 1999, but this did not work out and the plans were "put on hold."

Attempts at a Sister Congregation Relationship

One of the recommendations in the Davis report that had not been addressed was that

> A task force be appointed to contact other congregations who have or are experiencing transition from being primarily a Scandinavian-American parish to a more divergent one.

First Lutheran Church in Saint Paul was such a congregation. First Lutheran and Chisago Lake Lutheran were both started by Swedish immigrants in 1854. Over the years East Saint Paul has become home to many new immigrants: Black, Hispanic, and Hmong. For seven years Chisago Lake members had been collecting food items for the food pantry at First Lutheran. Attempts were made to make this a deeper relationship by sharing with each other. Pastor Peterson visited with the pastor at First Lutheran and discussed ways in which we could share and learn from each other. Ways discussed included an exchange of choirs, pulpit exchange, adult forums, women's groups exchanging programs, and youth activities such as our youth helping with a Bible school at First Lutheran and their youth coming here to enjoy our rural setting.

For some reason, these plans never worked out. Perhaps in the future these kinds of relationships with our "city cousins" will happen to increase our awareness of each other's needs and how we can be a blessing to each other.

The Davis recommendation task force was dissolved by the Church Council at their January 1997 meeting.

1997

Focus on Youth

With a full-time youth director on staff and the Youth Ministry Management Plan adopted, the youth program began to expand. The first area of emphasis was a Christ-centered ministry focus—to have the youth learn about the life and teachings of Jesus Christ, to practice Christian values, and to be closer to Christ and to God. The goal—that the youth be connected to Jesus and grow in that relationship of faith. This included Bible study, prayer, confirmation classes for 7th and 8th graders, and parent involvement.

The second focus was on service. This could be service to members of the congregation who needed help with washing windows or raking the lawn. It could be service to the community by cleaning the ditches along Highway 8 that are the responsibility of Chisago Lake Church. It could be outreach to the homeless such as the Union Gospel Mission in Saint Paul or to the elderly at Parmly.

PASTOR DALE PETERSON

The third focus was on fun and recreation such as volleyball, softball, ski trips, or swimming. These activities could be part of the cooperation with other area churches.

Another focus was on fine arts—participation in choirs, instrumental ensembles, or musicals. Youth from all three area Lutheran churches presented the musical *Live It To the Max*.

+ March 14 to 16, 29 youth and 11 adults from the Chisago Lakes area went to Youthquake, a synod-sponsored youth retreat in Saint Paul.
+ July 4 to 14, two teams of five adults and nine youth participated in the Appalachia Service Project in Panther, West Virginia.
+ From July 20 to 26, John Wind took three young people to Leadership Quest camp on the North Shore. The purpose of this wilderness camp was to develop young Christian leaders.

In John Wind's annual report presented January 25, 1998, we find these words:

1997

> The clearest theme I see in the Youth Ministry is developing spiritual community.... I am very encouraged as I see God bringing our High School Youth together in a spirit of unity and openness to God's Word. The High School Youth have collectively expressed a desire to get deeper in the Bible and to grow as Christians. Praise the Lord!

> My greatest desire for our Youth Ministry in 1998 is for a continued growing sense of working together. A sense among parents, grandparents, adults and youth alike that the Youth Ministry is OUR Youth Ministry, the goals OUR goals and we are committed to it.... this can be accomplished ONLY through the working of the Holy Spirit.... as we come together, the Holy Spirit will reveal the true areas of need among our youth and their parents. As we come together, the Holy Spirit will reveal those among us who God has gifted and called to help meet those needs. As we come together, the Holy Spirit will give us specific guidance in specific situations.... I pray for this working together in the Spirit.

(In 1998, responsibility for the confirmation program was turned over to the youth committee. This added new responsibilities for the youth director.)

Congregational Outreach

The council minutes for January 14, 1997, state "that we were able to pay all of our benevolences and bills by the end of the year (1996) due to increased giving by the congregation." Also, "we gave more than any other congregation in our Synod." The treasurer's report shows that the total amount given to benevolence from the general fund that year was $35,840.

At the annual meeting in January 1993, the memorial committee changed its name to "Memorial, Mission & Ministry." With this change, provision was made for a perpetual fund, which would be invested to bring in interest that could be used to provide for giving not included in the regular budget. The bylaws for the use of these monies state as follows:

1997

> Income from the Perpetual Fund shall be distributed annually and at such other times as deemed necessary and/or feasible to accomplish the following purposes:
> Minimum of 20% for outreach into the community and synod...
> Minimum of 20% for missions of the ELCA...
> Minimum of 20% for capital improvements, debt reduction, or a building program of CLLC.
> Up to 40% for any one or all of the above...

At the close of this committee's fiscal year, November 30, 1996, the interest earnings available for distribution were $6,910. This was distributed in the following manner:

$1,000	to Saint Paul Area Synod Budget
500	to Family Resource Center Food Shelf
900	to ELCA Vision for Mission
500	to ELCA Domestic Disaster Response Fund
4,010	to CLLC Nehemiah Project

Spring of 1997 was the time of the severe flood in the Red River Valley. Much of East Grand Forks was destroyed first by flood and then by fire. Of the more than 27,000 homes in East Grand Forks, all were flood damaged except for 28 Grand Forks and other cities along the river, including Fargo, also suffered severe damage. Crop land was under water for weeks. Lutheran Social Service coordinated volunteers who wished to help. Many busloads went as needed. Pastor Peterson and Bob Hawkinson were two from Chisago Lake who volunteered.

Chisago Lake set a goal of $2,000 to be sent to a needy church in the flood area. There was also the opportunity to send money directly to the Disaster Response in Fargo, North Dakota.

The goal of $2,000 was not quite reached, but $1,894.74 was sent to Pastor Jeff Sandgren, a son of Chisago Lake Lutheran Church, who was a pastor in Fargo. He agreed to manage the money and see that it would get to the persons where it could do the most good.

Chisago Lake Lutheran Church also received from the Elizabeth Aadland Estate $48,821.

1997

This was designated for anything that the church needed. Members of the congregation were asked to contribute their suggestions as to how the money should be used. Highest priority went to the purchase of a van that could be used for the youth or to transport senior citizens to church services and events. The first 10 percent, $4,882, was given to the Saint Paul Area Synod. The following committee, consisting of Matthew Wikelius, Gertrude Lindo, Chester Kukuk, Bonnie Anderson, John Wind, David Reed, and Don Bungum, tabulated the results of the suggestions received and recommended the following expenditures:

+ $25,000 for a van for church use.
+ $2,000   for insurance and maintenance of the van
+ $1,000   for flood relief
+ $1,000   for the pastor's discretionary fund to help the needy

- ✦ $1,000   for the Iringa project that Faith Lutheran Church in Forest Lake was sponsoring (the purchase of a farm for the college we had previously helped fund)
- ✦ $1,000   for Luther Point Bible Camp—facilities or programs
- ✦ $1,000   for new round tables for the Fellowship Hall
- ✦ $5,000   for building improvements
- ✦ $1,000   for parking lot improvements
- ✦ $4,000   for spiritual growth—to establish a Program Initiative Grant program
- ✦ $2,000   for a reserve fund if any of the above exceed estimates
- ✦ $3,500   of the Program Initiative Grant monies was set aside for the historical committee to have the history of the church since 1954 recorded for publication before the 150th anniversary celebration in 2004. The other $500 was given to Wendy Hickman to begin a women's Bible study fellowship.

On October 5, World Communion Sunday and also Lutheran World Federation Sunday, a special offering was received for the Moscow Soup Kitchen staffed in part by ELCA missionaries. This special offering amounted to $717.

1997

Larry Nelson and Pearl Nehl continued their work with the jail ministry. This ministry provides study of the scriptures on Sunday morning with any inmates who wish to participate. Those participating in this ministry have seen a number of inmates accept Jesus as their Lord and Savior and start the process of turning their lives around. In one case, an inmate was baptized at Chisago Lake upon his release.

Chisago Lake Church, through the W/ELCA channels has been helping to support a missionary for many years. Phil and Rene Johnson, who had been recipients of this support for the past several years were guests at Chisago Lake on Mission Sunday, February 23, 1997. They preached at both services and were a part of the Christian education hour for both the Sunday school and the adult forum. Following the second service, they participated in a congregational dinner.

The W/ELCA organization also began the project of making mid-wife kits for Global Health Ministries. Every container GHM sent overseas contained midwife kits, so there was a great need. During the first year of this project, 163 kits were completed. A kit consisted of one 36" square of muslin, one bath towel and wash cloth, a bar of Ivory soap, a stocking cap for the newborn, a kimono, a receiving blanket, plastic gloves, a cord tie, and a razor blade, all enclosed in a two-gallon size Ziplock™ bag.

Christian Relational Minister Added to Staff

In April 1997, the Christian education committee expressed to the Church Council the need for a part-time staff member to coordinate the Christian education program. They suggested that this person be on staff before September, and earlier if there was to be a vacation Bible school. The worship and music committee was also feeling the need for a music director as Mr. Bernas, the organist, had accepted the senior choir director position on an interim basis and there were no children's choirs. The committee was making decisions that were ordinarily made by the music director.

1997

At the May council meeting, a task outline for the position of Christian education coordinator was presented showing the need for the position of about 20 hours per week. The worship and music committee also presented a job description for a part-time music director.

A decision was made to establish a task force to study these proposals and to work out the financial estimates. Bonnie Anderson, Greg Solberg, Vicki Mickelsen, and Sue Leaf volunteered to serve on the task force.

Bill and Kristi Mitchell had joined Chisago Lake a few months earlier, and Kristi was already a member of the choir and often directed the choir for Woody Bernas. Woody was growing a little weary of

directing the choir with his "eyebrows" while he played the accompaniment. Kristi had a degree in music education and music therapy from
Wartburg College in Waverly, Iowa. For the
past four years she had been working as a
teacher in the Forest Lake School District.

A decision was made to hire Kristi
Mitchell full time to fill both the Christian
education and music positions. This new
position was given the title "Christian relational minister." This title was chosen because
the person in this position would have a key
role in building relationships with others to

Kristi Mitchell

help the programs grow and mature. These relationships would be
with the pastor, staff, volunteers, singers, cantors, teachers, musicians,
students, children, families, community, committee members, and
businesses. Kristi expressed this as an opportunity to educate others in
a new and exciting ministry at Chisago Lake Lutheran Church. She
began her work on August 15, 1997.

1997

As Kristi came on staff, she helped plan more efficient use of the
available office space and some new furnishings were purchased for the
office to accommodate the new computers and the additional staff.

Chisago Lakes Grief Support Coalition

In December 1996, Pastor Dale announced that a grief support coalition was beginning that would be sponsored by area churches, funeral
homes, social service agencies, nursing homes, the hospital, and hospice. Each organization would contribute $100 to the coalition. A six-
week "Growing Through Loss" series would be presented two or three
times each year. The series would be held in different churches. The
first series was held at Zion Lutheran Church, Chisago City, in April
and May of 1997. A second series was held at Saint Bridget of Sweden
Catholic Church in Lindstrom in September and October 1997. In

1998, the spring series was held at the Chisago Lake Ev. Free Church in Lindstrom, and the fall series was held at Chisago Lake Lutheran Church in Center City. At each meeting a guest speaker would present a lecture on a topic relating to grief, and then the group was divided into small groups according to the type of grief they were dealing with. Examples of loss included death, divorce, job loss, moving, etc. The purpose of this series was to provide an opportunity for individuals to obtain information and support for a variety of loss and grief issues. This coalition continues to function and provide support for those in need.

Faith Inkubators

Faith Inkubators of Stillwater, Minnesota, designed Christian education systems based on "faith from the family up." John Wind attended a workshop on the Faith Inkubators confirmation program. He returned inspired to adopt the program for this congregation.

1997

For several years Chisago Lake had used an intergenerational confirmation format with classes being held on Sunday mornings during the Sunday school hour. This was a program that Pastor Dale Peterson had brought with him from his church in Texas. Now it seemed the right time to move on to a new format.

Faith Inkubators is also intergenerational with many confirmed members participating and supporting the students in their studies. It is solid Lutheran theology but the method of teaching it is *relational* rather than *informational*. Volunteer guides direct the small group discussions and meet with the confirmands on a regular basis on Wednesday evenings. Prayer partners, mentors, and managers are involved in one-on-one Christian sharing. Families of each confirmand are given ideas for special family nights to use in their homes each month. Before he/she is confirmed, each student must write their own faith statement. This is a two-year program, which was introduced in the fall of 1997.

"Opening New Doors" Appeal for Luther Point Bible Camp

Chisago Lake is one of 74 congregations supporting Luther Point Bible Camp. Luther Point was started in 1946 and since that time thousands of people have been touched by the gospel while attending camp there. The board of directors of Luther Point felt that in order to continue to serve into the next century, improvements and additions needed to be made at the camp. Cabins would be winterized for year-round use, a new retreat center would be built, and a new well system would be constructed. For these improvements, a goal of $850,000 was set. During 1997, a committee consisting of Nancy Grossmann, Carol Hawkinson, and David and Virginia Johnson led the appeal for funds at Chisago Lake. The appeal was held in the fall with pledges made to be paid over a three-year term. The amount pledged by families or individuals was $16,770 over and above the regular support designated in the church budget.

1997

Church Property Annexed to City

On Sunday, August 17, 1997, following the Sunday service at 10:30 A.M. (summer services were held at 8:00 and 9:30), a special meeting of the congregation was held to take action on a request by the city of Center City to annex some property to the city of Center City. Previous to this time, only the property around the church building was in the city. The city wished to extend water and sewer services to the area north of Center City on County Road 9 in order to build a county garage on a site there. In order to do this, it was necessary to annex the Hillside Cemetery, the parsonage, and the wooded area north of the parsonage. The city would also need an easement for the purpose of installing and maintaining public utilities on church property (the Hillside Cemetery).

The minutes of this meeting show that the resolution for annexation passed by a unanimous voice vote. The annexation also included the Chisago Lake Cemetery and the area used as a ball field.

The city of Center City agreed to reimburse the church for any permanent losses (burial lots) at reasonable and customary rates. The cemetery committee determined that there would be a loss of 25 burial sites. The minutes of the October 14, 1997, council meeting state that:

> The sum of $8,160 was received, and that $5,100 should go to the Cemetery Fund to cover the cost of the lost lots, and that $3,060 should go to "undesignated funds" with a tithe of $306 going to the Synod "Making Waves" appeal.

This motion was passed.

Making Waves Appeal

1997

In 1996, the Saint Paul Area Synod approved a three-year funding appeal for mission. The appeal goal was $495,000 to strengthen the mission that congregations do together through the synod. The funds were to be used as follows:

- $150,000 for urban mission strategies
- $150,000 for new missions such as Thanksgiving Lutheran Church in Hugo
- $90,000 for continued assistance to Tanzania, our sister synod
- $60,000 for training in witness and outreach
- $45,000 to ELCA mission support

"Making Waves" envelopes were distributed to the members of the congregation for their contribution to this appeal. Later reports show that the goal of the appeal had been exceeded. Chisago Lake congregation pledged $15,000.

1997 News Shorts

- Ten members/relatives of Chisago Lake traveled to the Holy

Land in February to experience the sites in the land where Jesus lived. They learned firsthand about the Jewish/Arab differences and the Mid-East Conflict.

+ Chisago Lake Lutheran Church was used by the Cursillo movement for two weekends in April. Many members of Chisago Lake have participated in Cursillo weekends over the recent years. On these Sundays, Cursillo participants furnished the music for the worship services.

+ On May 8, the Cathedral Choir from Katarina Church in Stockholm gave a concert at Chisago Lake Church.

+ On May 14, the Captive Free Christian Band gave a concert, which was attended primarily by the youth.

+ The second service was held at 9:30 A.M. instead of 10:30 during the summer months.

+ A gift of $10,000 was received from Wenzel Bloom to be used for a fence around the Glader Cemetery where many of his relatives were buried. The fence was erected and there was enough money left to provide a new sign identifying the cemetery.

1997

+ The annual Swedish communion service was held on Thursday, October 9, with Pastor William Hyllengren officiating. A noon lunch was served following the 11:00 A.M. service, with 75 people attending.

+ Consecration Sunday was October 12, with Bob Armitage, CEO of the Board of Social Ministry, as speaker. Mr Armitage was a member of Christ Lutheran Church in Marine.

+ A new four-station computer system was installed which would be ready for the year 2000. The Shelby program was installed for congregation record keeping.

+ The social ministry team arranged for a Thanksgiving dinner on Sunday, November 23, with the Hmong community in Taylors Falls as guests. Several Hmong men and boys attended and the speaker for their group, William Vang, told about the suffering they had endured in escaping from their homeland. No women or girls attended. This community is within the local school district, so there are quite a number of Hmong children being educated in the local schools.

+ The annual "Sankta Lucia" and Festival of Light celebration was held in the fellowship hall on Saturday, December 13, at 9:00 A.M. Bob Nelson opened the festivities with the sound of his "Naverlur," a Swedish horn. The Kichi-Saga Swedish Club served Christmas breads, pepparkakor, coffee, and hot cider.

Endings and Beginnings

In December 1997, a letter was sent to all members of the congregation informing them that the church treasurer's report showed a shortfall of almost $82,000. This seemed to be an insurmountable amount. However, the November and December contributions to the general fund brought in an extraordinary $78,578 in congregational giving.

The annual report shows that 1997 benevolences were paid in full and all bills were paid up to date. In a letter sent to the members on December 31 we find these words,

> We thank God for leading and guiding us in times of need. Many prayers have been answered.

In looking forward to 1998, Pastor Peterson wrote in his annual report:

> My prayer is that 1998 will be a year in which we intentionally work to make our church climate a positive one for those who are committed to share this love of JESUS. We should listen and strive to become the community our children sing about: "They will know we are Christians by our love... by our love. Yes, they will know we are Christians by our love!"

In keeping with his goal for helping the members of the congregation grow in their love for and understanding of Jesus, Pastor Dale started a Bible study entitled, "Jesus—A Study of Our Lord." Sessions were held on the first and third Sundays at 4:00 P.M. This series continued until May.

In looking at minutes of the Church Council and various committee minutes for 1997, one finds a great deal of discussion taking place about the need for trained leadership in the congregation. Standing committees, W/ELCA, service groups, and the nominating committee looking for candidates for the Church Council all had difficulty recruiting people for leadership positions. Pastor Dale writes in his February 1998 newsletter article:

> Our primary 1998 focus is on leadership development. There will be opportunities for each of us to grow spiritually and significantly. At CLLC we are looking for solutions for the Leadership Crisis that surrounds us! Please pray for these solutions to be just as quick and thorough as the changes that engulf us.

As a result, early in 1998 several opportunities were offered to train leaders. Youth were encouraged to participate in TEC (Teens Encounter Christ) weekends. Youth were also offered the opportunity to participate in Leadership Quest Camp and to be a part of a youth ministry spiritual leadership team. The adult forum offered a series on "leadership skills that are led by the Spirit." On a Saturday in April, the Church Council and staff attended a one-day retreat at the seminary for the purpose of increasing their leadership skills. This continued to be a focus during the year.

1998

Repairs Needed

During 1997, the worship and music committee and the organist were struggling with an organ that needed repair. Some emergency repairs were made, but many stops were not working and two pedals didn't sound. In February and March 1998, the organ repairs were made. Cost of these repairs was just under $8,000.

There were also continued problems with the sound system. One of the main speakers at the front of the sanctuary shorted out. When it was replaced it shorted again and the trouble was found to be in the wiring. The amplifier also needed to be replaced.

The clock in the steeple stopped working and repairs were either unavailable or very costly. The carillon was not working properly and had not been repaired. (This would be taken care of in 1999 due to some memorial gifts and a generous anonymous gift by a member.)

The year 1998 was the year to finish the repairs to the building. The old roof was removed from the education building and a new roof installed. Krouse Construction Company was hired to re-roof the steeple, replace the louvers, and replace the wooden cross on the steeple with a metal one.

1998

Cost of these two projects was about $80,000. As the new cross was being hoisted to the top of the steeple, those who were watching thought about the hymn, "Lift High the Cross, the Love of Christ Proclaim."

During the summer of 1998 a garage was built for the church van. Cost of this proj-

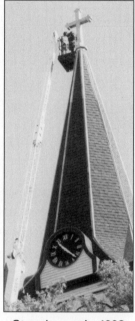

Steeple repair, 1998

ect was about $7,500. All labor was donated by members. Matt Wikelius took responsibility for getting the materials. Dormon Trippler helped organize the volunteer labor. The building was dedicated on Rally Day, September 13.

Another project was the replacement of the sidewalk around the church property. The cost was divided between the city of Center City and the church. The church's share of the cost was $5,000.

Saint Peter Tornado

On March 29, 1998, a devastating tornado ripped through Saint Peter, Minnesota, and raised havoc on the campus of Gustavus Adolphus College. All 29 buildings on the campus were damaged. Windows were broken, roofs were ripped off, more than 2,000 trees were uprooted, and the steeple on Christ Chapel was toppled. No college had received such extensive damage in the history of the United States.

The miracle? The students were home for Easter vacation and no one on the campus was killed.

Another miracle! Help came from many sources—the federal government, other colleges, alumni, friends. Portable buildings were brought in so that the students could complete their courses and graduate on schedule.

All carpeting had to be removed and replaced because of glass embedded it. All mattresses and upholstered furniture had to be replaced because of the broken glass. Sod around the buildings and on the football field had to be removed and replaced. The clean up was overwhelming. Over the summer months all of the buildings were put back into order and September 1998 saw the largest enrollment at Gustavus ever, including 700 freshmen. During the summer there was a "Plant a Tree" drive throughout the state to replace the trees on the Gustavus campus. Thousands of dollars were given and young trees planted to replace the trees that had been destroyed.

1998

By October, three new residential buildings were completed to house 220 students. On October 19, groundbreaking took place for the new student union to be opened in September 1999. On October 22, the spire was placed on Christ Chapel.

Chisago Lake Lutheran Church is a member of the Gustavus Adolphus College Association of Congregations. There are many programs connecting the college and the church that are available to us because of this membership. Several of our confirmation classes have used their facilities for confirmation retreats. The college will provide pulpit supply, adult forum presenters, youth outreach teams, and musical groups for member congregations requesting them.

At the time of the tornado, we had students at the campus. Fortunately, they were home for Easter break, and damage to their personal property was minimal. At least one of our members spent a day as a campus clean-up volunteer.

Growth in Chisago County

The 1990s were a period of great growth in Chisago County. Between 1990 and 1998, the population grew by 29.27 percent. Housing developments appeared on every road. The schools were overcrowded, but a bond issue passed and additions and renovations were made at every building site. Unfortunately, Chisago Lake Church membership did not reflect this increase in population.

1998

Summer Youth Activities

- John Wind took 11 students from the confirmation classes to Luther Point Bible Camp the week of June 28 to July 3.
- Five high school juniors and seniors accompanied John to Leadership Quest Camp July 12 to July 18.
- New Kids on the Rock gave a concert at Chisago Lake Lutheran Church on July 24. This was an inter-denominational Christian youth choir with two choirs in Minnesota and six choirs in Michigan. More than 100 voices joined together from these choirs to present this concert. A few of the choir members belonged to CLLC.
- Two Appalachia Service Project teams went to Leslie County, Kentucky, from July 24 to August 6. Each team was composed

of two adult leaders and five youth.

✦ H.O.P.E. (Hear Our Prayer Everywhere) was the theme for
the vacation Bible school August 10 to 14. Each day the children learned about a different country: Israel, Thailand,
Latvia, Namibia, and Chile. On Saturday, August 8, there was
an outdoor worship service on the parsonage lawn following a
campfire meal. The purpose of this congregational service was
to have children, parents, staff, and friends pray for the Bible
school and fellowship together. During the worship there was
a commissioning for the VBS staff. There were 50 students
who attended VBS.

✦ At Bible school and during the entire month of August, the
children collected items for school kits, which were given to
Lutheran World Relief.

Dawn Walker, Missionary

1998

For many years, Chisago Lake Church has contributed to the support
of a missionary or missionary family. Pastor Phil and Rene Johnson
had been receiving this support for several years as they worked in
Kenya. Pastor Phil took a three-year leave to return to the seminary in
order to prepare for teaching in a seminary in Africa. At this time, the
global ministry committee and the W/ELCA organization decided
that it was time to support another missionary in another country. The
W/ELCA organization had been making midwife kits to be sent to
overseas mission hospitals through Global Health Ministries. It
seemed to be the time to support a missionary in a health position.

Dawn Walker, administrator of Phebe Hospital in Liberia, was
chosen as the person to receive this support. In 1994, Phebe Hospital
was overrun and looted by rebels in the Civil War. The building was
not destroyed, but everything in the hospital was taken. The hospital
has since been completely renovated and gradually reopened as funds
and equipment became available and security increased.

PASTOR DALE PETERSON

Rally Day Mission Fair

During the summer, plans were made for a super Rally Day Fair on Sunday, September 13, 1998. Kathy Lindo and Kristi Mitchell organized the event. Nearly 60 committees, groups, and organizations of the congregation prepared displays to show what their mission was and how they were carrying out that mission. Brochures were prepared for distribution to all who were interested in participating in one or more of these committees or service groups. Each group offered an opportunity for members to sign up to participate and everyone was encouraged to take part in three things—one for spiritual growth such as a Bible study, one for service such as Stephen Ministry, and one for fellowship such as Christian Fellowship Club.

One service was held at 9:30 A.M. followed by the opportunity for everyone to visit the booths and displays. At 11:30 a pig-roast dinner was served to nearly 300 persons. David Reed provided the pig and roasted it. All food was provided and a freewill offering was received. There were games for children and a garage sale of obsolete church items in the newly completed garage.

1998

The day was beautiful, there was a large attendance and everyone enjoying the food and the fellowship.

Much planning was done by the pastor, the Christian education committee, and the Christian relational minister to provide educational opportunities for all ages. Five series of adult programs were offered to appeal to different age groups and interests. Sadly, not enough adults registered for these classes to even begin them.

Pastor Dale Peterson Resigns

On the last Sunday of August 1998 Pastor Dale presented his letter of resignation to the Church Council. The letter read in part:

> Today I want to communicate with you the recent plans Tamra
> and I have made for our future. I have accepted an appointment

from the Division of Outreach of the ELCA to develop a new mission congregation about 30 miles southwest of Houston, Texas. The project is called "Greatwood" after one of the planned communities' sub-divisions by the same name. It is an exciting opportunity and I am grateful that God has given me the Call to that ministry at this time in Christian history!

My intentions are to continue the ministry here with you until October 1, 1998.... God be with you and may your future be as great as your vision and faith!

On Sunday, September 27, the congregation held a farewell party for the Peterson family in the fellowship hall after the 10:30 A.M. service. The Petersons were surprised to see Bishop Mark Hanson, Saint Paul Area Synod, and several other friends from the community there.

The Church Council found out that Pastor Dale liked to play ping pong, and so they gave him a ping-pong table as a parting gift.

During his years at CLLC, Pastor Dale had been active in many committees and organizations in the community and synod. He served as chairman for the spiritual services advisory committee (SSAC) at the hospital. One of the responsibilities of this committee was the hiring of a hospital chaplain. Jack Hilger was chosen for this position. He served on the synodical global mission committee.

1998

September 5, 1998

PASTOR DALE PETERSON

Pastor Dale and Tamra became the sixth consecutive parsonage family to have a daughter married at Chisago Lake Church. On September 5, 1998, their daughter Angela was married to Craig Couillard.

Calling an Interim Pastor

Immediately after receiving Pastor Dale's resignation, the Church Council began the process of calling an interim pastor. Pastor Lawrence

Lystig was the pastor chosen, and he began his ministry at CLLC on November 1. Pastor Lystig had served as an interim pastor in a number of other congregations. Prior to that he had been an active duty chaplain in the United States Navy.

1998

Pr. Lawrence Lystig

During the month of October, there was no pastor at CLLC. Sunday worship services were conducted by guest pastors. On October 4, Worldwide Communion Sunday and Lutheran World Federation Sunday, the guest pastor was Rahila Stephen, a seminary student from Nigeria.

October 18 was Consecration Sunday with Bishop Herbert Chilstrom as guest. Grant Stevenson was the guest on October 25, Reformation Sunday. On Thursday, October 8, at 11:00 A.M., the annual Swedish language communion service was held with Pastor William J. Hyllengren officiating once again. Soloist was Bernhard LeVander. Lunch was provided after the worship service.

On October 24, a new fellowship group call ACT (Adult Christians Together), was formed for young married couples. The first meeting was a hayride and bonfire. This group continues to gather for Christian fellowship.

Earlier in the summer, the secretary, Liz Sterbentz, resigned after serving in the office for six years. Merrie Tolzman was hired as interim

Louise Angrimson

secretary beginning August 15. Louise Angrimson began as office coordinator on October 5.

Dick and Hazel Underhill relinquished their duties as custodians and the decision was made to hire a full-time janitor with regular daytime hours. Donna Anderson had served as morning janitor for many years, but this new arrangement meant the termination of her position.

Larry Olding

Larry Olding took over the responsibilities of full-time custodian in mid-November.

1998

Worship and Music

The worship and music committee developed the following mission statement: "To gather the people to worship and praise God; To proclaim the Word; To celebrate the sacraments; To inspire the people to serve as disciples of Christ's saving grace in their lives."

In 1998, a worship publication from the ELCA asked churches to take a look at how they were currently worshiping and how they might enhance, change, or continue quality worship within their churches. During the year, the committee researched, discussed, and planned according to the four areas of worship: Gathering, Word, Meal, Sending.

During the month of November, the committee held a series of adult forums to share with the congregation the results of their work. After the forum discussions, the committee presented a proposal to the Church Council that two different times of worship and Sunday school be tried during the period from February through May.

1. Family worship at 9:00 A.M. from Feb. 7 to Mar. 28. Children
   would come with their parents to the beginning of the worship
   service and be dismissed for Sunday school after the special
   music. Once each month the children would stay for the entire
   service so that they could participate in communion. A regular
   worship service would be held at 10:30 A.M.

2. Only one worship service, which would be at 9:00 A.M., followed by a Christian education hour for all ages from April 11
   through May.

A survey was included in the January 1999 newsletter asking the
congregation for their input. There was not much enthusiasm for trying these changes. The council decided that this was not a good time to
try something different and the proposal was not accepted.

Moving into a New Century

1998

As we neared the year 2000, everyone seemed to be talking about "moving into the new millennium." It was the subject of political speeches, it
was the worry of computer experts, and it was a theme for the church.
How can the church best serve the community as the new century
arrives? With the 150th anniversary of Chisago Lake Lutheran Church
just five years away, in 2004, it was a time to look back to where we had
been and a time to look forward to where we should be going.

The annual reports presented at the annual meeting on February
7, 1999, reflect this mood.

Gordon Grimm in his report for the Nehemiah Task Force
wrote:

This congregation can look back on these last three years with
great gratitude to God and its members for the work that has
been accomplished and give thanks to those who supported this

project.... As most of this task force's work is complete for the short term, we are disbanding.

The total amount of Nehemiah project was $235,836. Chaplain Grimm then went on to say that so far the Nehemiah project had been for "bricks and mortar" and that as we look to the future, we should concentrate on spiritual growth and outreach.

John Wind, youth director, wrote in his report:

In this report, I'd like to cast a vision for where our youth ministry could be in five years, which would bring us to our 150th anniversary year.... I envision a community of youth and adults hungry for God's Word and for his Holy Spirit. I envision Middle School and High School youth meeting in small groups—some adult-led, some youth-led — to share their real lives, to study God's Word and apply it to their lives, to pray together, and to be strengthened to share Christ with their world. I envision young people who have been built up strong in God's Word....

I envision Middle School and High School youth connected with adults in our congregation in one-to-one mentoring relationships. I envision not an isolation between the generations but sharing, growing, and serving together. I envision a church family.

I envision a whole community of churches working together for the cause of Christ in Chisago Lakes (Area). I envision churches united together to ensure that the next generation will know and will grow.

1998

John had a vision that could bind and heal our congregation—one that could make this a better place for our children, our families, our community, and our world.

The historical committee was already planning for a 150th anniversary celebration to be held on Sunday, May 9, 2004, the Sunday nearest to May 12, which was the date of the beginning of the Chisago Lake Church. They were making plans for this history to be written and for a cookbook to be published. They were planning their guest list of dignitaries to invite and commemorative items to be available.

When the resolution to adopt the budget as presented came to the floor, it indicated a decrease in the amount to be given to benevolences. Several members spoke against this decrease and a motion was made to amend the budget and increase it by $30,000, some money to prevent the benevolence part of the budget from being decreased, and some to provide money for more and better programs. The amendment was seconded and passed. The vote on the new budget of $375,950 was passed by with 52 voting yes and 33 voting no.

∾

1998

Pastor Lawrence J. Lystig
1999–2001

PASTOR LAWRENCE J. LYSTIG was born July 17, 1937, in Edmonton, Alberta, Canada, the oldest of six children. His father, the Reverend C. S. Lystig, at the time was pastor of Central Lutheran Church in Edmonton. The family lived in Edmonton until late in 1941 when they moved to Winger, Minnesota. In 1946 they moved to Minneapolis.

In 1955 Pastor Larry graduated from Edison High School. He attended Augsburg and Macalester Colleges before graduating from Concordia College, Moorhead, in 1959. For one year he taught English and plane geometry and served as dormitory resident head at what was then the West Central School of Agriculture at Morris, Minnesota.

Pastor Larry and Carolyn were married in 1964, while he was still a student at Luther Theological Seminary in Saint Paul, Minnesota. They have two children: Louise is married to Scott Fritchie and they live in Minneapolis; Ted is married to Sandy Schreyer and they moved from

Seattle, Washington, to Sweden in 2001. Pastor Larry's father died in 1971, his mother late in 1998. One sister, June, died in 1965.

Pastor Larry served Jackson Lake Evangelical Lutheran Church in Amboy and Faith Lutheran in Delavan, both in Minnesota, from 1965 to 1969. He then served as education pastor at Vinje Lutheran in Willmar, Minnesota, until September 1971, when he began active duty as a Navy chaplain. He had been commissioned as a chaplain while attending seminary in 1961.

In 1987 Pastor Larry retired from the Navy chaplaincy and began studying for a law degree at Hamline University School of Law in Saint Paul, Minnesota, finishing his work in December 1989. He continues to be a member of the Minnesota State Bar.

From November 1987 to June 1989 he served as visitation pastor at Christ the King Lutheran Church in Bloomington, Minnesota. Since 1989, Pastor Larry had served as an interim pastor in 13 congregations in Minnesota and Wisconsin.

1999

Pastor Larry began as interim pastor at Chisago Lake Lutheran Church on November 1, 1998. He accepted the call as an interim pastor with the understanding that he would not be a candidate for a permanent call. After a few months on the job, however, the pastor, the congregation's leadership, and Bishop Hanson agreed that a longer interim ministry was needed.

Pr. Larry & Carolyn Lystig

In March 1999, the congregation voted to issue Pastor Lystig a call for a four-year term, which he accepted since that was what the congregation wanted. The congregation also asked Pastor Larry and Carolyn to move to the parsonage. They agreed to this and the parsonage was made ready for them. Congregational members removed carpeting, painted walls, and cut down trees. Other people were hired to restore the maple floors and to eliminate the bats in the attic. A new refrigerator, washer, and dryer were installed.

Gift from the congregation

The Lystigs moved into the parsonage in May and Pastor Larry was installed as senior pastor on May 23, 1999, at the 9:30 A.M. worship service. Glendy Scully from the Saint Paul Area Synod officiated.

The responsibility of an interim pastor is to help the congregation move away from the pastoral style of the past and prepare to be open and receptive to the pastoral style and leadership of the future. With a four-year term call, he was required to assume the responsibilities of a senior pastor. This meant that in addition to preaching and teaching, he was involved with stewardship, staff supervision, property improvements, and all the other committee functions.

Pastor Lystig brought a new, more low-key style of ministry to the congregation. He delivered clear, honest sermons—often using imagery of ships and the sea—based on the texts for the day. He always spoke directly to the people without relying on notes. Pastor Lystig led thoughtful, erudite Bible studies during the adult forum.

1999

New Organist

Marilyn Wahlstrom

In June of 1999, Elwood (Woody) Bernas resigned after six years as organist of Chisago Lake Lutheran Church. During the summer, Ann Cebula, mother of Kathy Reed, was the interim organist.

Marilyn Wahlstrom was hired to begin her work as organist in October. Marilyn had visited Chisago Lake often as a child; she was

a descendant of the Linn family, early settlers of this community.
Several members of the family are still members at Chisago Lake,
including her mother, Marian Wahlstrom.

Marilyn had previously been assistant organist/director of music
at Central Lutheran Church in Minneapolis. She recalls when visiting
here how she had thought she would like to be the organist for this
church. Marilyn brings a wonderful
talent to Chisago Lake Lutheran
Church.

Another staffing change took
place when Sue Danielzuk was hired
to replace Jim Berling as part-time
accountant. Sue is married and the
mother of two children. The family
lives in Lindstrom.

Sue Danielzuk

1999   Called to Common Mission

At the ELCA National Convention held in Denver in 1998, the Called
to Common Mission statement was ratified. Throughout the ELCA
there were many people opposed to this document, the issue being the
historic episcopate, which became the hierarchical structure of the
ELCA when it approved full fellowship with the Episcopalian denomination. These dissenters formed a group called "Word Alone," a group
that Pastor Lystig joined.

In a letter written by Gerhard O. Forde and James A. Nestingen
at Luther Seminary, the concern of Word Alone was expressed that
"we were not remaining true to our Lutheran confession" and that "this
was a grave crisis for the Lutheran church."

One way to express disapproval of this ELCA action was to cut
back on financial support of its structure. As a result of this and to gain
better control of where our benevolence money was to go, a decision was

made at the annual meeting in January to give 10 percent of our offerings away and to divide our benevolence offerings as follows: 50 percent to the Saint Paul Area Synod of the ELCA; 12.5 percent to Lutheran World Relief; 12.5 percent to Lutheran Disaster Response; 12.5 percent to Lutheran Social Service; and 12.5 percent divided equally among Luther Point Bible Camp, Parmly Senior Housing & Services, Green Acres, and Family Pathways.

Other Highlights of 1999

+ Gordon Meland continued to record the service each Sunday. Videotapes of the services were aired on both Chisago Lakes and Forest Lake Cable TV.
+ Our mission support had been directed to Dawn Walker, administrator of Phoebe Hospital in Liberia. Dawn resigned from her position, married, and returned to the United States. Our support was then directed to Naomi Mahler and Todd Lynum, a married couple serving the Lutheran Church in Costa Rica.
+ Stig and Eva Ostlund from Skara, Sweden, presented a concert at our church. A free-will offering was received for the Ostlunds, which they chose to donate to the historical committee of our congregation. These funds were designated for the carillon repair fund.
+ During the summer the steeple clock, bell, and carillon were repaired and upgraded.
+ A bid was accepted to update the lighting system to increase efficiency and lower operating costs.
+ Each year the 3M Perpetual Fund interest is distributed for mission and outreach. In 1999, disbursements were as follows.
  1) Outreach in synod and community:
    $500 to Lutheran Seminary scholarship fund,

1999

$500 for the food shelf at Family Pathways,

$500 to the East Central Habitat for Humanity,

$500 to Thanksgiving Lutheran Church, a mission church in Hugo, Minnesota,

$500 to the Saint Paul Area Synod, above the congregation's commitment.

2) Gifts for missions of the ELCA:

$1,000 to Vision for Mission (Global),

$1,000 to Domestic Disaster Relief,

$500 to World Hunger.

3) $2,500 for unbudgeted capital improvements at CLLC.

+ Stacy Johnson, daughter of David and Virginia (Ginny) Johnson, received a master of arts degree from Luther Seminary, with an emphasis in youth and family ministry.

Stacy Johnson

1999

+ Kristi Mitchell, Christian relational minister at Chisago Lake Lutheran Church, was accepted at Luther Seminary. She started her seminary curriculum with a computer-based online course and followed that up with classroom courses in the fall.

+ The library committee did a complete inventory of the library and expanded it to the landing near the choir room. They also sponsored a book fair, which raised $267 worth of new books and materials for the library.

+ From July 3 to 10, a mission team of 18 youth and four adult leaders went to serve the Hispanic community in Denver, Colorado.

+ A garage sale was held in July by the social ministry committee, which raised $1,800. The earnings were divided between Family Pathways and East Central Habitat for Humanity.

- During the summer, a task force was formed to make plans for the 150th Anniversary of the congregation in 2004. The following people were accepted for the task force: Ade Akerlund, Bonnie Anderson, Lois Barott, Sally Barott, and Don Bungum, with Mark and Barbara Wikelius as co-chairs of the task force. Lois, Sally, and Don attended the Congregation Heritage Workshop at Luther College in Decorah, Iowa. The anniversary committee chose as their theme, "Pointing the Way to Christ Through All Generations."

- In August and September, pictures were taken by Olan Mills for a new pictorial directory.

- A Swedish communion service was held at 11:00 A.M. on Thursday, October 21, with Pastor William J. Hyllengren officiating and Pastor Larry assisting. Lunch was served after the service.

2000

- The fall stewardship fund appeal used the "Hot Potato" system. Commitment cards returned: 347; choosing not to pledge: 68; total pledged: $348,561.45. This was the strongest stewardship response in many years.

Pr. Bill Hyllengren

- Records show that at the end of 1999, there were 1,098 baptized members, and average weekly worship attendance was 268.

2000 · A Year of Change

In spite of all the concerns in the world for some kind of catastrophe when the new millennium began January 1, 2000, the change came without any serious problems. Computers continued to work, the electricity stayed on, and life on New Year's Day was the same as usual. The world breathed a sigh of relief!

PASTOR LAWRENCE J. LYSTIG

At Chisago Lake Lutheran Church, all was well and the congregation looked forward to the future with much hope and anticipation. However, it became a year of frustration, difficulty, and change.

In the spring John Wind, youth director, announced that he would be leaving on August 15. It was the intent of both John and his wife Rachel to further their education.

John Wind

In June Kristi Mitchell resigned. This led to an investigation by a congregational task force.

In early November Pastor Lystig was diagnosed with clinical depression and went on medical leave for two months. He resigned as senior pastor effective January 1, 2001, going on medical disability.

In a few short months, the youth director, Christian education director/music director, and pastor had resigned.

2000

A decision was made to continue to hire a full-time youth director and Carla Renner was chosen for this position. To prepare for this work, she attended the training offered by Tentmakers and financed by the congregation. She was commissioned on October 27, 2000, but she had been working part-time at the church while taking her training.

Carla Renner

Marilyn Wahlstrom took over the music director/senior choir director position in addition to her work as organist. Carol Hawkinson became the Sunday school coordinator. The Christian education committee directed the vacation Bible school, held August 7 through 11, with an enrollment of 50 students. Another change that occurred during the year was the cemetery recorder. John A. Nelson had served for several years and Dale Hawkinson assumed this responsibility.

It was at summer vacation Bible school that the ingathering for the Heifer Project began, spearheaded by Dawn Burger Sandberg. After Bible school, this became a congregational project that extended into the next year and resulted in more than $5,000 given to this important mission project.

Pre-Lent Every Member Visit

The evangelism committee decided to have an every member visit prior to Ash Wednesday. About 60 people were asked to distribute Lenten packets to their neighbors. All local resident members were contacted by this means. All packets included a schedule of events for the Lenten season, a Lenten devotion book, a coin folder, and a cover letter of invitation and explanation. Plans were to use any funds that came in from the Lenten folders for water pumps in Peru and for the ELCA program for nurturing new churches. The Church Council made a decision that all Lenten offerings should be used for mission work. This offering amounted to $5,200 and was distributed as follows:

2000

- ✦ Water pumps for Peru - $1,100
- ✦ Water pumps for Niger - $1,100
- ✦ Nurturing new churches - $2,000
- ✦ Water system for a hospital in India - $1,000

Youth Mission Trip to Toronto

From June 17 to 25, 24 youth and four adult leaders went to Toronto, Canada, to serve the inner-city community there. Toronto has one of the world's largest homeless populations, many of whom are teenage runaways. It is estimated that more than 10,000 teenagers are living on the streets. The youth fund-raisers and the sponsor families in our congregation raised more than $9,000 for this mission trip.

PASTOR LAWRENCE J. LYSTIG

Also April 7 to 10, Chisago Lake Lutheran youth hosted a Teens Encounter Christ retreat that was well attended.

Toronto Mission Trip

Other Bits and Pieces from 2000

+ At the annual meeting, a resolution was passed that the congregation pay full tuition for a member who attends the seminary with the intent of becoming an ordained pastor.
+ New robes were purchased for the senior choir.
+ A new sound system was installed by Kingdom Sound and Lighting at a cost of $22,000.
+ The historical committee published a cookbook with recipes from members of the congregation.
+ Center City and Hassela, Sweden, became sister cities. The first immigrants to this community came from Hassela in 1851. Tour groups exchanged visits during the summer and gifts were exchanged. Sally Barott arranged this wonderful exchange program.
+ Twelve teams from the Chisago Lakes area participated in the Relay for Life, raising more than $32,000 for cancer research. The Chisago Lake Lutheran Church team placed first in donations collected for the second consecutive year by raising more than $5,800.

- ✦ A church auction was held on September 10, which raised $8,537.25 for the sound system.
- ✦ The Reverend Marvin Palmquist was the speaker for Global Mission Sunday, October 1. Pastor Palmquist represented the Lutheran Orient Mission Society, which has a mission to the Kurds in Turkey and Iraq.
- ✦ The historical committee sponsored a Swedish communion service on Thursday, October 12, at 11:00 A.M. Pastor William J. Hyllengren officiated at this service, assisted by Pastor Larry. A luncheon was served following the service.
- ✦ Records show a membership of 1,114 baptized members at the end of 2000.

Transition

When Pastor Lystig was advised by his doctor to take a medical leave of absence, it became necessary to secure a pastor who could take over some of his duties. Pastor David Quarberg, recently retired as senior pastor at Grace Lutheran Church in Apple Valley, filled this need during November and December. Pastor Lystig submitted his resignation, effective January 1, 2001;

2001

Pastor Quarberg

Pr. D. A. Quarberg

agreed to continue as an "interim-interim" until a long-term transition pastor could be secured.

Pr. W. E. Strom

Pastor Bill Strom accepted a call to be the transition pastor for up to a year, and he arrived early in January. He had previously been the pastor at Our Saviour's Lutheran Church in Hastings, Minnesota. The main objectives during his ministry were to conduct a series of workshops called "Healthy Congregations," to develop a mission and vision statement, and to facilitate the formation of a call committee.

About 40 members participated in the workshops, which were held on four Sunday afternoons. Sessions were from 2:00 to 7:00 P.M. with a light supper break. The mission statement that was developed was "Guided by God's Spirit, Learning, Living, Sharing Christ's Love."

Early in the summer a call committee was formed. Those accepting this responsibility were Marcus Brottem, Holly Damm, Sue Leaf, Dorothy Neudahl, Tim Peterson, and Mark Wikelius. They worked long and hard with representatives from the Saint Paul Area Synod office to accomplish their task of finding a new pastor for the congregation.

During the Lenten season of 2001, Mrs. Gladys Peterson led the Wednesday 11:00 A.M. services using as her theme, "Jesus said, I AM."

2001

The Wednesday evening services were held at 7:00 P.M. preceded by a soup and sandwich supper served from 5:30 to 6:45 P.M. The evening services were "Grace Awakenings and Faith Stories" shared by five members on the congregation. This same format was used in Lent 2002 with Gladys Peterson using as her theme, "Walking with Jesus." The evenings again had soup suppers and faith story presenters.

Gladys Peterson

During the summer the youth went on two mission trips. One group went to Rapid City, South Dakota, and another group went to New Orleans, Louisiana.

Celebrating Settlers

In 2001, Center City celebrated the 150th anniversary of the first settlers in this community. To contribute to the Center City Heritage

Days, Chisago Lake Lutheran Church held a "Pioneer Worship Service" on the church lawn commemorating the first outdoor worship services held by the pioneers in the summer of 1851. This service was held on Wednesday evening, July 25, at 7:00 P.M. Special music for this service was provided by Barb Yotter and Nelda Abrahamson playing psalmodikons, which had been made by Elliott Hawkinson.

On Sunday, July 29, a Swedish smorgasbord was held at the church sponsored by the 150th Anniversary Committee and coordinated by Sally Barott. This event attracted former members, community residents, and church members and was very successful. Many, many Swedish foods were served. This fund-raiser had a net profit of $1,840.38 plus matching funds from Aid Association for Lutherans (AAL) of $400.00. This was the first fund-raiser since a new AAL branch was formed in our congregation in June.

The road going east from the church was scheduled for reconstruction and property owners had their property purchased for the right away needed. Property purchased from the church for this highway resulted in an amount of $24,370.00 being received. Of this amount, $2,450.00 went to the cemetery account. The balance of this fund was invested and will be discussed later.

2001

In August 2001, Susan Peterson began her work as half-time Christian education director. Susan was born and raised in Fergus Falls, Minnesota. She graduated from Concordia College, Moorhead, Minnesota, with a degree in art education. She taught in public schools for seven years and at a private preschool for four years. Susan is married to Dan Peterson and they have three children,

Susan Peterson

Elizabeth, Alice, and Benjamin. The family moved to the Shafer area in 1997 and has been active in the congregation since then.

Fall 2001

September 11, 2001, was a day to remember in the history of the world. On this day the World Trade Center in New York City and the Pentagon in Washington D.C. were struck by terrorists who had hijacked our commercial planes. A fourth plane crashed in Shanksville, Penn., as passengers prevented the plane from hitting a target in the Washington D.C. area, perhaps the White House or the Capitol. The church bell tolled at noon and a prayer service was held in the evening.

The Heifer Project goal was $5,000. This goal was reached with the total amount at $5,295.63. On Sunday, September 30, Jason Bergmann of Heifer Project International presented a plaque thanking the congregation for this donation. Also in 2001, the Women of the ELCA completed more midwife kits, sent through the Global Health Ministries to many places around the world. About 1000 kits have been donated in the past four years.

The annual Swedish communion service was held on Saturday, October 20, 2001, with a Swedish meatball luncheon served after the service. Pastor William J Hyllengren officiated with Pastor Russell Peterson assisting.

On Friday, October 26, from 6 to 8 p.m., the second annual all-church All Saint's party was held. This is proving to be a fun way to celebrate instead of "trick or treating." It was an evening of fellowship, food, and fun for all.

The annual Thanksgiving service and pie fest was held November 21 at 7:30 p.m. and the first annual holiday bazaar was held on December 1 from 10:00 a.m. to 4:00 p.m. These events brought many people together for fellowship.

2002

2001 Potpourri

+ Kid's Night Out, which was begun in 2000, continued to be a successful venture.

- Elementary children met from 6 to 8 P.M. one Friday evening each month. This was an opportunity for learning more about the Bible, for fellowship and fun. About 20 children were participating.
- Chester and Bonnie Kukuk continued to sponsor the Firefllies program. Students memorized Bible verses for points and prizes.
- Dorothy Neudahl continued as cradle roll coordinator. Materials are sent regularly to all children from baptism to 3 years of age. At that time they are eligible for Sunday school.
- The confirmation program was reviewed and changes made.
- On June 24, a new branch of AAL (Aid Association for Lutherans) was begun at Chisago Lake Lutheran Church. AAL offered opportunities for matching funds for many purposes.
- 325 copies of the *With One Voice* hymnals were purchased.
- Vacation Bible school was held August 6 through 10 with about 40 students attending. A new time was tried—5:30 to 8:15 P.M. Fall Sunday school enrollment was about 80.

2002

- Todd Lynum and Naomi Mahler, the missionary couple the congregation was helping to support, returned to the United States. In their place the support went to Pastor Pablo and Erika Obregon in Costa Rica.
- The youth program involved much more than the summer mission trips. There were Friday night events for students in grades 6 and up; Saturday service projects to help others; middle school Tuesday and Wednesday homework and youth room activities from 2:30 to 5:30 P.M.; Thursday evening Bible study for high school students; and much, much, more.
- A special request for funds at the end of the year resulted in offerings totaling over $55,000. This enabled the congregation to end the year in the black.
- Baptized membership at the end of 2001 was 1088.

Bridge Pastor

In January 2002, Pastor Strom received a call to become the transition pastor at Luther Memorial Church in South Saint Paul. He felt that the Chisago Lake congregation was well on its way to securing a new pastor and that he was ready to accept another call.

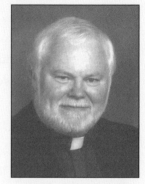

This made it necessary to find someone that would be the "bridge" pastor until the new permanent pastor came. Pastor Rob Englund came to Chisago Lake to fill this position. Newly retired, he had served for more than 22 years at Lebanon Lutheran Church in South Minneapolis. He began his work on February 24, 2002, working three-fourths time. Pastor Rob Englund was installed on March 17, along with the new council members.

Pr. R. R. Englund

2002

Special Congregational Meeting

A special congregational meeting was called for Sunday, May 19, 2002, for the purpose of extending a call to not one, but two pastors, Craig and Barbara Lundstad-Vogt. The couple had been co-pastors at First Lutheran Church in Pipestone, Minnesota, since 1986.

When the day for the meeting arrived, the church was well filled and the vote was unanimous to call the Lundstad-Vogts. Due to changes in the Synod office with a new bishop coming, the call was delayed for a time, but soon it was announced that the call had been accepted and that the pastors would begin their work at Chisago Lake Lutheran Church on August 7, 2002.

The Lundstad-Vogts were interested in living in the parsonage since they had lived in a parsonage previously. The people of the congregation busied themselves with preparing the parsonage, cleaning and painting, and with preparing the office spaces at the church. By the time the moving van arrived on July 16, all was ready.

This is by no means a full account of all the activities going on at the church. Many youth activities were held each week. During the summer of 2002 the youth went on a mission trip to Keystone, West Virginia. More than 20 people participated in this trip. Bible school was held at the end of July. The quilters made 240 quilts—a record number! Several hundred more midwife kits were assembled. Many more new members were received.

∽

2002

Pastors Craig and Barbara Lundstad-Vogt

34
2002

PASTOR CRAIG was born and grew up in Montana. Most of this time he lived on a farm near Bigfork; he also lived for a short time in Kalispell. He attended Concordia College in Moorhead, Minnesota, and received his bachelor of arts degree in 1974, with a major in math and a minor in Greek. During the summers he worked for a local lumber yard.

Pastor Barb grew up on a farm near Grinnell, Iowa. She attended Iowa State University and received a bachelor of science degree in 1973, with majors in public service and administration in agriculture, outdoor recreation resources, and public recreation. During the summers she worked at state 4-H camps in Iowa and Minnesota. Following graduation, she lived in Humboldt, Iowa, working as a 4-H and youth extension agent in Pocahontas and Humboldt Counties.

Both went to Luther Seminary in Saint Paul in the fall of 1974, where they met. Pastor Craig spent his internship year in Avoca, Iowa, at Trinity Lutheran Church (1976–1977). He worked in construction during the summers. Pastor Barb spent her internship year in Saint Petersburg, Florida, at Garden of Peace Lutheran Church. She worked one summer in extension and one summer at Holden Village in Chelan, Washington.

On May 28, 1978, they both received their master of divinity degrees from Luther Seminary. The following day, May 29, they were married. On August 6, 1978, they were ordained at Pastor Craig's home church, Bethany Lutheran Church, Bigfork, Montana. For the next three years, they lived in South Dakota with Pastor Craig serving two congregations—Our Savior's Lutheran Church, Menno, and Our Redeemer Lutheran in Irene, and Pastor Barb serving Trinity Lutheran, Yankton. They continued serving in South Dakota, working together from 1981 to 1986 at First Lutheran Church, Mitchell.

In 1986 they were called to First Lutheran Church in Pipestone, Minnesota, where they served until accepting a call in 2002 to Chisago Lake Lutheran Church, Center City, Minnesota.

2002

The Lundstad-Vogts have two daughters. Kari is a 2003 graduate of Augsburg College in Minneapolis and Amy is studying at Hamline University in Saint Paul.

The Lundstad-Vogts were installed on Sunday, September 8, 2002, with the Reverend Charles Anderson, advisor to the bishop, Saint

Kari, Pr. Craig, Amy, Pr. Barb, 2001

Paul Area Synod, officiating. It was a festive day. There was one service at 9:30 A.M. followed by Rally Day, a mission fair, book fair, fellowship hour, and then a pot-luck picnic dinner on the church lawn. A ball game was planned for the afternoon, but it was shortened because of the hot weather and the wet ground.

The pastors stated their wish to spend the first few months getting acquainted with the church program, the members, and the community. They attended many committee meetings and visited many members in their homes.

Pastors Barb & Craig Lundstad-Vogt at Holy Communion   2002

Music Series Concerts

In the spring of 2002, the worship and music committee reported that an appropriate piano, a Kawai baby grand, had been found for the fellowship hall to replace the clavinova that had been used there the past few years. It was purchased with memorial gifts, donations from members, and monies from a bequest. The piano was dedicated on Sunday, June 9, 2002, with the organist, Marilyn Wahlstrom, presenting a piano concert. Nelda Abrahamson also participated in this program.

This concert was the first of a series of musical events presented during the next few months. On September 22, 2002, the second concert featured Lois Barott and Richard Bloom, accompanied by Marilyn Wahlstrom, singing favorite sacred, classical, Swedish, and Broadway musical songs.

Pastor Bill Strom, accompanied on the piano by his wife Sara, presented the third Music Series Concert on February 9, 2003. Pastor Strom had soloed in church several times during his ministry in our congregation and was warmly welcomed back.

The next Series Concert was held on May 4, 2003, and featured the children's choirs with three of the youth as soloists. Maria Anderson and Kristine Weise were vocal soloists and Aaron Peterson played his trumpet.

A new season of Music Series Concerts began on September 28, 2003, with Ellie Hawkinson, soprano, as featured soloist. Ellie is a 2003 music graduate of the Perpich Center for Arts Education in Golden Valley and will be attending the American Music and Dramatic Academy in New York City beginning in October 2003. Also participating in this program was a friend of Ellie's, violinist Lia Ubl.

These concerts have been enjoyed by those who have attended and plans were made to have them continue.

2002

During these past two years, new *Lutheran Book of Worship* books have been purchased to replace the old worn ones, and the congregation has also begun the use of the *With One Voice* hymnal supplement.

Worship and music committee members in 2002 were Nelda Abrahamson, Lois Barott, Chris Ruser, Kathy Olson, Ellen Hawkinson, Matt Wikelius, and Marilyn Wahlstrom.

Milestone Ministries

Milestone Ministries is a new program at Chisago Lake started by the Christian education committee and the pastors, and involving the entire congregation. The purpose of this program is to bring the family and the congregation together in celebrating milestones of our children as they grow to adulthood. It can also be carried on into adulthood by continuing to recognize special times of life.

The first milestone for a child is Holy Baptism. At this time the child receives a Faith Chest. Ideally this chest is made of wood by a volunteer member of the congregation and includes the name of the child and any other appropriate decorations. The candle, book, and napkin given at the baptism are placed in this chest.

For the first three years, the child receives several mailings through the cradle roll program. These items can also go into the chest. At three years of age the child is ready to begin Sunday school and this will be celebrated with a Teddy Bear Tea for children and their parents. As the program develops, each year will have some special event.

At the present time a milestone already being observed is when third graders receive their Bibles. Another one is their first Holy Communion in fifth grade. Plans are to give a quilt made by the women of the church to each graduating senior.

Milestone Ministries is meant to show each child that there is a place for them in the church and to help each one to grow in his/her relationship with Jesus Christ.

A Picture of God's Grace   2003

Lenten services in 2003 centered on the Last Supper. A set was made by volunteers to represent Leonardo daVinci's painting of the Last

Supper. Pastor Craig played the role of Jesus, and members of the congregation took the parts of the 12 disciples. Each week two disciples were introduced. The first were Andrew and Peter—"Fishers of

Men and Women." They took their place at the table. By Maundy
Thursday, all 12 disciples had been seated at the table and Jesus joined
them to observe the Passover meal and institute the Lord's Supper.

Pr. Barb, Pr. Craig, and the 5th graders, 2003: Quiana Quam,
Briana Johnson, Brittany Bettcher, Joey Reed, Bradley Johnson,
Jacob Christensen

2003

Fifth graders, who were having their first Holy Communion, and
their families were the first to participate in the Lord's Supper. It was a
very special time for all.

Planning and Anticipation

The year 2003 was a year of planning for the celebration of the 150th
anniversary in 2004. The anniversary committee had recommended a
fund-raising campaign to raise $1,000 for each year the congregation
has existed, a total of
$150,000. This rec-
ommendation was
u n a n i m o u s l y
accepted at the
annual meeting in
January and plans
were made for the
fund appeal. Three

150th anniversary committee: Ade Akerlund,
Lois Barott, Barbara Wikelius, Mark Wikelius,
Bonnie Anderson. Not pictured: Don Bungum,
Sally Barott

people were selected as co-chairs of this appeal; Kathy Lindo, Sue (Mrs. Ron) Johnson, and Don Bungum. They then secured other workers for the appeal.

The appeal was made during the month of April, with a Celebration Sunday on May 4. Total amount of cash and pledges by that date amounted to more than $132,000, with some monies continuing to come in.

The funds were specified as follows:

+ 30 percent for the structural integrity of the building;
+ 30 percent for painting and decorative artwork of the sanctuary;
+ 20 percent for mission start outreach ministry;
+ 10 percent for anniversary year activities; and
+ 10 percent for future positioning and fund-raising administration.

For many years the church has been plagued by water damage from rain water seeping into the building. In some places mold was found. It was vital that something be done to cure this problem. With monies received in the fund appeal, it was possible to begin replacing the gutters and downspouts on the building and putting in new curbs, gutters, and sidewalks on the south and west sides of the structure. To prepare for new landscaping, old trees and shrubs were removed.

2003

During the summer the sanctuary walls were painted and decorative painting begun.

The congregation designated by the Saint Paul Area Synod for our ministry start outreach assistance was the Minnesota Faith Chinese Lutheran Church in Saint Paul. This congregation serves mostly students from Luther Seminary and the

Minnesota Faith Chinese
Lutheran Church

University of Minnesota. The university has the largest number of Chinese students of any school in the nation.

To supplement the monies received through the fund appeal, other fund-raisers were sponsored. One of these was a Victorian Tea and Style Show held on Saturday, April 26. Tickets were sold for $15 each and more than $2,000 was raised to help with the decorative painting. Another event was a yard sale held July 10 to 12, which netted more than $1,000 for the church. Other events were an ice-cream social and an outdoor worship service.

2003

Senior choir with Marilyn Wahlstrom, organist/director

Plans were made to celebrate the 150th anniversary throughout 2004, with various congregational committees and organizations helping to host special events each month during the year

Ilula Congregation in Tanzania: Our Companion

A new and exciting adventure for our congregation is becoming a companion to the Ilula congregation in Mazombe, Tanzania. The Saint Paul Area Synod has been a companion to the Iringa Diocese in Tanzania for a number of years. Several individual congregations within the synod and diocese have become companions. Last year our congregation was asked to be a companion to a church there that was begun by Swedish missionaries more than 50 years ago. This was approved by the Church Council.

Bell tower at Ilula

The Ilula congregation has a total membership of 1,439 members, with 557 adults and 882 children The parish is divided into five preaching points served by Pastor Elay A. Mwinuka. The main economic activity is agriculture. Maize and millet are grown as food crops; tomatoes, onions, and sunflowers as cash crops. Because they are near a paved road, they are able to do trucking.

As a companion congregation we will donate $2,000 per year for building assistance. Of the five preaching points, only one has a permanent worship building at the present time. Plans are to build three more structures in the next three years. We can help by providing funds for the roofs, which they cannot afford.

Scholarships are another way we can help. Tuition for a student to go to high school is $250 per year. We are asked to support a minimum of five students each year, a total of $1,250. This can be done by the congregation as a whole, by groups, or by individual families. Support for one student for four years of high school is $1,000.

2002

The third part of this companionship is communication. We can reach them by e-mail or regular mail. They also invite us to send members of Chisago Lake Church to visit them and also to provide money for some of their members to come to visit us. The people of Ilula are as excited about getting to know us as we are to get to know them. We can look forward to this cultural exchange with other Lutherans.

As we close this chapter in our history, we look forward to God's leading us on in this century, and by the power of the Holy Spirit and God's grace, Chisago Lake Evangelical Lutheran Church will continue to be a beacon on the hill, proclaiming the gospel of Jesus Christ in this community and throughout the world.

PASTORS CRAIG & BARB LUNDSTAD-VOGT

Pastors Who Served

Chisago Lake Evangelical Lutheran Church
the Next 50 Years

J. W. Kempe 1945–1954

Hugo Thoreme 1954–1955

W. Burdette Benson 1955–1969

James A. Almquist 1970–1980

Robert S. Knutson (associate) 1980–1987

Russell A. Peterson 1981–1988

Paul H. Knutson (interim, 8 months) 1988

Dale L. Peterson 1989–1998

Marilyn Witte (4 months) 1991

Ernest Mwaluvinga (exchange, 3 months) 1992

John Voelker (associate) 1993–1995

John E. Fahning (interim, 3 months) 1996

Lawrence J. Lystig (interim, 5 months) 1998–1999

Lawrence J. Lystig (term call, 21 months) 1999–2001

David A. Quarberg (interim, 2 months) 2000

William Strom (interim, 12 months) 2001–2002

Robert R. Englund (interim, 3 months) 2002

Craig Lundstad-Vogt 2002–present

Barbara Lundstad-Vogt 2002–present

Pr. J. W. Kempe

Pr. Hugo Thorene

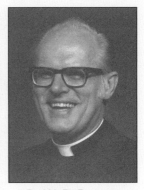

Pr. W. B. Benson

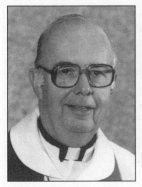

Pr. J. A. Almquist

Pr. R. S. Knutson

Pr. R. A. Peterson

Pr. P. H. Knutson

Dr. D. L. Peterson

Pr. M. Witte

PASTORS WHO SERVED

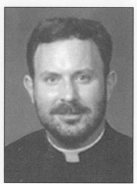

Pr. E. Mwaluvinga   Pr. J. Voelker   Pr. J. E. Fahning

Pr. L. J. Lystig   Pr. D. A. Quarberg   Pr. W. E. Strom

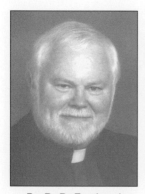

Pr. R. R. Englund   Pr. C. Lundstad-Vogt   Pr. B. Lundstad-Vogt

Organists Who Served

Chisago Lake Evangelical Lutheran Church

Peter Shaleen 1858–1898

P. R. Melin 1898–1909

Emil Anderson 1909–1918

Carl Malmstrom 1918–1925

J. A. Walllin 1925–1938

Miss Agda Wennerbreg 1938–1953

Faylon W. Geist 1953–1956

Glen Lovestrand 1956–1960

Roger Crary 1960–1963

Hazel D. Tkach 1963–1966

Kathleen DeBolt 1966–1978

Rita Knutson 1978–1987

Ron Crowl 1988–1988

Janelle Schauer/Anderson 1988–1993

Elwood (Woody) Bernas 1993–1999

Marilyn Wahlstrom (below) 1999–

Chisago Lake Church, Center City, Minnesota • October 2003

CHISAGO LAKE EVANGELICAL LUTHERAN CHURCH